STUDIES IN IMMIGRATION AND CULTURE
Royden Loewen, Series editor

# STORIED LANDSCAPES

## Ethno-Religious Identity and the Canadian Prairies

*Frances Swyripa*

UNIVERSITY OF MANITOBA PRESS

University of Manitoba Press
Winnipeg, Manitoba
Canada R3T 2M5
www.umanitoba.ca/uofmpress

Printed in Canada on chlorine-free, 100% post-consumer recycled paper.

Cover and interior design: Frank Reimer

Front cover: Pilgrimage, Our Lady of Mount Carmel shrine, St. Peter's Colony, Saskatchewan, 1939 (Archives of the Order of St. Benedict, St. Peter's Abbey).

Back cover: Russo-Greek Orthodox Church of St. Mary at Shandro in the Ukrainian bloc, east-central Alberta, 1906 (Provincial Archives of Alberta, B2738).

**Library and Archives Canada Cataloguing in Publication**

Swyripa, Frances, 1951–
    Storied landscapes : ethno-religious identity and the Canadian Prairies / Frances Swyripa.

(Studies in immigration and culture series, 1914-1459 ; 5)
Includes bibliographical references and index.
Also issued in electronic format.
ISBN 978-0-88755-720-0 (pbk.).—ISBN 978-0-88755-191-8 (bound)

    1. Immigrants—Prairie Provinces—History. 2. Minorities—Prairie Provinces—History. 3. Prairie Provinces—Social conditions. 4. Prairie Provinces—Emigration and immigration. I. Title. II. Series: Studies in immigration and culture ; 5.

FC3209.I4S99 2010          971.2'02          C2010-902848-1

The University of Manitoba Press gratefully acknowledges the financial support for its publication program provided by the Government of Canada through the Canada Book Fund, the Canada Council for the Arts, the Manitoba Department of Culture, Heritage, and Tourism, the Manitoba Arts Council, and the Manitoba Book Publishing Tax Credit.

# Contents

My father, whose idea of a Sunday afternoon during my prairie childhood was a long drive visiting country churches, reading the tombstones, and letting me and my cousin pick strawberries from around the graves.

My mother, who, in keeping with that tradition, accompanied me on many of the journeys that led first to an idea, then to more serious fieldwork, and finally to the manuscript that became this book.

# ILLUSTRATIONS

## PHOTOGRAPHS

## CREDITS AND PERMISSIONS

MAPS: The mapping of ethnic settlement on the prairies is a very interpretive and inexact art. The first disclaimer here is that, in the interests of clarity, only groups dealt with in this book have been mapped. Consequently, there is no indication of British settlement other than the Barr Colony and no indication of French, French-Canadian or French-Métis settlements. The second disclaimer is that these maps are not based on any specific criteria or systematic census data. Rather what these maps represent is the synthesis of a wide variety of both historical and interpretive mapping found in the sources noted below. Lastly, it should be mentioned that identifying areas with a particular ethnic group does not mean that other ethnic groups were not also present, only that the preponderance of settlers came from the group indicated. The base map was prepared by Gerhard Ens and reformatted for publication by Weldon Hiebert. It was constructed using Atlas of Canada base maps provided by GeoGratis © Department of Natural Resources Canada. All rights reserved.

The sources on which the maps are based include: C.A. Dawson, *Group Settlement: Ethnic Communities in Western Canada* (Toronto: Macmillan, 1936); Howard Palmer and Tamara Palmer, eds., *Peoples of Alberta: Portraits of Cultural Diversity* (Saskatoon: Western Producer Prairie Books, 1985); John Warkentin and Richard L. Ruggles, eds., *Historical Atlas of Manitoba: A Selection of Facsimile Maps, Plans and Sketches from 1612 to 1969* (Winnipeg: Manitoba Historical Society, 1970); Ka-iu Fung, Bill Barry, and Michael Wilson, eds., *Atlas of Saskatchewan, Millennium Edition* (Saskatoon: University of Saskatchewan, 1999); D.G.G. Kerr, ed., *A Historical Atlas of Canada* (Don Mills: Thomas Nelson and Sons, 1966); Lubomyr Luciuk and Bohdan Kordan, *Creating a Landscape: A Geography of Ukrainians in Canada* (Toronto: University of Toronto Press, 1989); Orest Martynowych, *Ukrainians in Canada: The Formative Period, 1891–1924* (Edmonton: Canadian Institute of Ukrainian Studies Press, 1991); Orest Martynowych, "The Ukrainian Bloc Settlement in East Central Alberta, 1890–1930," in *Continuity and Change: The Cultural Life of Alberta's First Ukrainians*, ed. Manoly Lupul (Edmonton: Canadian Institute of Ukrainian Studies and Alberta Historic Sites Service, 1988); John Lehr, "The Process and Pattern of Ukrainian Rural Settlements in Western Canada, 1891–1914" (Ph.D. dissertation, University of Manitoba, 1978); John Lehr, "Peopling the Prairies with Ukrainians," in *Canada's Ukrainians: Negotiating an Identity*, ed. Lubomyr Luciuk and Stella Hryniuk (Toronto: University of Toronto Press, 1991); James Darlington, "The Ukrainian Impress on the Canadian West," in *Canada's Ukrainians*, ed. Luciuk and Hryniuk; Brigham Card et al., eds., *The Mormon Presence in Canada* (Edmonton: University of Alberta Press, 1990); John Warkentin, "The Mennonite Settlements of Southern Manitoba" (Ph.D. dissertation, University of Toronto, 1960); William Schroeder, *Mennonite Historical Atlas*, 2nd ed. (Winnipeg: Springfield Publications, 1996); Wilhelm Kristjanson, *The Icelandic People in Manitoba: A Manitoba Saga* (Winnipeg: R.W. Kristjanson, 1965); Carl Tracie, *"Toil and Peaceful Life": Doukhobor Village Settlement in Saskatchewan* (Regina: Canadian Plains Research Center, 1996).

# ACKNOWLEDGEMENTS

No book, including this one, gets written without help. A number of people sitting in the archives, behind a microfilm reader, or before a computer assisted with important aspects of what is always unglamorous but necessary primary research. They were Krzysztof Lada, Dawn Nickel, Larissa Sawiak, and Andriy Zayarnyuk—all graduate students in the Department of History and Classics at the University of Alberta—as well as Orest Martynowych of Winnipeg and Olena Plokhy of Edmonton. My travelling companions on my journeys into rural Alberta, Saskatchewan, and Manitoba as part of the fieldwork for the book undoubtedly had a much more enjoyable time. I would like to recognize the following in particular: Audrey Swyripa; John, Stefan, and Roman Sokolowski; Larissa and Allan Sawiak; Marshall and Lorraine Kotowich; Orest Martynowych; Alan Meech; Crystal Willie; Dushan Bednarsky. Among the many knowledgeable and generous people I met along the way, Abbot Peter Novecosky, OSB, and Fathers Martin Brodner, OSB, and Demetrius Wasylyniuk, OSB, of St. Peter's Abbey in Muenster deserve special mention. More often, however, nameless strangers provided directions when I flagged them down on a dirt road, guided me through their local museum, or stopped to give an impromptu history lesson when they saw my car parked beside a local landmark. Several individuals are acknowledged in the notes for sharing specific insights or pieces of information. A timely McCalla Research Professorship from the University of Alberta provided the teaching release that allowed me to focus on the manuscript. In addition to the two anonymous readers, I would also like to thank Ryan Eyford, Julie Rak, and Daniel Stone for commenting on the sections on Icelanders, Doukhobors, and Jews respectively. A special thank you goes to Gerhard Ens, my colleague at the University of Alberta, who not only critiqued the finished manuscript but also offered to create the map for the book. Finally, the patience and professionalism of the staff at the University of Manitoba Press are greatly appreciated.

Concentration of non-British and non-French settlement on the rural prairies

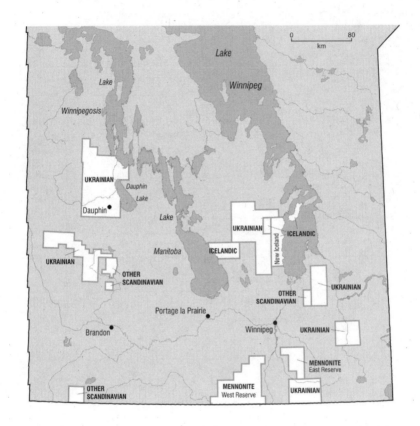

Ethno-religious settlement patterns, selected groups, Manitoba

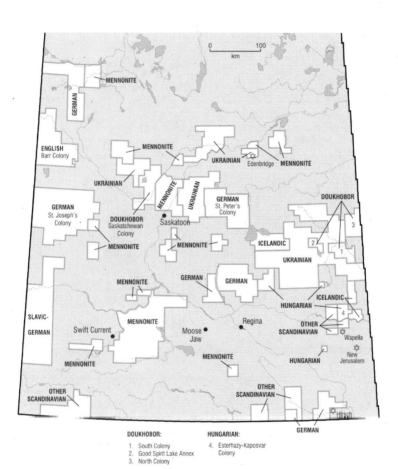

0       100
km

MENNONITE

GERMAN

ENGLISH
Barr Colony

MENNONITE

UKRAINIAN
Edenbridge

MENNONITE

UKRAINIAN

MENNONITE

UKRAINIAN

DOUKHOBOR

GERMAN
St. Joseph's
Colony

DOUKHOBOR
Saskatchewan
Colony

Saskatoon

GERMAN
St. Peter's
Colony

3

MENNONITE

MENNONITE

ICELANDIC

2

1

UKRAINIAN

MENNONITE

GERMAN

GERMAN

ICELANDIC

SLAVIC-

GERMAN

HUNGARIAN

4

MENNONITE

Swift Current

Moose
Jaw

Regina

OTHER
SCANDINAVIAN

Wapella

New
Jerusalem

MENNONITE

MENNONITE

HUNGARIAN

OTHER
SCANDINAVIAN

OTHER
SCANDINAVIAN

Hirsch

GERMAN

DOUKHOBOR:

1. South Colony
2. Good Spirit Lake Annex
3. North Colony

HUNGARIAN:

4. Esterhazy-Kaposvar
Colony

Ethno-religious settlement patterns, selected groups, Saskatchewan

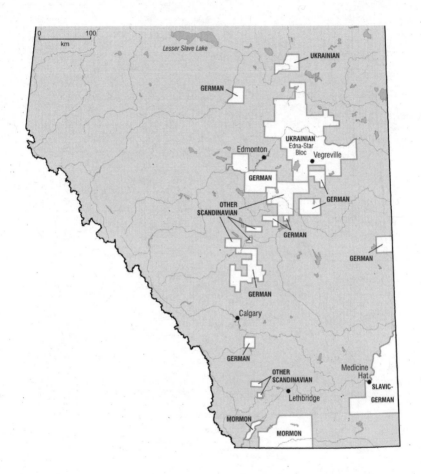

Ethno-religious settlement patterns, selected groups, Alberta

# STORIED
# LANDSCAPES

# Introduction

IN SOME RESPECTS, THIS BOOK BEGAN during my prairie childhood in east-central Alberta during long Sunday drives on dirt roads, rain or shine, looking for nothing in particular, eyes peeled for whatever the countryside offered. If we went east from our farm at Kitscoty outside Lloydminster, we immediately entered English Barr Colonist territory and soon after that, Saskatchewan. If we went west, we found ourselves in the largest Ukrainian bloc settlement in Canada, where my paternal grandparents had settled in 1901–2 and where family graves were scattered throughout. If we went north across the North Saskatchewan River, there were French communities at Bonnyville and St. Paul and a succession of Indian reserves whose residents we would encounter travelling in convoys of horse-drawn wagons. Oddly, we never went south, except the ten miles to visit my mother's sister and her family. We also never took a camera, both because the places visited constituted our own backyard (which still did not preclude getting lost), and because everything in them was familiar and would last forever. Essential stops included close-up inspections of particularly impressive crops; tramping about—and yes, trespassing—in abandoned houses, marvelling that people could just go and leave their dishes, furniture, and even curtains in the windows; buying ice cream cones in country stores with oiled floors; and checking out every church and cemetery we came across. Rural churches were unlocked in those days, their congregations unworried about vandalism or theft, and my father always slipped a dollar bill under the collection plate "for whoever finds it." The only boring bits, from my perspective, were the endless lakes and bush north of the river, when I read a book, and the endless waits when the car broke down and limped into a garage whose absent owner knew better than to open on Sunday.

These trips gave me an appreciation of my own roots in the prairies and the land. They also alerted me, however fuzzy my understanding at the time, not only to the existence and importance of ethnic and religious differences but also to their visual impact on the landscape. Ukrainians built onion-domed churches and plastered, whitewashed cottages. Natives preferred teepees that could be moved from place to place. The English and French lived in clapboard houses, sometimes two storeys high, while their churches were distinguishable by the square turrets of the former and the pointed spires of the latter. The prairie historian that I became as an adult expanded and refined these observations to question both the nature and the implications of ethno-religious identity in the Canadian West, specifically among the European immigrant settler peoples who arrived in the region between the 1870s and the 1920s. This study examines how their sense of identity or belonging was shaped by the complex interplay among a physical and emotional attachment to the land at personal and group levels, the particular ethno-religious group experience, and the history group members shared with other westerners. It also examines how that sense of identity or belonging, among both the original immigrant generation and its descendants, was influenced by (and, critically, in turn influenced) a series of relationships internal and external to the prairies. These relationships were with prairie society at large, the Canadian nation, group members in the rest of Canada, and the homeland and its diaspora. Ultimately, the study demonstrates the importance of ethnicity and religion to prairie identity, especially the little-explored intersection between "ethnic" and "mainstream," as well as the importance of the prairie West to ethno-religious identity both within the region and nationally.

Apart from its findings about specific ethno-religious groups and the West, the study addresses broad questions pertaining to Canadian identity and hinterland-metropolis relationships, past and present. First, how do ethnicity and religion inform our understanding of Canadian regionalism, or the dynamics between region and nation? Second, to what extent does the character of ethno-religious regionalism depend on and vary with the specific group immigration and settlement experience? Third, as a phenomenon within the national group experience, does prairie-based ethno-religious regionalism echo traditional alienation of the West, contest subordination, or privilege the

West? Finally, when and why does ethno-religious identity remain localized and confined to the group, and when and why does it transcend group boundaries to influence the self-image of westerners and Canadians more generally? Chapter 1 provides the framework for examining these questions and the themes of individual chapters. While not ignoring traditional emphases in the peopling of the land like settlement patterns, numbers, and reception by the host society, it highlights other factors. They are the presence or absence of a unifying collective consciousness, ideology, or way of life; the presence or absence of recognized leaders to provide initiative and direction; and the nature of the movement abroad.

Chapters 2 to 5 are organized around the idea of widening spheres of identity. Chapter 2 begins with the immediate or local, or how the immigrant generation domesticated its surroundings and became attached to the land. This grassroots identity crystallized around place naming, particularly in ways that evoked the homeland or the immigration and settlement experience; Christianization of the landscape via old-world saints, churches, and shrines; and creation of burial grounds for the dead. Chapter 3 moves to the evolution of a regionally based group consciousness among successive generations, at grassroots and elite levels, in which the construction of collective memory around founding stories and landmark anniversaries of settlement both reflected and reinforced identification with place. Chapter 4 shifts to the role of prairie-based ethno-religious identity within Canada as a whole. In some cases the prairie experience subsumed the national experience, in effect elevating the prairies to the group's Canadian homeland. In other cases the prairies were marginal to the overall group consciousness, or had to compete with national origins and origins myths that predated western settlement. Sometimes the prairies kept the group's founding story but were otherwise displaced by mass abandonment of the region or new immigration to other parts of the country. Chapter 5 probes the impact of international ties—with the homeland, a worldwide diaspora, its American component. Of special interest are the implications of a tradition of serial migration, alienation, exile, and martyrdom for the experience and identity of ethno-religious groups on the Canadian prairies.

The final three chapters examine how the immigrants' descendants, group members untouched by the western settlement experience, and the ethno-religious community at large internalized the prairie pioneer legacy in public and private space. The symbols of prairie ethnicity (Chapter 6) were curiously divorced from lived experience, favouring instead popular homeland images easily recognized by both insiders and outsiders. The pioneers were remembered, however, in a self-conscious return to the land (Chapter 7) that not only reasserted their possession of it, and thus the extended group's rights to it and its history, but also preserved their imprint by erecting cairns, ennobling surviving landmarks, and renaming the map. In contrast to the settlement period, when ethno-religious groups constructed communities and identities parallel to mainstream prairie society, certain symbols and landmarks were stripped of their ethno-religious exclusiveness and adopted by westerners as a whole to express their regional identity. Chapter 8 discusses how the land itself became "sacred ground," as ethno-religious communities transformed arrival sites, pioneer shrines and cemeteries, and the graves of their founding fathers into places of group pilgrimage and commemoration.

For almost 150 years the prairie West has been a place of remarkable ethno-religious diversity, making it unique in the history of Canada. In no other region of the country was settlement not just accompanied but defined by the simultaneous arrival of many different peoples who established themselves on the land in distinct enclaves. That this diversity emerged in conjunction with the formative period of the modern era on the prairies, and revolved around ownership and occupation of the land, was crucial to the subsequent identity of both the region and individual groups. On the one hand, regardless of the ethno-religious hierarchy that privileged some peoples and penalized others, groups and their members could not help but feel that they mattered, had a legitimate stake in the unfolding venture, and deserved to have their contribution recognized. On the other hand, and again regardless of an uneven privileging and penalizing, the pervasiveness and weight of ethno-religious diversity could not help but affect the character and self-image of prairie society, both positively and negatively. Without the frontier, however, neither phenomenon would have been possible.

Americans traditionally saw their West as a steadily progressive frontier settled by restless migrants from points further east, with the immigrant merely filling in empty spaces. The Canadian prairies, in contrast, were settled quickly via the railway and with the immigrant (and especially the non-British immigrant) regarded as a major player. A "foreign" and "immigrant" frontier alienated and alarmed Canadian migrants, who resolved to secure their patrimony through assimilation of the newcomers, but it also automatically made the newcomers participants and encouraged a sense of place and belonging. The other impact of the frontier was its fluidity. Although the dominance of the British element was never in jeopardy, the initial absence of entrenched interests, shared memory, and a consensus as to spiritual or secular authority created a vacuum. It meant that immigrant settler peoples, their patchwork of ethno-religious settlements, and their related institutions enjoyed more latitude than they would have had entering established regional societies in the Maritimes, Ontario, or Quebec. This advantage bred visibility and confidence. It also positioned ethno-religious communities to help define that elusive concept, the regional mainstream—reconfiguring and far surpassing their imprint in those areas where, thanks to numbers or profile, they set the tone. While taking care not to overstate the case, the multiculturalism that existed in the West—decades before Ottawa declared a more toothless version the cornerstone of Canadian identity—touched the core of the regional society.

The American frontier, argued Frederick Jackson Turner in 1893, acted as a levelling influence, encouraging equality, democracy, and individualism. The preceding comments tend to support his thesis, but suggest that the Canadian reality is more complex. Rather than being erased or minimized, ethno-religious differences became more pronounced and ethno-religious diversity became legitimized as part of the physical landscape and western character. If the frontier was a levelling influence, then the levelling applied not to difference and diversity but to opposition to them. Thus, and this point is critical, frontier equality and democracy benefitted groups *as* groups, even as they jeopardized the hold that groups *as* groups exerted over individual members.[1] The West's experience also urges historians who shy away from integrating non-British, non-French ethnicity and ethno-religious communities into the Canadian nation-building story as meaningful forces to return to J.M.S. Careless's notion of Canada as a series of "limited identities." While comfortable with the traditional regionalism he used to test his idea, Careless himself retreated before ethnicity, fearful that too great a focus on the trees, that is, particularist identities, risked obscuring the forest or nation. What must be recognized and incorporated into the analysis, however, is that in the prairie West the limited identity defining the region owed much of its distinctiveness to its peculiar ethno-religious history.[2] That the region's ethno-religious distinctiveness emerged from and described the rural West, outside the urban centres with which the countryside maintained a symbiotic relationship, was also significant. It ensured that the rural West retained an inflated importance in the collective imagination well after large-scale urbanization reduced its impact in everyday life.[3] This enduring relevance, both to the ethno-religious groups represented by immigrant settler peoples and as an explanation for the character of prairie society, challenges Gerald Friesen's suggestion that by the late twentieth century the idea of the traditional prairie West was passé.[4] Although it might have lost much usefulness as a conceptual tool for analyzing contemporary politics, for example, the traditional prairie West remains a valid framework for understanding the construction and expression of ethno-religious identity, past and present.

To appropriate Benedict Anderson's now ubiquitous phrase, the identity that ethno-religious groups on the prairies cultivated over the course of a century or more described "imagined communities." Individuals who did not, and indeed could not, all personally know each other nonetheless saw themselves as creating distinct and emotionally valuable units, defined by a shifting combination of shared language, borders, faith, race/ethnicity, historical memory, current events, and symbols.[5] As immigrant settler peoples on the prairies illustrated, it was possible to belong to several overlapping, even incompatible and competing, imagined communities at once: local, regional, national, diasporic. In fact, emigration and the peculiarities of frontier settlement forced a wide range of new constellations and identities onto individuals and groups for whom an equally complex mix of old-world constellations and identities no longer sufficed. Also, immigrant settler peoples were not monolithic. Nationalist and communist ideologies, for instance, could be as powerful as Catholicism and Protestantism (or class) in creating smaller imagined communities within the overarching rubric of the ethnic group. Even the notion of the "prairies" or the "West" imposed at times an artificial unity, as ethno-religious groups were also affected by their specific experience in each of Alberta, Saskatchewan, and Manitoba.

The best access to these imagined communities, especially the narratives and assumptions that transcended internal divisions, is through milestone anniversaries of immigration and settlement. While the identification of such landmarks ordered the collective experience and defined its common touchstones, the associated celebrations—from rhetoric and "invented" traditions to physical memorials—often had presentist goals.[6] The deliberate cultivation of a group consciousness and sense of achievement around a particular interpretation and valuation of the past enabled immigrant settler peoples not only to explain and justify who they were but also to argue for their uniqueness and importance. In so doing, they moved from the realm of history, with its emphasis on objectivity and fact, into the realm of heritage, constantly invented and reinvented, always subjective and selective. "Legends of origin and endurance, of victory or calamity," wrote David Lowenthal in *The Heritage Crusade and the Spoils of History*, "project the present past, the past forward; they align us with forebears whose future we share and whose vices we shun. We are apt to call such communion history, but it is actually heritage. The distinction is vital. History explores and explains pasts grown ever more opaque over time; heritage clarifies pasts so to infuse them with present purposes."[7] Heritage also relies heavily on the material as well as the imagined past, its artifacts ranging from embroidered folk costumes in the museum to picturesque ruins, historic buildings, and old monuments on the land. The association among heritage, the land, and ethno-religious identity is central to this book, hence its title *Storied Landscapes*. The landscapes are both physical places and places of the mind, the stories the multilayered, sometimes contested narratives and material legacies that immigrant settler peoples mobilized in shaping and claiming those places.[8]

Settlers, whether immigrant or migrant, and their rural descendants defined the prairie West for over half a century after 1870, as, with the active input of the Dominion government, they turned their backs on the fur trade in favour of agricultural occupation of the land. Such an observation begs clarification as to what the book is about in terms of its human actors. First, it is about immigrants, so that the country's two "charter peoples" appear infrequently, either as part of specific overseas movements or as transplanted Canadians possessing advantages and privileges that non-British and non-French "foreigners" lacked. It is also about European immigrants, whether coming directly from overseas or via the United States, and thus ignores the comparatively few American Blacks and even fewer Asians who went to prairie farms. Second, the book focuses exclusively on settlers on the land. This emphasis pushes to the fore ethno-religious groups that established a visible presence around identifiable colonies or blocs, regardless of their size and whether or not they typified the group's prairie experience as a whole, and disregards urban and resource-based communities. Ownership of the soil (especially on reserved tracts of land), family settlement, and the shared feat of pioneering fostered a sense of permanence and place and belonging that simultaneously celebrated and transcended ethno-religious differences, and which eluded the transient and often male-dominated populations of mining towns or prairie cities. Third, the book is about both ethnicity and religion, acknowledging the inseparability of the two in the makeup of European immigrant settler peoples in western Canada. Faith was often a critical feature of their ethnic identity and distinguished one group from another, just as religious divisions could destroy ethnic unity or denominational ties create bonds across ethnic lines.

Also, the book is an exploration of themes rising directly or indirectly from the self-images ethno-religious groups cultivated and not a history of the groups as such. The reader expecting to find "the story" of his or her people will therefore be disappointed. Given the focus on themes, individual groups weave in and out of the discussion, mobilized when pertinent to the topic or point under review. The mix includes both the scattered few and the concentrated many; both the widely accepted and easily integrated and the highly suspect and marginalized; and both those with strong collective identities and narratives and those with weak ones. It also includes distinct and sanctioned ways of life together with more loose associations based on voluntary and ill-defined ties; controlled emigrations together with the leaderless movements of individuals; and histories of national and/or religious oppression and uncertain survival together with histories of old-world statehood and security. That said, by virtue of the robustness of their imagined communities and invented traditions predicated upon the immigration and settlement experience, four peoples dominate. They are Ukrainians, Mennonites, Icelanders, and Doukhobors. Other Scandinavians (Swedes, Norwegians, and Danes) and other eastern Europeans (Poles, Romanians, and Jews) join them, as do American Mormons and Finns. Three peoples—Hungarians, German Catholics, and English—are represented by single settlements: the Esterhazy-Kaposvar, St. Peter's, and Barr colonies. A handful of other groups make cameo appearances.

Finally, and most importantly, the book is about how people see themselves, as individuals and as members of ethno-religious groups whose immigrant ancestors settled the Canadian prairies and created a particular type of westerner—different from other westerners and group members elsewhere, yet sharing features with each. These people and the myths, symbols, commemorative traditions, and landmarks underpinning their identity deserve respect and recognition, even as I have taken the liberty of subjecting them to the historian's gaze. The fieldwork for the book took me across Alberta and Saskatchewan and Manitoba, far beyond the backyard of my childhood. Much of the time I was by myself, driving down unfamiliar roads (in Alberta now often paved, although not in Saskatchewan or Manitoba), still open to whatever the landscape offered, but simultaneously, these many years later, armed with a plan. There were still boring bits, but sitting behind the wheel, I could not read a book. The car never broke down, but if it had, I could have summoned the Canadian Automobile Association on my cellphone, twenty-four hours a day. Of course I carried a camera, self-consciously recording the surviving reminders of communities built by the immigrant settler generation. Sometimes I enjoyed the comradeship of travelling companions, inevitably impressed with the treasures on their doorstep; and everywhere I met the proud descendants of the pioneers, still living on the land and always ready to accommodate an inquisitive stranger.

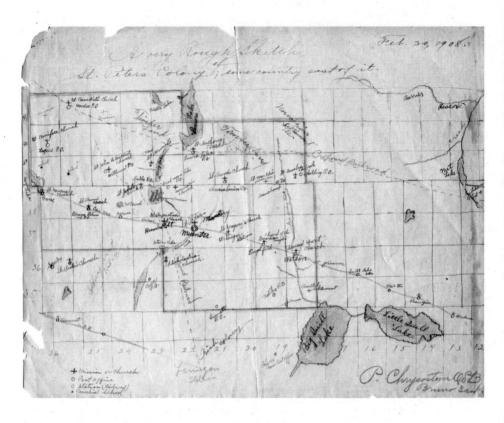

**1.1.** A "sense of place"—landmarks in the five-year-old St. Peter's Colony as identified by Benedictine priest, Father Chrysostom Hoffmann, 1908.

# Ethno-Religious Settlement:
# The Canadian Prairies in Context

IN 1998 ROMANIANS IN ALBERTA celebrated their centennial with a special service at St. Mary Orthodox Church, a ninety-three-year-old structure in the heart of the group's old settlement of Boian, east of Edmonton. Following a lunchtime banquet in nearby Willingdon, area residents, descendants of the pioneers, and more recent Romanian immigrants to the city returned to the crossroads below the church for ceremonies at the outdoor pioneer museum. A plastered and whitewashed cottage, restored to reflect early twentieth-century Romanian homestead life, delighted visitors who might not have noticed a small, incongruous calendar from Adler's Department Store in Vegreville hanging on the wall. Dated 1991, it featured a picture of the Sacred Heart of Jesus, a devotion meaningful to local Roman Catholic Poles but not Byzantine-rite Romanians. Saints' days, feasts, and fasts on the calendar appeared in Ukrainian. The Adlers themselves were Jews, one of several families to have opened businesses in the area among fellow immigrants from eastern Europe.[1]

This chapter lays the groundwork for explaining a multicultural curiosity like the Adler calendar, its unremarked presence in a Romanian pioneer museum, and the broader implications for ethno-religious identity on the Canadian prairies. It does so using four frameworks, each representing one of the many relationships that shaped European settler peoples in the West. The first situates the settlers in the traditional narrative of Canadian nation building, in which the prairies took a prominent place in a young Dominion destined to own the twentieth century, as Prime Minister Sir Wilfrid Laurier boldly predicted. Over several generations, commentators and historians sharing the pro-British biases and agenda of nation builders produced a story of prairie immigration and settlement that silenced the voice of the "foreigner." The priorities and narratives of individual ethno-religious groups, dignifying the immigrant as actor, inform the second framework. This section tells the story of prairie immigration and settlement from the vantage point of the newcomers and isolates factors that over the next century influenced the construction of their local and regional identities. The third framework locates ethno-religious groups on the prairies within the immigration and settlement history of their people in Canada as a whole. The fourth considers those same stories in the context of the emigration history of the homeland.

## Nation Building and Prairie Settlement

The surrender of Rupert's Land by the Hudson's Bay Company in 1869 paved the way for the fledgling Dominion to finally stretch "from sea unto sea," as its motto boasted. By the outbreak of war in 1914, which ended the settlement rush that followed, the West had long shed its image as an inhospitable wilderness suited only to the fur trade. Led by British Ontarian expansionists, it became instead a virgin and fertile land promising redemption, regeneration, and material wealth. At the same time, fuelling future western alienation, Ottawa retained control over natural resources, while the National Policy of the 1880s and later promoted the region as the hinterland of the country's manufacturing, metropolitan centres.[2] Events on the prairies, as well as the prejudices of French Quebeckers and their priests (the former unconvinced of the richness of the soil, the latter fearing denationalization), also meant that the West was seen as the patrimony of Anglo-Protestant Ontario.[3] The resulting ethno-religious hierarchy and emphasis on immigrant assimilation dictated who would be wanted as settlers and who would not, and whether newcomers were accepted and quickly integrated or treated with suspicion and marginalized. A final assumption was that the land in the West would be occupied by independent farmers living with their families on "free" homesteads of 160 acres each.

By 1901 one-third of the West's population was foreign born compared to 3 percent in the rest of Canada, a sign that the prairies would not replicate the East even though the British and French enjoyed special privileges as European first-comers, dominating the region's elites and its official narrative.[4]

However, large-scale internal migration from Ontario and the Maritimes, coupled with the strength of Great Britain as an overseas donor, ensured the ascendancy of the British element and heritage. Until mid-century, over half of prairie residents claimed British origins, while the French hovered around 6 percent, below new German, Scandinavian, and Slavic immigrant groups.[5] British immigration combined individual initiative with a handful of government-supported colonization schemes of varying success that produced distinctive ethno-religious communities. The most patriotic venture was the Barr Colony, named for the Anglican clergyman, Isaac Barr, who in 1903 led some 3000 English "greenhorns" to what became Lloydminster on the Alberta-Saskatchewan border in a bid to keep the prairies British.[6] French settlement drew on modest internal migration and overseas immigration, plus the repatriation onto prairie homesteads of former Quebeckers living in the United States. The priest-colonizers behind this movement, backed by the Roman Catholic hierarchy, founded French-speaking communities at points across the West.[7]

Despite commitment to individual homesteading, Ottawa was clearly receptive to group colonization, whether to attract the right type of settler, ease the burden of pioneering, or stimulate immigration in the 1870s and 1880s when disappointingly few settlers came on their own. After 1896, as Liberal minister of the interior responsible for immigration, Clifford Sifton de-emphasized cultural and racial considerations that had favoured Britain, northwestern Europe, and the United States. Preferring experienced farmers used to adversity, he solicited peasants from central and eastern Europe, convinced that their affinity with the soil would encourage assimilation and identification with the new homeland. Opponents dismissively labelled the newcomers "Sifton's pets" and condemned the influx and bloc settlement of Slavs in particular.[8] Central and eastern European settler peoples, Catholic or Orthodox in faith, were preferred to Jews (who came from the same part of the world) and even less-wanted Asians and Blacks. But they ranked well below the British, French, Germans, and Scandinavians, with their broadly shared values and histories.[9] Succeeding Sifton in 1905, Frank Oliver tried to reverse the trend and promote British immigration, as did the Conservatives after 1911. Yet both attempts proved vulnerable to industry and business, so that the decade before the Great War saw a rise in "foreign navvies" coming not to farm the western prairies but to lay sewers, build railways, and work in mines.

Ottawa first attempted to attract settlers to the prairies through reserved blocs of land. In 1874 German-speaking Mennonites left the Russian empire, where they had moved in the late eighteenth century, for the treeless Manitoba plain. Self-segregated pacifists who practised communal landholding without rejecting private property, they had successfully farmed the Ukrainian steppe and were seen as law abiding and hard working. Ottawa thus willingly made concessions, known to Mennonites as the "Canadian Privilegium" after the similar Privilegium under attack in Russia. They received land grants—the East and West reserves—on either side of the Red River; exemption from military service and the oath of allegiance; religious freedom; and, to preserve their language and culture, control over education. The latter lay outside Ottawa's authority, but Manitoba grudgingly instituted bilingual schools that lasted until the anti-foreign hysteria of the Great War. Homesteading requirements were also altered to permit Mennonites to reside in their traditional villages, instead of the quarter sections registered to male heads of households, and share the land. By the time the reserves were opened up in 1898, more individualistic Mennonites had moved onto their own farms.[10] Impoverished Icelanders fleeing a harsh environment were the second group to receive an exclusive land grant in this period. Established in 1875 in what became the District of Keewatin, and absorbed by Manitoba when it extended its boundaries in 1881, New Iceland consisted of some nine townships of often swampy land on the west shore of Lake Winnipeg. The territory was self-governing with its own constitution, laws, and elected officials until 1887, and it remained closed to other settlers until 1897. Anglo-Canadians regarded Icelanders as ideal immigrants—progressive, democratic, educated—although local preconceptions were less positive. Anticipating the first contingent headed for New Iceland, Winnipeggers expected people "about four feet [tall], rather stout and thick set, with long black hair and much like the Eskimos."[11]

In the 1880s group settlement shifted from closed colonies, with their negative implications for nation building, to more informal clusterings. In 1887 American Mormons seeking religious freedom trekked north from Utah, their most recent sanctuary, to escape prosecution following the criminalization of polygamy. They took homesteads and purchased land in southern Alberta in an area between the Rocky Mountains and the Blood (Kainai) Reserve.

**1.2.** Mennonite village with windmill partially visible, perhaps Reinfeld, southern Manitoba, c. 1898. ARCHIVES OF MANITOBA, MENNONITES 66, N11766.

By 1900 success with irrigation had tempered hostility to a group believed to undermine the moral foundations of Canadian society.[12] Also fleeing religious persecution and never recruited by Canada were Jews from the Russian empire, as government-condoned pogroms and restrictions escalated after the assassination of Tsar Alexander II in 1881. Despite generalized anti-Semitism and doubts about Jews' farming ability, fifteen "colonies" were established, particularly in southern Saskatchewan (originally the District of Assiniboia), between 1884 and the Great War. They were small, only a few score homesteads each, and had a precarious existence; other Jewish immigrants became independent farmers.[13] In 1886, after a settlement attempt at Huns Valley in Manitoba the previous year, Assiniboia also welcomed Hungarian peasants increasingly reduced to labouring on Hungary's landed estates. The Esterhazy or Kaposvar Colony, founded with a loan from the Canadian Pacific Railway, also contained some Slovaks.[14] The decade brought other economic emigrants as well. Swedes founded New Sweden or Scandinavia

**1.3.** Icelandic farmstead (note the Red River cart), New Iceland, Manitoba, n.d.
ARCHIVES OF MANITOBA, NIC 237, N11244.

on reserved land at Erickson, Manitoba, in 1885 and New Stockholm next to Esterhazy-Kaposvar in 1886. In 1888 Finns established New Finland next to the Hungarians. Scandinavian immigration, augmented by Danes and especially Norwegians, swelled over the next two decades, enlarging existing settlements and producing new centres. Anglo-Canadians welcomed these immigrants for cultural reasons as well as the fact that they often had money and often preferred purchasing land (to the delight of the railway with its unsold acres) over homesteading.[15]

The largest of the controversial peasant peoples courted by Sifton, Ukrainians soon epitomized the evils of his immigration policy. The first permanent settlers arrived in 1892, taking homesteads east of Edmonton near Ukrainian-speaking Germans in what became the Edna-Star colony. As new immigrants chose the comfort of this growing bloc, Ottawa tried to restrict its size and impact by creating alternate nuclei—to which end agents adopted novel tactics, even locking the railway cars that transported the immigrants west. By 1905 a series of Ukrainian settlements of varying size crossed the parkland from southern Manitoba near the Mennonite East Reserve to just outside the Alberta capital. Sifton defended the "Galicians," a pejorative term derived from Ukrainians' place of origin, saying, "I think that a stalwart peasant in a sheepskin coat, born on the soil, whose forefathers have been farmers for ten generations, with a stout wife and a half-dozen children, is good quality."[16] Polish and Romanian peasants—like Ukrainians, land squeezed, impoverished, and nationally oppressed—often settled nearby; they, too, laboured under the unflattering "Galician" stereotype.[17] The experience of Russian Doukhobors was more complicated. A pacifist and simple-living communistic sect that rejected a mediatory priesthood, all sacraments, and secular authority, they had had a tumultuous relationship with the Russian state since the eighteenth century: exiled to Taurida and Transcaucasia, imprisoned in Siberia, and finally forced into military service. In 1899, championed by Count Leo Tolstoi and the English Quakers, and enjoying broad public sympathy, Doukhobor peasants received four reserves in the districts of Assiniboia and Saskatchewan. They became the North and South colonies and Good Spirit Lake Annex near the Manitoba border, and the Saskatchewan Colony near Prince Albert. Like Mennonites, Doukhobors were exempt from military service. Pro-Doukhobor sentiment soon soured, sparked by conflicts with the government and other settlers over living in traditional villages rather than on their homesteads and by the growing extremism among some members.[18]

One final land grant prior to the Great War accommodated German Catholics in St. Peter's Colony east of Saskatoon, beginning in 1903. A second German Catholic settlement, St. Joseph's Colony, established southeast of Lloydminster in 1908, evolved as an informal bloc or ethno-religious cluster. In both cases individual homesteads were the norm. More generally, German immigration and settlement tended to be at once individualistic and oriented towards other Germans, producing widely dispersed but identifiable communities in all three prairie provinces. Anglo-Canadians welcomed Germans for their perceived sobriety and industriousness, although four years of fighting for Mother Britain against the hated "Hun" in the muddy, rat-infested trenches of Europe had tarnished this positive image.[19]

By the time of the special prairie census in 1916, war had ended the region's first and largest wave of immigration and settlement. As Benedict Anderson writes, both the census, which counts and classifies group members, and the map, which defines their geopolitical territory, are crucial to a sense of nation.[20] However, if Anglo-Canadians exulted in the wash of red over the globe that symbolized the British empire, the map of their own country, particularly its western interior, caused unease. A welter of ethno-religious islands attested to the success of physical nation building but they also warned of the need to weld diverse peoples into a regional society and to make them Canadian. Belying Anderson's argument as to its unifying powers, the census reinforced such concerns, dividing the population according to ethnic origin, religious affiliation, immigrant versus Canadian born, country of birth, naturalized versus unnaturalized, and mother tongue. In 1916, out of a prairie population of 1,698,220, Germans and Ukrainians constituted by far the largest "foreign" ethnic groups, Romanians and Finns the smallest. As ethno-religious minorities, Doukhobors and Mormons comprised less than 1 percent of prairie residents, Mennonites considerably more. The big Anglo-Protestant denominations—Anglican, Presbyterian, and Methodist—mustered a bare plurality. They were challenged by the Roman Catholic Church, expanding from its French base to absorb Irish, Poles, Germans, Hungarians, Italians, and others; Scandinavian, German, and Finnish Lutheran churches; and the Byzantine-rite Catholic and Orthodox churches of Ukrainians, Russians, and Romanians. Looking again at the map, nation builders shuddered to note how religious boundaries reinforced ethnic ones.

The census behind the ethno-religious map hid and misled as much as it revealed. Often the generic "Scandinavian" substituted for individual peoples. Canadian ignorance of eastern Europe, plus the fact that the identity of Ukrainians was in flux, meant that Ukrainians appeared under five names: "Austrian," for the empire of which they were subjects; "Galician" or "Bukovynian," for the provinces from which they originated; "Ruthenian," the old word for themselves; and the increasingly preferred "Ukrainian," first listed on the census form in 1916. Both imperial and provincial designations inevitably included Poles, Romanians, and Jews who also self-identified in those terms.[21] The "Russian" designation did not include all Doukhobors, as perhaps most still refused to register with the state, especially as relations with Canadian officials deteriorated. "Russian" was also a legitimate imperial option for Poles, Jews, and Ukrainians from tsar-ruled territories; attractive to Russophile and Orthodox Austrian Ukrainians; and, in 1916 and 1921, popular among Ukrainians from Austria-Hungary trying to elude the wartime stigma of enemy aliens. Both "Romanian" and "Hungarian" included Jews; "Finnish" included

**1.4.** Typical broad central street in a Doukhobor village, South Colony, Saskatchewan, early 1900s. SASKATCHEWAN ARCHIVES BOARD, S-A135.

Swedes living in Finland; "Mennonite" from 1921 included Hutterites; and "German" included a host of peoples having no direct contact with Germany. The German experience highlights the problems with the census not only in counting and classifying but also in establishing the boundaries of a "Canadian people." The passions of the Great War that temporarily made ethnic Germans suspect were reflected in prairie Germans' response to the question about ethnicity. In 1911 a total of 147,638 individuals claimed German origins; after two years of hostilities, the number dropped to 136,968; by 1921 it had dropped again, to 122,979.

In the 1920s, as Canada refocussed on domestic issues and absorbed the lessons of the war years, assimilating the country's undigested foreign masses received high priority. At the same time, immigration to the West resumed. Shrinking homestead lands plus unsold railway grants favoured both farmers with capital and labourers for the crews that large-scale market production demanded. Anglo-Canadian nativism and the pre-war ethnic hierarchy also combined to categorize donor countries as "preferred" and "non-preferred." Ottawa retained control over preferred immigration, which included assisted

British settlement schemes, but in 1925 handed the selection, monitoring, and sponsorship of immigrants from non-preferred sources—the new states of Austria, Hungary, Poland, Romania, Bulgaria, Yugoslavia, Czechoslovakia, and the Soviet Union—to the railways. When the Great Depression ended this agreement in 1930, Ukrainians had been its greatest beneficiary.[22] Interwar immigrants reinforced the existing ethno-religious map, although they also contributed to emerging settlement areas. Displaced persons from the Second World War, European immigrants in general over the next two decades, and the visible minorities (from Asia, the Caribbean, and Africa) who followed preferred central Canada.[23] By then the Anglo-Canadian vision of nation building in the West and the campaign to assimilate one-time foreigners had long been abandoned. In fact, the "old West" relished its diversity, proudly proclaiming cultural pluralism one of the defining features of the regional society.

## Prairie Settlement and the Ethno-Religious Experience

Whether the catalyst was religious persecution, national oppression, grinding poverty, or, as immigration historians have increasingly argued, frustrated ambition and expectations, the factors pushing peoples from their homelands were at least as strong as Canada's desire to attract settlers. Members of ethno-religious groups came to the prairies as part of international movements embracing a wide range of experiences, motivations, and decision-making processes that affected group identity both then and later. One variable involved the nature of the initial immigration: the role of a preliminary scouting party; organized movements under recognized leaders versus those that were not; and compact movements from a limited source, arriving within a short time frame, versus those from diverse and widely dispersed sources that spanned many years. A second variable concerned the nature of the original settlement experience, both its rural character and the repercussions of settling in official colonies, informal and voluntary blocs or clusters, or individual scattered homesteads. How the profiles of individual groups evolved in subsequent decades depended on yet other variables. They included group size, regional distribution patterns, the impact of new immigrations, ideological and religious divisions, and changing rural-urban relationships.

When Isaac Barr selected the land on which to erect his outpost of the British empire, he used a map. He was lucky, and the naive city dwellers who relied on him fortunate, that he chose well. Otherwise, agricultural disaster would have joined the charges of mismanagement that led to his ouster before the English colonists reached their destination. As it was, individual settlers were unhappy with their quarter sections, allotted on-board ship using yet another map.[24] Barr was unusual for leaders of organized colonization initiatives, or even more general group movements, in his hands-off approach to site selection. More commonly, an advance party visited the West to check out the options and make recommendations. Sometimes scouts returned to lead their people to Canada; other times they faded to the background, relinquishing active leadership of the movement they instigated or never emigrating at all.

Both Mormon settlers and St. Peter's Colony of German Catholics had advance scouts-turned-leaders who played major roles in the formative stages of their communities. In 1886 the Mormon Church in Utah sent Charles Ora Card to investigate British Columbia as a haven for the persecuted faith. Unimpressed with the available land, he visited and recommended southern Alberta instead, and the following year led the first settlers to the site. Card continued to be prominent in Mormon life, and in 1895 became first president of the Alberta Stake.[25] St. Peter's Colony began when St. John's Abbey in Minnesota dispatched Father Bruno Doerfler to western Canada to find land suitable for a homogeneous "closed" settlement under the Order of St. Benedict.[26] This wish coincided with the desire of the priory at Cluny, Illinois, to relocate to a healthier climate, giving the colony an immediate leadership in the monastery founded at Muenster in 1903. Father Bruno became its second prior in 1906, and in 1911 its first abbot. Occupation of the land reserve—whose settlers came from the United States and Europe—represented a unique blend of ecclesiastical initiative and control through the Benedictines, homesteading through the Catholic Settlement Society, and land purchase through the German American Land Company. Otherwise, St. Peter's Colony was like the many church-focussed and clergy-led settlements, Catholic and Protestant, that marked so much German immigration. The men who chose or arranged for their location, brought out the first settlers, and shepherded the pioneers in their early years never acquired more than local reputations.[27]

German speaking and faith based, the Mennonite immigration of some

7000 persons in the 1870s differed in scale, magnifying the role of the advance party of 1873 that toured southern Manitoba, inspected the land, and met with officials to receive the Canadian Privilegium. In fact, three delegations were dispatched, connecting en route to investigate the American Midwest as well, but some representatives preferred western Canada with its specific guarantees.[28] One of these men, the Reverend Heinrich Wiebe, accompanied the first settlers in 1874 and eventually located in the West Reserve, but as a spiritual leader in an increasingly fractured community he lacked the stature of Card or Father Bruno. The most prominent figure in the advance party was Jacob Shantz, a Swiss Mennonite farmer and businessman from Ontario. At Ottawa's urging, Shantz was targeting his co-religionists; not only had he previously visited Manitoba and written a pamphlet promoting the province, but he also pushed Canada over the United States, helped the Russian Mennonites with their journey abroad, and worked thereafter on their behalf on many fronts. The immigrants, like the delegates who selected Manitoba, were less prosperous and more conservative Mennonites from Chortitza, one of two original colonies on the Ukrainian steppe, its daughter colonies of Bergthal and Fürstenland, and the Kleine Gemeinde colony of Borozenko.

New Iceland also originated in a preliminary scouting mission that included an individual who shaped the establishment and early life of the colony. Departing for North America in 1872 at age twenty, Sigtryggur Jónasson chose to settle in Ontario over following Páll Þorláksson, a Lutheran theological student studying in Missouri, to the United States. He promoted Icelandic immigration to Ontario on behalf of the provincial government, although a visit to Nova Scotia made him discourage settlement in that province. Then, in 1875 he joined a delegation—financed by Ottawa and accompanied by Icelandic delegates from Wisconsin—to explore sites for an Icelandic colony in the West. Jónasson subsequently helped negotiate the terms for New Iceland, toured his homeland as a federal immigration agent, and recruited and led the bigger of two parties forming the "Large Group" that arrived in 1876. He also served as the first chairman of New Iceland's colony council. Immigration to the colony was erratic and only ever numbered several thousand, dominated by the 1200-member "Large Group" driven abroad by volcanic eruptions in the Dyngja Mountains. Epidemics and out-migration competed with incomers, so that the population fluctuated widely: from 1500 settlers in 1877, for example,

**1.5.** Ukrainian homestead, with traditional thatched, plastered, and whitewashed cottage and wattle fence, Smoky Lake area, Alberta, c. 1927.
PROVINCIAL ARCHIVES OF ALBERTA, G184.

it dropped to 250 in 1881 before recovering to 1557 by 1894.[29]

Ukrainians best illustrate the scenario where the first men to explore settlement possibilities in western Canada acted independently and soon slipped into obscurity. In 1891 Ivan Pylypiw, a peasant entrepreneur from the village of Nebyliv in Galicia, and his one-time employee, Vasyl Eleniak, came to check the free land east of Edmonton touted by a German countryman. Not only did Pylypiw's enthusiasm inspire the first permanent settlers a year later, also from Nebyliv, but his German connections determined the site of the Edna-Star colony. Both Pylypiw and Eleniak eventually settled there with their families, but neither man remained active in Ukrainian emigration or became a leader in the pioneer community. Ukrainians, however, also typify the scenario where an instigator of the movement to the Canadian prairies did not join it. In 1895 Dr. Osyp Oleskiv, one of the Galician intelligentsia distressed by the lot of the Ukrainian peasantry, toured Canada and unsuccessfully tried to interest Ottawa in an assisted settlement scheme. His advice to peasants (he, too, preferred east-central Alberta) and two popular pamphlets turned the trickle after Pylypiw and Eleniak into a flood. But Oleskiv himself never returned to Canada and ill health ended his emigration work by 1900.[30] As Ukrainian immigration became a mass movement reaching 170,000, in which parties of varying size travelled together, unconnected to other parties coming at different times, it lacked overall direction and leadership. Also, while dominated by the provinces of Galicia and Bukovyna in Austria-Hungary, it drew as well from adjacent territories in the Russian empire.

In different ways Hungarians, Doukhobors, and Jews offer better examples of the absent or displaced leader. Founder of the Esterhazy-Kaposvar Colony, the self-styled "Count" Paul O. d'Esterhazy was a Hungarian patriot and soldier—and an ambitious and purportedly compassionate, if not always practical man—who had emigrated to the United States after 1848. He returned south of the border after leading the first contingent to the site he had personally inspected and chosen, but continued to dream of a "New Hungary" in western Canada and intervened with both Ottawa and the Canadian Pacific Railway on behalf of the colony and its residents. In 1902 he also toured the area for the Department of the Interior to research a promotional pamphlet to lure more Hungarian immigrants.[31] Esterhazy's initial settlers came from Pennsylvania, and he paid much attention to the United States, whether to rescue Hungarian peasants from its coal mines and foundries and bring them back to the land, or to convince new arrivals at Ellis Island of the benefits of Canadian homesteads over American cities.

Propelled by a strong collective consciousness forged over a century of persecution, the entire 7400-strong Doukhobor immigration occurred over six months, in only four shiploads, and went to a fixed destination. The immigrants' leader in Russia, as head of the majority group formed in the schism that succeeded the powerful Lukeria Kalmykova, Peter "the Lordly" Verigin guided his followers from exile in Siberia. Although playing no part in the exodus to Canada other than acquiescing in the choice and continuing to lead from afar, after his release in 1902 he joined the group in Saskatchewan. The very idea of Canada as a refuge emerged by chance, when a supporter read about the terms won by Russian Mennonites. The subsequent delegation under Tolstoian follower Prince Khilkov and the Quaker Aylmer Maude to find suitable land included two Doukhobor peasants who, unusually, brought their families to reassure Canadians about the people being proposed for the West. However,

Sifton's opponents resisted their selection of a single bloc near the Ukrainians at Edna-Star, making the dispersed reserves further east a disappointing compromise.[32] Doukhobors were unique in that the movement to Canada had a single catalyst—the symbolic burning of arms on St. Peter's Day 1895 in defiance of the reimposition of conscription and the brutal repression that ensued. Also, by the time the refugees arrived, the majority group (reconstituted as the Christian Community of Universal Brotherhood), did not necessarily support all aspects of Verigin's idea of a Christian communist utopia that included vegetarianism and sexual abstinence.

The major figure in Jewish immigration to the rural prairies was the German-born and Paris-based Baron Maurice de Hirsch—industrialist, financier, and philanthropist. He founded the Jewish Colonization Association in 1891, a London-registered stock company backed by Jewish leaders in England and western Europe, and committed large sums of his own money to establish agricultural colonies in South America, the United States, and western Canada for persecuted European Jews. Modest Jewish settlement initiatives in Saskatchewan and Manitoba predated Hirsch's involvement, but the Jewish Colonization Association provided invaluable funding and security to the colonies founded with its support. Hirsch died in 1896, precluding a personal hands-on approach even if he had been so inclined. At the grassroots level, Jewish colonies looked to local leaders, much like the small and scattered German settlements. The immigration stories of other groups—from Danes, Swedes, and Norwegians to Poles and Romanians—were similar, in that localized settlement initiatives and leaders deprived the overall movement of dominating or unifying events and figures.

As Canadian nation builders intended—and as the immigrants expected, even if ill prepared for farming or pioneering—newcomers to the West settled overwhelmingly on the land. Jews, who preferred the burgeoning city of Winnipeg, were the exception. In rural areas, and reflecting the English immigrants' urban origins, the immediate creation of Lloydminster to service the surrounding agricultural community set the Barr Colonists apart. All settler peoples also had to adapt to the Canadian requirements of occupying the land, which changed how they lived and related to others. Although Mennonites and Doukhobors received permission to recreate their traditional villages, no mechanism existed to force group members to comply, and the village

**1.6.** Norwegian homestead on the bald prairie (the ploughed strip in the foreground is a fireguard), Bawlf, Alberta, early 1900s.
GLENBOW MUSEUM, NA-3618-3.

system crumbled as the independently minded withdrew to their own land.[33] Ukrainian and other eastern European peasants who had also lived in villages, often in extended families, and gone out to till their small plots, had not only to cope with the isolation that faced all homesteaders on their quarter sections but also to invent an alternative to the village and its services. The answer was a multitude of rural "crossroads" clusters: a combination of churches, halls, general store, blacksmith shop, and mill; and, from the outside world, post office and school.[34] Such clusters, like their counterparts among other settlers, eclipsed the towns that sprang up in conjunction with the railways as the focus of community life. Finally, while peasants used to subsistence on one or two acres had to learn to farm commercially on a quarter section, the English greenhorn and the Jew from the ghetto started from zero and had to learn to harness a team of horses.

Despite adjustments demanded by the homestead system, settlement in either official colonies or informal blocs surrounded residents with their own kind and cushioned them against prejudice and discrimination. Yet the same colonies and blocs splintered along a number of lines. The most common division was physical, as new immigrants sought out family members and fellow villagers, or at least people from the same district in the old country, configuring the landscape around old-world places of origin and old-world identities. At the same time, the frontier threw together people from a wide range of backgrounds, obliging them to renegotiate their collective sense of self. Years later, a pioneer in the Jewish colony of Edenbridge northeast of Saskatoon recalled the settlers gathering in the tiny post office to discuss events in revolutionary Russia. "There, in that waiting room," he wrote, "I encountered Jews who came from all over the world. There were Africans, Europeans, Americans, and a new breed called Canadians. Each had his own distinguishing feature: the African wore a light shirt; the Lithuanian, tall boots; the American wore a leather jacket; and the Canadian, a fur cap with flaps pulled down over his ears and Edenbridge-style overalls—a checkerboard of patches. All of them had one thing in common—beards; some short ones, and some long, full beards."[35] Outside influences, particularly a new rail line with service centres at regular intervals along its tracks, also caused individuals and communities to reorient themselves.[36] Other divisions were invisible but profound in their impact. Religious and ideological differences—between Catholic and Orthodox or nationalist and communist Ukrainians, for example, or within Mennonite and Doukhobor ranks—produced at times volatile factions. Such disputes also left their imprint on the landscape in the form of rival churches, halls, and cemeteries.

By 1931 it was clear that, except for the British and French, prairie settler peoples had dispersed unevenly across the region. Only Ukrainians—with roughly a third of group members in each of Manitoba, Saskatchewan, and Alberta—mirrored the "founding nations." Their distribution pattern no doubt owed much to the series of blocs, established roughly simultaneously and with government direction, that from the start embraced all three provinces. Almost 90 percent of Mennonites (Manitoba, Saskatchewan) and over 80 percent of both Swedes (Alberta, Saskatchewan) and Finns (Saskatchewan, Alberta) crowded into two provinces. Mennonites, for example, had expanded into Saskatchewan on a large scale beginning in the 1890s, either as daughter colonies of the Manitoba reserves or drawing from further afield: Ontario, the

United States, Russia, and Prussia. Most groups disproportionately favoured a single province: Manitoba for Icelanders, Jews, and Poles; Saskatchewan for Doukhobors, Hungarians, Romanians, Norwegians, and Germans; and Alberta for Mormons and Danes. Hungarians, for example, preferred to create new settlements within Saskatchewan, while Icelandic expansion westward never challenged the Manitoba base.

In 1931, and again in 1971, Saskatchewan was more multicultural than its neighbours, with a larger proportion of residents neither British nor French in origin. Over the intervening forty years, however, internal migration, relocation to the prairies from other parts of Canada, and new but uneven immigration had redistributed individual ethno-religious groups. After the Second World War the most wealthy and buoyant prairie province, Alberta gained the most. In 1971 almost half of westerners of British origin, and over half of Norwegians, Swedes, Dutch, and Finns in the West lived there, joined by some four in ten westerners of Hungarian, German, Ukrainian, Romanian, French, and Polish origin. Six in ten Mennonites lived Manitoba, while a handful of groups concentrated in the same province they had four decades earlier: Icelanders and Jews in Manitoba; Doukhobors in Saskatchewan; and Danes and Mormons in Alberta.

Between 1931 and 1971 urbanization also transformed the West. Two years into the Great Depression the prairies remained predominantly rural (although less so in Manitoba than in Alberta or especially Saskatchewan) and considerably more rural than the country as a whole. Forty years later, all three provinces were predominantly urban: Alberta close to the national figure, Manitoba and Saskatchewan some distance behind. Ethno-religious groups underwent a parallel transformation. Taking Jews as one extreme, as the Depression hammered their remaining farming settlements, even in Saskatchewan only one in five Jews lived in rural areas; in Manitoba and Alberta fewer than one in ten did so. By 1971 that ratio had halved in Saskatchewan, more than halved elsewhere. At the other extreme, eastern European agriculturalists like Ukrainians and Mennonites were appreciably more attached to the land in 1931 than the provincial population generally, although the gap was less in Saskatchewan. By 1971 Ukrainians reflected the Saskatchewan and Manitoba provincial figures but remained slightly more rural in Alberta. Over half of Mennonites, however, remained not only rural

**1.7.** Jewish immigrants from Romania posing outside their prairie home, Lipton, Saskatchewan, n.d. ARCHIVES OF MANITOBA, JHS 408.

but markedly more rural than the provincial population generally, albeit less in Saskatchewan; in Alberta the gap had actually widened in favour of rural Mennonites. Scandinavians also demonstrated strong staying power on the land, especially compared to more rapidly urbanizing Ukrainians, confounding the stereotypes and expectations of early twentieth-century nation builders. Finally, in both census years, the British were more urban than anyone else, although by 1971 the gap had narrowed; more rural than either the British or provincial populations, the French approximated the "foreign" immigrant profile.

## The Prairie Experience and the Nation

Most histories of ethno-religious settlement on the prairies take as their starting point either Canadian nation building or the group's regional immigration and settlement story. The second approach often begins by sketching previous contacts with Canada, from shadowy individuals lost in the mists of time to already existing communities in other parts of the country. Rarely do these histories pursue the relationship between the prairie segment of the group and members elsewhere. But situating the prairie story within the context of the group's immigration and settlement experience within the nation as a whole invites a broader perspective. Did the West represent the first, largest, or only movement to Canada, or merely a change of location in a long tradition of choosing the Dominion or its pre-Confederation territories? As for later immigrants, did the West continue to attract group members in significant numbers, and for how long? Furthermore, what was the impact of migration within Canada on the profiles of prairie ethno-religious groups? General demographic trends, such as economic relocation from the prairies to Ontario during the Great Depression or Second World War, or from across Canada to Alberta during the oil boom of the 1970s, were one factor. More important here was organized and mass abandonment of the prairies by substantial portions of ethno-religious groups for what they hoped would be more congenial surroundings.

Instances in which the prairies were a group's first sustained, and ultimately permanent home in Canada generally reflected the non-traditional immigrant sources promoted by Sifton. They included Ukrainians and Doukhobors, as well as Hungarians and Romanians, all of whom went directly to the land in the West. They did not, however, include Poles or Jews. The Canadian predecessors of Polish peasants on prairie homesteads were a handful of individuals in New France/Lower Canada; political émigrés fleeing the abortive insurrection against Russia in 1830–31; and, beginning in the 1850s, immigrants from Prussian Poland, who settled in Upper Canada/Ontario. The Canadian ancestors of the Ashkenazi Jews in the West were a few Sephardim trading in New France; the soldier settler Aaron Hart who served under General Amherst at the British Conquest; and more general Sephardic immigration, between the 1840s and 1880s, of Jews from Germany who also went to central Canada, especially Quebec. Nor were prairie Mennonites—from Russia, and more distantly from Holland and Germany—the first of their co-religionists in Canada, although, like Jews, their forerunners represented a separate historical trajectory. Swiss German Mennonites had moved north from Pennsylvania in

1786 after the American Revolution to what became Upper Canada, seeking land but equally certain of finding more religious tolerance under the British Crown than in the new republic. More general German roots dated from the 1750s and the founding of Lunenburg, Nova Scotia, by the British as a "foreign Protestant" foil to the Catholic Acadians. Loyalist refugees in the 1770s and 1780s and thousands of arrivals between the 1830s and 1880s, all favouring Upper Canada/Ontario, made the movement to the prairies the fourth wave of German immigration to Canada.

For other settler peoples, the West was not the first Canadian stop, but it quickly eclipsed prior initiatives elsewhere in the country. For example, although a few Mormons could be found north of the border prior to the 1880s, any Mormon presence in Canada was negligible until the coordinated migration to southern Alberta under Card. Icelandic settlements at Rosseau and Kinmount in Ontario predated New Iceland, and in fact provided its first residents, but the Manitoba colony and Winnipeg immediately became the magnet for new immigrants. Similarly, the first permanent Danish settlement in Canada was New Denmark in New Brunswick, founded in 1872 as part of a provincial plan to develop the interior and become self-sufficient in food, but the size of subsequent immigration to the prairies refocussed Danish attention west. Norwegian and Swedish preferences for the prairies also soon overshadowed previous or contemporary attempts at settlements elsewhere.[37] At the other extreme, the Canadian origins of prairie Finns lay to the east, and at the turn of the twentieth century the prairie region (and its land) attracted only a fraction of immigrants from that group.

Interwar immigration reinforced existing patterns among both those already inclined towards the prairies and those for whom the region was marginal. The great majority of 67,000 Ukrainian immigrants (and especially the 55,000 arriving under the Railways Agreement) went, at least initially, to farms in the West. The great majority of 24,000 Mennonites, refugees from the Bolshevik revolution and civil war in Russia, who also came under the Railways Agreement, likewise settled in the rural West. Swedish and Norwegian immigrants also augmented existing populations on the prairies, while Jews and Finns continued to prefer the urban centres or resource towns of Ontario and Quebec. After the Second World War, the West claimed only a minority of Europeans coming to Canada as economic immigrants or displaced persons, even among groups traditionally attracted to the region. Initially uprooted by war and now fleeing Soviet communism, Ukrainian displaced persons gravitated to Ontario while Russian Mennonites opted for cities and towns in both the West and Ontario over prairie farms. Canadian labour requirements and large-scale development projects, plus the composition of the immigrant workforce, dictated the shift: Ontario Hydro jobs for Ukrainian men, domestic service jobs for the women prominent among Mennonites. The prairies never again drew European immigrants as they had in the past, and those who did come favoured the region's cities over smaller centres or the land. Proof that the rural West had had its heyday, most of the 30,000-plus Hungarian refugees (a large proportion of them Jews) immigrating after the failed anti-communist revolution of 1956 went to central Canada. Although the prairies received some of the young and well-educated newcomers, few contemplated farming.

Census statistics support these observations. In 1911 an astonishingly high percentage of some groups lived in the three prairie provinces. Among Icelanders, Ukrainians, and Mormons the figure was well over 90 percent; among Doukhobors, other Scandinavians, Hungarians, and Mennonites it was at least 70 percent, sometimes considerably more. The next six decades recorded a steady decline—to less than half of Doukhobors, Danes, Hungarians, and Swedes, but still robust numbers for Mormons, Norwegians, Ukrainians, Mennonites, and Icelanders. The staying power of the last three groups was particularly impressive. The proportion of Romanians and Poles in Canada living in the prairie region also fell during this sixty-year period, from over half in both cases to some two-fifths for Romanians and one-third for Poles. In 1971 the prairies claimed just over 40 percent of all ethnic Germans. Among smaller groups, during the settlement era about one-quarter of Finns and Jews lived in the region; six decades later, one in ten did so.

Unsurprisingly, not only was Ontario historically the most popular alternative to the prairies but the proportion of ethno-religious group members living in the province also rose over successive censuses, just as it did for Canadians generally. Mennonites were the notable exception, in that the original Swiss German base in Upper Canada proved unable to keep pace with the growth, fed by three separate immigrant waves, of the German-Dutch "Russian" Mennonites in the West. As a result, while just over one-third of Canadian Mennonites lived in Ontario in 1901, less than one-quarter did so in

1971. That same year, reflecting out-migration from the prairies plus the bias of post-war immigrants, one-quarter of Ukrainians, one-third of Romanians and Germans, and nearly one-half of Poles and Hungarians lived in Canada's most populous province. Among Finns, who had always preferred Ontario, and where roughly half of them lived at the turn of the twentieth century, the figure hovered around two-thirds. Given Anglo-Protestant nation-building prerogatives in the half century after Confederation, Quebec hardly registered in the consciousness of ethno-religious groups headed for the prairies between the 1870s and the 1920s. In fact, by 1971 still only a tiny fraction of Mennonites, Icelanders, and Ukrainians lived there. However, in 1911 two-fifths of all Jews lived in the province, concentrated in Montreal; sixty years later the figure had hardly changed, and Quebec and Ontario together accounted for almost the entire Jewish population in Canada.

Finally, some groups with strong prairie roots favoured British Columbia over Ontario as descendants of the original pioneers left the region and post-war immigrants chose other parts of the Dominion. By 1971 between one-fifth and one-third of the four Scandinavian peoples lived in the West Coast province, attracted, like other Canadians, by its climate, economic opportunities, and reputation as a retirement haven. British Columbia also drew significant numbers of Mormons, both regular church members crossing the mountains along with other Albertans and breakaway fundamentalists, including open supporters of polygamy, headed for the mountain valleys of the interior.[38] However, the Doukhobor–British Columbia relationship was the most important. In 1901 every Doukhobor in Canada resided on the prairies, mostly in Saskatchewan; by 1911 only eight in ten did so, and sixty years later a mere two in ten. Meanwhile, the proportion of Doukhobors living in British Columbia soared to more than seven in ten. The Doukhobor exodus from Saskatchewan to the Kootenays constitutes the sole mass, ideologically motivated movement of a prairie settler people from its original location to another part of the country. Driving the exodus were escalating tensions with the Canadian government over the Doukhobor reserves, land registration, the oath of allegiance, and the education of Doukhobor children. Verigin's ongoing instructions from Siberia, and then events set in motion after his arrival, fanned the general restlessness.

## The Canadian Prairies and the Homeland–Diaspora

For many ethno-religious groups, the impact of the homeland extended far beyond its role as a source of new immigrants. This complex, ongoing relationship—shaped by unfolding domestic and world events—had several facets. One was how the movement to Canada, and the prairies specifically, fit into the emigration or migration history of the group overall. Whether the ethno-religious group as a Canadian prairie phenomenon represented the pre-emigration society (in terms of class, gender, or regional composition) and mainstream culture in the homeland, or reflected a particular fragment, also mattered. Sometimes contact with the homeland after emigration, or participation in its diaspora tradition, involved organized return movements or organized relocation to yet other areas of the world. Finally, proximity to the United States and diaspora ties across the border had the potential to overshadow or complicate the connection with the homeland and encourage a north-south orientation that competed with forces identifying the group as Canadian.

During the great European migrations of the late nineteenth and early twentieth centuries, Canada and the prairies were not the first choice of most peoples seeking a new life in a new place. The reason lay, in part, in the timing of the opening and serious promotion of the West for settlement, especially compared to industrial expansion in the United States or competing frontiers in South America and the American West and Midwest. Prior to the Great War, for example, under 2 percent of Hungarian emigrants chose Canada, over 90 percent the United States. Both Ukrainians and Icelanders had gone to Brazil before turning to Canada. In fact, it was Oleskiv's resolve to find an alternative to the unhealthy jungle and slave-like plantations that redirected Ukrainian peasants to western Canada. Doukhobors' supporters tested several places for relocation, including Brazil, but only the British colony of Cyprus responded. So high was mortality among the 1126 souls who went to the island that a year later the survivors joined the movement to Canada.

The United States outstripped all alternate destinations. In the 1870s, although Russian Mennonites toyed with places as far apart as Turkestan and Australia, over one-third of them left for North America. But while 7000 chose southern Manitoba, 10,000 others chose the adjacent American plains. The following decade, Esterhazy's scheme saved Hungarian peasants from the mines, foundries, and factories of Pennsylvania. Thereafter both the United States and new immigration from the homeland fed the Hungarian population in Saskatchewan. New Finland was also founded with immigrants from the United States (where most Finnish emigrants went), and drew heavily from south of the border, notably Michigan, as well as Finland; a few settlers came from other parts of Canada. The catalyst behind St. Peter's and St. Joseph's colonies was the desire for compact German Catholic enclaves to preserve the language, traditions, and faith eroded among an earlier generation of immigrants dispersed in the Dakotas, Minnesota, Nebraska, and Kansas. Later German Catholic settlers also came from both the United States and overseas. Some of New Iceland's original residents went initially to Wisconsin, while in 1888–89 immigrants disillusioned with Wisconsin and North Dakota established Markerville, the first Icelandic settlement in Alberta. They included Stephan Stephansson, destined to become Iceland's most famous poet, who had been among those landing in Quebec in 1873 but proceeding on to the United States. In the early 1900s North Dakota and other states, as well as Manitoba, supplied settlers for new Icelandic enclaves in Saskatchewan.[39] The founders of the Danish settlement at Dickson, just south of Markerville, came from Nebraska. Lastly, the immediate point of departure for thousands of Swedes and Norwegians was not Sweden or Norway but one of several American states, where high land costs and rising debt made the new frontier to the north attractive.

Scandinavians in particular tended to think continentally: proceeding immediately to the United States upon reaching Quebec or Winnipeg; relocating freely between the two countries; and, in the case of New Iceland, uprooting and moving south of the border en masse not long after establishment. Nor were Canada-focussed settler peoples like Ukrainians and Doukhobors immune to the lure of the United States. A handful of Ukrainian idealists experimented with a socialist commune in California, and agricultural labourers made seasonal sojourns to the states below the Canadian prairies. Disenchanted Saskatchewan Doukhobors also flirted with seeking utopia in California before deciding to move to British Columbia. Disenchanted Russian Mennonites, however, looked farther afield. By the 1930s, after the group lost control over education in the anti-foreign backlash following the Great War, some 7735 Manitoba and Saskatchewan Mennonites had fled to Mexico and Paraguay. There, they again hoped to find the isolation and state guarantees essential to survival. Physical hardship and religious schism brought many back to Canada almost immediately; return from Mexico gathered momentum after the Second World War, reinforcing a Mennonite rural way of life albeit not always in the West. In the late 1940s another 2000 Mennonites left Manitoba for Paraguay, although a third returned within three years; many Mennonite post-war refugees who initially went to Paraguay also relocated to Canada.[40]

Other organized and ideologically motivated departures targeted the homeland. The Bolshevik victory and commitment to building a workers' paradise in the new Soviet state inspired Ukrainian, Finnish, and Jewish communists across Canada, as part of pan-North American movements, to join the venture. In the 1920s prairie Ukrainians and Doukhobors helped to establish "Canadian" communes in Soviet Ukraine; a fortunate few managed to return to Canada before the Stalinist purges of the 1930s decimated their ranks.[41] During the Great Depression, joining a much larger migration of disaffected Finns (mostly from the United States), a small band of Finnish farmers left hard-hit Saskatchewan for Soviet Karelia; again, the lucky ones returned.[42] Also in the 1930s prairie farmers were among those Canadian Jews who debated emigrating to the Jewish Autonomous Region of Soviet Birobidzhan, although few actually went.[43] However, the great majority of members of eastern European ethno-religious groups condemned the Soviet state, ruling out return movements. In addition, difficult access created an unnatural relationship with the homeland that only the collapse of the Iron Curtain in the 1980s and 1990s reversed. Ukrainians, the largest group affected, campaigned tirelessly for an independent Ukraine and condemned human rights abuses, while Russian Mennonites, Doukhobors, and Jews— not interested in states of their own—still tried to help their co-religionists. Although eastern Europe was the immediate homeland for most prairie Jews, Palestine or Israel was the homeland of both historical memory and the future. Between the wars over 100 Zionists left for Palestine, where they expected to use their Canadian farming experience to benefit the Jewish people in a Jewish state; again, many returned or tried to return to Canada, although not necessarily to prairie farms.[44]

For its part, the Canadian prairie diaspora was often uniquely significant.

During Canada's Centennial in 1967, the president of Iceland noted that "in Canada more people of Icelandic descent have their homes than anywhere in the world outside Iceland."[45] Two-thirds of them, in fact, lived in the three prairie provinces, mostly descendants of late nineteenth-century immigrants to the region. By 1920, when three-quarters of Canadian Mennonites lived in the three prairie provinces, the Canadian Mennonite community was the fourth largest the world, after the United States, the Soviet Union, and Holland.[46] Two more immigrations from Soviet-controlled territories and decimation among those who remained reinforced Canada's importance among the German-Dutch wing. At the time of the collapse of the USSR in 1991, one perhaps optimistic estimate put the Canadian descendants of nineteenth-century Doukhobor immigrants, whether still practising Doukhobors or not, at over 30,000, split evenly between British Columbia and the prairies. Fewer than half that number were believed to remain in the late Soviet Union after decades of harassment and persecution.[47] Canada's Ukrainians became the largest national Ukrainian community outside the Soviet Union,[48] and, as the second-largest ethnic group in the country (after the British and French), exercised considerable influence, particularly on the prairies, where they constituted one out of ten residents.

New immigrant waves also had an impact, revitalizing existing ethno-religious communities, but also reorienting them and, at times, introducing tension and discord. Different attitudes towards shared ethnicity and religious faith reflected Canadianization on the one hand and changing values and events in the homeland on the other. Moreover, no immigrant wave duplicated the old-world society, so that the ethno-religious group as a Canadian prairie phenomenon became a distortion of the whole. This bias was evident in the self-selection that propelled the poor and the restless and not the comfortable and the complacent overseas, and in the gender considerations that sent more men than women to the West, even among peoples headed for the land. The same self-selection lay behind the emigration of more conservative Mennonites and Doukhobors. Unlike the older Sephardim in central Canada, prairie Jews were Ashkenazi from eastern Europe; moreover, they came from diverse sources, notably the Pale in the Russian empire, Austria-Hungary, and Romanian territories, but also including previous stopping places from London to South Africa. The Russian Mennonite movement of the 1870s also introduced geographical distinctions: Canada drew from Chortitza and its daughter colonies, the United States from Molotschna, the second mother colony on the Ukrainian steppe. The 1899 Doukhobor contingent originated in three Transcaucasian sites: the Wet Mountains in Georgia, Kars, and Elizavetpol. In the early twentieth century they were joined by a few hundred Siberian exiles and a handful of non-Veriginites.

In fact, regional peculiarities characterized virtually all prairie settler peoples arriving before 1914. Most significantly, given that by 1921 Germans outnumbered all but the British, only some 12 percent of German immigrants originated in Germany proper. Over half—more if adding relocation from the United States—came from the Russian empire. Besides Mennonites, they included both Catholics and Lutherans from widely separated German colonies in the Black Sea area, the Volga region, and Volhynia. While most Ukrainians lived under Russian rule and were Orthodox, Byzantine-rite Catholics from Galicia in Austria-Hungary dominated the movement to Canada. Eighty-five percent of Romanian immigrants also came from Austria-Hungary (Transylvania, Bukovyna, the Banat) and not the Romanian kingdom of Wallachia and Moldovia. Austrian and Russian portions of the old Polish-Lithuanian Commonwealth, and not the Prussian sector, provided the bulk of Polish immigrants. Danes ventured abroad from the southeastern islands and northern Jutland in particular; in the decade before the Great War city dwellers outnumbered farmers. Immigrants to New Iceland came largely from the north and northeast of the island, the precise location affected by volcanic activity. Swedes had more varied origins as immigrants from Swedish-speaking parts of Finland, for example, joined long-time residents of Sweden. South-central Sweden supplied the greatest number of overseas emigrants, but during the heyday of Canadian prairie settlement, Stockholm and the north were important sources. Finland was different again: two-thirds of Canada-bound immigrants came from one province, Pohjanmaa (Ostrobothnia) on the western coast, a farming area undergoing industrialization.

\* \* \*

In the final analysis, the multicultural curiosity hanging in a pioneer museum in rural Alberta was the product of a specific time and place, in which overlapping local, regional, Canadian, and transnational ethno-religious identities formed a complex web. From the beginning, huge variations in size, distribution, and outside relationships influenced how European settler peoples saw themselves as imagined communities with a common heritage and purpose and how they related to others. Romanians, Jews, Poles, and Ukrainians brought a tangled and fraught history from eastern Europe to western Canada, and those tensions never entirely disappeared over the next century as each group retained its distinctiveness. But perhaps it was at the local level, where people had been thrown together to put down roots and survive on the land, that the tensions were erased most completely.

**2.1.** Stry post office, named after a Ukrainian village in Galicia, east-central Alberta, 1920s. COURTESY OF TERRY WINNICK.

# Possessing the Land:
# The Secular, the Sacred, and the Dead

FEW IMMIGRANTS WHO BOARDED THE TRAIN in the ports of Halifax or Quebec knew how to read the western landscape—the bald prairie susceptible to drought, the scrub bush hiding rocks that would have to be picked, the richness of the earth beneath the grass and trees. Sometimes they misjudged and made mistakes. Practice had taught Ukrainians that trees meant good soil for growing crops, so many chose homesteads in the infertile Interlake region of Manitoba. Cultural conditioning since emancipation from serfdom in 1848 also convinced them of the desirability of land with trees, as it meant access to wood for building or heat without having to pay the landlord, so they passed over the plains in favour of the parkland that required intensive labour to clear.[1] In ways more profound than the derogatory label of an unwelcoming host society, they were indeed "foreigners." But at least the Ukrainian peasant possessed some frame of reference. The Englishman from Leeds who had earned his living in a factory cutting cloth for men's suits had nothing in his own past on which to draw for guidance, regardless of whether the choices he made were ultimately wise or foolish ones. Perhaps the Mormons, Scandinavians, and Germans who trekked north across the forty-ninth parallel from the Midwestern and western states were best equipped to make sound decisions based on first-hand experience. Even migrants from Ontario and the Maritimes had more to learn about a physical environment vastly different from the one they knew in central or eastern Canada.

All settlers responded to their surroundings through a cultural filter based on the norms and values of the home society. When this filter failed, they had to adjust their thinking. Although Christian for centuries, many European rural folk still lived alongside and interacted with more ancient gods and spirits, both good and evil, that inhabited the mountains, fields, woods, and streams. The reluctance of these familiar supernatural beings to follow them to Canada forced an entirely new relationship with the environment. It also exaggerated the typical newcomer reaction to the landscape as simultaneously a place of staggering beauty and an intimidating wilderness. For their mental well-being, the immigrant settler generation had to claim and define the land according to their own criteria, reconfiguring it around their experiences and populating it with their heroes and stories.

They did so on one level through actual ownership of the soil, 160 acres for every man who applied. Moreover, when settlers planned their homesteads—setting out fields and gardens, choosing seeds to plant, situating the house in relation to the barn or sun, designing their homes—they copied what they knew and what their culture required. At the same time they made concessions to the terrain and local resources (trees versus sod for building, for example) and the grid survey that overlay the entire region. Possessing and ordering the land beyond the homestead combined personal and collective priorities. It occurred, first, through the creation and naming of new communities, especially the rural clusters of churches, halls, stores, post offices, schools, and cemeteries that acted as focal points of local activity and identity while distinguishing members from neighbours a few miles away. Second, it occurred through Christianization of the landscape, as settlers constructed churches, named them after old-world saints, and erected shrines and crosses in the countryside. And finally, it occurred through the creation of places for the dead, where the certainty that they would rest apart from their ancestors, their bones becoming literally part of the new land, drove home the finality of the decision to uproot and relocate. As individuals and groups internalized the implications of asserting their presence on the land, a grassroots identity emerged in which they began to see themselves as westerners. The same processes nurtured a separate ethno-religious consciousness forged around both their old-world heritage and shared immigration and settlement experience.

## Place Names

Newcomers often failed to realize that western landforms already had aboriginal names that told stories, explained the universe, and oriented Natives as they moved about their vast territory. Certainly, many newcomers entertained preconceived notions of Indians or embraced local stereotypes after arriving in the West, images that ranged from noble savage to bloodthirsty and shiftless. But most probably seldom saw a Native up close to compare image with reality, or to appreciate that their freshly ploughed field once held a Native summer camp. In fact, the words settlers used to describe the West—empty, virgin, alien, unpeopled—ignored the indigenous presence as they set about creating their own landmarks and claiming this space as their own.[2] Long before the settlement era, European exploration and the fur trade that pitted the English at Hudson Bay against the French (and later Scots) along the St. Lawrence had imposed a second cultural imprint on the West. A name like Portage la Prairie, on the French route between the Assiniboine River and Lake Manitoba, highlighted the relationship between geography and the fur trade. One like Fort Pitt, commemorating the British prime minister and statesman, registered imperial sensitivities. Those forts that survived the transition to settlement to become towns and cities were the most identifiable legacy of the era; Edmonton, dropping the "fort" as its ambitions grew, emerged as the largest of them. European exploration and the fur trade also preserved many earlier Native names even though their meaning was invariably lost. Those retained in the original language became simply words (Saskatchewan), but even if translated (Swift Current) the words were divorced from the cultural context and stories that had produced them.

Migrants from Ontario and the Maritimes would have recognized many place names encountered in the West, traces of the familiar tempering their sense of alienation. Such recognition was particularly true of Ontarians, educated by years of expansionist propaganda and events like the North-West Rebellion of 1885, which some 8000 volunteers rushed to help quell. Incoming Canadians became the major players as the settlement era added a third layer of meaning to the prairie landscape. Altario in Alberta acknowledged their old and new identities, while Manitario, Saskatchewan, reflected a two-stage westward journey. The place names these transplanted Canadians chose, including their own names and those of their hometowns, represented Canada's British heritage and underlined the French and Native retreat before the agricultural frontier that replaced the fur trade. Yet place naming was more complicated than that. Residents of Old Wives, Saskatchewan, for example, not only named their community after an Indian legend but insisted that their choice be restored when it was changed to Johnstone, in honour of an English aristocrat who visited the district to hunt.

British immigrants joined Anglo-Canadians in naming the landmarks that came to define mainstream prairie society. Moreover, familiarity with the old-country references behind many other place names lessened the dislocation of uprooting. The Alberta cities of Edmonton and Calgary and the national mountain park at Banff were the most grand reminders of home. Dozens of railway stops—like Maidstone, Kitscoty, and Islay straddling the Alberta-Saskatchewan border along the Canadian Northern line completed in 1905— also had namesakes in Britain. Another set of railway stops, in central Alberta on the Canadian Pacific line, commemorated the coronation of George V in 1911: Throne, Veteran, Loyalist, Consort, and Coronation itself. Similarly proclaiming the bonds of empire were three Manitoba settlements (Baden, Powell, Mafeking) named after the Boer War hero and founder of the Boy Scouts. British immigrants also belonged to an extended Anglo-American world. An Englishwoman applying to operate a post office from her Saskatchewan sod house named it Nokomis after Hiawatha's grandmother in the Henry Wadsworth Longfellow poem, because her new surroundings conformed to her romantic image of the world inhabited by the North American Indian. Such ties found common ground with transplanted Americans as well as Ontarians and Maritimers, and let British immigrants access their environment on a level impossible for settlers ignorant of English and the English-speaking heritage.

Without the tools to access the names of places they saw from the train going west, passed through on the way to their homesteads, or visited periodically for supplies and services, non-British immigrants had to memorize words that had no meaning outside their immediate context. Edmonton, for example, was a brash young city on the banks of the North Saskatchewan River, not a venerable English village on the outskirts of London. With major landforms and commercial centres already named before they arrived, and largely excluded from the establishment of railway stops, "foreigners" could

**2.2.** Russo-Greek Orthodox Church of St. Mary at Shandro in the Ukrainian bloc, east-central Alberta, 1906. PROVINCIAL ARCHIVES OF ALBERTA, B2738.

expect to influence the settlement-era map only through the communities that defined their own enclaves. Two exceptions merit mention. Because of New Iceland's early appearance and remoteness, many topographical features had not acquired British or French names, or European-sanctioned Native names, and official surveyors and cartographers acknowledged Icelandic input. This input included Gunnar Rock, Hecla Island (although the original settlers called it Mikley or Big Island), and Hnausa Reef in Lake Winnipeg; the Icelandic River; Bjarnason Island in Lake Manitoba; and Solmundsson and Thorstenson lakes.[3] Then there was the Mennonite Post Road, constructed across the West Reserve in the late 1870s. A series of posts erected at seventy-five-pace intervals on the open prairie, it guided travellers along the "Mennonite" portion (Emerson to Mountain City) of the Boundary Commission and North-West Mounted Police trails. Significantly, the Post Road represented not pioneer "civilizing"

**2.3.** Lutheran church shortly after construction in the Icelandic community of Gimli, Manitoba, early 1900s. ARCHIVES OF MANITOBA, NIC 107, N11131.

of the land in the sense of community building but a more primitive struggle for survival in a monotonous and often suddenly hostile environment. It also implied rejection of the isolation Mennonites craved by connecting the villages on its path to the outside non-Mennonite world.[4]

Whether they acted as members of larger ethno-religious groups, or simply as individuals fighting homesickness in a strange land, "foreigners" also domesticated the wilderness in terms that were meaningful and familiar. An unconscious exercise, it totally disregarded Anglo-Canadian ideas of political and cultural hegemony, immigrant assimilation, and supremacy of the English language. Only a few communities were ever renamed to sound less foreign or to appease nervousness about immigrant loyalty. Wartime passions, for example, transformed Kreuzburg, Manitoba, into Fraserwood (after the wife of an early non-German settler); and perhaps influenced the change of Huns

Valley to Polonia, although the "Huns" in question were the area's original Hungarian settlers not Kaiser Wilhelm's soldiers. Non-British immigrant place naming could reflect communal decision making or tensions between aspiring leaders and the mass of settlers, but tended to fall to the better educated, the more progressive, and the more experienced in dealing with Canadian society. It tended as well to be a male prerogative, and thus revealed a primarily male world view. Place naming could also involve contested identities, particularly in ethnically mixed areas or areas where latecomers of another origin prevailed over the original settler core. This happened in Polonia, as incoming Poles engulfed the remaining Hungarians. Ukrainians and Mennonites, who formed compact blocs and spread out over a large area, left the most widespread and permanent imprint on the prairie map. But whatever names they and other "foreigners" picked, their choices collectively illuminated the delicate balance between old and new worlds.

The most popular old-country place names were nostalgic reminders of villages, friends, and relatives left behind, suggesting that people's local identity mattered most. Mennonite villages in the East and West reserves routinely bore the names of parent villages on the Ukrainian steppe. They included Altona, Blumengart, Gnadenfeld, Kronsthal, Rosenort, and Steinbach (which emerged from the settlement period as the largest Mennonite centre in Manitoba). The Canadian prairies were the third stop for many of these place names, originally transplanted from Prussia when Mennonites accepted Catherine the Great's invitation to settle in the Russian empire in the 1780s. Some of them, like Steinbach, would appear again on the Canadian prairies, as residents of the Manitoba reserves established new colonies in neighbouring Saskatchewan. The names of around forty Ukrainian villages and districts in the Austro-Hungarian empire emerged across the prairie provinces, confirming a settlement pattern that saw families, villagers, and people from the same area seek one another out. Adopting the name of the district over the village of origin attested to both a larger regional identity and its power to transcend parochial divisions. The distribution of old-country Ukrainian place names also illustrated how different regions of the prairies attracted settlers from different regions in Galicia. Thus, Manitoba had Terebowla, Saskatchewan had Tarnopol, and Alberta had Brody, although other Galician place names (such as Buczacz and Jaroslaw) sprang up in more than one province. Alberta boasted the largest Ukrainian Bukovynian settlement, which included a pocket of Romanians whose crossroads community at Boian preserved another imported place name.

Other settler peoples also named tiny prairie communities after places at home, among them cities with international reputations: Reykjavik and Bruxelles in Manitoba, Stockholm and Amsterdam in Saskatchewan, and Venice in Alberta. It was one of the ironies of the uneven appeal of prairie homesteading that three of the nationalities represented—Belgians, Dutch, Italians—had limited impact on the settlement map, while Ukrainians and Mennonites coloured chunks of it. Malmo in Alberta—named by settlers from Malmo, Nebraska (itself named after a village in Sweden)—captured the serial migration of Scandinavians who came north from the United States rather than directly from Europe. The most potent old-country village memorialized on the prairies, Bogdanofka in the Doukhobor North Colony, commemorated the site of the burning of arms that set in motion the movement to Canada and became the defining moment in the immigrant sect's collective psyche. A few old-country names elicited no personal emotions. According to one account, an official decided what to call the Hungarian settlement in Saskatchewan by stabbing a map of Hungary with his finger and announcing "Kaposvar!" And Norway House in Manitoba had nothing to do with Norwegian immigration in the settlement era; a Hudson's Bay Company post, it recalled the Norwegian axemen hired in 1814 to construct a winter road north of Lake Winnipeg to York Factory.

Settler peoples also expressed a common national identity. Some place names—Magyar in Saskatchewan, Neerlandia in Alberta, and Scandinavia in Manitoba—stood by themselves. Others—like New Iceland (Manitoba), New Finland (Saskatchewan), and New Norway (Alberta)—deliberately distinguished between the homeland and its western Canadian diaspora, revealing people torn between emigrant and immigrant. Ukrainians were unique in that the national awakening underway in Austria-Hungary played out in the names given prairie communities. Ruthenia in Manitoba suggested a pre-modern self-image, but each province also had a Ukraina or Oukraina, evidence of a crystallizing pan-Ukrainian consciousness. The fact that Ukraina, Manitoba, originated with the pioneer intelligentsia, however, cautions against equating such choices with grassroots thinking. Ukrainians also chose politically charged names that resonated in Ukrainian history and inspired nation-building efforts in the present. In Manitoba, Bohdan honoured the Cossack leader whose revolt against Polish rule in 1648 produced the Ukrainian Cossack state, and Szewczenko the nineteenth-century serf whose poetry embodied the suffering and yearning of his captive people. Myroslaw in Alberta, named for the university student who assassinated the Polish governor of Galicia in 1908, tied emigrants overseas to contemporary events in the homeland. Although firing Ukrainian consciousness on the prairies, such place names imported ethnic tensions that had historically poisoned eastern Europe. Myroslav Sichynsky was no hero to Polish settlers, whose collective memory gave them rights to Galicia, just as the excesses associated with Bohdan Khmelnytsky's uprising made him hated among Jews. Place names with old-country associations, then, could impede the coalescence of a common regional society and identity in western Canada.

Icelandic immigrants were particularly drawn to the old world of the imagination in Norse mythology. Brunkild, Manitoba, evoked the Valkyrie, the god Odin's handmaidens who escorted slain warriors to Valhalla (heaven). As the entrance to hell, Hecla was perhaps better suited to the volcano in Iceland than the island in Lake Winnipeg that also bore the name. But given the role of volcanic eruptions in the Dyngja Mountains in emigration to New Iceland, the Manitoba island served as a constant reminder of why the colony existed. While Icelandic place naming as a communal activity never equalled that of Ukrainians and Mennonites,[5] New Icelanders' tradition of individually naming private farms ordered the wilderness and claimed the land at the most intimate level. Some farm names were nostalgic reminders of home, recalling farmsteads or communities left behind. Others revealed, if not vanity on the part of male property owners, at least the desire to immortalize themselves in relation to their land, using their own names to make a more public and assertive declaration of possession than a routine entry in a government ledger allowed. The majority of New Icelandic farm names described the property itself, highlighting natural features that underscored how much water, as well as land, shaped the Icelandic experience. Less popular but similarly present minded were names (like *Kjarni*, or choice land) that expressed immigrant hopes for a new life.[6]

Immigrant settler peoples as groups also looked forward when they christened their prairie communities. Like Waldheim (German for home in the forest) in Saskatchewan and Arbakka (Icelandic for riverbank) in Manitoba, some names simply described the physical environment. Others flatly denied the notion of Canada as the promised land. Although named after a homeland village, Komarno in Manitoba (*komar* is mosquito in Ukrainian) reminded everyone of the insects that Ukrainians across the prairies insisted sucked more blood than their old landlords ever did. Surprise, Saskatchewan, originally settled by Germans from the Dakotas, registered the contrast between rosy government propaganda and the bleak treeless plain of reality. More typically, place names echoed pre-emigration imagery of a land of freedom and plenty, whether or not contact sustained the fantasy. Yet other images stressed new beginnings to reinforce the Ontarian expansionist vision of the regenerative and purifying powers of the frontier. Saskatchewan Jews founded New Jerusalem, their Doukhobor neighbours the village Ooteshenia (*uteshenie* in Russian means comfort or consolation). Alberta Ukrainians established Myrnam (peace be with us) and Vilna (freedom). Valhalla, Alberta, equated the settlers' new home with the paradise where Vikings killed in battle feasted with Odin for eternity. Gimli, Manitoba, was the Norse "great hall of heaven" or home of the gods.

A significant number of place names referred to settlements' human actors. Among the dozens of communities honouring the first settler, the first baby, or the first postmaster were those expressing broader group sentiments. Bruderheim (in German, home of the brothers) in Alberta was named for three siblings who spearheaded Moravian settlement in the area in 1893–94. And, belying the notion that the Ukrainian-Jewish relationship was universally antagonistic, Meleb in Manitoba was an amalgam of Melnyk and Leibman, for the Ukrainian farmer and Jewish shopkeeper who donated land for the Canadian Pacific Railway station. Certain immigrant traditions disapproved of the conceit implied by personalized claims to place. Winkler, Manitoba, was named for a local businessman and politician who exchanged one of his quarter sections for land the Canadian Pacific Railway had bought from Mennonite Isaac Wiens. The Mennonites objected not only to Wiens selling his land to an outsider but also to the unseemly worldliness of the railway's original proposal to name its townsite after him.

Lastly, place names celebrated a group's founding fathers. Viking, Alberta,

**2.4.** Roman Catholic Cathedral in Muenster, Saskatchewan, 1928, during silver jubilee celebrations in St. Peter's Colony. ARCHIVES OF THE ORDER OF ST. BENEDICT, ST. PETER'S ABBEY.

**2.5.** Doukhobor prayer home and residence of Peter "the Lordly" in Veregin, Saskatchewan, 1928. SASKATCHEWAN ARCHIVES BOARD, S-B870.

delved into the distant past for such figures, but most were personally involved in the immigration and settlement process, even if they never visited or lived in Canada, or led the immigrants they sponsored or encouraged to come. Many place names acknowledged purely local individuals (for example, the priest or pastor founders of specific colonies), but others honoured men prominent in the larger group story. They included Hirsch, Saskatchewan (after German-Jewish philanthropist Baron Maurice de Hirsch), Cardston, Alberta (after reconnaissance scout and Mormon churchman Charles Ora Card), and Esterhazy, Saskatchewan (after enigmatic Hungarian immigration promoter "Count" Paul O. d'Esterhazy). The only one of this coterie to settle among his followers was Peter Verigin, the Doukhobor spiritual leader for whom Veregin, Saskatchewan, was named. In fact, Doukhobors celebrated his arrival by rechristening the village of Poterpevshee (past suffering), where his mother lived, to Otradnoe (joy).[7] The foregoing examples demonstrate at least an embryonic sense of collective identity and shared formative experience at the time of immigration and settlement. Founding fathers of Ukrainian settlement, Vasyl Eleniak and Ivan Pylypiw never loomed large enough in the consciousness of their contemporaries to merit a place name. Yet both Manitoba and Alberta perpetuated the name of Dr. Osyp Oleskiv, suggesting that the man whose 1895 tour set in motion the mass Ukrainian movement to Canada did capture the immigrant imagination.

Place naming by non-English-speaking immigrants was a rural phenomenon tied to settlement on the land. Groups and individuals attracted to urban centres put their own names on the storefronts of their businesses, just as they called their socialist halls after old-country proletarian heroes and their churches after old-country saints. But they did this naming in private space, even though their foreign-language signage, especially in a place like Winnipeg's North End, had a strong public impact. Moreover, Anglo Winnipeg supplied the North End label that became synonymous with everything unsavoury in immigrant life: immorality, crowded and unsanitary dwellings, totalitarian and superstitious churches, socialist agitation. The prerogative of antipathetic outsiders, the public naming of ethno-religious space in western Canada's cities, towns, and resource communities separated "them" from "us." Coal mining centres had their Slavtowns, for example, while Regina's "foreign" district was Germantown.[8] Denied ownership of the land, and the creation and christening of prairie communities, urban immigrants were also denied the sense of belonging and building a new western society that came to mark their rural counterparts.

Why immigrants chose the place names they did was forgotten by subsequent generations, wrapped up in their everyday lives. Similarly, the Canadian born increasingly forgot the historical or political significance behind the place names they inherited. Of the two "foreign" groups most active in place naming, only Ukrainians systematically set out to recover where their prairie place names came from and why. Perhaps Mennonites found the exercise unnecessary. The penchant for transplanting village names from Mennonite colonies on the Ukrainian steppe made the question of origins seldom a mystery, while Mennonites' religious conscience and shared emigrant/immigrant experience produced a cohesiveness and awareness of their history that Ukrainians, with their diverse backgrounds, lacked. Yet it is noteworthy that old-country Ukrainian place names were collected and recorded not by a descendant of the pioneers but by a linguist immigrating as a displaced person after the Second World War.[9] The psychological grounding provided by place, always exaggerated among emigrants, had special appeal to those whose uprooting was involuntary and violent. For both Ukrainian and Mennonite refugees arriving in the aftermath of two world wars in Europe, so many recognizable place names out of context would have been disorienting but comforting.

## Saints and Shrines

As European settler peoples imposed order on their surroundings, they also redefined the land as Christian space, reinforcing fragmentation of the map around ethnicity. This religious filter added a further layer of complexity in that denominational divisions not only imposed their own boundaries but could also cut across common ethnic heritages or even transcend ethnic differences. The ordering of the prairie landscape around Christian images— Catholic, Protestant, Orthodox—reflected both grassroots priorities and the agenda of a clerical elite whose own predecessors were fur trade missionaries proselytizing among the Natives. Christians also inherited a territory central to the millenarian vision of Métis leader Louis Riel as he led his people, rocked

**2.6.** Shrine erected in 1917 by Ukrainian immigrant, Ivan Wintonyk, on his Saskatchewan homestead. COURTESY OF ELIZABETH HOLINATY.

by the demise of the fur trade and the buffalo and encroaching settlement, into rebellion in 1885. Just as God had chosen the Métis to save the human race, Riel contended, so he had chosen the Canadian West to save a corrupt Catholic Church and inaugurate the 1000 years of happiness ending with the Second Coming of Christ and Last Judgement.[10] While avoiding Riel's heretical musings, immigrant religious leaders and their flocks often shared his belief in the powers of the prairie frontier as the recurring motif of a "New Jerusalem" attested.[11] For incomers, however, the West as Christian space complemented rather than replaced the religious legacy of Europe.

Claiming the land they stood on for the Christian God, churches were often the first community institutions to be built. For those propelled to the prairies by religious persecution (which included Jews as well as Christians), or whose colonies were clergy led, religious services marking their arrival and the construction of places of worship were priorities. Thus, the Benedictines who spearheaded St. Peter's Colony in Saskatchewan offered Mass immediately upon reaching what became Muenster, the site of their monastery and centre of the German Catholic settlement, on the Feast of the Ascension in May 1903. By September a log church, built by the settlers at the Benedictines' bidding, had been completed.[12] But even homesteaders who came without religious leaders, or religion as the unifying and motivating factor behind their emigration, held services in their homes, organized parishes, and erected churches. Forced to rely on volunteer labour, local talent, and available materials, these first buildings were modest structures reflecting small populations preoccupied with survival.

More substantial churches, built as settlers prospered, introduced a profusion of architectural styles following old-world spiritual and cultural traditions. Natural and unremarkable features in the homeland, however, acquired inflated ethnic connotations on the prairies, among both outsiders and groups eager to distinguish themselves from others. Some communities erected massive structures that drew the eye and redefined both the surrounding countryside and people's mental maps. Often taking years to complete, they were intended to inspire awe and reverence as well as remind their beholders of ecclesiastical power and authority, even on the newly settled Canadian prairies. Many, like Ste. Philomène (1919) at Gravelbourg in Saskatchewan, represented French Roman Catholic communities.[13] Of their "foreign" equivalents, the Hungarian Our Lady of Assumption Roman Catholic Church (1908) at Kaposvar, Saskatchewan, consuming over 1600 wagon loads of local fieldstone, was the earliest; the multi-domed Ukrainian Catholic Church of the Immaculate Conception (begun 1930) at Cooks Creek in Manitoba was the last. The most unusual, the twin-towered frame St. Peter Roman Catholic Church at Muenster (1910) became a cathedral in 1921 with the creation of an Abbacy Nullius, or independent diocese, under the Benedictines corresponding to St. Peter's Colony.[14] One of only two ever established in North America, the Abbacy Nullius existed to 1998, giving Muenster and its church a profile in Catholic circles well beyond the local community.

When settlers chose a feast day and name for their church, they not only reiterated that sacred space on the rural prairies was also ethnic space but underscored denominational divisions as well. Protestants rarely named churches after the Virgin Mary or Mother of God, a favourite among Catholics and Orthodox; nor did they choose names like Ascension and Transfiguration or Sacred Heart (a purely Catholic devotion). The universal popularity of other saints spoke to a common Christian inheritance across Europe. Settlers from all branches of Christianity and a wide range of ethnic groups dedicated churches to St. John. They included both English and French—from St. John Anglican built by the Barr Colonists a year after their arrival in Lloydminster to the Roman Catholic St. Jean-Baptiste (1908) serving the farming settlement of Morinville north of Edmonton.[15] They also included "foreign" churches like St. John Evangelical Lutheran (1893) in New Finland; the Ukrainian Catholic St. John the Baptist (1907) at Dolyny, Manitoba; and the Polish Roman Catholic St. John the Baptist (1910) at Kopernik, Alberta. Yet even St. John took on ethnic traits. To French Catholic migrants from Quebec he was the province's patron saint, his symbol the beaver, emblematic of the fur trade on which New France, and Canada, were founded. Morinville made these connections explicit in the dedication of one of the church's bells, and especially in the small brown beaver crouched at the feet of the statue of St. Jean-Baptiste on the roof of the adjacent rectory. At the same time, a second bell—dedicated to St. Boniface, the eighth-century evangelizer of Germany and patron saint of German Catholics— recognized that the parish was not exclusively French.

In the homeland, Catholicism, Orthodoxy, and various branches of Protestantism often represented national churches whose saints were not just holy men and women but kings, queens, bishops, and others who played crucial roles in the history of the secular nation. When immigrants and their clergy brought these old-country figures to pioneer prairie churches, they expressed a politicized religious consciousness as well as faith, and drew a line with worshippers of the same faith but other nationalities. One of two Roman Catholic churches in Wakaw, Saskatchewan, was called St. Elizabeth after the thirteenth-century Hungarian queen known for her care of the sick, identifying its parishioners as Hungarian and different from other Catholics in the village.[16] Conceivably among these mostly Catholic saints, only the Irish St. Patrick struck a chord with the predominantly Anglo-Protestant population in the West. The rest were simply unknown and perhaps faintly threatening for the alien ideals and collective memory they embodied. To those concerned, their familiar national saints represented continuity and an old-world political identity in the process of becoming a Canadian ethnic one. Other saints, like

**2.7.** Our Lady of Lourdes shrine at Skaro, Alberta, flanked by St. Michael Roman Catholic church and cemetery, 1920s. PROVINCIAL ARCHIVES OF ALBERTA, MISSIONARY OBLATES, GRANDIN COLLECTION, OB2182.

St. Nicholas, patron of travellers, provided special comfort and guidance to make a daunting journey and a strange and often hostile land less forbidding.[17]

Just as Hungarian parishes chose St. Elizabeth of Hungary (or St. Laszlo, the eleventh-century Hungarian king and statesman) as their patron saint,[18] so other groups selected individuals from their national pasts. Ukrainians named churches after Sts. Volodymyr and Olha, the Kievan prince and princess who converted medieval Rus', the precursor of modern Ukraine, to Christianity in 988; Norwegians picked their contemporary, the king and Christianizer St. Olaf, later patron of Norway.[19] Poles preferred St. Stanislaus, the eleventh-century bishop martyr and symbol of Polish unity, or St. Casimir, benefactor of the poor and Poland's patron saint.[20] St. Peter's Colony drew on Germanic or northern European saints: St. Boniface, St. Bruno, St. Hubert, St. Oswald, and St. Gertrude—none of whom would be found in a Ukrainian parish, just as Olha and Volodymyr would never grace a German church. Yet church naming in St. Peter's Colony wove the specific immigration and settlement experience into old-world religious figures and traditions. Both the community of St. Bruno and St. Bruno parish were named for Father Bruno Doerfler, whose scouting mission had been the impetus for the colony. St. Oswald parish honoured Prior Oswald Moosmueller, the founder and head of Cluny Priory in Illinois, whose death led his Benedictines to relocate to Saskatchewan. Over time, the religious landscape of St. Peter's Colony shifted. In the 1930s the Church of the Canadian Martyrs, commemorating seven Jesuit priests killed by the Iroquois in their wars with New France, replaced the defunct St. Hubert.[21] This Canadianization of German immigrant Catholicism involved adopting a pan-Canadian religious identity that transcended the prairies, crossed ethnic lines, and integrated the new homeland into local devotions.

Catholic settler peoples in particular also Christianized the prairie landscape in ways more intimate and interactive than building churches and naming them after old-world saints. As private gestures—to assert their faith, find solace, remember family and villages back in Europe, give thanks for the new land—individuals erected crosses and family shrines on their homesteads or by the road at the edge of their property. As collective gestures, whole communities erected other crosses and shrines that could be as much political and secular statements as sites for worship. Created from perishable materials, most of these expressions of pioneer religiosity eventually succumbed to the ravages of time and disappeared. While they stood, however, they served as reminders not only that God lived on the prairies but also that he could be found wherever one looked.

A handful of such crosses and shrines did survive, if not always in their original form. Constructed of concrete, at some point painted white with blue trim, the family shrine erected by fifty-five-year-old Ukrainian immigrant Ivan Wintonyk on his homestead in the Sokal district north of Wakaw was made to last. Nestled in shrubs down a gentle slope from the house, it consisted of a cross atop a large hollow base holding a miniature altar accessed through a framed glass door. The inscription on the cross said, in Ukrainian, "Save Thy People, O God, Year 1917." A wire fence and ten concrete posts decorated with crosses surrounded the site, defining and enclosing what was clearly a holy space. Family members used the shrine for private prayer, but on Sundays and major holy days, especially before the local church was built, they invited neighbours for informal services with Wintonyk acting as deacon.[22] A second private Ukrainian shrine—a three-barred wooden cross erected in 1900 in Halicz district near Calmar southwest of Edmonton by Ivan Borys, three years after the family came to Canada—did not last and was eventually replaced by stone. Located at the crossroads, landscaped with spruce trees, and surrounded by a picket fence, the original cross was a companion to the one Borys had put up in his village in Galicia prior to leaving. As personal statements on the emigrant/immigrant condition, the Borys crosses not only documented their maker's departure from one place and arrival in another but also served as reminders of his presence in and thus rights to both.[23] A third private cross, erected in the early 1900s and inscribed "To the Glory of God," marked the arrival of Hungarian immigrants in the Prud'homme area south of Wakaw. In 1928 Janos Miskolczi (on whose land it stood) substituted a second wooden cross that, in turn, was eventually replaced with metal and transferred to nearby St. Laszlo Roman Catholic Church for safekeeping.[24]

Other crosses had greater community, and even secondary secular, functions. A large wooden cross inscribed "Gateway to St. Peter's Colony, 1903" on the northern edge of the land grant marked the site of the settlers' first Mass.[25] The four rogation crosses erected in St. Joseph's Colony, also German Catholic and also in Saskatchewan, by Father Francis Palm one-half mile in each direction from the Grosswerder church became the sites for annual prayers "for good crops and protection from bad weather."[26] In neighbouring Manitoba, a Ukrainian "cross of freedom" constructed from a poplar tree was erected on a hill overlooking the river on the homestead of Ivan Gereliuk in 1897, a year after seven families settled in the area they named Trembowla after their native village. Similar crosses or roadside shrines had appeared in the Galician countryside following the emancipation from serfdom in 1848. In blessing the Trembowla cross, the Reverend Nestor Dmytriw, the first Byzantine-rite Catholic priest to visit the fledgling Ukrainian settlements, not only evoked the freedom won in 1848 but also compared it to the "genuine" freedom from both landlords and rulers found in Canada.[27] Markers of faith in the new land, this and other such Ukrainian crosses thus also had secondary secular functions linking the settlers' pre-emigration past with their post-emigration present, in which "freedom" became identified with a particular piece of consecrated ground.

Catholic immigrant settler peoples also established a handful of major public shrines that became both physical landmarks, often visible for miles, and magnets for pilgrims from near and far. The joint spiritual and secular role these sites came to play in group consciousness echoed that of a major Native predecessor at Lac Ste. Anne mission northwest of Edmonton, established by the Oblates in 1844. As a Christian phenomenon, the lake's waters revealed their healing powers in 1889, transforming the mission into a pilgrimage centre and absorbing both a Native site, attractive to traditional healers, and a popular gathering spot before the annual buffalo hunt, into Catholic belief and practice.[28] The heyday of ambitious Catholic shrine construction among immigrant settler peoples occurred several years, even decades, after the first settlers arrived, and in some respects represented the harnessing or culmination of earlier religious activity. The principal shrines emerging before the Second World War were Our Lady of Lourdes (Polish, 1919) in the rural community of Skaro in Alberta, Our Lady of Mount Carmel (German, 1922) in St. Peter's Colony, and the Grotto Golgotha (Ukrainian, 1935) in the village of Mundare in Alberta. All three shrines realized the dreams of local clergy, making their origins elitist, yet each became the focal point of annual pilgrimages that drew large numbers of people to interact with the land as a holy place and to proclaim their ethnic identity.

The Polish shrine at Skaro came about when the parish priest, Father Antoni Sylla, decided that a church alone was not enough and proposed the construction of a scaled-down replica of the famous grotto in Lourdes, France, so people could stop and pray as they had done in the old country. Over the next year, Sylla persevered with his project, despite the sometimes flagging enthusiasm of his flock who provided the labour around working their own farms. They also provided the 600 wagonloads of rocks—the curse of agricultural progress, now transformed—that went into building the shrine. Furnished with statues of Mary and St. Bernadette, the peasant girl before whom the Virgin appeared in 1858, and topped with a tall cross, the structure "tower[ed] ... over the whole countryside and [could] be seen from far." At Sylla's suggestion, the first pilgrimage at the shrine, and the second for the adjacent church, was held in August 1919 on the Feast of the Assumption. It drew an estimated crowd of 4000, mostly Poles from rural areas plus the cities of Edmonton and Calgary, but including Ukrainians for whom there was a special service. In future years Skaro acted as both a spiritual centre for Alberta Poles and the ceremonial focus of community identity and life, embracing also urban immigrations far removed from the peasant pioneers.[29]

Proximity to the newly completed church, and not miracles or related phenomena, dictated the location of the Skaro shrine. Our Lady of Mount

Dedication of M* Carme
Sept 10 1922

**2.8.** Dedication of Mount Carmel shrine, St. Peter's Colony, 1922.
ARCHIVES OF THE ORDER OF ST. BENEDICT, ST. PETER'S ABBEY.

Carmel in St. Peter's Colony, on the highest point of land in the district rising ninety-five feet above its surroundings, had quite different origins. Known as Mount Carmel—after the home of the prophet Elijah in the Holy Land and an important site of Marian devotion—since surveyed in 1886, the hill immediately struck the pioneer Benedictines as auspicious. In his memoirs, Father Chrysostom Hoffmann recalled his first glimpse of it in summer 1903, and how in 1921 he obtained eleven acres from homesteader John Bunko for a shrine. Moreover, he said, since most of the colonists had been "invested in their childhood with the scapular of Our Lady of Mount Carmel ... it was but natural that when they came within sight of Saskatchewan's Mount Carmel they should think 'what a fine place for a shrine of Christ's Holy Mother! If we could make it into as holy a place as the Mount Carmel mentioned in the Bible!'"[30] At the first pilgrimage to the shrine in July 1922, attended by 3500 people, the entire territory of St. Peter's abbacy was dedicated to Mary. As time passed, the shrine grew from a simple altar to include a monumental white marble statue of the Virgin (9000 pilgrims witnessed its blessing in 1928) on the summit, and, by the 1950s, a Way of the Cross circling the hill, a stone chapel, and two stone confessionals. Also distinguishing Mount Carmel from Skaro, the site came with its own history and stories, both Christian and Native. Members of the 1902 scouting party not only climbed the hill, and contemplated its suitability for a Marian devotion, but also replaced the poplar cross they found. Travellers had mentioned such a cross since the early 1870s, giving rise to the name Hill of the Cross. In one version, echoing the lives of the virgin martyrs, it was erected in memory of a young Catholic woman (in some accounts Métis, in others Irish Scottish), buried nearby, who had swallowed poison rather than marry the man, a non-Catholic, her parents chose for her.[31]

The presence and agenda of the Benedictines in nearby Muenster clearly shaped Our Lady of Mount Carmel. The Ukrainian Order of St. Basil the Great had a similar impact on the Grotto Golgotha. A monastic order from Galicia, the Basilians settled in the growing Ukrainian bloc east of Edmonton in 1902 to thwart inroads by Russian Orthodox missionaries and Anglo-Protestant assimilationists. After a few years in the countryside, they took up residence in the new railway stop of Mundare, where the grotto next to the monastery marked their last big stamp on the village until after the Second World War. In contrast to the pioneer origins of Skaro and Mount Carmel, the idea for a grotto originated with an interwar immigrant priest, Father Petro Bodnar. The first Divine Liturgy at the shrine was celebrated in 1935 on the Feast of Sts. Peter and Paul, patron saints of the local church. Thereafter not only did the grotto provide a devotional focus for pilgrims gathering annually in Mundare on that day since 1910 but such occasions also acquired a secular dimension, tied to landmark anniversaries of Ukrainian immigration and settlement. At the Grotto Golgotha, the close relationship between its pioneer clergy and the French-dominated Roman Catholic hierarchy exaggerated the influences of Polish Roman Catholicism found in Galicia. While Byzantine-rite Catholics allowed only two-dimensional images, the devotional features of the vine-draped grotto with its catacombs and chaplets included (in addition to the Stations of the Cross) statues of Christ, the *Pietà*, and a kneeling St. Bernadette before the Virgin Mary.[32]

Proclaiming the land for Catholicism through the construction of countryside shrines that identified certain places as special and holy persisted over several decades and involved communities across the prairies. Father Sylla marked his transfer to the Polish parish at Rama, Saskatchewan, during the Great Depression with a second Marian shrine (1939), visually reminiscent of the Skaro grotto and likewise dedicated to Our Lady of Lourdes.[33] German Catholics at Kronau in the extreme south of the province had constructed their version of Lourdes, tucked into the hillside beside the church, already in 1917; Hungarians at Kaposvar waited until 1942. Also in Saskatchewan, the Ukrainian Catholic Our Lady of Sorrows (1911) near Cudworth had popular miraculous origins in repeated sightings of a wandering light on a nearby hill, followed by the vision of three children of "a beautiful sad-looking lady ... carrying a chain and dragging a gold cross."[34] In 1956, reinforcing the ethnic specificity of Catholicism, Poles at Webster in northern Alberta built a shrine to Our Lady of Częstochowa—after the miraculous icon known as "Healer of the Sick, Mother of Mercy, and Queen of Poland" purportedly painted by St. Luke and brought to Poland in the fourteenth century.[35] By the late twentieth century, prairie shrines numbered in the dozens, from elaborate Church-run complexes to solitary statues and crosses maintained privately. Their defining characteristics remained the dominance of Marian devotion and links to the countryside or small towns and villages rather than prairie cities. Most could no longer be considered "ethnic," although the biggest pilgrim draws continued to be Native shrines like those at Lac Ste. Anne and St. Laurent and the shrines constructed by ethno-religious communities in conjunction with settling and breaking the land.[36]

Catholicism's traditional intimacy with its surroundings—through local saints, roadside shrines, and pilgrim routes wending through the countryside—equipped it to establish a similar, although less pervasive, intimacy with the new land. With its greater austerity and often outright rejection of graven images, Protestantism was less suited in this respect to be an emigrant church. For their part, Mennonite and Doukhobor martyrs for the faith were not treated as saints and they did not cross the ocean to name prairie churches or populate outdoor shrines. But even mainstream Anglo-Protestant denominations—Anglicans, Methodists, and Presbyterians—were largely cut off from the spiritual connections with the land that Catholic devotional vehicles provided, putting mainstream prairie society outside this specific attempt at domesticating the wilderness. Saints and shrines, of course, never came close to dominating the prairie landscape. Yet in claiming the land on which they stood, shrines in particular performed a dual function. Communal pilgrimages to the site not only reaffirmed faith and bestowed the gift of grace but also reaffirmed the ethnic community in its primal connection to a specific place and its history.

## Cemeteries and the Dead

When progress forced the main character in Gabrielle Roy's touching short story, "Where Will You Go, Sam Lee Wong?" to give up his restaurant in Horizon, Saskatchewan, the villagers assumed that he was going back to China to die. Thus they were puzzled when he boarded the train heading east. They did not see him get off the train, in an identical village on the opposite side of the faraway hills that dimly reminded him of home, where he opened another restaurant.[37] Roy did not say where Sam Lee Wong eventually died, but like other Chinese sojourners who sought their Gold Mountain on the Canadian prairies, every month he paid a small sum of money to a Chinese society in Vancouver to transport his coffin across the ocean so that he could rest among his ancestors. Sam Lee Wong wanted nothing less; Chinese tradition expected nothing less. Not all Chinese sojourners, however, made that journey home and were buried instead among strangers in alien soil, in cemeteries that represented a wrench with the past. But for immigrant settler peoples, and even migrants from other parts of Canada, who perceived their move as permanent and put down roots in the land, cemeteries and their dead helped create psychological and physical bonds to the new country.[38]

Pioneer graveyards were much more than necessary disposal sites for human remains, inevitable by-products of the settlement process, or consecrated ground to receive the body from which the soul had departed. To those born elsewhere, burying their dead on the Canadian prairies forged deep emotional ties with the soil that sheltered them, and thus to a specific place. It also nurtured a broader sense of belonging and community in that cemeteries symbolized the coming together, through their dead, of individuals originating in often different countries, different regions in those countries, or, when all else was equal, different villages. Public cemeteries in ethnically mixed areas illustrated this phenomenon best, but even in ethnically closed and inward-looking communities, cemeteries reflected settlement patterns that could draw

**2.9.** Ukrainian Basilian Fathers beginning construction of the grotto next to their monastery, Mundare, Alberta, c. 1933. BASILIAN FATHERS MUSEUM, PH000709.

from a vast area in the homeland as much as a single village or district. Ethnic exclusivity among the dead, strengthened by religious exclusivity in graveyards attached to country churches, fused a group consciousness onto a more general regional identity. Simultaneously, ethnically or religiously exclusive cemeteries served as statements of distinctiveness and separation from other settlers. Cutting across a shared homesteading experience, they proclaimed as premature a shared vision of building a common prairie society.

In the beginning, settlers' reaction to the unexpectedness of death, and their makeshift burial of the dead in the absence of clergy and formal cemeteries, consciously or unconsciously revealed a sense of rootlessness and detachment from place. "We were unprepared for such a tragedy," wrote a Norwegian immigrant of her childhood in the Nose Hills district of central Alberta, recalling the death of her newborn niece. "However," she continued, "in traditional frontier fashion, we did the best we could.... Dr. Little baptized the baby, Papa built a little coffin which I padded and lined while Sam dug the grave in the corner of the yard. It was a strange funeral; only three of us present.

Papa read the twenty-third Psalm and said a prayer. I placed a bunch of wild flowers on the casket and finally Sam planted a little wooden cross which he had made and inscribed to mark the grave."[39]

Marking countless graves both on private land and in communal burial grounds, the wooden crosses or posts surviving the wild fires that periodically torched the countryside ultimately succumbed to the elements and rotted away. Countless other settler graves went unmarked, or were identified by a rock or shrub, so that eventually only a slight depression in a pasture remained of their presence. As cemetery grave markers in particular became increasingly substantial and permanent, they reflected not only a family's economic position but also the specific ethno-religious tradition (a truncated tree mourning the loss of a young Jew, for example) and local skills like working with glass mosaics.[40] Most striking were the iron crosses forged by artisan blacksmiths popular among German Catholics from the Russian empire; in St. Joseph's Colony they dominated cemeteries like St. Anthony at Grosswerder and Holy Rosary at Reward.[41] Among eastern Europeans especially, the luxury of a camera joined custom and personal taste to put photographs, framed and protected by glass, on the headstone: stern moustached men and women in kerchiefs, sometimes already in their open coffins.

Whatever the nationality, inscriptions appeared in the immigrants' own language, reinforcing the ethnic character of cemeteries as places apart from the dominant Anglo prairie culture. Language barriers, which an unfamiliar script or alphabet magnified, also barred outsiders from the collective identity cemeteries represented and the personal stories they told. The words themselves could be scratched with a nail or crudely hand painted, or, as individuals and communities prospered, exquisitely engraved. Awkward letters and ungrammatical text, especially in the early days among peasant peoples, testified to limited literacy. Some inscriptions provided just name and year of death, suggesting other preoccupations or their own estrangement from place on the part of the living. Some inscriptions noted the deceased's European birthplace, tying the dead to a faraway home and claiming personal identities that were broadly national, regional, or highly specific.[42] Even Jews, whose villages and ghettoes of eastern Europe represented a displaced homeland, reaffirmed who they were and where they came from in this way. Old-world origins also enabled individuals in unfamiliar surroundings to identify

**2.10.** Ukrainian cemetery northwest of Rossburn, Manitoba, 1908.
ARCHIVES OF MANITOBA, SISLER 15, N9663.

themselves in relation to their new neighbours. Other inscriptions, like one at Bangor, a settlement of "Patagonian Welsh" relocated to Saskatchewan from Argentina, expressed identities shaped by serial moves: "From the pampas to the prairies. Johanna Jenkins Davies, 1864–1917," it read, next to a delicately etched Welsh dragon.[43] Finally, some inscriptions conveyed the centrality of the emigration/immigration experience to the life story they recorded: meticulously adding the day, month, and year the person arrived in Canada, or, for immigrant parents burying a child, inserting the phrase "born in Canada."[44] The second generation, buried where they had always lived, would not be so concerned to affirm place. Responsibility for their parents' tombstones also meant that those inscriptions increasingly reflected how they, and not the immigrants, identified with both old-world and pioneer heritages.

Certain ethno-religious traditions stressed the relationship between the living and the dead, which promoted a sense of community and continuity and thus spiritual bonds with the new land. At a 1908 celebration for the dead in St. Peter's Colony, the *Liberia* was sung "for the deceased of the parish" in a church "completely draped in black [with] the symbolic coffin ... standing in the middle

**2.11.** Memorials on the land: (from left) Unidentified grave marker made of sturdy materials, New Finland, Saskatchewan, 2002; Crudely chiselled stone marker recording the deceased's details, New Stockholm, Saskatchewan, 2002; Exquisite workmanship of iron crosses in Grosswerder cemetery, St. Joseph's Colony, Saskatchewan, 2006. PHOTOS BY FRANCES SWYRIPA.

surrounded by many burning candles."[45] Ukrainian traditions involved the land directly. Every Christmas Eve peasant families put out a sheaf of wheat saved from the harvest, whose kernels, they believed, contained the souls of their ancestors; on New Year's Eve they burned the sheaf in the field to return the souls to the soil. Thus, when immigrants brought a treasured sack of grain from Ukraine, their forbears came too, literally mingling with the Canadian earth. For Ukrainians, the newly dead were as important as the distant dead, making the liturgical calendar and pioneer cemetery pivotal to forging a sense of attachment to the land. In the Orthodox and Byzantine-rite Catholic churches, Easter was followed by memorial services for the dead, when people brought baskets of food to their tidied family plots, the priest blessed both graves and food, and those present then feasted together (and symbolically with their dead). In one 1940s photograph from Alberta, family members enjoyed bottles of beer and a game of cards next to the braided bread and Easter eggs set on the tombstone.[46] The annual spring ritual of assembling in the cemetery did two things. It emphasized shared national origins alongside a shared prairie settlement experience; and it bound increasingly remote ancestors in villages back in Ukraine with immigrant Canadian ancestors, buried in their adopted land.[47] The Polish custom during the Skaro pilgrimage of placing lighted candles on family graves in the adjacent cemetery likewise united the living and dead and identified the former with their pioneer roots.

The theological rationale behind the Ukrainian tradition was saving souls from purgatory. All immigrant Orthodox and Catholic faithful adhered to this doctrine in some form, although not always with formal and collective prayers for the dead focussed on the cemetery itself. However, the sixteenth-century Protestant Reformation rejected the notion of purgatory or damnation in favour of justification by faith alone. Its immigrant heirs in western Canada— Mennonites, Dutch Calvinists, German and Scandinavian Lutherans, English Anglicans and Methodists, Scottish Presbyterians—dwelt on the salvation of the living. Cemeteries might be places that family members visited privately, but they were not transformed into places of communal ritual and symbolism focussed on the dead. As such, they did not serve as a constant reaffirmation and reminder of the immigrant generation and their legacy or as a claim on the land and its history.

Despite their agricultural way of life, the theology of more conservative Mennonites actively discouraged a three-way relationship binding the living and the dead through the cemetery to foster a sense of place in the land. Arguing that it was enough for God to know where the dead lay, they sometimes forsook even markers, producing cemeteries like the one in Reinland in the West Reserve: a large expanse of apparent emptiness held the remains of those wishing to be buried anonymously.[48] Doukhobors also preferred unmarked burial mounds; some early settlers believed that they should be eventually ploughed and seeded, mixing the dust of the dead with the dust of the earth.[49] Symbolically, this custom empowered their descendants to feel part of the land of western Canada if not the Canadian state, and respected the Russian peasant's intimacy with the soil. It also undercut the tradition of forced migration and exile that informed Doukhobors' collective memory and identity and hampered attachment to place. When they existed, Doukhobor cemeteries and tombstones could be highly sensitive to place and belonging, in self-consciously establishing the credentials of the immigrant generation. Grave markers routinely identified individuals not only as Doukhobors dedicated to "toil and peaceful life" but also, if having suffered personally for their beliefs, by the formulaic "exiled by the Russian autocratic government." Deliverance, in the form of Canada, also figured in the story. One man, buried outside

Veregin, Saskatchewan, "gained his freedom [from ten years' exile in Siberia after refusing military service] by coming to Canada where he prospered for 11 years" before dying in 1917 at age forty-two.[50]

Judaic religious law and practice meant that in the western Canadian cities where they settled Jews established private Hebrew cemeteries. The situation in smaller centres was less clear cut. Although the Jews who opened shops in the Ukrainian bloc in Alberta maintained a synagogue in Vegreville, they buried their dead in Edmonton's Hebrew cemetery.[51] The rural-urban interplay and broader ethno-religious regional consciousness that this decision reflected had no parallel among other prairie settler peoples, whose local burials proclaimed and reinforced a strictly local identity. Founded in Winnipeg in 1894, Shaarey Zedek was the largest Jewish cemetery on the prairies. It also accommodated co-religionists perhaps too few in number or too scattered to have their own burial ground. Among the Jews it brought together from points in Manitoba and Saskatchewan was Sam Korbin, described in his 1917 epitaph as "an upright Jew and worthy citizen, four years mayor of Canora, Sask."[52] That tombstones named these towns and villages hinted at a certain tension between the comfort and correctness of a final resting place among fellow Jews and burial in a city far from the prairie homes where the deceased and their families had put down roots.[53] In contrast, Jewish rural colonies—for example, Sonnenfeld, Hoffer, Edenbridge, Lipton, and Hirsch (all in Saskatchewan)— frequently and very early in their existence established local cemeteries that functioned like those of other settler peoples to foster feelings of belonging in the land.

On one level, attitudes towards old-world ancestors, contemporary "Canadian" dead, and the place where the latter, as the bridge between past and present, were laid to rest, reflected individual decision making and sentiments acting in concert with custom and religious belief. On a second level, but less universally, they involved collective activity and memory, including a sense of community and identity crystallizing around shared experience and roots in new surroundings. The beautification projects undertaken by the Women's Institute in interwar Alberta illustrated how cemeteries in the larger prairie society became part of an evolving consciousness of place and permanence, with general responsibility for their care.[54] When prairie dead shared space, the resulting sense of community and identity transcended ethno-religious

**2.12.** Ukrainian fellowship around a family grave during prayers for the dead, east-central Alberta, 1948. PROVINCIAL ARCHIVES OF ALBERTA, G746A.

boundaries, but when self-imposed exclusiveness or external prejudices kept them apart, cemeteries and their associated rituals reinforced difference.

Because emigration attracted the young, most pioneers never died in the settlement period, or even the 1920s and 1930s. Perhaps the greatest number of "old-timers" were buried between the 1950s and 1970s, precisely those decades when rural areas faced large-scale out-migration and the decline of their communities. Burials in country cemeteries became increasingly infrequent, confined to the older settler generation and their descendants who stayed on the land. Other cemeteries closed and were swallowed by grass or brush. Some never survived the pioneer period. A mere thirty years after one of the first Mennonite villages was established in 1874, the farmer who took over the abandoned land noted how he "could easily pick out the evidence of fourteen or sixteen house cellars and a larger building which may have served as a Sunday School. The Cemetery was on the north west corner of the village—one of my implements caught the corner of a casket or rough box."[55] The dead from other country cemeteries were dug up and moved closer to where local activities had shifted. As the settlers' clusters of churches, schools, stores, and post offices lost their reason for being and the buildings were demolished or sold and hauled away, only the cemetery remained as a reminder of a once flourishing community with a clear identity. Some of these graveyards would be carefully maintained, still part of the lives of area residents and more intermittently of descendants returning for special events and services. Others awaited a generation curious about its Canadian origins, and an ethno-religious group anxious to acknowledge its pioneers, to be rescued from decay and neglect.

\* \* \*

Communities and churches, names bridging old and new worlds, wayside crosses and shrines, cemeteries. All showed the immigrant settler generation imposing order and meaning on the prairie landscape at the most basic and human level. This grassroots activity and the localized identity it promoted became the vehicle through which subsequent generations accessed both their prairie roots and their specific ethno-religious pasts. The immigrant settler generation's physical and emotional intimacy with the land also became the foundation for group mythologies that transcended the personal and local in the construction of widening spheres of identity, beginning with a regional consciousness that looked to group founding stories for its inspiration.

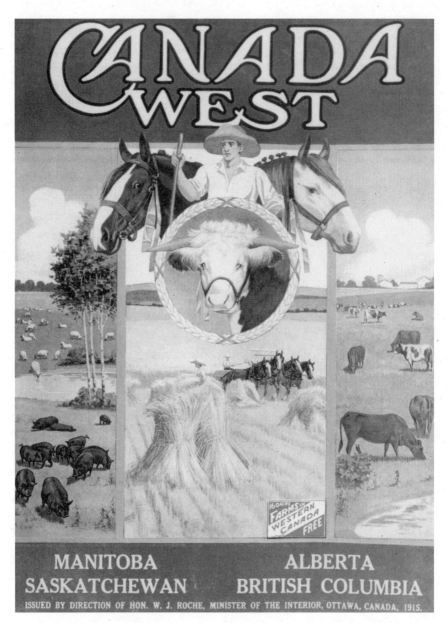

**3.1.** Advertising western bounty, n.d. GLENBOW MUSEUM, NA-789-159B.

# Founding Stories and Founding Fathers: Beginnings, Place, and Belonging

*CANADA*. THAT WAS THE NAME PRISONERS in the Nazi death camp at Auschwitz gave to the barracks holding the belongings stripped from new arrivals. Jews from the ghettoes and villages of eastern Europe, "they associated the sheer amount of the loot and its mind-boggling value with the riches [the country] symbolized."[1] It was a place that most of these victims of the unfolding Holocaust would never see, but it existed in their imagination and dreams. A similar image, of a biblical Promised Land that abounded in material plenty, also animated immigrants to the western prairies. On a personal level, pre-emigration fancies of boundless wealth tended to be culturally specific, identified with coveted scarce commodities in the homeland. The Ukrainian girl, who yearned to see the country that a former neighbour's letters convinced her had "borders ... braided with sausage [*kovbasa*] like some fantastic land in a fairy tale," illustrated not only the poverty of would-bè emigrants but also their ideas of affluence. Her particular dream of gorging every day on a rare holiday treat evaporated when she recognized the wizened crone scratching in her garden outside a hut as the wife of the man who had enticed them with his talk.[2]

Garlic sausage was a poignant but hardly beautiful metaphor for Canada and never entered a general Ukrainian mythology. Yet notions of a land "flowing with milk and honey" influenced countless private decisions to uproot and relocate. They also facilitated the construction of group-based founding stories around such expectations and the handful of individuals, as founding fathers, who promoted or epitomized them. The resulting collective consciousness, rooted in the West and identified with beginnings, went beyond the localized identity that place names, old-world saints and shrines, and cemeteries represented. Two additional factors affected the evolution of prairie founding stories, among first the settler generation and then its descendants, as the foundation for regionally based group identities. They were the existence and character of a pre-emigration group consciousness, and the nature of the immigration and settlement experience. It mattered profoundly if immigration was well defined and controlled (clear leaders, narrow source base, limited time frame, pre-assigned destination) and represented a distinct world view or way of life. Such conditions produced a singular experience whose points of reference resonated personally with the immigrant generation and immediately informed a collective group memory. It mattered equally profoundly if immigration was unstructured and leaderless, extended over years or decades, had multiple destinations, and drew from a wide geographical area whose residents emigrated as individuals, even when travelling with fellow villagers or compatriots. These conditions produced a generic experience, devoid of a formative moment with which a majority of immigrants personally related, and translated into collective memory only over time. Unlike the first scenario, where the group's origins were known and unambiguous, the founding story and its actors had to be recovered, publicized, and secured against alternate versions or individuals.

Canadian immigration propaganda promoted the West's natural bounty as the Promised Land and unarguably coloured the perceptions and decision making of intending immigrants.[3] Outsiders' rosy faith in the "last best west," however, had little impact on ethno-religious founding narratives. Invariably, a group's founding fathers drew attention to the region, scouted and passed judgement on the land, negotiated the terms (if any) of settlement, and led their people to their new home. Assuming the mantle of prophets guided by the hand of Providence, these men introduced an inevitability and purpose to the western Canadian venture that precluded error or betrayal and exacted a commitment to progress and success. Aversion to mistakes and failure turned problematic if events proved the prophets to be human, their followers fickle, the land unsatisfactory, or government promises retractable.

## Group Founding Stories—the Highlights

The founding stories and founding fathers behind the collective identities of immigrant settler peoples in the West were predicated upon "first" arrivals and where and when they settled. These firsts drew in part on remote and isolated individuals, meaningful to the group alone and useful only symbolically, but they relied primarily on later mass movements significant also to the general prairie narrative. Anniversary milestones and their trappings thus reflected not only internal group dynamics and priorities but also regional landmark events, stressing shared pioneering credentials on the land and in province building. In fact, the arrival and dispersal of group movements from overseas defined the contours of the settlement frontier, beginning with the Scottish crofters brought to Red River by the Earl of Selkirk in 1812, in a way that the steady and larger stream of undifferentiated Canadian migrants could not.

Immigrant settler peoples illustrated the importance of founding dates and first arrivals when, in the twentieth century, rival groups turned to the Selkirk colony for evidence to claim deep roots in the region. Pitting Poles against Ukrainians, and relying on "corrected" spellings of the men's names and birthplaces, the prize was ownership of a handful of Slavic soldiers who joined the fledgling settlement following military service in Upper and Lower Canada during the War of 1812.[4] None of these men—who left no trace of Polish or Ukrainian consciousness and had no link to the communities later immigrations established—could ever be more than symbolic firsts. Yet despite their admitted short stay in Red River, the Polish members of the De Meuron regiment became "persevering colonists and valuable settlers,"[5] tying them to both the birth of agricultural settlement in the West and subsequent Polish homesteaders on the land. In critiquing Polish claims to the ex-soldiers, Ukrainian Paul Yuzyk laid bare the implications of discontinuity. "Had there existed the link between these pioneers and the later Polish immigration in the 1890s," he wrote, "it would have given the Poles priority rating as co-builders of Western Canada. As it turned out, the Slavs who hold this honour are the Ukrainians."[6] One-upmanship aside, the distinction between firsts as figureheads, in the form of distant and obscure individuals, and mass movements able to sustain meaningful founding fathers and founding myths was crucial.

By the opening years of the twenty-first century, a spate of centennial anniversary celebrations acknowledged the fruits of immigration and settlement policies implemented many years earlier. For some groups, the festivities denoted a new stage in their identity in that previous anniversaries had passed unnoticed or unmarked. For others, the centenary capped a tradition of observing major landmarks in their collective life. Attitudes towards beginnings, and whether or not they were transcribed in carefully crafted narratives with larger-than-life players, varied. The experience of some immigrant settler peoples created strong bonds from the outset. This category included Mennonites and Doukhobors, sensitized to and protective of their distinctiveness, who emigrated en masse in orderly and ideologically motivated movements and settled in compact reserves. It also included those lacking the same consciousness and commitment, and with more diverse geographical origins, but who also settled as communities on designated land: New Iceland, the Hungarian colony at Esterhazy-Kaposvar, St. Peter's Colony of German Catholics, and the English Barr Colony at Lloydminster. Finally, it included Mormons and rural Jews, who shared features of each type. A second category of immigrant settler peoples initially did not possess strong bonds—their movements were broadly based and leaderless in any practical or visionary sense, sharing nationality but not a dictated or desired way of life, dispersed on lands to which they had no privileged claim. It included Ukrainians, whose founding story had to be retrieved and made relevant to immigrants and their descendants in the deliberate creation of collective memory. It also included Swedes, Norwegians, Poles, Romanians, and others who never developed all-embracing myths of coming to and establishing themselves in the new world. The discussion that follows explores how groups in both categories dealt with their prairie beginnings, focussing on selected aspects of the narratives that emerged.

Mennonites produced no figures from the movement to Canada or the creation of prairie communities who dominated the group consciousness to the exclusion of all others. Nonetheless, although they never pushed the claim, they alone among immigrant settler peoples possessed a Canadian founding father, Jacob Shantz. The Swiss Mennonite businessman-farmer from Ontario visited the prairies on behalf of the Russian Mennonites in 1872 and joined the 1873 scouting mission. The Mennonite founding story highlighted the

**3.2.** Ontario Mennonite Jacob Shantz, likened to eighteenth-century French explorer La Vérendrye, n.d.
MENNONITE ARCHIVES OF ONTARIO, 1989-5, ID#26.

arrival of the first sixty-five families aboard the sternwheeler the *International* in 1874 and their short overland trek from the junction of the Rat and the Red rivers to the East Reserve. The West Reserve was settled the following year (and officially designated only in 1876), handicapping it in terms of actual beginnings but producing a secondary, parallel strand to the regional founding story that addressed its own experience and identity. That both Shantz and the Reverend Heinrich Wiebe, one of the Russian delegates, eventually settled in the West Reserve also enhanced its position. The centennial history of the village of Reinland called Shantz "the West Reserve's La Verendrye," instrumental in selecting the site and convincing doubtful newcomers that, despite the absence of wood, "the earth itself was 'excellent good land.'"[7] Subsequent developments confirmed the East and West reserves as joint participants in the regional founding story and a homeland themselves, as Manitoba Mennonites

**3.3.** Peter Vasilevich ("the Lordly") Verigin, released from exile prior to leaving for Canada, Russia, 1902.
ROYAL BC MUSEUM, BC ARCHIVES, C-01470.

established new settlements in Saskatchewan and Alberta, recreating their old-world pattern of mother and daughter colonies.

The Russian count Leo Tolstoi and Doukhobors' own spiritual leader, Peter "the Lordly" Verigin, dominated that group's founding story. Tolstoi's role—winning sympathy and respectability for the Doukhobors, facilitating their exit from the Russian empire—largely ended with emigration. Verigin, however, ruled from exile in Siberia before his release in late 1902, then again in person until tensions with the Canadian state drove the most disaffected in the Christian Community of Universal Brotherhood to British Columbia. Verigin's authority waned among the rising Independents, but he remained a force and bond among all factions until his murder in 1924, recognized as the group's

**3.4.** Doukhobors burning arms to protest the Great War, Veregin, Saskatchewan, 1920s. SASKATCHEWAN ARCHIVES BOARD, S-B9695.

first (and ultimately only unanimous) leader in Canada. He also established the village bearing his name, on land purchased along the Canadian Northern rail line, residing in the imposing "palace" that became his headquarters. "Clad in the English style, wearing a silk hat," he would sally forth, "in the summer in a phaeton, in winter in a sleigh, drawn by pure-bred horses," to visit his followers in their villages.[8]

The Doukhobor founding story also pivoted on two dates. One was 1899, when the first immigrants sailed into Halifax in late January aboard the SS *Lake Huron* en route to the West. This initial party split between the North and South colonies and so privileged neither in terms of beginnings (the Saskatchewan Colony received its first settlers in June). The more important date was the ceremonial burning of arms in 1895 at Bogdanovka on the Feast of Sts. Peter and Paul in defiance of the tsarist authorities. A single symbolic act that brought renewed persecution and served as the catalyst to the journey abroad, it had no peer among other immigrant settler peoples. To successive generations of Canadian Doukhobors, Petrov Den (Peter's Day), observed on 12 July on the Julian calendar and then on 29 June, had triple significance. It was both Peter Verigin's birthday and his name day, facilitating identification with

**3.5.** Sigtryggur Jónasson, first Icelander in Canada and "Father of New Iceland," n.d. ARCHIVES OF MANITOBA, NIC 292, N11296.

the Doukhobor leader. It was also the day on which their ancestors had chosen the path of the Christian martyrs, and in remembering their deed, Canadian Doukhobors reaffirmed their own pacifism and willingness to suffer for their beliefs. In the 1920s, for example, the village of Veregin re-enacted the burning of arms with a bonfire as a protest against the recently concluded war, when the sect's position attracted animosity.[9] As the twentieth century closed, communal gatherings on Petrov Den opened the legacy of the burning of arms around a commitment to honour the courage of the 1895 generation by promoting world peace. Finally, Petrov Den separated those who gambled on a new life in a new country, "where they could live without sacrificing their principles," from their co-religionists who elected to stay where they were.[10] Petrov Den, in other words, created the phenomenon of Canadian Doukhobors, who henceforth followed a different trajectory within the sect. If 1899 was about the move to Canada and the prairies, the wisdom of which could (and would) be debated,

1895 involved principled decision, personal danger, and faith.

Like the Mennonite reserves and Doukhobor colonies, New Iceland became the foundation for a regionally based group founding story and identity. There were also other similarities. While lacking Shantz's credentials, Sigtryggur Jónasson as New Iceland's founding father and head of its first governing council brought Canadian experience to the venture in the West, having spent three years in Ontario. He left the colony in 1880, for first Selkirk and then Winnipeg, but continued to serve its interests, especially after election to the Manitoba Legislature in 1896, and was rewarded during his lifetime with the title Father of New Iceland. The colony's 125th anniversary celebrations in 2000 recalled Jónasson as a "visionary leader, entrepreneur, [and] statesman," rising "by sheer initiative and ability" from "stalwart and gifted farm folk."[11] Mennonite and Icelandic founding stories also mirrored each other in their identification with a fixed time and place of first arrival, although the Icelandic landing site lay within the group's allocated tract. The Icelandic story also entailed great drama. Travelling north on Lake Winnipeg on flat boats towed by a Hudson's Bay Company steamer, the *Colville*, the settlers were cut adrift when the captain feared a pending storm; they poled their way to shore, disembarking at Willow Point on 21 October 1875.[12] Gimli became the undisputed "capital" of the colony, eclipsing Winnipeg, and, as "the cradle of our race in the New World," eventually the capital of all Icelanders in North America.[13] While not driven by a formative crucible like Doukhobors' burning of arms, the Icelandic founding story also boasted an explicit old-world catalyst—the volcanic eruptions of 1876 that differentiated the Large Group from economic emigrants whose poverty was unpunctuated by a single life-changing disaster. Survival in the face of a second devastation, the smallpox epidemic of 1876–77 that attacked both Icelandic settlers and their Native neighbours, also featured in the Icelandic founding story.

Hungarians at Esterhazy-Kaposvar, German Catholics in St. Peter's Colony, and the English Barr Colonists at Lloydminster also possessed clear territorial bases and unambiguous leaders of immigration and settlement. However, given the long-time English and German presence in the country and region, only the Hungarian founding story—constructed around the controversial "Count" Paul O. d'Esterhazy, who chose the site and assisted the early colony without living there—had more than local potential. Established shortly

**3.6.** Hungarian "Count" Paul O. d'Esterhazy in elegant surroundings, n.d. FROM *KAPOSVAR: A COUNT'S COLONY, 1886-1986*, 30.

after Huns Valley in Manitoba, Esterhazy-Kaposvar soon overshadowed its predecessor, and on its golden jubilee in 1936 proudly declared itself "Canada's First Hungarian Colony." That Esterhazy-Kaposvar was Roman Catholic, and later Hungarian settlements often Protestant, did not seem to affect its pre-eminence in terms of group beginnings or its self-styled status as the "mother colony." Yet a coalescing regional consciousness dislodged Esterhazy-Kaposvar in relation to Huns Valley, so that by its centennial it had adjusted its sights to become the first Hungarian settlement "west of Manitoba."[14] Home to the original log church, the massive stone rectory and Our Lady of Assumption Church built the following decade, and the adjacent cemetery, rural Kaposvar constituted the physical and spiritual focal point of the Hungarian colony.

Also Roman Catholic, and also boasting an individual (Father Bruno Doerfler) essential to the settlement, St. Peter's Colony differed in key respects. Crucially, it had a sharper and more enduring definition, especially after elevation to an Abbacy Nullius. The Benedictines' pervasive presence also magnified the colony's religious character. It ultimately produced a two-pronged founding story—the transfer of the order from Illinois to the banks of Wolverine Creek and the settlement of homesteaders on the land—as well as a group narrative centred on Muenster, the Benedictines' base. Doerfler, who died suddenly in 1919, was the ideal figure of a founding father. He not only headed the search for a site for a German Catholic farming enterprise but also, as prior and then abbot, shaped the colony as a religious undertaking. It was inconceivable that the Benedictines would let Father Bruno be forgotten or not institute a tradition of celebrating the colony's beginnings.

In his account of his 1902 scouting mission, published the following year, Father Bruno noted how approval for "a large colony for German-American Catholics" had provoked a demand for "a similar undertaking for Englishmen in order to save Canada from being 'swamped.'" By then the English colony was a reality and its inspiration, the Reverend Isaac Barr, already banished for what Doerfler termed "vampire-like extortions" that inflated prices the colonists paid en route for goods and services.[15] Barr's replacement, the Reverend George Exton Lloyd, who had accompanied the immigrants as their chaplain, carried no negative baggage as a second founding father. But although they rewarded his competence in naming the townsite "Lloydminster," and officially chose the name Britannia for their settlement, it remained the Barr Colony to all intents and purposes. Barr himself was rarely expunged from the founding story, even as defenders and critics debated his merits, perhaps because his vision and energy underpinned the entire venture. Other features of the story included the "nerve-racking" trip aboard the SS *Lake Manitoba*, the arduous trek from Saskatoon, and the hurdles facing inexperienced farmers. Unusually, the latter were embraced not rejected—their naïveté (as in the tale of the greenhorn who thought potatoes "had to be planted in pairs in order to 'produce'") gently mocked.[16]

**3.7.** Father Bruno Doerfler, aged thirty-six, with his bed roll in western Canada, 1902.
ARCHIVES OF THE ORDER OF ST. BENEDICT, ST. PETER'S ABBEY.

In the context of the foregoing groups, Mormons were unique in that Charles Ora Card fit into a pre-existing tradition of colonizing founding fathers. As leader of the trek by covered wagon to southern Alberta, he became "Canada's Brigham Young," successor to the man who four decades earlier had guided the Latter-day Saints across the Mississippi River to a hoped-for sanctuary in the Salt Lake basin. Also unique to Mormons was the towering role in the collective consciousness played by the settlement's principal centre, Cardston. Here the settlers observed their first communal sacrament in a tent, the pulpit "a packing case, with boxes, kegs and bags of oats serving as seats for the congregation." The first Mormon temple outside the United States was also early prophesied for the site; dedicated in 1923 after a decade of construction, the massive Cardston temple came to act as a magnet for Mormons from across Canada.[17]

In that most Jews settled in Winnipeg rather than on the land, the Manitoba capital and not the handful of Jewish colonies drove an essentially urban group narrative, whose rural counterpart Saskatchewan dominated. Rural Jews knew of their debt to Baron Maurice de Hirsch, their European benefactor, as the colony bearing his name testified; and its residents in particular saw the tie to "Our Father" as personal.[18] Winnipeg and the rural West shared both the first arrivals of 1877 and the mass movement of refugees from the Russian empire starting in 1882 (although the first rural settlement, New Jerusalem, was not established until 1884). The precarious footing and eventual demise of the rural Jewish colonies meant that none took control of a regional founding story based on agriculture that could parallel the more rewarding Winnipeg storyline. The spotlight instead shifted among Hirsch, Wapella, and Edenbridge. Yet the rural colonies represented an important aspect of the regional group experience, suggesting that place in the land, regardless of its uncertainty, provided prairie Jews with an identity and validation that city roots alone could not.

The second category of immigrant settler peoples, those initially without strong bonds, had no obvious candidates for founding fathers (who often turned out to be ordinary settlers) and no clear start to the prairie adventure. Founding stories thus appeared after the fact, if at all, and were often limited in scope. Prairie Finns—numbering only a few thousand, divided between church-goers and socialists/communists, scattered in small settlements—never privileged a particular storyline. Even New Finland, their oldest settlement, made no regional claims, and on the eve of its centennial remained uncertain about the details of its own establishment. Settler David Kautonen was the colony's acknowledged founding father, but whether he arrived in 1888 (when he filed his homestead) or earlier remained in doubt; in the local history he was merely listed as one of the men and women who arrived between 1888 and 1933.[19] Three times more populous than Finns, prairie Danes did privilege their oldest settlement—Dickson in Alberta, the province where one in every two Danes lived. Despite far larger numbers and territorial bases, neither Norwegians nor Swedes constructed regional founding stories and identities. Gulbrand Loken hinted at one explanation for both groups in his 1980 study, *From Fjord to*

**3.8.** "Discovery" of Ukrainian founding father Ivan
Pylypiw, Lamont, Alberta, 1932. UKRAINIAN CANADIAN
ARCHIVES AND MUSEUM OF ALBERTA, P78-1-498.

*Frontier,* when he complained that multiculturalism came too late to "save"
Norwegians, who had assimilated.[20] In addition, the two trajectories—from
the homeland and the United States—that characterized immigration and
settlement for Norwegians and Swedes precluded a single founding story that
resonated with a majority of group members.

Romanians and Poles, who often settled in pockets among much bigger
Ukrainian populations, also never developed regional identities around
overarching founding stories and narratives. In the 1990s, however, reflecting
the impact of the larger prairie society on identity formation, the Alberta

wings of the two groups celebrated provincial centennials. Each accepted that its founding fathers were not the first of their people in the West. Alberta Romanians conceded that honour to Saskatchewan, where the first documented Romanians arrived in 1896, two years before the Ichim Yurko family and Elias Ravliuk took homesteads east of Edmonton. The first Polish settlers in Alberta, identified by Father Antoni Sylla, were Stanisław and Maria Banach, who came from Washington state in 1895 and spent time in Strathcona before homesteading at Round Hill.[21] In both instances a sense of roots in the land centred on religious sites fewer than forty kilometres apart: St. Mary Romanian Orthodox Church at Boian and the Polish Our Lady of Lourdes at Skaro. But while the Romanian celebrations took place in the countryside at Boian, many of the Polish events (including a banquet in honour of the "first pioneers") were held in Edmonton.

Ukrainians epitomized the confusion that could plague a founding story when immigration and settlement were untidy and unfocussed. The group marked its golden jubilee in 1941, with celebrations centred on the prairie provinces and a founding story that began with the arrival in 1891 of Ivan Pylypiw and Vasyl Eleniak, who later settled in the Edna-Star colony in Alberta and whose stories mirrored those of thousands of their peers. Although every subsequent anniversary took its cue from the 1941 celebration, in 1928 Alberta Ukrainians had boldly marked thirty years of life in the province and country, giving an arrival date after 1891. The Edmonton-based Ukrainian Pioneers (Old-Timers) Association made the anniversary its inaugural project. It also opted for maximum exposure in the city—a Cossack-led parade down Jasper Avenue, official greetings from all three levels of government, a gala concert and picnic—over the rural bloc where most Ukrainians lived.[22] The celebrations acknowledged no special individuals, although the Winnipeg-based newspaper *Kanadiiskyi farmer* noted the 1895 scouting mission of Dr. Osyp Oleskiv. The celebrations also vacillated between a firm time frame of thirty years and a more ambiguous transition at 1898 from limited immigration (starting six years earlier, when Edna-Star received its first settlers) to a mass movement.[23] Not long thereafter, Ivan Bobersky, a Galician activist and intellectual who spent time in Canada between the wars and launched a search for the first Ukrainian in Canada, rescued Pylypiw and Eleniak from oblivion beyond oral tradition and local memory. Having visited the duo in Alberta in 1932, he published their stories, told in their own words, in 1933 (Eleniak) and 1937 (Pylypiw, who had died the previous year).[24] Such publicity and certainty assured fiftieth anniversary celebrations in 1941.

Ethno-religious groups' own agenda, and not external factors, provided the impetus to a search for roots. Similarly, groups' own immigration and settlement experiences, and not those of the larger society, furnished the elements of the resultant founding stories recited and reinforced on important occasions. Yet mainstream platforms like the Alberta and Saskatchewan golden jubilees in 1955 tested those narratives and the group credentials they ostensibly conferred. Alberta's personalized Senior Citizen Scrolls, given to every non-Native residing in the province in 1905 or earlier, accepted one-time "foreigners" into the ennobling fraternity of pioneers, yet recognition did not extend to the ethno-religious groups to which the individuals belonged. The government refused to translate the scrolls into French, both because French was not an official language in Alberta and because it would then have "to print others in Ukrainian, and other languages as well."[25] The 1955 commemorative stamp issued by the Post Office underscored the Anglo bias in those controlling the settlement narrative: its female pioneer wore a sunbonnet, her kerchief in the original design deemed too foreign.[26] The three women chosen to portray the pioneer generation in the Esterhazy jubilee celebrations affirmed the hierarchy in the settler experience even as they acknowledged group contributions. The "queen" represented the English founders of nearby Sumner Colony established in 1883, the two "princesses" (the elder in a kerchief) stood for the Kaposvar colony begun three years later.[27]

Ethno-religious groups also used such anniversaries to insert themselves into the provincial narrative. As examples, Ukrainians in 1955 and Icelanders during the Manitoba centennial in 1970 each had a strong sense of place in the land and role in building the West. Ukrainians stressed that they had lived in the West fourteen years before the creation of Alberta and Saskatchewan, putting the peasants who broke the land (and whose descendants testified to the material progress the jubilees celebrated) among the region's true pioneers.[28] Icelanders could not boast origins predating Manitoba, but, as the cabinet minister reminded his listeners in a speech at Gimli, they had been there for ninety-five of its 100 years. Moreover, he continued, tying the provincial milestone to Icelanders' own story, "five years from now the Centennial of

**3.9.** Home of Charles Ora Card, "Canada's Brigham Young," Cardston, Alberta, 1889. GLENBOW MUSEUM, NA-147-1.

the Icelandic settlement on the shores of Lake Winnipeg, upon the very spot on which we meet today, will be celebrated ... a fact that we ... must prepare to observe in a fitting manner."[29] Among Ukrainians, however, 1955 injected artificial divisions, forcing celebrants in Saskatchewan to borrow the still-living Eleniak to claim the regional founding story that eclipsed more localized ones. But the ninety-six-year-old, residing on the family homestead at Chipman, enabled Alberta Ukrainians to internalize the jubilee, situating their founding story and founding father in the provincial narrative and cultivating a parallel identity.[30]

## Patterns and Implications

The founding stories that evolved from mass movements to the Canadian prairies beg a number of observations. Perhaps most striking was the irrelevance of group size. Both Ukrainians with their huge numbers and Icelanders and Doukhobors with their small ones cultivated strong traditions, while groups far larger than Icelanders or Doukhobors—such as Poles, Norwegians, and Swedes—developed rudimentary narratives at best. Also, while a well-organized movement and identifiable tracts of land mattered, Ukrainians showed that immigration could proceed haphazardly and that the tracts did not have to be officially designated or secured. Nonetheless, a sharp sense of place distinguished peoples whose journey, arrival, and settlement were highly structured affairs with clear destinations. Mennonites and Icelanders came to identify strongly with the East and West reserves and New Iceland respectively as both real and imagined places. Ukrainians never felt the same about their amorphous bloc settlements, not even Edna-Star. "Bloc" itself was a term used by academics and often critical outsiders, not part of the vocabulary and imagination of local residents; and, although home to the group's founding fathers, the Alberta colony was established after 1891, divorcing arrival from settlement. The place with which Doukhobors most identified, the village of Veregin, was likewise divorced from beginnings. Indelible events signalling the journey's end and a new start also dominated the consciousness of certain groups: the first Mennonites leaving the *International* where the Rat joined the Red, the first Icelanders landing at Willow Point, the arrival in Halifax of the first party of Doukhobors aboard the SS *Lake Huron*. In contrast, Ukrainians attached little significance to when and where Pylypiw and Eleniak set foot on Canadian soil (7 September 1891 in Quebec) or how they got there (on the SS *Oregon*). When interviewed by Bobersky, neither man recalled the details of their arrival, and future generations repeatedly insisted that they landed in Halifax.[31]

A second observation concerns the relationship between a sense of beginnings and place and contemporary documentation. A written account of the search for suitable land in the Canadian West shaped the subsequent movement, gave an automatic structure to the founding story, and identified its principal actors. Such texts included Shantz's *Narrative of a Journey to Manitoba* (1873), Oleskiv's *O emigratsii* (1895), Doerfler's eighteen-part "Across the Boundary" (1903), and *A Peculiar People: The Doukhobors* (1904) by the English Quaker Aylmer Maude, who joined the 1898 scouting party and helped negotiate the terms of admission.[32] Other texts—like the diary, published in 1905, of the young Russian aristocrat in charge of the first shipload of Doukhobors—recorded the inaugural journey itself.[33] The nature of the contemporary documentation could also colour how the founding story was viewed. Addressing the Manitoba Historical Society in 1990, Jewish community

**3.10.** Mennonites arriving in Winnipeg aboard the *International*, 31 July 1874.
GLENBOW MUSEUM, NA-264-1.

historian Abraham Arnold complained about "the lack of knowledge or forgetfulness by Jewish leaders in Montreal and London of the two-year wait for land." It threatened, he said, to cast the New Jerusalem pioneers "in the role of another 'lost tribe,' … like the ten tribes of ancient Israel."[34]

A pioneer press increased the chances that how and why the group came to the prairies would be written down and canonized by repetition, while the agenda of those in control dictated how the account would be moulded and managed. *Framfari* (progress), edited by Sigtryggur Jónasson, began publication two years after New Iceland's establishment, while *St. Peter's Bote* (messenger) appeared within nine months of the Benedictines' arrival in St. Peter's Colony. Moreover, neither newspaper had to contend with competitors in the surrounding hinterland, and each took a lively and influential interest in settlement affairs. Ukrainians had no press of their own until over a decade after immigration began, and several rivals jockeyed for readers spread over three provinces. Doukhobors, whose intertwined history and faith were preserved orally in the "Living Book," addressed their past in both Russia and Canada through an evolving repertoire of hymns.[35] New Icelanders also used a familiar form, the saga, to tell their immigration and settlement stories, published in *Framfari* or, after 1895, the annual *Almanak*, which became the guardian of Icelandic memory for all North America.[36]

An intrigued Canadian media commenting upon the initial arrival also facilitated founding stories. It could never occur with a Pylypiw or a Eleniak, two anonymous men stepping off a boat onto a train heading west, but it could and did occur with large group movements. Both Canadian and British presses charted the journey of the Barr Colonists from England to the North-West Territories. Western Europe and North America also followed the travails of the Doukhobors, so that when the first party sailed into Halifax, curious reporters awaited. In addition, photographers caught the immigrants aboard ship, creating for posterity a series of images of both journey and arrival; other photographers waited in Yorkton, Saskatchewan, to catch them detraining in the West. The Winnipeg press also captured the arrival in December 1902 of Peter Verigin, en route to Yorkton where 300 faithful met him at the station.[37] The first parties of Icelanders and Mennonites to reach Winnipeg had aroused similar curiosity and commentary. Outsiders could also empower a particular storyline, as when in 1901 the Historical and Scientific Society of Manitoba invited Jónasson to speak to its members about early Icelandic settlements in Canada.[38]

A third observation concerns the relationship among founding stories, major anniversaries of immigration and settlement, and the evolution of a historiographical tradition. The link was negative in the case of Swedes and Norwegians. The absence of an overarching regional identity fashioned around common points of reference paralleled a dearth of studies, beyond a few articles often written by Americans and/or appearing in American publications.[39] Where founding stories and historiographical traditions coexisted, anniversary milestones stimulated both scholarly research and popular jubilee histories. The prairie Mennonite and Ukrainian-Canadian centennials each produced excellent studies that situated group developments in the West in their national contexts.[40] Popular histories—sporting pictures of monarchs and church hierarchs and greetings from political worthies—preferred bald fact over analysis and celebrating the group and its achievements over critiquing them. As catalysts to the collection, ordering, and prioritizing of information, however, such projects had no equals. St. Peter's Colony produced its first history in 1928 as part of its silver jubilee celebrations, Hungarians at Esterhazy-Kaposvar their first history in 1936 in conjunction with their golden jubilee.[41] As befit two Roman Catholic settlements, both books were church dominated, focussing on male and female religious and institution building at the expense of ordinary settlers. The Benedictines retained control of the narrative on St. Peter's golden jubilee, but for its centennial the laity published local community histories with huge family biography sections that emphasized the people themselves. The centennial history of the Hungarian colony showed the same shift in authorship and priorities.[42] The local history format—pioneer churches and clergy, schools and teachers, businesses and entrepreneurs, and generations of settler families—attracted peoples and places without larger group founding stories. Like *Life in the New Finland Woods*, many appeared in conjunction with not only anniversaries of immigration and settlement but also the late twentieth-century impulse across the prairies to record a vanishing era in the countryside.

While the above publications expressed a local consciousness, the centennial histories compiled by Poles and Romanians in Alberta attested to provincial identities within a larger group framework. Both books followed the local community history format, but differed in how they imagined their provincial communities and in who controlled the narrative. Among Romanians, and mirroring the centennial festivities themselves, control lay with the descendants of the immigrant settler generation still living in the original settlement area. Although incorporating Edmonton institutions, individuals, and events after 1945, reflecting rural-urban migration and new immigration from overseas, the story focussed on the countryside, the church and school at Boian as its hub, and the pioneers and their offspring. The Polish story, like much of the celebrations, was dominated by newer immigrants and urban intellectuals. Edmonton was an important player from the beginning; Polish communities from the Peace River district in the north to the Coal Branch in the south complemented the settlement core east of Edmonton; and interwar and especially post-war urban immigrants received as much attention as settlers on the land.[43] Other provincial peculiarities included the local histories produced in St. Peter's Colony as part of the 2005 Saskatchewan centennial, or the 1980s republication of Father Bruno's scouting report as a contribution to "the beginnings of Saskatchewan."[44] The historiographical traditions fostered by some regional founding stories also privileged a particular province. Far more works appeared on Mennonites and Icelanders in Manitoba than in Saskatchewan and Alberta. Also, despite Paul Yuzyk's pioneering *Ukrainians in Manitoba*, the Ukrainian group's subsequent obsession with the Alberta bloc left the provincial experience in Manitoba and especially Saskatchewan largely unexplored.[45]

Milestone anniversaries of immigration and settlement also spurred non-literary initiatives. Doukhobors' oral tradition lent itself to outdoor pageants and re-enactments, staged near Veregin on the fiftieth and seventieth anniversaries of immigration and settlement in 1949 and 1969. The Ukrainian Pioneers Association of Alberta (it had no counterpart in Manitoba or Saskatchewan) was founded in 1941, on the group's golden jubilee, with unrealized plans to write a history of Ukrainian settlers in the province. The Jewish Historical Society of Western Canada had similar origins, in interest generated by the confluence of the ninetieth anniversary of the arrival of the first documented Jews in the West in 1877 and the Canadian Centennial in 1967.[46]

A final observation concerns the use of biblical language. It appeared very early in a name like New Jerusalem, suggesting that the colony's Jews had ended their wanderings. In 1902 it appeared in Father Bruno's description, after days of disappointing land, of finding a pastoral paradise at what would become St. Peter's Colony. It appeared again in 1936 when Ukrainians in Fraserwood, Manitoba, addressing the visiting governor general, compared the move to Canada to Moses leading his people out of the wilderness into "a land of wheat, and barley, and vines and fig trees, and pomegranates; a land of olive oil, and honey; a land wherein thou shalt ... not lack any thing." And it appeared on Doukhobors' golden jubilee, when they likened fleeing the Russian empire under the tsars to the "flight of the Israelites from Egypt under the pharaohs."[47] As succeeding generations mobilized the Promised Land motif to paint their founding fathers as wise and prophetic and their ancestors, through labour on land so providentially chosen, as successful and secure, they validated the decision to relocate on the Canadian prairies. This imagery could be purely local, as with "Moses of Rabbit Hill," the Polish family patriarch who was also patriarch of his small Alberta community.[48] It could also be broad and generic. In the Ukrainian version, the peasants Pylypiw and Eleniak came ahead and selected a site at Edna-Star. They found the soil good, trees plentiful, and Galician Germans nearby for employment and familiarity. In the Icelandic version, five delegates came ahead and selected a site north of the Manitoba boundary at a place the pioneers called Gimli, or great hall of heaven, where "the country was wooded, there was hayland at Icelandic River, and ... fish in Lake Winnipeg."[49] In the Mennonite version, a small party came ahead and selected a site in what became the East Reserve. It resembled the treeless steppe of southern Ukraine with which they were familiar, offered the isolation they craved, and, if the delegates did not necessarily choose excellent land, Mennonite labour and skill soon proved it blessed.

Material prosperity represented the rewards and wisdom of long-ago decisions. Perhaps in part because of the delay in ensconcing Pylypiw and Eleniak as founding fathers, Ukrainians agonized little over the accuracy and optimism of Promised Land imagery. Jaroslav Petryshyn's 1985 *Peasants in the Promised Land* illustrated its allure even in academic circles. The communist minority did question its veracity and self-fulfilling destiny, but they took care not to disparage a heroic pioneer generation or the figures of Pylypiw and Eleniak.[50] Mennonites, in contrast, knew directly upon the return of the 1873 scouting party that not all delegates had been impressed with the soil, or conditions more generally, in Manitoba.[51] The plentiful wood, hayland, and fish of the Icelandic myth were first evoked in an address to Governor General Lord Dufferin in 1877, in the context of cautious optimism for the future against a shaky present.[52] Finally, it is important to note the limitations of a Promised Land imagery at the group level. While the local priest writing on the Esterhazy-Kaposvar golden jubilee saw the hand of Divine Providence as one of deliverance, the Royal Consul of Hungary in Winnipeg regretted that it had taken Hungarians from their mother country.[53] Mennonites and Doukhobors qualified the Promised Land in another sense. Their identity shaped by recurring persecution and migration, and seeking more than free land in western Canada, they often framed their story as a "search for utopia" and not necessarily its discovery.[54]

## Problematic Founding Stories and Founding Fathers

"If it were not for the d... mosquitoes," Paul O. d'Esterhazy wrote his wife from Kaposvar in 1902, "the country would seem to have been marked out by the hand of God for a second paradise." A Ukrainian priest likewise complained of the swarms of mosquitoes that "sat on the face, neck, and arms and greeted everyone in the name of Canada." And, when Doukhobor radicals set off naked on foot to find a new paradise in the sun, the North-West Mounted Police opened the doors to the detention building in Yorkton and lit lamps, so that the mosquitoes would succeed where the state had failed and force the pilgrims to put on their clothes.[55] The insect was a perfect metaphor for the possibility that the Promised Land might disappoint, or at least severely test, those whom it lured to the West. Sometimes a group's prophets did not choose providently or well, caused dissension and turmoil, or fled the scene. Sometimes the settlers failed and betrayed their prophets, abandoning this Promised Land for a better one. More rarely, betrayal involved the Aboriginal population that immigrant settler peoples and their founding stories displaced.

In explaining groups' origins and confirming their entitlement to the land, founding stories inevitably impinged on the counterclaims of prairie Natives. Personal memoirs described encounters with Indians and jubilee histories acknowledged their presence as part of the pre-settlement landscape, but otherwise they seldom disturbed group narratives or consciousness. Icelanders offered a partial exception. On the one hand, harmony between New Iceland's first settlers and local Natives, as they braved a forbidding environment, became a point of congratulation. For example, when queried about her experiences with the surrounding Indians, one of the colony's original settlers spoke touchingly of the death of her small son and the Indian father who asked to bury his dead daughter beside him. "We thought," she said, that "this was a beautiful idea."[56] On the other hand, and apparently without tension or irony, New Icelanders proudly embraced the Viking "discovery" of North America. Of greater immediacy, as Ryan Eyford argues, the decimation of local Indian bands from smallpox in 1876–77, plus the quarantine boundaries imposed by the Keewatin Board of Health, "resulted in their dispossession, and the appropriation of their land and resources by the Icelanders."[57] Natives also figured in the Mennonite founding story. Not only had the 1873 scouting party put aside its pacifist principles and armed against a crowd of hostile Métis, nervous about white settlement, but the non-Christian West also appealed to a missionary impulse. If his fellow deputies saw fit "to have their people come to this wilderness," wrote one delegate, appalled by the quality of the soil, "then I could only accept this as a work of God's sovereign mercy that through these people the poor Indians should see the light of the gospel."[58] The rights and wrongs of complicity in destroying the Native way of life, and of profiting from expropriated Indian land, hounded the 1974 centennial celebrations. Some Mennonites voiced contrition on behalf of their ancestors; some sought atonement in Native outreach; others expressed gratitude for the involuntary sacrifice that had let Mennonites pursue their own freedom.[59] No other immigrant settler people compromised its centennial celebrations with such soul searching, although a First Nations representative read a message of friendship to Doukhobors during ceremonies in Saskatoon on the 100th anniversary of the burning of arms.[60]

Unlike Native rights, internal group divisions did challenge ethno-religious narratives. In such situations, founding stories and founding fathers retrieved retroactively fared better than those informing the group consciousness as immigration and settlement unfolded. With no contemporary sense of a common venture and expectations and no contemporary press to debate and censure any deviations, Ukrainians as new arrivals never had to deal with inadequacy or failure in the form of disgruntled settlers. Belatedly vaulted into the limelight, Pylypiw and Eleniak also escaped both blame for the disappointments of their fellow immigrants and criticism for any shortcomings of their own. But groups that recorded events as they happened, and whose founding fathers figured prominently in the immigration and settlement process, could not easily expunge embarrassing episodes or ignore leaders plunged into disrepute or controversy. Fortunately for the Barr Colonists, the Reverend Lloyd waited in the wings to save both venture and founding story from Isaac Barr's betrayal. Doukhobors' Peter Verigin not only physically removed himself from the prairie narrative but also contributed to the tensions that doomed its peculiar experiment. Other disputes pitted immigrant factions against each other and questioned the integrity of the colonies they established or even the very choice of the Canadian prairies. Large-scale exodus by those who condemned the move and their fellow settlers as misguided shook the confidence and threatened the survival of those who remained. Quitters, whingers, and weaklings also queried the group as quality pioneering stock distinguished by their perseverance and progress. Finally, if the group began prairie life in well-defined colonies, perhaps with legal standing, animated by a sense of purpose or destiny, defectors not only betrayed the collective investment in the journey to the Promised Land but also denied its existence, at least in western Canada. Icelanders, Hungarians, and the German settlers at St. Peter's Colony illustrate these issues best.

By the late 1870s New Iceland was torn by a multilayered dispute over the location of an all-Icelandic colony as a bastion of Icelandic identity in North America. The specifics focussed on the merits of the Canadian settlement on the isolated wooded shores of Lake Winnipeg versus the open prairie of Minnesota or Dakota.[61] Religion complicated matters. Allegations of destitution amid claims of unattainable prosperity, and departure for the United States without repaying a government loan, became identified with the American Norwegian Synod, which most settlers spurned for independent Icelandic churches. The centrepiece of the quarrel was what New Iceland's defenders called the "begging letter," written by the Reverend Páll Þorláksson to his synod asking for help for destitute New Icelanders. A second flashpoint, after months of simmering tensions, a "secret deal letter" co-authored by Þorláksson defended the exodus, proposed a solution to the debt issue, and criticized the role of government agents (notably Sigtryggur Jónasson) in the matter of the loans.[62] The repercussions for myth making were threefold.

First, to its defenders, the negative attacks—harsh climate, poor soil, isolation, impassable roads, too many trees and too few meadows, no money-earning potential—hurt New Iceland's image and stability and had to be rebutted. Thus, the soil was good, meadow land existed, and the nearby lake teemed with fish; trees provided lumber for building and firewood for use and sale; isolation preserved Icelandic identity; water transport was available year round; and the awaited railway to the south presaged a great future.[63] Second, that New Iceland's founding father was assailed for his actions as Ottawa's agent, and felt pressed to respond in the pages of *Framfari*, undermined his authority and reputation. Later he would be rehabilitated—as the force that "sustain[ed] 'New Iceland' during and after the painful bloodletting of the 'Great Exodus'" and enabled the settlement to "finally [take] root and flourish."[64] Third, the need for government assistance, the "public begging" in Þorláksson's letter, and leaving New Iceland before clearing the loan with Ottawa were seen as a disgrace to the colony and snub to Canadian generosity, casting doubt on the self-reliance and honesty of Icelanders as settlers and citizens. Jónasson himself suggested that events vindicated the officials who wanted to withhold the funds "on the grounds that Icelanders had become ... degenerate ..., lacking the strength, vigour and patience other people had, and which were essential in overcoming the difficulties of pioneer life." But Jónasson also planted the seed that allowed those who stayed and persevered to wrest the founding story from the quitters. The people of New Iceland, he said, faced perhaps greater adversity than if they had settled elsewhere or among other nationalities, overcoming great obstacles to survive economically and to preserve their Icelandic identity.[65]

Departure by the discontented or unsuited also disrupted St. Peter's Colony. Again, controversy over the exodus—in which the press reflected the views of its Benedictine publishers—centred on ethno-religious identity and the disadvantages of the settlement site, especially the climate and weather related to its northern location. "Our settlers are contented with their new country, and many are quite enthusiastic," wrote St. Peter's Bote in 1904, basking in the conversion of one of the colony's critics: "There still may be one or the other doubting Thomases, but most are overjoyed that Western Canada, even though it is not the promised land overflowing with milk and honey, it is still an area where all manner of grain, except corn, and all kinds of vegetables will flourish. They have come to the happy conclusion that, especially, St. Peter's Colony is by and large a very fruitful piece of land."[66] Unhappy settlers complaining to friends and relatives back in the United States about harsh winters, early frosts, and erratic rainfall affected opinion in the very places where St. Peter's hoped to recruit more German Catholics and which periodically sent excursions to inspect the Muenster area.[67] Doubts about economic returns thus affected the colony's ethno-religious character, and its defenders agitated for new immigration to prevent other nationalities, and particularly Protestants, from settling on unclaimed land. They also faulted settlers who had grown ashamed of being German in the United States and now opposed German names for their parishes and schools. "We wish nothing less," said one critic, "than [that such people] turn their backs on our colony."[68] Then there were the "German Michels" and "kickers." Lazy, whining ne'er-do-wells, they damaged the colony's reputation and hindered the progress that came from "German handicraft, German stamina, German industry ... German diligence, German tenacity ... German willingness to sacrifice and German piety."[69] By St. Peter's silver jubilee in 1928, erasing the dissension of the early years, these traits had metamorphosed into the heroic pioneer of the founding story the Benedictines popularized:

> The trials and difficulties of the one were the trials and difficulties of the other. There were the hardships arising from isolation, from the rigorous climate, from the tardy seasons, from the pesky mosquitoes. The beginnings indeed were no rosy path of ease. Undaunted courage and constant industriousness were necessary for success; but these essential qualifications adorned the hardy pioneers. The progress and development of the land they undertook to form into a home, the thriving towns and villages, the well organized parishes, the flourishing educational and charitable institutions are a standing testimony to the courage, foresight and work of these men.[70]

The problem was that the hardships necessary for heroic pioneers required the same adverse conditions about which the doubters and quitters had complained and that the jubilee's predecessors had dismissed as exaggerated or non-existent.

The exodus of settlers from Esterhazy-Kaposvar differed in two respects. First, the defections were massive. Despite government assistance for travel and homesteading, an estimated two-thirds of the original settlers, from New York and Pennsylvania, had gone by 1887, to be replaced the following year by immigrants from Hungary. Second, as later renditions of the founding story pointed out, the first colonists included Slovaks as well as Hungarians, so that the two groups shared responsibility for the unfit pioneer.[71] Much like Jónasson in New Iceland, the government immigration official who visited shortly after the exodus helped transform the settlers who stayed into good pioneers. "So far as I have been able to ascertain," the colony's centennial history quoted him saying, "those who abandoned the land were not a desirable class, being for the most part rough and uncultivated and in some instances vicious and criminal. And it is the generally expressed opinion that Canada is better off without them." But, he insisted, the settlement "is a flourishing one and promises to rapidly grow in wealth and numbers," with the settlers "as a class ... frugal, industrious and persevering."[72]

The above offical also queried the judgement of Esterhazy, with whom a disillusioned Ottawa had severed links over both the instability of the colony and his patronage ties to the Canadian Pacific Railway. The colony's architect and focus of its founding story, Esterhazy was an enigmatic figure with a checkered career whose true identity, including his right to the aristocratic Esterhazy name, was debated at the time and remains a mystery. His financial arrangements with the railway to assist the settlers, which left them heavily in debt, and the quick departure of so many whom he had handpicked, also hurt his reputation. Yet Esterhazy avoided the entanglements that embroiled Jónasson in New Iceland and remained widely respected. Residence in the United States kept him out of local disputes, free to act as advisor, adjudicator, and government intercessor (most notably for compensation for the settlers after his chosen administrator misappropriated funds intended to register homesteads). According to historian Martin Kovacs, when Esterhazy visited in 1902, "he was treated like a leader blessed with almost miraculous powers to propitiate the moody bureaucratic 'deities' of far-away Ottawa."[73] Although invited, Esterhazy pled ill health and did not attend the 1911 silver jubilee celebrations of the colony he founded; he died the following year. By Esterhazy-Kaposvar's golden jubilee, he had been totally rehabilitated as the patriot concerned for his countrymen's welfare, carefully divorced from settler hardship and the massive defections that followed the first harsh winter; his personal claims accepted at face value. Fifty years later, distance no doubt explained both the official centennial history's more cautious assessment of the man and its openness to dissension and irregularities in the settlement process.[74]

In none of the above cases did rejection or betrayal of the Promised Land successfully sabotage the affected ethno-religious colonies or fundamentally contest their founding stories. Nonetheless, dissatisfaction with the prairies persisted among immigrant settler peoples, as did the solution to uproot and leave. The most striking parallels to departure during the founding years were the environmental and economic factors that coalesced during the Great Depression. It was during this decade, for example, that Jewish farming colonies like Hirsch failed. But, by and large, people tended to move as individuals rather than as part of ethno-religious groups. Also, the dirty thirties did not then or later seriously dent the optimism of ethno-religious founding narratives, as success and progress dominated their storylines. In fact, local histories contended that the 1930s, like the settlement years, tested westerners' resolve; that they passed with flying colours proved the Depression generation worthy heirs of their pioneer ancestors.

Yet Canada sometimes reneged on its promises of abundance in the land and material wealth. In response, an alternate set of myths countered the themes of economic opportunity and social justice. These myths were especially popular within groups prey to severe ideological rifts, prejudice and discrimination, or exaggerated disappointment with Canada and the prairies.[75] Socialism and then communism, for example, attracted many Finns, Jews, and Ukrainians. A storyline that indicted Canada as the Promised Land, and stressed capitalist exploitation of a powerless proletariat and the poverty and impotence of prairie farmers, resonated during the Depression.[76] While countless Finns, Jews, and Ukrainians abandoned their farms independently of politics, the Red Finns of the Coteau Hills in Saskatchewan quit the West (and the country) for ideological reasons. In concert with 10,000 Finns from across North America, albeit mostly waged workers, some 250 persons headed for Soviet Karelia on the eastern border of their homeland, hoping to help build communism and found a Red Finland based on collective farming. Soon disillusioned, the luckier ones escaped the Stalinist terror that claimed many of their comrades and returned to Canada.[77] Among Ukrainians, ideological divisions affected the fortunes of the group's founding fathers. The communist minority gravitated to Pylypiw, who became Russian Orthodox and had descendants involved in the communist movement, outside the mainstream of community life. The rest adopted Eleniak, who remained staunchly Ukrainian Catholic and thus represented the group's centre.[78] Overall, communist counter myths posed less threat to dominant group narratives than the troubles that temporarily destabilized the young colonies of New Iceland, St.Peter, and Esterhazy-Kaposvar and cast a shadow over their self-images as pioneers.

\*  \*  \*

In the prairie context, ethno-religious founding stories were positive tales that emphasized the settling of the land, and in which progress and success rewarded struggle and sacrifice. Communist-driven narratives with their national thrust, pessimism and negativity, and emphasis on urban workers could have only limited impact. Over time, the founding stories and founding fathers of some peoples became the basis of regional group narratives expressing regional group identities. Those of other peoples remained locally confined. Even within groups without a discernible overarching narrative or identity, individual communities still expressed a sense of roots and beginnings focussed around their specific experience on the land. Regardless of how broad or narrow, such an identification defined immigrant settler peoples as westerners for whom the region behaved as a Canadian homeland much like the St. Lawrence Valley for French Quebeckers or the Red River Settlement of the fur trade era for Métis. Finally, the notion of the West as a Promised Land pervaded contemporary and subsequent imagery, but not without qualification, feelings of guilt and betrayal, and detractors. Sometimes fickle settlers were the problem, sometimes imperfect founding fathers. Sometimes the land produced thistles and rocks instead of milk and honey; other times fertile and free land was secondary to the freedoms that the country itself represented.

# Region and Nation:
# Situating the Prairie Experience
# within National Narratives

ON CANADA'S CENTENNIAL IN 1967, the Winnipeg-based *Canadian Mennonite* published a four-part editorial of thanksgiving. It first acknowledged God, whose creation and land Canada was. Natives, who shared that land "with us, conquerors and immigrants from foreign countries," came next, followed by the colonizers' own intrepid French, English, and Mennonite forefathers. Finally, there was Canada itself, the best of many stopping places Mennonites had known in their earthly wanders. "We would like to get on Henry Derksen's buggy to thank you," the author said, coyly incredulous that readers might not have heard of the man:

'Tis true, he isn't in the history books, but he lives in our memories. He was a Mennonite farmer-preacher, died in the early thirties, or somewhere there. He was a Chortitzer, which didn't help him to get into the books either. He was poor and he had a large family, and those facts were against him too. But so overwhelmed was he during World War I by Canadian freedom—which allowed every Mennonite, even the bums, to be COs [conscientious objectors]—that every year for years he would pay his thanks.... Once in 12 months, so the story goes, he would hitch his horse to the buggy, drive the 30–40 mile trip to Winnipeg, and thank the Queen through the Manitoba premier and lieutenant governor for one more year of grace, freedom, and privilege. And then he would go home again.[1]

An often multilayered national identity developed alongside the regional roots of immigrant settler peoples. For most it reflected the desire of outsiders to be accepted as partners in Canadian nation building and integrated into the national narrative.[2] As such, they stressed the values of freedom and democracy, exploiting Canada's much vaunted self-image as a "free country" to illustrate ideals shared with the British parliamentary tradition and Anglo-Canadian establishment. A homeland history of struggle against oppression or persecution, augmented by a record of good citizenship (especially sacrifice on the battlefield), provided concrete proof of commitment to the principles underpinning the Canadian nation and thus the worthiness of the group and its members. As Henry Derksen suggests, some immigrant settler peoples elevated Canada's promises of freedom and democracy to group-serving covenants between themselves and the nation, or the British Crown. Others evoked them on behalf of group missions dedicated to enriching and safeguarding the Canadian way of life. Inevitably, the prairie experience coloured how those in the West defined their relationship with the nation. The regional story could also colour how the ethno-religious group at large saw its Canadian birthright.

Moreover, the prairie experience informed the collective memory and identity, and thus national narratives, of individual ethno-religious groups. The precise nature of this relationship between the group and its prairie segment, and the extent to which the West figured in the group's imagination and agenda, varied. Among Ukrainians and Icelanders, prairie settlement and stories of regional origins dominated the national picture, in effect elevating the West to the group's Canadian homeland. In contrast, Mennonites' Canadian origins predated prairie settlement, producing a regional story that competed confidently, albeit not without tensions, with the national narrative. Jews were concentrated historically in Quebec and later Ontario. Sometimes subsequent immigration and/or migration (as with Hungarians) or voluntary abandonment (the Doukhobor exodus to British Columbia) displaced the prairies and prairie roots in the group consciousness.

## Integrating into the Canadian National Narrative

In 1915 the Ontario-born journalist and author Agnes Laut warned that "the presence of the ignorant and irresponsible foreigner in hordes," especially from eastern Europe, endangered Canadian democracy. It "need not surprise us," she said, if people formerly restrained by bayonets and "suddenly plunged in freedom ... run amuck."[3] Clearly, to a nervous host society, Canadian freedom entailed more than equation of the West with free land. Laut's own fears demonstrated ignorance (Austria-Hungary, the main source of her troubling hordes, was a constitutional monarchy with freedom of speech and assembly, and, by 1907, universal manhood suffrage). Yet immigrants to the prairies shared her appreciation of the ideals that made Canada a haven from oppression and injustice. For some, the move to the Dominion meant the right to practise their faith according to their conscience or to use their native tongue without persecution or penalty. For others, it meant the right to cultivate national institutions and political loyalties forbidden in the homeland. Affected groups included Russian Jews fleeing anti-Semitic pogroms; Ukrainians in the throes of a national awakening; Icelanders governed by Denmark; and Mormons, Mennonites, and Doukhobors intent on preserving their way of life.

Canada as a "free country" also compared favourably with the United States. In his pioneering study of ethno-religious settlement on the Canadian prairies, C.A. Dawson argued that America-bound Mennonites in the 1870s "put fertile land above complete sectarian freedom, while those who insisted upon religious liberty at any price" opted for Canada. Mennonite historian Frank Epp later insisted that committed pacifists also went south of the border, but he agreed that conscientious objection and German culture were pivotal to those selecting Canada.[4] The German Catholics of the Midwest who founded St. Peter's Colony likewise equated the Dominion with a better chance of cultural survival. And Mormon founding father Charles Ora Card pointed out the irony in his American ancestors having fought for freedom from a tyrant English king only for their grandchildren to seek freedom under an English queen.[5] The queen, of course, was Victoria, who, together with governors general Dufferin in the 1870s and Tweedsmuir in the 1930s, shaped the mythologies of immigrant settler peoples on the prairie. As the Crown became the source of a contract or covenant between the group and the Dominion, it bestowed legitimacy, recognized a group's special needs, and validated members as upstanding citizens.

In 1873 the lieutenant governor of Manitoba tried to sway the Mennonite scouts touring his province by stressing Queen Victoria's Germanness.

However, the knowledge that Canada lay under her protection, giving weight to its guarantees of exemption from military service and control over religion and education, impressed Mennonites more.[6] Among Doukhobors, Victoria's purported intercession on behalf of the sect translated into an article of faith. On the golden jubilee of their immigration in 1949, Saskatchewan Doukhobors noted how England alone had listened when Count Leo Tolstoi appealed to the world to save their ancestors. "Good Doukhobor people," they reported Victoria saying, "even though I am a queen I have a good soul and a maternal heart. I love you for refusing to kill, for being vegetarian ... for looking after your poor, and for eschewing alcohol and tobacco." She then promised free land and asylum in Canada for as long as they kept the peace.[7] In his 1968 history of Canadian Doukhobors, George Woodcock dismissed "the legend,"

> later put out by Peter Verigin, and to this day believed by many Doukhobors, that Queen Victoria personally declared that the Doukhobors were to live in Canada for ninety-nine years free from all earthly laws. The queen is not on record as having expressed any opinion about the Doukhobors, and even a democratic country like Canada could hardly countenance an island of theocratic autonomy in the midst of its territory.[8]

Yet as the Doukhobor centennial approached, hardcore believers worried that they would have to reapply for military exemption. "How do such myths begin," an insider asked, "and why would the Doukhobors revere this Queen, the aunt of their energetic tormentor and author of their miseries and suffering, Czar Nicholas II? ... And this coupled with the irony of losing their Saskatchewan lands because they refused to swear allegiance to her son, Edward VII?"[9] Victoria's allure evokes intriguing parallels. One is the image among Russian peasants of the good and just tsar, kept ignorant of their misery by corrupt officials, who would do right if they could only speak to him directly. The other is Victoria's own image, among her Native subjects in the West, of the Great White Mother who personally concerned herself with their welfare.

If Queen Victoria acted as a concerned and benevolent protectress for Canada-bound Doukhobors, Lord Dufferin's vice-regal tour of Manitoba and the District of Keewatin in 1877 validated Mennonites and Icelanders as settlers and future citizens. The governor general also confirmed Mennonites in their Canadian Privilegium. "Beneath the flag whose folds now wave above us," he told a crowd in the East Reserve, "you will find protection, peace, civil and religious liberty, constitutional freedom and equal laws." Two world wars tested the covenant Dufferin symbolized, but until then, according to Epp, Mennonites kept "their part of the bargain—proving the agricultural potential of Canadian prairie farmland and the rightness of a liberal immigration policy."[10] No such complications beset Icelanders, who seized Dufferin's speech in Gimli as recognition of the qualities they valued in themselves. He singled out the intellectual resources that offset inexperience with forested land, the books found in every "hut or cottage ... no matter how bare the walls or scanty its furniture," and the link between Icelandic "freemen serving no overlord" and Canada's democratic ideals.[11] On the 125th anniversary of New Iceland in 2000, Governor General Adrienne Clarkson resurrected her predecessor's words to pay tribute to the prized love of learning and democratic tradition that Icelanders brought to Canada.[12] In fact, Canadians' claims for their country on the back of the British parliamentary heritage fared poorly against what a special millennium section of the Winnipeg-based *Lögberg-Heimskringla* described as the "unique democratic commonwealth" founded in Iceland in 930 by "the first national democratic legislative assembly in the world." It was this legacy that "became the backbone of the Icelandic Settlement at New Iceland."[13] Indeed, for several years after 1875 popular myth insisted that a sovereign Republic of New Iceland, with its own democratic constitution, existed on the shores of Lake Winnipeg.[14]

Dufferin also told New Icelanders that in "becoming Englishmen and subjects of Queen Victoria," they need not forfeit the "time-honoured customs" of their ancestors.[15] Permission to remain Icelandic while becoming Canadian never, however, acquired the authority of similar comments by Lord Tweedsmuir to Ukrainians at Fraserwood, Manitoba, in 1936. His statement, "You will all be better Canadians for being also good Ukrainians," became simultaneously a pledge by the Crown to honour Ukrainians' dual identity as the basis of full personhood and a charge not to abandon their Ukrainian consciousness and commitment. Given their goals of a free Ukraine in Europe and integration in Canada while preserving their language and culture, Ukrainians needed a definition of Canadianness that included group membership and its obligations. Writing for the seventy-fifth anniversary of

Ukrainian immigration in 1966 and the Canadian Centennial in 1967, Senator Paul Yuzyk extracted a further point from the dictum that good Canadian citizenship rested on Ukrainian patriotism. "A person shunning his cultural background," he said, citing Tweedsmuir, "is empty, with little, if anything, to offer Canada's cultural heritage. A person having pride in his ancestry, on the other hand, already has appreciation of cultural values and strives for higher spiritual goals, that will benefit not only him but his country."[16]

Tweedsmuir also commended Ukrainians for their centuries-long commitment to freedom, selflessly protecting Europe against repeated Asian invasions. His tribute contrasted sharply with Laut's crisp remark two decades earlier that if foreigners truly valued and were worthy of freedom, they would have fought for it in their homelands like Britons and Americans had done.[17] However misguided, Laut voiced a widely held opinion about military service and blood sacrifice as proof of patriotism and moral fibre. Anglo-Canadians long cast the two world wars as watersheds in the creation of a Canadian people and nation, united in a righteous cause and tested on the battlefield. Yet these same conflicts cast doubts on the loyalty of suspect ethno-religious groups, underlined the fragility of Canadian freedom and democracy, and eroded special compacts with the Canadian state. All non-pacifists nonetheless aspired to a "good war," in which enviable enlistment numbers, decorated bravery, and the willingness to die for Canadian ideals—especially in the face of prejudice or legal impediments—reflected positively upon group members as a whole.[18]

Both Icelanders and Ukrainians honoured their veterans of the two world wars with commemorative books that also served as records of the military service and blood sacrifice that proved their patriotism and good citizenship.[19] But the two groups reached this common ground via very different relationships to nation building. During the Great War, when Icelanders toasted their soldiers at their annual festival in Winnipeg, they stressed how participation in the war effort demonstrated not only loyalty but also "our determination never to forget how well we were received and how good our new country has been to us." However, the same war turned unnaturalized Ukrainian subjects of Austria-Hungary into enemy aliens (over 5000 were interned) and stripped thousands of others of their franchise, making a mockery of the rights naturalization professed to confer. Stung by the betrayal, Ukrainian leaders in Canada responded that their people deserved recognition and respect as full citizens—earned, first, as invited manpower, and now, despite their treatment and the risks, by volunteering in the thousands to die for their country.[20]

Concentration on the prairies made the two world wars a regional story for Icelanders and Ukrainians but otherwise region mattered little. The same could not be said of the North-West Rebellion, three decades earlier, that pitted western Natives and Métis against Ottawa and galvanized Anglo-Ontarians to rush to save their patrimony in the West. For Icelandic immigrants to be able to redeem their promise to Lord Dufferin "to defend our land, and faithfully fulfill the obligations England expects of every man,"[21] especially on the new homeland's own soil, meant a great deal. Thus, they joined the torch parade that welcomed General Middleton's forces to Winnipeg, and some twenty men, mostly from the city rather than remote New Iceland, volunteered; at least one was wounded at Batoche. Commended by their commanders and immortalized in Kristinn Stefansson's ode to victory and the bravery of the Ninetieth Battalion in which they served (read at the Icelandic banquet held in Winnipeg on their return), the soldiers earned their people an honour never to be forgotten.[22] Icelanders' choices in 1885 embraced the biases of Anglo-Ontario and automatically cast Louis Riel as the villain. Riel's changing fortunes in the West in the late twentieth century therefore alienated the Icelandic-Canadian myth of blood sacrifice from a major symbol of western identity, leaving them tied to an unpopular, centralist interpretation of the region's place within the nation.

A second rallying point for identification with Canadian nation building and values was Dominion (later Canada) Day on 1 July. It celebrated political nationhood and increasingly the creation of a Canadian people characterized by remarkable cultural diversity. Aware of their centrality to this mosaic, ethno-religious groups used both Dominion Day and landmark anniversaries of Confederation to assert their membership in the Canadian family around not only shared beliefs and goals but also their specific contributions. Costumed dancers posed no threat to Anglo-French hegemony, prejudices, or views of the past, but more serious integration into the national narrative required rethinking the parameters of nationhood. As groups redrew those parameters, manipulating the annual commemoration of Confederation in the interests of their own agenda, they built support for traditions and narratives in tension with traditional Canadian ones.

Sometimes the symbolism of coincidence sufficed. Ukrainians conflated the seventy-fifth anniversary of their own arrival in 1966 with the Canadian Centennial in 1967, seizing the opportunity to promote their physical role in nation building, led by settlers on the land in the West.[23] Prairie Jews identified more with the mass movement to the region beginning in 1882 than with isolated arrivals in Winnipeg and the Qu'Appelle Valley in 1877. But the latter provided a nicer symmetry with 1967, making Jews co-builders of the West for ninety of the 100 years of Confederation.[24] Alberta Poles found symmetry with 1967 in the homeland to express a tripartite identity linking Poland, Canada, and themselves as westerners. "In honour of the Polish pioneers of Alberta on the occasion of the Polish millennium of Christianity and Canadian Centennial" read the plaque on the monument outside Holy Rosary Roman Catholic Church in Edmonton, the city's Polish parish since 1913. A scroll presented to Premier Ernest Manning by the millennium committee made the monument's message explicit. Alberta Poles were not only proud heirs of Poland's tradition of "Christian ethics, tolerance, and personal freedom" but also "equally proud to be able to share in the growth of our new homeland— Canada—a country ... founded on the same principles of human rights."[25]

For Doukhobors, Dominion Day brought strain and division. Its nation-building rhetoric clearly clashed with the rejection of secular authority and conflicts with the Canadian state over title to their Saskatchewan lands, yet the date also helped to distinguish the purists who left for the Kootenays from those who stayed on the prairies. The fiftieth anniversary of Doukhobor immigration in 1949 saw major events staged at Blaine Lake and Veregin/Kamsack in Saskatchewan and Grand Forks in British Columbia. The Grand Forks celebration occurred over two days culminating on 1 August, the date in 1934 when the Union of Spiritual Communities of Christ adopted the declaration laying out the principles of internal Doukhobor affairs and withdrawal from civic life. Scheduling at Blaine Lake, a long-time Independent Doukhobor stronghold, pitted Petrov Den on 29 June against Dominion Day on 1 July. The former would stress Doukhobors' old-world heritage, history of persecution and insecurity, and separate identity. The latter would firmly attach them to Canada and Canadian nation building. In the end, Blaine Lake kept Petrov Den for observing the burning of arms and marked the jubilee on Dominion Day. As the assembled crowd remembered their immigrant ancestors and thanked

God for the past fifty years, one speaker remarked how patriotism rested not on the power of man over man but on the peaceful life Doukhobors practised.[26]

Dominion Day, punctuated by landmark anniversaries of Confederation, provided regular and ritualized occasions for ethno-religious groups to proclaim their patriotism and for Canada to reach out to them. The single most significant occasion in Canada's evolution towards nationhood, however, occurred at midnight as 1946 rolled into 1947 and over 12 million born or naturalized British subjects became Canadian citizens. In early January, at a national citizenship ceremony at the Supreme Court in Ottawa, twenty-five individuals led by Prime Minister Mackenzie King received special certificates and swore the oath of allegiance. "Into our equal partnership of English-speaking and French-speaking Canadians," King said, "we have admitted thousands who were born of other racial stocks, and who speak other tongues. They, one and all, have sought a homeland where nationhood means not domination and slavery, but equality and freedom.... So long as we continue to cherish the high ideals of our common citizenship, our country will make a great, and, it may be, a decisive contribution to the preservation of human freedom, and, to the establishment of enduring peace."[27]

The remaining recipients acknowledged the country's regional and cultural diversity. Inconceivable a few decades earlier, all three prairie representatives came from eastern Europe and were identified as old not new Canadians. From Manitoba, "Mrs. Stanley Mynarski of Winnipeg, the Polish-born mother of the late P.O. Andrew Charles Mynarski, second to win the Victoria Cross in the history of the RCAF," as she was invariably described, obviously substituted for her more worthy son. "Both proud and scared at the thought of the trip and the ceremony," Annie Mynarski "bore herself with complete poise," and, her son's medal pinned to her dress, attracted more applause than the prime minister.[28] The other two individuals made the list on their own: Vasyl Eleniak, "the first of 400,000 Ukrainians to come to Canada," from Alberta; and Gerhard Ens, "born in Russia of German parentage," from Saskatchewan. Eighty-three-year-old Ens had spent a lifetime serving the community of Rosthern as well as working as a government colonization agent and sending two sons and three grandsons to war. Eighty-seven-year-old Eleniak, who walked to the bench "with faltering but determined steps" and "beamed with happiness" as he returned to his seat, earned his certificate simply by deciding to come to Canada. In fact, his unsung ordinariness made him the archetypal pioneer. "Through hard work and thrift," the *Edmonton Journal* wrote, Eleniak "became a successful and prosperous farmer. His children and grandchildren have become worthy and respected Canadians; five of them served in the forces during the last war and others are business and professional men. Mr. Eleniak's story is typical of the hundreds of thousands of central and eastern Europeans who helped to open the Canadian west, and found new homes and new opportunities for themselves in the process."[29]

Neither Mynarski nor Ens entered or emerged from the citizenship ceremony as factors in Polish and prairie Mennonite identity and legitimization. Mynarski's brief fame came vicariously, via motherhood, while Ens arrived too late (1891) to play the role of founding father except locally and personally for those he helped to settle. Also, his worldliness violated Mennonites' traditional separation from the surrounding society, just as his family's military service violated their pacifism.[30] That his Mennonitism appeared nowhere in the publicity materials suggests that Ens was chosen more for his Liberal connections and mainstream activities than as a regional ethno-religious symbol, at least in a way meaningful to Mennonites. In contrast, Eleniak's invitation to participate in the citizenship ceremony cemented his pre-eminence as Ukrainians' founding father to the chagrin of Ivan Pylypiw's son. In an interview some months later, he stressed how Pylypiw had been the leader, his employee Eleniak the follower.[31] Yet the Ukrainian community made less of the implications of the occasion for group legitimization than might have been expected, and much commentary was perfunctory.[32] During the Commons debate on the bill, Ukrainian Member of Parliament Anthony Hlynka (Vegreville) alluded to Ukrainians obliquely when he applauded the eligibility for citizenship of all prairie pioneers regardless of the language they spoke. "Virtually with bare hands they cleared the land, and out of the wilderness they made the land blossom," he said. "They have earned their place in this country by their industry and devotion to Canada, and by their sons' sacrifices in World War II."[33]

As immigrant settler peoples stressed their Canadian citizenship and values, group milestones became occasions for expressing gratitude and thanksgiving for Canada's gifts. The right to live without fear and to worship, speak their mother tongue, and practise their cultural traditions freely was especially important to nationally oppressed peoples like Ukrainians, or to those like Mennonites and Jews with long histories of religious persecution. In 1974 the main character in a dramatized meditation on the arrival of the Russian Mennonites in Manitoba 100 years earlier uneasily recalled the ambivalence of the scouting party as to the quality of the soil. "But," he reminded himself, "there would be *freedom* in Canada, freedom to live and worship our God as we saw fit. And most important of all: under the protection of the gracious Queen Victoria, who looked so much like a Mennonite Ohma [grandmother] in the pictures we had seen of her, our young men would never have to put on uniforms and fight no matter what happened."[34] Writing from the perspective of 1974, the Steinbach *Carillon* in the East Reserve confirmed the fulfillment of that promise, concluding that the "new country was to become the most wonderful homeland ... [Russian Mennonites] and their forefathers had ever dreamt possible."[35] Similarly, although mindful of anti-Semitic undercurrents, the Winnipeg Jewish press extolled the "exceptional advantageous conditions" under which Jews lived in Canada. They were not just permitted but encouraged to "maintain their native customs and traditions ... in complete freedom, and with a benevolence and tolerance not known in countries from which they came to these shores."[36]

But Canada's gifts carried obligations beyond gratitude and thanksgiving, or even the supreme sacrifice of a group's sons, to include the everyday activities of hard-working, law-abiding citizens. To this end, immigrant settler peoples emphasized the "unique" and "special" qualities that defined their collective character, underpinned their contribution to nation building, and led them to work for a better Canada and world. While independent of time and place, these qualities were typically forged by the pre-emigration experience and most identified with the initial immigrant generation (and often its role in opening the West). They also avoided negative stereotypes while embracing imagery that flattered. In evoking immigrant ancestors and appropriating mainstream values, imagery, and rhetoric to insist upon their innate worth and contribution to nation building, ethno-religious groups emulated two well-established traditions: the cultivation of a United Empire Loyalist myth among Canadian imperialists between Confederation and 1914; and, in the same period, the elevation by westerners of the Red River Selkirk settlers to regional founding fathers.

First, to strengthen their own position, Canadian imperialists exalted the Loyalists as the founders of British Canada and the conservative values, fundamental to a healthy society and national greatness, for which they had suffered. In this way, Canadian imperialism gained indigenous roots together with "an almost indescribable sense of mission and destiny" that made Canadians heirs to the British empire, rightfully sharing its power and "overshadow[ing] ... the republic from which their ancestors had fled."[37] Second, while Ontario envisaged the West as its hinterland, primed to lift Canada from colony to nation and even empire, by 1900 a crystallizing regional consciousness replaced Canadian annexation in 1870 with the establishment of the Red River Settlement in 1812 as the decisive moment in western history. As founding fathers, the Selkirk settlers affirmed the intrinsic value of the West and preserved it for Confederation to make the dream of a transcontinental nation possible. By internalizing the sense of mission contained within expansionism, they facilitated the rejection of an imposed subordinate role in nation building. Not only would they create the promised superior society in a virgin land, but in their "toil and sacrifice ... lay the rights of present-day westerners to full equality in the Dominion."[38]

In a similar manner, the immigrant ancestors of ethno-religious groups embodied the fundamental commonality of values between their people and Canada, and provided for the Canadianization of the ideals and personal strengths imported in their cultural baggage. Thus, Ukrainians came to Canada to find the liberties for which their forebears had "fought and died." Nazi and communist rule reinforced Polish immigrants in "their traditional democratic attitude," making them better Canadian citizens. And Norwegian egalitarianism and humanitarianism were recognized when Canada adopted an ombudsman.[39] But ethno-religious groups also had to show these qualities actively at work in the choices and lives of the immigrant generation. They did so selectively through success stories measuring personal achievement and integration, and as collective attributes marking group members as singularly valuable, even superior, builders of Canada. Ultimately, however, the ancestors of ethno-religious groups operated on a more modest scale than the United Empire Loyalists or Selkirk settlers, eschewing grand principles in favour of humble traits.

Perseverance, fortitude, endurance. Industry, thrift, resourcefulness, enterprise. Sacrifice and self-denial. Sobriety, humility, rectitude. Religiosity, hospitality, lawfulness. The qualities that settler peoples on the prairies ascribed to their immigrant ancestors, and which Canadian establishment figures trotted out on special occasions, were the only ones readily available to groups whose primary contribution to Canadian nation building entailed hard physical labour.[40] Their sameness also undercut the distinctiveness and special merit they aimed to confirm. Nevertheless, groups saw these traits as their own, part of a collective or national character born of adversity, sustained over centuries, and admirably suited to the demands of pioneering in western Canada. They could even vault so-called inferior peasants over less tested peoples higher in the hierarchy. Their special qualities, claimed a Centennial-year history of Poles in Manitoba, enabled Clifford Sifton's maligned men in sheepskin coats to tame the "uninhabited, wild and inaccessible lands" that had "baffl[ed] even the most courageous settlers before them."[41]

Before prairie Jews could access such an argument, they had to answer settlement-era accusations that their people made poor farmers and soon reverted to type, becoming pedlars and vagabonds. Thus, the settlers' defenders maintained, the original colony of New Jerusalem failed not only because of inexperience and inadequate preparation but also because of fluctuating markets and environmental disasters that crushed even seasoned farmers and private land companies. Also, they said, given the two-year gap between the arrival of the first Jews in Winnipeg and the start of the colony, many potential homesteaders did indeed take up other occupations, putting New Jerusalem's so-called vagabonds among the West's first entrepreneurs. More generally, the prospective Jewish farmer turned pedlar was held to illustrate the special qualities of Jewish immigrants on the prairies. They were more mobile and versatile than agricultural peoples like "Mennonite farmers, Scottish crofters, ... [and] Ukrainian peasants" who "knew no other calling" and stayed on the land rather than cut their losses and move on to something else.[42]

Ukrainians most aggressively pursued a regionally based group myth based on ownership and cultivation of the soil. In short, the backbreaking toil and sacrifice of their peasant pioneers—without government assistance, on often sub-marginal land, and in the face of prejudice and discrimination—made Ukrainians a founding people of western Canada. Yuzyk put it bluntly:

> The outstanding and everlasting contribution of the Ukrainian
> pioneers is the bringing under cultivation of millions of acres of
> virgin soil in the Canadian West and the bringing of civilization and
> prosperity to this vast, hitherto unsettled region. The significance
> of this contribution can be fathomed when a comparison is made:
> the Ukrainians brought under cultivation considerably more land
> (... approximately 10,000,000 acres) in seven decades than the French
> Canadians in Quebec (over 3,000,000 acres) in over 300 years....
> Together with the British and French, the Ukrainian [sic] are builders
> of Western Canada and have every right to be recognized as partners.[43]

By rooting their demand for partnership in their role in opening the West,
Ukrainians acted much like westerners in the Selkirk settler tradition who
adopted expansionist rhetoric to demand equality in Confederation. In
the settlement era Ukrainians with their blocs, peasant ways, and diaspora
mentality received such scrutiny precisely because they were participants in
western expansion, the endeavour deemed to spell national success or failure.[44]
The Ukrainian peasant pioneer myth with its corollary of progress and success
also paralleled the Selkirk settler tradition in its wide resonance within the
group. It appealed especially to the upwardly mobile children of the pioneers
(Yuzyk's generation), anxious for acceptance in a country where British
ancestry mattered most. But the myth also appealed, for example, to the post-
Second World War displaced persons immigration, as illustrated by the poems
"Conquerors of the Prairies" and "The Three." In the latter, John (English), Jean
(French), and Ivan (Ukrainian) all came West. Improvident and incompetent,
the first two left after killing a few score Indians. Ivan stayed; then after he had
broken the virgin soil, John and Jean "returned to carry the empire's name."[45]

While Ukrainians shamelessly exploited their pioneering in the prairie
West to identify with nation building, Doukhobors had come to Canada not
to be citizens but to live by the promises in their "contract." In this respect,
the prairies disappointed. Within a decade, Ottawa had abolished Doukhobors'
land reserves, insisted upon individual registration of all homesteads, imposed
an oath of allegiance for final patent, and moved to confiscate the land of
those who refused. The more individualistically minded, concentrated at
Prince Albert, accepted and even welcomed the changes, but the Christian

Community of Universal Brotherhood in the North and South colonies resisted. The "English clothes" and defiance observed among young men working on the railway also encouraged conservatives to equate the prairies with moral lapse and go again into exile. Beginning in 1908, led by Peter Verigin, two-thirds of Saskatchewan Doukhobors abandoned an increasingly vulnerable way of life for purchased land in the interior of British Columbia where they hoped to live undisturbed. They were joined by the radical Sons of Freedom, some of whom found inspiration in events of origins from 1902 when Verigin wrote from Siberia describing a paradise where the devout and the abstinent gave up their worldly possessions and did no work. This vision appealed to radicals and poorer villagers, and some 2000 pilgrims released their livestock, burnt objects made of leather, threw away all metal, shed their clothes, and set off on foot to find this promised land.[46]

Woodcock's study applauded the achievements of the communitarian experiment of the Verigin years and regretted the lack of an "imaginative compromise" to secure it. "Arriving at a crucial time in the history of the prairies," he said, echoing the rhetoric of other settler peoples, "Doukhobors played a considerable part in the opening of the west, not only by breaking and cultivating large areas of land, but also by building many miles of the vital railway links, often under conditions that other workers were unwilling to accept."[47] The group's own attitudes were mixed. The conviction among British Columbia exiles that Doukhobors had been wrongfully stripped of their Saskatchewan lands—thousands of acres worth millions of dollars settled and cultivated in good faith—and the right to follow their conscience alienated them from their roots. Expressing pride in their pioneers, Doukhobors who had stayed on the prairies identified with the settlement saga that gave their own history continuity.[48] By the group's centennial in 1999, Canadianism had triumphed among mainstream Doukhobors regardless of where they lived, although a residual sense of injustice remained. Some members used the occasion to explore redress for their land losses, first in Saskatchewan and later in British Columbia where the province had bought the property of the bankrupt community. Compensation, they argued, would both avenge past wrongs and help ensure the group's cultural survival and growth.[49]

## Creating Ethno-Religious National Narratives

Whether prairie settler peoples of British and French origin, immigrant or migrant, coalesced around founding stories and group-based roots in the land depended on several factors. The Barr Colonists' experience of travelling and settling together instantly encouraged a localized collective identity around place, ethnicity, and religion. The single Englishman coming to homestead with his bachelor brothers, the Quebec family pioneering alongside repatriated French from New England, and the Anglo-Ontarian farmer applying his business acumen to prairie agriculture initially had no founding story other than their own and those of the local communities they helped build. Yet the British and French pervaded both the western story and Canadian national narrative. Common points of reference ranged from the British imperial loyalties of the Barr Colonists and English bachelor brothers to the western patrimony of Quebeckers in the explorer La Vérendrye and of Anglo-Ontarians in expansionism. Within this context, arguably only former Quebeckers and their descendants saw themselves as part of a specific national ethno-religious community rooted outside the region. In the late twentieth century, Quebec separatism threatened to shatter those ties, cutting French in the West from their national group narrative.

Like transplanted Quebeckers, non-British and non-French settlers on the prairies constituted regional fragments of ethno-religious groups with larger national identities, and, in fact, derived part of their own identity from that relationship. In turn, to varying degrees and in different ways, these larger groups were influenced by their prairie wings. Landmark anniversaries of immigration and settlement crystallized the interplay between a group's national collective memory and self-image and regional or local identities that defined important segments of the group. They did so through a founding story and narrative meaningful to members regardless of when they came or where they lived. But although religion and ethnicity were thus shown to be regionally sensitive, the nature of ethno-religious regionalism depended on the specific group experience.

Ukrainians were the ultimate example of the prairie founding story and settlement experience subsuming an ethno-religious group's national narrative and identity. Virtually the entire initial immigration, which dwarfed later waves, went to the West, settling in blocs that claimed huge hunks of territory as Ukrainian. Well into the twentieth century relatively few Ukrainians lived outside the prairies, and they often had contacts or roots there. Emphasis in the mainstream Canadian narrative on opening the West, and on Ukrainians' impact, reinforced a sense of place and importance as a prairie people. It also generated a huge popular and scholarly literature devoted to the peasant pioneer experience to the neglect of Ukrainians in other provinces.[50] Not surprisingly, the golden jubilee of Ukrainian immigration and settlement in 1941 was observed primarily in the West, suggesting that the group origins story featuring Pylypiw and Eleniak had not yet penetrated widely. At the same time, establishing the pattern for later jubilees, Ukrainians in the West celebrated fifty years in Canada not only as a regional, often grassroots-level milestone that touched them personally but also as a national event that included Ukrainians and Ukrainian life elsewhere in Canada. Prairie Ukrainians' easy conflation of their regional story with the national narrative perhaps explained why, in contrast to prairie Jews and Mennonites, they were slow to create specifically regional historical societies to study and preserve their heritage.

By the centennial of Ukrainian immigration and settlement in 1991, the arrival of Pylypiw and Eleniak and their status as the group's founding fathers had been internalized by Ukrainians across Canada. In addition to commemorations on the prairies, anniversary monuments and statues appeared in places as far apart as Kelowna in British Columbia, Timmins in Ontario, and Lachine in Quebec. That Ramon Hnatyshyn, a grandson of pioneers homesteading in Saskatchewan, happened to be governor general of Canada, representing them and their achievements, was a bonus. The Ukrainian Philatelic and Numismatic Association of Montreal issued a special centennial envelope bearing his photograph, while the Ukrainian Professional and Business Club masterminded the construction of Hnatyshyn Park in Sudbury, Ontario.[51] More fundamentally, over the preceding quarter century non-communist Ukrainians had aggressively politicized their turn-of-the-century prairie pioneers and the resulting regional (and national) narrative. As a founding people of western Canada, they argued, Ukrainians had earned the right to enlist the Canadian state to ensure the group survival—language and culture maintenance, unfettered scholarship—jeopardized in their Soviet-ruled homeland.[52]

The prairie West also came to dominate Icelanders' self-image, merging regional and national narratives, although it faced outside competition for the story of group origins. More immediate and serious rivals than the distant Vikings, Icelandic settlements had been established in 1874 at Kinmount, Ontario, and in 1875, prior to the founding of New Iceland, at Markland, Nova Scotia. A number of advantages assured New Iceland victory as the cradle and focal point of Icelandic-Canadian life. First, Kinmount and Markland soon folded while New Iceland survived a shaky start to eventually prosper as part of the nation-building adventure in the West. Second, not only did the original Ontario immigrants feed the Lake Winnipeg colony but its founding father—Sigtryggur Jónasson—also abandoned Ontario for New Iceland, where he played a pivotal albeit controversial role. Both the Vikings and Kinmount/Markland occupied the fringes of the national narrative, treated as the prelude to Icelanders' arrival in Manitoba and the beginnings of real Icelandic-Canadian history. At the same time, as a regional narrative, the Manitoba story fit into a larger Icelandic-Canadian story that started with its Viking and eastern Canadian predecessors.[53] Third, validating Manitoba's dominance in the national narrative and collective memory, the Icelandic-Canadian experience was largely a Manitoba one. During the period covered by the Canadian and Icelandic centennials, one of every two Canadians of Icelandic descent still lived in the province and two-thirds of all Icelanders lived on the prairies. Nonetheless, the millennium in 2000 spurred efforts to commemorate New Iceland's predecessors at Kinmount and Markland, pulling them into the origins story and asserting Icelanders' historical roots in Ontario and Nova Scotia. The erection of memorials in both places never intended to displace New Iceland, and indeed its presence was felt at both sites. A formal delegation from Gimli attended the Markland unveiling, while the Kinmount ceremony perpetuated the settlement's image as a prelude to real Icelandic-Canadian history. Its 352 inhabitants, reported *Lögberg-Heimskringla*, "settled [there] briefly ... before moving on to found New Iceland at Gimli."[54]

In contrast to Ukrainians and Icelanders, the 1874 arrival of Russian Mennonites in the West constituted a purely regional origins story, yielding the national narrative to the German Swiss who came to what is now southern Ontario in 1786 from the United States. The two stories existed side by side, producing robust historiographies that reflected different ethnic bases and histories, both before and after coming to Canada, and strong separate identities as a result. The formation of the Manitoba Mennonite Historical Society in 1958 also illustrated this division. The first attempt to create a single national narrative around regional, ethnic, and ideological diversity— by Manitoba-born Frank Epp, covering 1786 to 1920—appeared in prairie Mennonites' centennial year. One reviewer stressed the interdependence of the two strands of Canadian Mennonitism, arguing that the presence and good reputation of the 1786 immigration paved the way for the movement from the Russian empire. He applauded how, as a result, "a people of common origin, whose paths had diverged in the 1530's, were brought together again on another continent over three centuries later." Such optimism aside, parallel Mennonite stories in North America persisted to affect the Ontario-driven bicentennial celebrations of 1986.[55] The two anniversaries offer insights into the self-image of prairie and Ontario Mennonites, their views of each other, and the regional component of their relationship.

In 1974 prairie Mennonites seldom qualified "Mennonite Centennial," implying great confidence in their own identity and sense of place as well as detachment from the national origins story and Mennonite community in Ontario. Old-world differences feeding separate trajectories to Canada were partly to blame, but the Canadian experience also had an impact. Prairie Mennonites often had more in common with Russian Mennonites from the same 1870s emigration settled in neighbouring American states. Also, as a regional force, prairie Mennonites mattered. In 1996, the 500th anniversary of the birth of Anabaptist Menno Simons, Manitoba claimed "a higher percentage of Mennonites ... than ... any other jurisdiction in the world."[56] Thus, they had little incentive to subordinate their story to that of their eastern counterparts, regardless of its claims of precedence, and every reason to identify as *western* Mennonites with a well-merited reputation in their pioneers. The author of a centennial editorial clearly held such a view. He recalled with pride a history of Manitoba, written "when it was still fashionable to give credit to United Empire Loyalists for really settling Canada," that reworked the mainstream nation-building narrative and credited Mennonites with developing prairie farmlands.[57] Finally, although Ontario migrants helped build Mennonite communities in the West, Manitoba was a more important source for expansion westward, making 1974 significant to Mennonite identity across the prairies and in British Columbia.

In the prairie Mennonite centennial, the immigration and settlement story was central. It included a strong consciousness of place identified with the point of disembarkation at the junction of the Rat and Red rivers and with the East and West reserves. For Ontario Mennonites, their trek along the Conestoga Trail from Pennsylvania to the Niagara peninsula played a lesser role. The monument the Mennonite Bicentennial Commission erected in 1986 at the site of the first meeting house at Vineland, Ontario, reflected a localized sense of place associated with faith not roots in the land. Moreover, the historical dramas at the dedication—remembering the migrations of 1786, the 1920s, and the 1940s but not the prairie movement of 1874—dismissed the West's peculiar experience in the bicentennial vision.[58] Yet the bicentennial actively embraced the cultural and ethnic richness of Canadian Mennonitism, from its two European traditions to more recent Chinese and Hispanic additions, even as it stressed their interdependence and the centrality and universality of faith. Unity in diversity lay behind both the design of the maple leaf of the official bicentennial logo and the symbolism of the Vineland memorial: fieldstones from Mennonite communities across Canada, wagon wheels for the 1786ers, and roses from Russian folk art for the nineteenth- and twentieth-century immigrations.[59] More concretely, at the wheel of their Menno Van, Reg and Kathy Good took the bicentennial's message to some 350 communities across Canada. Heading west from Ontario armed with the friendly caution, "Watch out for those Manitoba Mennonites," the Goods discovered a new world on the prairies. Repeatedly, they said, they found themselves defending their own Mennonite surname and explaining a bicentennial that followed so quickly on the heels of the centennial the prairies celebrated in 1974. "Why should we celebrate a Bicentennial?" they were asked. "What does an anniversary of Swiss Mennonites coming to Ontario have to do with us?"[60]

If prairie Mennonites saw their regional story as fully competitive with the group's national (Ontario) narrative, and Ukrainians and Icelanders privileged the West, prairie Jews mirrored the traditional hinterland-metropolis relationship, including its sense of western grievance. The group's national origins story predated Jewish settlement on the prairies by over a century. Concentration in central Canada (no more than a fifth of Jews ever lived on the prairies; often it was much less) marginalized the prairie experience within a national narrative dominated by Montreal and Toronto. Also, within the region most Jews lived in Winnipeg. Prairie Jews were thus not only sensitive to their subordinate status vis-à-vis central Canada but also conscious of the imbalance in their own story. Small numbers, with even smaller numbers settling on the land, affected how Jewish historians—in studies that emanated from and focussed on central Canada—packaged the prairies within the national narrative. The farming colonies emerged as an intriguing, even exotic experiment in rural life and agriculture, and important to the group's roots in the West, but ultimately theirs was a finite storyline in a narrative carried by Winnipeg.[61]

In 1959–60 the Jewish national bicentennial commemorations centred on Aaron Hart, who settled in Trois-Rivières, Quebec, after assisting in the British conquest of New France. Its focus on Quebec origins complicated the Jewish founding story. Aaron's son Ezekiel (elected to the Legislative Assembly of Lower Canada) could and did unite Jews and French—the former basking in his political achievement, the latter in the tolerance of their society. But although Aaron served as a valuable symbol of shared vision in the "Anglo island" of Montreal and English-speaking Canada, he aligned Jews with the victorious British against the vanquished French, making him a potentially divisive figure.[62] Furthermore, Quebec and Ontario dominated the celebrations, with Toronto taking charge of the group experience in English-speaking Canada.[63] This bias carried into Louis Rosenberg's bicentennial chronology of important dates, which credited the arrival of the first refugees from the Russian empire in 1882 with greatly augmenting small Jewish communities in Montreal and Toronto but ignored its impact on Winnipeg and the West. Still, the founding of the "oldest existing Jewish farming settlement at Hirsch" in 1892 did merit mention.[64] Meanwhile, prairie Jews used the bicentennial to advance their regional story and secure its place in the national narrative. They deplored the preoccupations of a Quebec-obsessed historiography, "so that Central Canada, the Maritimes, and the huge West have been practically neglected, particularly as in recent years the Quebec metropolis has served as the seat of all national organizations."[65] They also insisted that Canadian Jewish history began properly not with the modest Sephardic movement to Quebec but the Ashkenazi influx from eastern Europe, which was their own story. Moreover, that story ensconced Jews in Canadian nation building. They, too, broke the "virgin soil in the wild prairies," and although few remained in farming colonies "built with Jewish sweat and blood," their legacy remained in the rich fields and prosperity of their current owners.[66]

Writing in 1967, another observer took prairie distinctiveness further. Jews, he said, had contributed to western pluralism through not only the efforts of eastern European Ashkenazi after 1882 but also the absence of an entrenched "assimilationist German or Sephardic element." Its different experience also excluded the West from Montreal novelist Mordecai Richler's indictment of Canadian Jews as would-be Americans, their cultural capital New York, bereft of homegrown leaders, and invisible in the larger society.[67] Western Jews' sense of place and belonging was underscored in the early 1970s when the Jewish Historical Society of Western Canada (JHSWC) clashed with the Manitoba Museum of Man and Nature over the exhibit "Journey into Our Heritage." The museum had suggested "New World Odyssey" as a title, only to be told that odyssey (wandering) "no longer applied to the Jews living in Western Canada."[68] Founded in 1968 under the auspices of the Canadian Jewish Congress, Western Region, the JHSWC objected when the formation of the Canadian Jewish Historical Society (CJHS) in 1975 appeared to ignore western sensibilities. It complained about lack of consultation, and, until receiving assurances that its independence and identity were safe, refused to be submerged by a national organization run (it was implied) from Toronto and Montreal.[69] Fifteen years later, the West claimed to have the only active historical societies in the country and took upon itself the rescue of a floundering CJHS.[70]

For prairie Jews, 1982 was the anniversary date that mattered. Well in advance, their most prolific historian and media voice, Abraham Arnold, urged Jews across Canada to make the decade special. Binding regional and national narratives, he identified as its chief milestone the 1882 arrivals who inaugurated Jewish settlement on the prairies, revitalized the Jewish communities of Montreal and Toronto, and launched the huge eastern European influence on Jewish-Canadian life. His second milestone, the centennial of Jewish settlement on the land, bound the two stories through the support settlement had received from Jews in Montreal and Toronto.[71] As 1982 unfolded, Arnold criticized the indifference, even in Winnipeg. He also resented the ceremony in Quebec City that year in honour of the 150th anniversary of Jewish emancipation in Quebec (incidentally, omitted from his own list of milestones). The Canadian Jewish Congress participated in that event, Arnold noted, but "no Jewish organization, west or east, has so far seen fit to mark the Centennial of the 1882 newcomers in an appropriate manner." Their coming, he continued, was "surely just as important to the major Jewish centres in eastern Canada, which played a part in organizing it, as to Winnipeg and the West where the largest number of the 1882 arrivals first settled."[72]

Hungarians represented yet another scenario, in which the prairies kept the group origins story but lost control of the national narrative through abandonment of the region and much bigger new immigrant waves that went elsewhere. For over three decades after 1886, Esterhazy-Kaposvar supplemented by other centres, also mostly in Saskatchewan, effectively defined the national Hungarian-Canadian experience. The first and only history of the group, written for the Generations Series of ethnic histories produced in the 1980s, called the years before the Great War "The Saskatchewan Era." In 1921 over two-thirds of Hungarians still lived in the province. Although interwar immigrants preferred Ontario and the Depression depleted the prairie communities, the old settlement core remained "one of the foremost centres of Catholic Hungarian influence not only in Saskatchewan but in the whole of Canada."[73] Despite further out-migration and the preference of the 1956 refugees for cities in central Canada, Saskatchewan continued to have more people of Hungarian origin than any province except Ontario. By then, however, the centres of Hungarian-Canadian life lay far from the rural prairies, and except for the descendants of the pioneers, Esterhazy-Kaposvar resonated little with urban Hungarians in central Canada or even Winnipeg, Calgary, and Edmonton. Nor, judging by the jubilee books prepared for its fiftieth and 100th anniversaries, did Esterhazy-Kaposvar seek to situate itself within a larger national narrative. Other than claiming the title "Canada's First Hungarian Colony" in 1936, both were local histories, their frame of reference proudly Saskatchewan.[74]

Finally, Doukhobors' large-scale exodus from Saskatchewan after less than a decade left the prairies with the group origins story but otherwise produced two parallel narratives, intersecting at points and dominated by British Columbia. The latter's ascendancy rested, in the first instance, on the fact that the Christian Community of Universal Brotherhood and Sons of Freedom in the Kootenays represented committed Doukhobors, while the Independents, who dominated on the prairies, grew more relaxed towards both their Doukhoborism and the larger society.[75] In 1959, for example, the government of Saskatchewan erected a commemorative cairn at Petrofka Ferry, the first time in Doukhobor history that the sect and the state interacted in this way.[76] For Doukhobors in British Columbia, the prairies cast an unwelcome shadow even after their voluntary exile. Peter Verigin feared the Independents' growing prosperity and unity, tempting the young men under his authority in particular, and in 1913 he apparently forbade interaction with them. During the Great War he also tried to have prairie Independents exempted from conscientious objector status, telling Ottawa that they were not Doukhobors.[77]

Perhaps the best evidence of attitudes at mid-century towards the prairies by the British Columbia sector was the play *Kavalkada*. Depicting pivotal episodes in Doukhobor life in Canada, it was performed for the golden jubilee of Doukhobor immigration in Grand Forks in 1949. After 1908, when state actions negated Doukhobors' pioneering labour in Saskatchewan and drove the committed across the Rockies, the prairies simply disappeared. Reinforcing the regional divide as British Columbia took over the narrative, the play organized its story around the Community faction's leaders.[78] British Columbia, in other words, had appropriated the national narrative and skewed it in a specific direction. The province also came to dictate what Canadian society equated with Doukhobor life and values. The Sons of Freedom formed only a small minority of Doukhobors in the province, but the decades of hunger strikes, nude marches, and arson attacks that reflected both internal group tensions and clashes with the state over a variety of issues, among them the education of Doukhobor children, dominated the public image. From Doukhobors' perspective, their centennials in 1995 and 1999 highlighted common ground and were an incentive to bring together the threads in the group narrative: Community, Independent, Sons of Freedom; prairies and British Columbia. The experience encouraged working towards a more permanent structure to speak and act with a united voice on matters, like their pacifism, on which they agreed.[79]

\* \* \*

That immigrant settler peoples on the prairies accessed the nation through the ethno-religious group confirmed its importance to their own identity plus their conviction that ethnicity and religion acted as positive forces in Canadian society. That their self-image as westerners and their prairie experience informed both their relationship with other group members and the national group narrative underscored the impact of region on ethno-religious identity. It also situated ethnicity and religion alongside freight rates, natural resources, and equalization payments as factors shaping the relationship between the West and the nation as a whole.

# Outside Connections:
# Homelands, Diasporas, and the
# Forty-Ninth Parallel

ON THE FIFTIETH ANNIVERSARY OF Doukhobors' arrival in Canada, a British Columbia correspondent to *Iskra*, organ of the Union of Spiritual Communities of Christ, took issue with remarks from Blaine Lake, Saskatchewan, about the jubilee. Rather than celebrate freedom and the good life, he said, the occasion should remind Doukhobors that their time in Canada was up. Never had they lived more than fifty years in one place and now, as people chosen by God to witness to the world, they must heed their ancestors' example and move on.[1] Immigrant settler peoples less conflicted about coming to Canada also looked outward as well as inward, maintaining multifaceted relationships that ranged from personal contacts in the ancestral village to public campaigns on behalf of wartorn or oppressed homelands and persecuted co-religionists. Some incorporated landmark events and rituals of the homeland into their communal life. Alberta Mormons, for example, celebrated Utah Pioneer Day on 24 July, the date when the Latter-day Saints reached Salt Lake in 1847. In 1955 local Mormon communities combined this American holiday with festivities, some of which included "a salute to the USA," marking Alberta's golden jubilee.[2] More broadly, every March Ukrainians in western Canada joined Ukrainians across the globe to honour Taras Shevchenko. The poet's famous epistle to "my countrymen, the dead, the living, and the not yet born, in Ukraine and outside it" proclaimed the essential unity of all Ukrainians for all time and all places.[3]

In addition to being westerners and Canadians, prairie dwellers belonged to homeland or diaspora communities that also shaped their behaviour and identity, and to which Canada and the West contributed. A sense of otherness was strengthened when the homeland or diaspora believed in all-embracing membership and reciprocal benefits and obligations—especially if accompanied by ongoing oppression or persecution, and if the Canadian prairies mattered in the diaspora consciousness. Marginalized and subjugated peoples already possessed the mindset and mechanisms for group survival, unlike newcomers from sovereign states who acquired "ethnic" and "minority" status only in emigration. A tradition of serial migration potentially weakened ties to the Canadian prairies, feeding, if not return movements to the homeland, then relocation to other parts of the world. Large-scale abandonment by segments of an ethno-religious group affected the profile of those who remained, including how they approached their immigration and settlement story and constructed their regional and national identities. Finally, close ties with the United States, whether as a supplier of immigrants or through shared institutions, produced a special category of immigrant settler peoples whose orientation differed profoundly from that of groups whose primary external point of reference was Europe.

## Homeland Ties

European homelands, both sovereign nation-states and aspiring or thwarted ones, exerted a hold on their western Canadian diaspora long after the immigration and settlement period ended. Often the attraction was mutual, as homelands continued to claim the loyalty of long-gone emigrants and their descendants, or derived pride or practical assistance from the achievements of former countrymen. The president of the Hungarian World Congress visiting Esterhazy-Kaposvar between the wars reported himself "deeply impressed with the good name of Hungarian settlers" who, "through long years of toil and perseverance ... turned the wilderness into flourishing settlements ... [and] added honour and glory to the Hungarian name."[4] A secure nation-state at home made for a relaxed old-world relationship, nostalgic and cultural in nature (and thus inoffensive to Canadian nation builders), and facilitated by unhindered communication across the Atlantic. It also tended to mute the diaspora consciousness that promoted a robust group identity and mobilization around survival. Except for the Second World War years, Norwegians fell into this category, as the prairie-focussed *From Fjord to Frontier* reflected. Not only did its author complain that multiculturalism came too late for the assimilated Norwegians, but, in fact, multiculturalism and not the Norwegian community was the catalyst for the book, commissioned in the government-sponsored Generations Series. Among Ukrainians, survival was not an option: living in a free country demanded that they work actively to liberate Ukraine and its people and to preserve the language and culture in peril in the homeland. This type of old-world relationship, further complicated by barriers to open communication, created tensions within Canada because of its external political agenda. It also, however, produced a vibrant community defined in part by a strong historiographical tradition tailored to its needs and goals.

Icelanders typified another type of old-world relationship, in which the departure of so many countrymen and their choice of destination affected the mentality of the homeland. Laying a wreath at the Manitoba Legislature on 17 June 2002, Independence Day in Iceland, Iceland's minister of agriculture articulated the themes that had characterized his country's attitudes towards its overseas diaspora for well over a century. Quoting the lines, "Every road away from home/Is also a road home," he remarked on the strength of Icelandic identity in Canada; his country's desire for vigorous ties with the descendants of long-ago emigrants; and Iceland's own evolution from extreme poverty to relative riches.[5] The context for such sentiments was two-fold, beginning with Canada's boasting the largest Icelandic population outside Iceland and its concentration in Manitoba. This fact resulted in the successful campaign for a community-funded chair in Icelandic at the University of Manitoba in the 1950s, coinciding with the seventy-fifth anniversary of the founding of New Iceland. Fostering a shared intellectual heritage with the homeland, the chair fulfilled both "the dreams of the pioneers" and Lord Dufferin's admonition, issued in Gimli in 1877, to "continue to cherish for all time the heart-stirring literature of your nation."[6] Second, emigration to Canada was regarded not as an unprecedented anomaly in the history of Iceland and its people but as part of a tradition of mobility and an identity as serial migrants and adventurers. These phenomena began with the move to the desolate North Atlantic island in the ninth century, included Viking voyages to the new world, and spurred Icelandic expansion across North America.[7] Less positively, at the time of the acrimonious exodus from New Iceland in the late 1870s, founding father Sigtryggur Jónasson conceded that the colonists' relocation in hopes of something better honoured Icelandic tradition, but warned that such decisions often proved unwise and that "this constant migration and moving, not the land," kept them poor.[8]

Nothing better illustrated how the Icelandic diaspora in North America, and in Canada and Manitoba in particular, constituted an extension of Iceland's own imagined community than the terms *Vestur Ísland* (West Iceland) and *Vestur Íslendingar* (West Icelanders). Initially applied to nineteenth-century emigrants, whom the many opponents of emigration identified with disloyalty and betrayal, the terms remained a century later to define fourth- and fifth-generation Canadians and Americans, regardless of their own identity. Demonstrating this sense of organic unity, the government of Iceland and Icelandair donated new translations of the Icelandic sagas to North American libraries, while the Icelandic-Canadian documentary heritage was repeatedly said to belong to Iceland and thus should be physically housed there.[9] The frequency with which homeland dignitaries visited the prairie communities—commending their progress and Icelandic consciousness, exhorting them to maintain their heritage and contacts with Iceland—was unusual among immigrant settler peoples. Iceland was also regularly represented at the annual Icelandic festival in Gimli, Manitoba, whether through special guests or the ritual toast to Iceland and mythical *fjallkona* (Maid or Mother of the Mountains) who presided as the incarnation of the homeland. In her address the *fjallkona* typically evoked the dark days when Iceland "drank the dregs from the cup of humiliation and helplessness," eventual independence, and the loss of the country's children overseas who, nonetheless, remained "cherished members of our Icelandic family." In 1951 she celebrated their achievement in the new Icelandic chair at the University of Manitoba, telling them that "your glory has been my glory," but half a century later expressed concern for the future of the Icelandic language and literature among them.[10] Despite her authoritative voice as Iceland, the *fjallkona* came from the emigration and over the decades inevitably reflected its ritualized views of the homeland relationship. It would also be incorrect to exaggerate the prominence of the West Icelanders in the homeland's world view; Iceland's national museum, for example, never saw the mass nineteenth-century emigration as integral to the story of the nation it told.[11]

Sometimes external events and Canada's role on the world stage, rather than their own interaction and history, determined the relationship between a Canadian diaspora and its homeland. For certain peoples, the negative impact of homeland politics on their reputation lay behind protestations of loyalty during the two world wars. For others, a solidarity of interests and cooperation between the homeland and Canada reinforced a positive image of possessing the right values. Norway's airmen training in Edmonton under the British Commonwealth Air Training Plan not only demonstrated Canada's commitment to liberating the Nazi-occupied country but also assured Norwegian Canadians that they could campaign for their homeland with impunity.[12] The same did not hold for the mainstream of interwar Hungarian Canadians, who, at Hungary's urging, pushed for the dismantling of the hated Treaty of Trianon, responsible for a large expatriate population outside a truncated Hungarian state. That the return of lost territories in 1938–39 came via Adolf Hitler, and that Budapest's wartime foreign policy allied the country with Nazi Germany, created further problems.[13] Polish Canadians, in contrast, self-righteously denounced enemy-alien status during the Great War, given that they "had reasons to claim that their nation had been at war with the Central Powers much longer than Canada." In fact, according to one commentator, Polish patriotism with its goal of a restored independent Poland in 1914–18, and Allied guarantees to Poland in 1939–45, explained Polish-Canadian loyalty and support of the Canadian war effort in both conflicts. From this perspective, the fate of post-war Poland, stripped of its non-Polish borderlands and under the communist yoke, was a tragedy.[14] But the Cold War reinforced the traditional harmony of interests between Canada and its Polish citizens, just as it allowed non-communist Hungarian Canadians, their homeland also caught behind the Iron Curtain, to agitate openly on behalf of now popular old-world causes.

Among Ukrainians, homeland politics drove community agenda, creating friction with other Canadians. The unresolved Ukrainian question in Europe not only soured relations between them and the "charter" British and French but also thrust a wedge between them and ethno-religious groups with competing agenda. Nationalists' expectations that the two world wars would liberate Ukraine relied on dismemberment of the Russian empire (1914–18) and the Soviet Union (1941–45), both Canadian allies. It also required restricting a resurrected Poland, whose integrity the Allies and Polish Canadians championed, to Polish ethnic territories rather than the old multinational commonwealth. That some interwar Ukrainians pinned their hopes on Nazi Germany deepened concerns about whether they shared the ideals of their adopted homeland. But the sudden transition of the Soviet Union from foe to friend in June 1941 gave Ukrainian communists, for the only time in their history, common cause with and positive notice within the Canadian mainstream. The Cold War redeemed Ukrainian nationalists, whose anticommunism and demand for the destruction of the USSR aligned them squarely with post-war Canadian foreign policy and the country's democratic values.

However, when Ukrainian nationalists tried to bring the Ukrainian question to Canadian soil, they discovered the limits to group missions empowered from overseas. Ultimately, it had been Ukraine's predicament that caused them to lobby for a multiculturalism policy to serve what they saw as their special needs as a fully functioning microsociety aided by public funds and access to government institutions and programs.[15] It was also for this reason that Ukrainians claimed full partnership in Confederation as a founding peoples of western Canada. Moreover, governments in the prairie provinces responded. In the 1970s they approved Ukrainian-English bilingual schools, while a Canadian Institute of Ukrainian Studies at the University of Alberta, "the cap on the Ukrainian educational ladder," acted as a bulwark against the "twin perils of Russification abroad and Anglo-Americanization at home."[16] But Ukrainians failed in their primary goal, to have minority language rights entrenched in the 1982 Constitution. "I am not surprised we lost," wrote a disillusioned academic and activist. "Indeed, I would have been surprised had we won. The non-ethnics who govern us have never been willing to take seriously the difficult 'Ukrainian Question.'"[17] Thus, while the group myths erected around the peasant pioneers managed to achieve closer integration with Canadian nation building, as a political tool for peculiarly Ukrainian ends they witnessed major defeat.

The collapse of the Soviet Union and Ukraine's declaration of independence in 1991—coinciding with the centennial of Ukrainian immigration and settlement in Canada—resonated on both sides of the ocean. Canada was the first country to recognize independent Ukraine, while

Governor General Ramon Hnatyshyn visited his ancestral homeland in his capacity as the Queen's representative. On both counts, the new Ukrainian state derived vicarious status and legitimacy from long-ago emigrants and their Canadian descendants. For Ukrainian Canadians, the new political reality overseas—dislodging the communist minority from favoured status, vindicating decades-long campaigning by nationalists—inaugurated a vastly altered relationship with the homeland. In 1966, on the group's seventy-fifth anniversary, communists and nationalists had celebrated separately. Also, only the communists had incorporated the contemporary homeland into their official program, with ritualized greetings from the Soviet Union (including the village of Nebyliv from which Ivan Pylypiw and Vasyl Eleniak came) and declarations of fraternal ties.[18] But in 1991 nationalists took the celebrations home, where the Ukrainian-Canadian centennial became something of an "event," especially in intellectual circles freed from the ideological restraints of the Soviet regime. Repackaging the Ukrainian emigrant experience around the notion of *nasha diaspora* (our diaspora) made it a continuing part of the history of the Ukrainian nation, and, by extension, the emigrants' descendants part of reborn Ukraine.[19] In the context of a fragile independence and need for financial assistance, moral support, and practical expertise, the motivation behind *nasha diaspora* clearly went beyond a way of framing the past. Still, the idea had an uneven ride among Ukrainian Canadians as it forced them to think about who and what they were. Most receptive were those with roots in the post-war displaced persons immigration; least receptive were the grandchildren and great-grandchildren of the pioneers on the prairies.

## Martyrdom, Alienation and Exile, Migration

For three immigrant settler peoples from eastern Europe—Jews, Mennonites, and Doukhobors—Canada spelled another stop in a long series of moves, voluntary and involuntary, triggered by hostile church and secular authorities. Even though Doukhobors were Russians living in the Russian empire and Jews and Mennonites had put down deep local roots, all three had complicated relationships with the "homelands" left behind. Persecution and martyrdom, a sense of alienation, and migration and exile had become dominant motifs in their collective memory and identity. Jews also claimed an ancient homeland (modern-day Palestine or Israel), integral to their faith and self-image, from which they had been expelled and to which they hoped to return. Large-scale emigration from the Russian empire in the nineteenth century, augmented by flight from and attrition within the Soviet Union in the twentieth, created the unusual situation of as many Doukhobors living in Canada as in the successor states to the USSR and proportionately more Mennonites living in Manitoba than anywhere else in the world.[20] How, then, did the prairie experience affect core elements of Mennonite, Doukhobor, and Jewish identity? Was Canada yet another temporary home producing its own story of persecution, martyrdom, alienation, and exile, or had uprooting and relocation ended? To those who said the latter, Canada became a permanent homeland and they its pioneers— although an end to the adversity that had historically forged their character and identity meant re-evaluating their self-image. To those who said the former, the Canadian sojourn constituted a short and often unhappy chapter in a history unattached to place.

When nineteenth-century Canadian expansionists looked at the West, they saw a virgin land capable of regenerating a tired and corrupt civilization. This image of innocence and purity lost in older societies made the region unique and uniquely attractive to both migrants and immigrants seeking not simply a new start but salvation of the soul and a better world.[21] Quite independently, the notion of renewal and redemption also animated immigrant settler peoples cast as perpetual pilgrims and pioneers on a succession of frontiers. Historically, however, while a tradition of successful frontier pioneering gave immense satisfaction and often dug deep roots in the land, recurrent persecution tempered the sense of attachment and made the group wary of becoming too comfortable or complaisant.

Russian Mennonites who settled on Manitoba reserves beginning in 1874 were well acquainted with serial migration and agrarian colonization, having moved to the Russian empire and then founding satellite or daughter colonies. Their more distant ancestors originated in Holland. The newcomers also brought a history of martyrdom, dating from the Anabaptist followers of Menno Simons immortalized in the *Martyrs Mirror*, originally published in 1660 and treasured next to the Bible in Mennonite homes.[22] While not martyrs in the same sense, and escaping the Soviet-era persecution of non-emigrating co-religionists, the prairie pioneers nonetheless made sacrifices for their faith, labouring once again to break the land, build homes, and create communities.[23] The prominence and exclusivity of this cumulative experience could alienate co-religionists who did not share it, prompting one outsider to its heritage to warn against letting the prairie-dominated Russian Mennonite storyline overshadow the faith struggle itself.[24] But the 1874 narrative did not turn inward. Prairie Mennonites incorporated interwar and post-war refugee movements from the Soviet Union into their story and noted (albeit sometimes rather vaguely) that they had been preceded in Canada by Mennonites moving north from the United States.[25] Finally, as the homeland of prairie Mennonites, both Russia and Ukraine had negative connotations: Russia for dishonouring the Privilegium and its Soviet successor for the horrors of collectivization; Ukraine for the excesses of its state-building attempts after 1917, especially under Nestor Makhno. But while their initial frame of reference was Russia and not the world of the surrounding Ukrainian peasantry, by the late twentieth century prairie Mennonites increasingly equated their imagined homeland with Ukraine.

Doukhobors' familiarity with serial migration, coupled with pioneering for the state they rejected, transplanted well to both colonization of the prairies and later resettlement in British Columbia. The move to Canada thus exemplified the continuity of Doukhobor history and an interlude in a much longer journey. Equation of the old place with corruption of Doukhobor ideals and the new place with spiritual renewal also transplanted well. By abandoning their latest home, where many felt Doukhobors had become too quarrelsome and materialistic, they could start again with a clean slate on virgin land across the ocean. Doukhobors also possessed a defining martyrology,[26] often welcoming suffering and martyrdom because that was what being Doukhobor meant. Such thinking consciously or unconsciously invited conflict and coloured both the sect's reaction to Canada and the interpretation of its Canadian experience.[27] Significantly, too, Doukhobors brought their martyrs to Canada—the men beaten, imprisoned, and exiled for refusing to bear arms. On the fiftieth anniversary of their immigration and settlement in 1949, for example, they not only remembered this cohort collectively but also honoured by name the survivors who joined their co-religionists in Canada. Doukhobors preserved the memory of old-world persecution, martyrdom, and exile in their orally transmitted hymns, some composed in Canada by veterans of the struggles or their descendants, and still sung a century later.[28]

As the most recent stop in the group experience, Canada and the prairies could have unexpected repercussions. Mennonite historian Frank Epp marvelled at the unprecedented factionalization among North American Mennonites, blaming the frontier and the religious and economic individualism of the larger society. Similarly, George Woodcock noted how the extremism of the Sons of Freedom was peculiar to Doukhobors in Canada, as much the product "of stresses generated in a society emerging from the pioneer stage, as any of their more conformist neighbours." Like the Métis, he wrote, they were "representatives of simple cultures caught in the trap of a closing frontier, with nowhere farther to go in their efforts to escape from the modern state."[29] Both Mennonites and Doukhobors, however, also responded to the strains and disappointments of the prairie West in traditional fashion, simply pulling up stakes and leaving.

Nor was abandonment confined to groups with a history of migration and exile. As with the Red Finns of Saskatchewan during the Depression, disillusionment could precipitate an ideologically driven return to the homeland. In the 1920s several hundred Ukrainian communists (primarily labourers from across Canada but including prairie farmers), as well as anti-Marxist Doukhobors (mostly Independent farmers from Saskatchewan), answered the call to help build a Soviet paradise. The Bolsheviks particularly valued the North American money, equipment, and mechanical expertise that the returnees brought to the handful of collective farms they established. Although progress on the Canadian communes impressed local peasants, Soviet ineptitude and dishonesty and general backwardness led to disenchantment and defections. When Doukhobors' military exemption was revoked in 1928, most returned to Canada, inspiring the comment that the experience should make for greater contentment than in the past. Ukrainians who waited too long to return paid the price in the purges of the 1930s.[30] Also between the wars, some 100 Jews—committed to the Zionist dream and craving a Jewish milieu that their colonies could not provide—left the prairies for Palestine. They saw their anticipated rural settlements as benefitting from their hard-earned Canadian farming experience, cash, and skills, but their criteria for success, drawn from the prairies, proved impractical for local conditions.[31]

Doukhobors' restlessness went well beyond both the exodus from the prairies to British Columbia and the modest return to the Bolshevik-ruled homeland in the 1920s. In 1924 Doukhobors from Saskatchewan and the Kootenays founded a grape-growing cooperative in Manteca, California; selling its produce under the name Ruscol (for Russian Colony), it survived almost two decades. The fascination with a mythical "warm idyllic land to the south ... where the snow never fell, where fruits of all kinds ... grew abundantly, and where the wages were twice those of Canada," went back to 1900, when the first attempt to establish a colony in California failed after a few months.[32] Leaving Canada became a constant theme in Doukhobor life, and although the desire to leave appealed to prairie Doukhobors less and less as the century progressed, it periodically burgeoned in British Columbia.

One catalyst was disillusionment with British Columbia. The province delivered neither prosperity, as the Depression destroyed the jam factory run by the Community Doukhobors, nor freedom, as compulsory schooling inflamed uncooperative, mostly Freedomite parents. Staging nude marches and destroying not only their own but also others' property, and imprisoned in the hundreds, the Sons of Freedom actively courted and won martyrdom. The crisis atmosphere also spurred a fruitless search for a sympathetic country (including the Soviet Union) willing to accept them.[33] A second factor in Doukhobor restlessness was the widespread conviction that Canada represented a temporary stay. Many believed that another uprooting, perhaps back to Russia, would be the last of three great events foretold for their people, the first being the break with the Russian Orthodox Church, the second the pacifist stand of 1895. Many also believed that Lukeria Kalmykova, Peter Verigin's predecessor, had predicted that Doukhobors would prosper in Canada but that the materially uncorrupted would return to Russia. For their part, proponents of the ninety-nine-year covenant with Queen Victoria feared the uncertainty of what would happen, especially to military exemption, when it ended.

As events in the 1920s illustrated, regime changes in the homeland stimulated return movements among Canadian Doukhobors. After the 1905 revolution, Verigin toyed with taking his people back to a liberalized Russia; similar ideas attended the collapse of the Soviet Union in 1991.[34] A further catalyst to return movements came from landmark anniversaries of immigration and settlement. Doukhobors' golden jubilee in 1949 aroused passions over not only the meaning of the past fifty years—security and prosperity, steadfastness in the face of persecution, loss of principles and distinctiveness—but also whether there would be another anniversary. Against those grateful to their ancestors for choosing Canada, others held that to save themselves Doukhobors had again to become pilgrims and pioneers prepared to suffer for their ideals.[35] In the late twentieth century the end of the Soviet Union and the Doukhobor centennial prompted Community Doukhobors to explore a return to the homeland, briefly encouraged by an apparently softening stance on military exemption. Spearheaded by an older generation worried about assimilation, the notion appealed to those raised in the belief that after a hundred years of exile and prosperity they would go back to the land of their birth. Quoted saying, "Move to Russia? Don't be silly," Doukhobor youth appeared less thrilled.[36]

Rather than return to Europe, in the 1920s disaffected prairie Mennonites relocated within the new world, choosing to pioneer anew in Mexico and Paraguay. When wartime Canada broke its promise to accommodate conscientious nonresistance and German culture, Frank Epp wrote, these conservative Mennonites proved themselves ready to "forsake their land, even in a developed state, for their cherished values."[37] In the 1940s a smaller exodus joined them, for a total of some 10,000 persons. The two emigrations affected both subsequent prairie Mennonite identity and Mennonite history more generally. By adding Canada to the list of countries from which Mennonites had been forced or voluntarily fled, the departees reinforced the group character and consciousness as a worldwide diaspora independent of place. They also ensured that the Mennonite imagined community in the West, as a Canadian phenomenon, included emigrants as well as individuals who stayed.

The regional centennial in 1974 sparked reflection on the implications. Some ranked the departees among other Mennonite martyrs, including the celebrants' own Canadian ancestors, who moved rather than disobey their conscience. Frank Epp suggested that it was wrong to applaud the 1874 movement while criticizing those who stayed behind in Russia or later left Canada for Latin America. Because of the departees' resolve in response to the breaking of the covenant of 1874, another commentator mused, the remaining Mennonites perhaps enjoyed "greater freedom in this land" than they would have had otherwise.[38] And the son of interwar emigrants took issue with the attitudes of "enlightened" Mennonites towards their "conservative" brethren. "*They*," he wrote of the latter, went to Canada in 1874 when we, who stayed in Russia, were just entering our most prosperous half century. *They* moved to Mexico, when we had made our peace with the "national" school system. *They* left Canada because of its intolerance, just when we were coming into Canada as the haven of liberty from our own oppressed state in Communist Russia. And we continue to look down just a bit on them, on the conservatives.... And when they move into Bolivia or to British Honduras, we say: "They are still trying to run away from the world."[39]

Yet, he stressed, it was the departees of the 1920s with their "biblical sense of pilgrimhood" and not the materially mobile enlightened Mennonites who had lessons to teach. A final commentator raised the point that although Mennonites in the West had much for which to be proud and thankful, the leaders of 1874 might reconsider the decision to go to Canada if they could see the changes wrought over 100 years.[40]

The last individual's observation flirted with a central issue confronting ethno-religious groups moulded by martyrdom, alienation and exile, and serial migration. The great majority of Mennonites (and Doukhobors and Jews) not only stayed in Canada but also came to see their ancestors' move to the country, and shared experiences and values with other Canadians, as positive. In other words, Canada was home and the journey over. Historically, survival and a sense of peoplehood had relied on voluntarism and moral suasion strengthened by the bonds of persecution. Now, however, group membership depended on voluntarism and moral suasion in a society that valued individualism and material success and neither routinely oppressed nor insisted upon a melting pot.

By the 1980s one-third of prairie Mennonites resided in large metropolitan centres compared to 42 percent still on farms.[41] Participation in Canadian society, especially entry into its middle class threatened to undermine the principled nonconformity and will to witness that had brought Mennonites to Canada and defined them. According to Winnipeg sociologist Leo Driedger, the very tolerance of Canadian society—as well as sharing a language, jobs, and cultural values with other Canadians—hurt Mennonite identity. No longer feeling like strangers or pilgrims, and without the customary cultural clash that set them apart, Mennonites neglected their theology and faith and lost their sense of differentness, separation, and martyrdom. In any event, he added, collusion in the dispossession of prairie Native peoples had already compromised their self-image as martyrs. Pessimistic about the number of Mennonite martyrs to be found in Manitoba in 1974, other than those "prepared to die for their businesses or their land," another commentator concluded that rather than actively witness, Mennonites assuaged their guilty consciences with generous contributions to charity. Perhaps, he suggested, they needed the unifying and galvanizing force of adversity.[42] Ultimately, as believers in a worldwide Mennonite community, past and present, prairie Mennonites could claim the group martyrology (from the Anabaptists of the *Martyrs Mirror* to victims of Soviet aggression), but the decision to stay in Canada and become Canadians meant that they would rarely contribute to it.

Disrespectful youth adopting English clothes and habits and rebel farmers removing their homesteads from the communal village first signalled breakdown among Canadian Doukhobors, which accelerated over the twentieth century. The Canadian experience also provided genuine martyrs (jailed hunger strikers, arsonists, and nudists in British Columbia), reinforcing that aspect of the group identity and providing continuity with the pre-emigration past. But mainstream Doukhobors distanced themselves from radical behaviour and beliefs. Becoming Canadian and being accepted by other Canadians thus meant denying not only an ongoing tradition of alienation, exile, and migration but also the peculiar contribution by a segment of the group to its tradition of martyrdom. Opened in 1996, the Doukhobor centennial exhibit at the Canadian Museum of Civilization avoided the dark side or controversial and "un-Canadian" aspects of Doukhobor life, including mention (and thus contextualization) of the radical fringe. It focussed instead on children, clothing and textile displays, food preparation, working together, and the transmission of values through songs. Perhaps inevitably, controversy erupted between the *Ottawa Citizen*, whose reviewer criticized the omissions while accepting that no group deserved unfair stereotyping, and the guest curator, Doukhobor historian Koozma Tarasoff.[43] Nonetheless, collaboration with an arm of the state to tell the Doukhobor story testified to the distance mainstream Canadian Doukhobors had travelled since 1899. Yet the interest that the centennial stimulated in an umbrella organization embracing all three Doukhobor factions revealed enduring differences. Sons of Freedom delegates at the unity conference held in Calgary in 2001 objected to including "Canada" or "Canadian" in the name of the proposed body. Doukhobors were pilgrims of the world, they maintained, and the words implied a patriotism they could not condone.[44]

Two late twentieth-century developments had a further impact on the identity of eastern European Jews, Mennonites, and Doukhobors. One was the return to Canada of thousands of Mennonites from Central and South America, augmented by the resettlement of Soviet Mennonite refugees who had gone to countries in South America after the Second World War. Both movements redeemed Canada's image from freedom betrayed and promises broken. The returnees specifically, many of whom established farming communities in the West, validated the mainstream Mennonite regional narrative that their ancestors' departure in the 1920s had rejected. The other development, the fall of the Iron Curtain, facilitated interaction with not only co-religionists still resident in the former Soviet Union and neighbouring states but also the actual places long-ago immigrants left. The possibility of return tempted Doukhobors more than Jews and Mennonites, but members of all three groups travelled to the "old country" as tourists or pilgrims. To an extent unknown since 1939, Canadian Jews could visit ancestral cemeteries that had escaped destruction in the Holocaust, Canadian Doukhobors could visit the site of the burning of arms at Bogdanovka, and Canadian Mennonites could visit the remains of the colonies whose village names dotted the prairies. One scheme involved not only the documentation of surviving Mennonite buildings in Ukraine but also their restoration as accommodation for overseas visitors or summer schools for overseas Mennonite colleges.[45] The new opportunities for physical contact coincided with a quest for old-world roots tied to Canadian beginnings; as such, these places no longer represented only flight, or persecution, or exile. Rather, indifferent to and cutting across the nation and state building that thrived on post-communist territories, they became meaningful homelands.

Doukhobors' most ambitious undertaking to mark the centennial of their coming to Canada was the Yasnaya Polyana project on the former estate of Leo Tolstoi. The money raised would establish a bakery and restaurant on the site, now a museum, as well as support a flour mill at Archangel in Siberia, where the descendants of one-time exiles maintained a Doukhobor presence. This gesture to honour the group's nineteenth-century patron on his own soil while contributing, however modestly, to the welfare of non-emigrating Doukhobors accompanied a shift in attitude towards emigration to Canada—from exile to escape. "Think about what your life is like today, and what it could have been had your grandparents stayed in Russia," wrote a supporter of Yasnaya Polyana, urging "every individual of Doukhobor descent" to back the project. "Give thanks to Leo Tolstoy for … saving you, your parents, and grandparents from the Holocaust of the Russian Revolution, World War 2, and the agony that the Russian people are going through today."[46] The site of the burning of arms at Bogdanovka in 1895 also gave the Doukhobor centennial a very specific and emotionally potent focus in the homeland. A recording of traditional hymns and songs by Doukhobor elders from the village was another anniversary project, the proceeds of sales going to support Doukhobors in the former Soviet Union.[47] But Bogdanovka, the post-Soviet village renamed Ninotsminda, lay in the independent Republic of Georgia. Canadian Doukhobors who wished to access their religious and Russian heritages in person thus had to look outside the borders of Russia for the formative place in their memory and identity. Ironically, the exercise rooted them voluntarily, if retrospectively, in the Russian imperial framework that their ancestors had rejected. Although post-Soviet Russian and Georgian governments cooperated in relocating many of the Bogdanovka Doukhobors, the site where, locals believed, all Doukhobors would reunite at the world's end, remained outside new Russia's borders.[48]

## The Forty-Ninth Parallel

Many immigrant settler peoples in western Canada defined themselves, at least in part, in juxtaposition with their counterparts south of the border—often, but not necessarily, in the role of a satellite or junior partner. Other groups barely registered the American presence or dynamic. Under what circumstances, then, did the forty-ninth parallel matter, and what were the implications for the construction of ethno-religious identity on the Canadian prairies? The United States figured in the imaginations of immigrant settler peoples on the prairies in three contexts: as a perceived utopia for the restless and the disgruntled; as the immediate and thus "displaced" homeland for thousands of newcomers; and as the source of institutional bonds, primarily denominational. Such denominational bonds reflected shared ethnic and religious identities, yet north of the forty-ninth parallel could evoke distinctly Canadian reactions over values and control. In many instances, the American impact on Canadian religious life compounded the transformation of once-powerful Catholic, Orthodox, and Lutheran churches in the homeland, in which faith was synonymous with nationality, into minority "ethnic" churches in Canada.

Different kinds of group movements characterized the notion of the United States as a perceived utopia or sanctuary or simply pragmatic alternative to the Canadian prairies. The rancour-filled exoduses from New Iceland, St. Peter's Colony, and Esterhazy-Kaposvar shortly after their founding involved the return of American emigrants, their interlude homesteading in western Canada ruled a mistake and temporary aberration. In the case of Icelanders especially, it also included first-time immigrants to the United States making not only economic choices but also a decision about where to create an enclave in North America. As seen in Doukhobor circles, with their image of a warm refuge in the sun and attempts to establish colonies in California, a second type of movement involved a collective and utopian vision. A third type also entailed a collective and utopian vision but without seeking to perfect an existing religious communalism. Rather, the handful of Ukrainians who forsook the prairies for the United States—also to a commune in California, on land owned by a fellow Ukrainian and renegade Orthodox priest from Kyiv, Ahapii Honcharenko—were propelled by secular socialist ideals.[49] The Ukrainian Brotherhood, as they called their egalitarian venture established in 1902–3, also differed from the Doukhobor initiative in its elitist nature, attracting future leaders of the pioneer Ukrainian-Canadian intelligentsia. But unlike the doomed Doukhobor experiment in the same period, whose participants' return to the prairies in early 1901 the *Edmonton Bulletin* heralded with the headline "No Place Like Home," the Ukrainian scheme never entered the public radar, so that its collapse after a few months attracted no notice.[50]

The notion of the United States as the immediate or "displaced" homeland of prairie immigrants also involved different types of movements. In this respect, Mormons were unique. The faith that defined them emerged out of the American experience; their history, including the serial march west to escape prejudice and persecution, was a purely American one; and they themselves were "ethnically" American. As a group shaped by internal exile and migration without complicating ethnic divisions, they closely resembled Russian Doukhobors. But if "refugees from the American crusade against Mormon polygamy"[51] who sought freedom under the British Crown had mixed emotions towards the United States as the homeland, the state of Utah was another matter. In the settlement era, concerned nation builders recognized and feared its influence as the wellspring of Canadian Mormonism. A 1909 map of North America depicting the "octopus of Mormonism" showed the head of the beast imbedded in Utah, one particularly thick tentacle curling into southern Alberta.[52] The cross-border organization and contacts of the Church of Jesus Christ of Latter-day Saints, as well as invented Utah traditions like Pioneer Day, constantly reminded Alberta Mormons of the importance of both Utah and the Mormon American experience. The back-and-forth flow of individuals who kept feet firmly planted in both places reinforced the tie at family and local levels.[53] Yet Mormons in southern Alberta clearly came to see themselves as Canadian (and as "not American"), while Mormon scholars attempted to explain the differences between Canadian and American Mormonism that so intrigued them. They also pursed the implications of Alberta as the "Canadian Utah" for a regional sense of ethno-religious peoplehood, especially with the twentieth-century expansion of Mormonism across the country.[54]

For other immigrants from south of the border, the United States proved to be a temporary stop in a journey that began in Europe, sometimes one or two generations earlier but often in the newcomers' own lifetimes. Many such serial immigrants had not only passed through Canada on their way to the United States but also never intended to be sojourners, just as many of their children and grandchildren had never intended to be anything but Americans. In terms of identity, as the immediate but "displaced" homeland, the United States competed with more distant overseas countries of origin like Sweden, Norway, Denmark, Iceland, and Germany. Scandinavians squeezed for land tended to come north for economic reasons, even as they gravitated to their own kind,[55] but a settlement like St. Peter's Colony owed its existence to dissatisfaction with the United States as a place for German Catholics to preserve their ethno-religious character. Also, not everyone emigrated, so that an American identity and influence persisted within the Canadian settlements. These same settlements, however, simultaneously attracted immigrants straight from the old world. Untouched by an American interlude and alienated from an American-based founding narrative, they looked not south but across the Atlantic for emotional support. The religious institutions that shaped pioneer communities could also straddle old and new worlds. The Benedictine founders of St. Peter's Colony represented an American movement, but the German-speaking female religious they invited to provide health care and education came from Austria (Sisters of St. Elizabeth, 1911) and Germany (Ursulines, 1913).[56]

In contrast, despite interaction in terms of individuals, homeland causes, and organizational ties, Ukrainian Canadians rarely juxtaposed their experience against that of Ukrainians in the United States. Their roots clearly lay in Canada and the West, confirming the centrality to the group's identity of the time and place of its great immigration. Despite their numbers, Ukrainian Americans—initially lured as unskilled workers to the eastern seaboard—lacked Ukrainian Canadians' nation-building pedigree and thus collective consciousness and confidence.[57] Here, then, was a case in which the Canadian experience eclipsed its American counterpart. The same held true in the western borderland, where small Ukrainian farming communities in North Dakota seldom dented the east-west gaze of the huge Ukrainian blocs in neighbouring Manitoba. However, for these American Ukrainians, whose daily lives had more in common with Ukrainians in western Canada than in Pennsylvania or New York, the north-south axis supported their ethnicity.[58] The Ukrainian religious picture was more complicated. In the late nineteenth century the celibate Roman Catholic Irish hierarchy in the United States secured a ban on married Ukrainian Catholic priests throughout North America, which greatly affected the organization and profile of the Ukrainian Catholic Church in Canada. At the same time, except for itinerant priests from south of the border in the pioneer period, it drew its clergy from Europe not the United States. But in 1924 the fledgling Ukrainian Greek Orthodox Church of Canada chose Archbishop Ioan Teodorovych of the Ukrainian Orthodox Church in the United States as its head. It eventually parted with Teodorovych, in part because he did not consult it over his controversial reconsecration, yet the fact that he resided abroad gave the Canadian church valued independence and latitude.[59]

The Ukrainian Greek Orthodox experience had little to say to St. Peter's Colony, which, as an Abbacy Nullius after 1921, was jurisdictionally independent even though maintaining contacts with Benedictine communities south of the border. The interesting comparisons came from the Lutheran churches of Scandinavian and German immigrants, often served by American pastors in denominational structures that reflected the American experience and were headquartered in the United States. In the pioneer period, the controversy scarring New Iceland was predicated in part on differing religious visions for the colony. One favoured independent Icelandic churches, the other affiliation with the American Norwegian Synod. New Stockholm Lutheran Church, established in 1889 in southeastern Saskatchewan, relied on the Swedish Augustana Lutheran Synod in the United States for literature, hymns, Swedish and English Bibles, and pastors. The original congregation joined the Minnesota Conference of the Augustana Synod, which provided financial support, and in 1913 participated in the formation of the Canadian Conference of the Augustana Synod. Repeatedly affected by reorientation within Lutheran ranks in the United States, New Stockholm became a "Canadian church" only in the 1980s, joining the newly formed Evangelical Lutheran Church in Canada.[60]

Identifying Lutheranism as one of the principal markers of Norwegianness in Canada, author Gulbrand Loken directly addressed the impact on the Norwegian Lutheran Church of membership, until 1967, in "a larger continental church body" headquartered in Minnesota. The establishment, in 1911 and 1915, of Lutheran colleges in Camrose, Alberta, and Outlook, Saskatchewan, he saw as positive influences. However, the Canadian church's insistence well into the interwar years on the Norwegian language, which attracted more conservative, less assimilated pastors from south of the border, highlighted significant national differences. According to Loken, the presence of an American-trained and transient ministry ignorant of Canadian conditions fanned nationalist sentiments culminating in a Canadian theological seminary in Saskatoon in 1939. The US-driven reorientation within Lutheranism in the 1960s affected Norwegians as well as Swedes. Disaffection with the "American" in the name of the new merger and the subordination it conveyed, Loken noted, prompted Norwegian churches to help form the new (and autonomous) Evangelical Lutheran Church of Canada in 1967. He also complained of middle-class conformity, formality, and liberal values in late twentieth-century American Lutheranism—and commented on Canadian resistance, especially in central Alberta, where the agenda of certain American faculty shook Camrose Lutheran College.[61] Finally, Norwegians also illustrated the American impact on secular organization within Scandinavian communities in Canada. Founded in Minneapolis in 1895, the Sons of Norway was transplanted to the Canadian prairies during the settlement period. Moreover, its Alberta and Saskatchewan lodges remained in the American orbit, joining Montana and North Dakota in an international District Four.[62]

The United States figured strongly in the consciousness of both Russian Mennonites on the prairies and their Swiss Mennonite predecessors who settled in Upper Canada after the American Revolution. The prairie storyline, however, had its own American connection, based on the split in the 1874 emigration between Canada and the United States and evolving in a purely western context. One aspect, discussed previously, was that better educated, more economically advanced and prosperous Mennonites from Molotschna went south of the border, while Canada attracted those who put religious freedom first, largely more conservative Mennonites from Chortitza.[63] The religious versus economic motivations behind the two streams became a matter of some debate. Writing on the prairie Mennonite centennial, one commentator acknowledged the role of nonresistance in the movement to North America, but queried its understanding in conservative circles and stressed the impetus of land shortages amid population growth on the steppe.[64] A related issue involved post-emigration factors shaping the 7000 Mennonites who went to Canada compared to the 10,000 who went to Midwestern states. Examining the adaptation over three generations of the conservative Kleine Gemeinde, who settled in both Manitoba and Nebraska, historian Royden Loewen dismissed military exemption as the primary reason for their emigration. He also concluded that the physical environment and economic realities within the continental Great Plains region, more than government policies, explained the similarities and differences that emerged. For example, poor soil in Manitoba and excessive rain in Nebraska in the 1870s encouraged a shift from wheat to oats in the former and to corn in the latter. Larger dairy herds resulted, affecting the nature of women's work.[65]

That Russian Mennonites in Canada and the United States observed the same landmark anniversaries of immigration and settlement reinforced a regionally based continentalism involving essentially equal old-world fragments. The question of a continental approach to conceptualizing Mennonite history in North America also arose more generally. An obvious flashpoint was the Russian Mennonite prairie centennial in 1974, particularly the appearance of Epp's *Mennonites in Canada*, which told a national story beginning with the first Mennonites arriving from the newly independent United States. One reviewer objected to calling Mennonites' post-1786 ties with Pennsylvania and Ohio a continentalist outlook, which "suggests a political and geographic awareness ... hard to substantiate" when "they simply operated transnationally and apolitically." Another reviewer pointed out that spiritually and intellectually Canadian Mennonites had always looked southward, citing the examples of Winnipeg and Kitchener, long unable to wrest "continental" seminaries from the American centres where they had located.[66] A second catalyst for conceiving of the Canadian Mennonite experience in continental terms was the Swiss-based national bicentennial in 1986. During the Menno Van's western swing, students in an unnamed Manitoba Mennonite school confidently named Russia as the source of the first Mennonites in Canada, and never guessed the United States when the Goods said they were wrong; the anecdote astounded Mennonites in the East. Teaching prairie Mennonites about their national story with its continental roots thus became one goal of the Menno Van. Another was to "cultivate a 'healthy nationalism'" among those with direct origins in the United States, for whom "the lesson of varied but equal stories is just as significant ... as for the Canadian Russian Mennonites."[67]

The Icelandic experience differed from the preceding cases in that Canada and not the United States dominated the relationship. In terms of numbers alone, the 15,000 Icelanders living in Manitoba in 1950, New Iceland's seventy-fifth anniversary, significantly surpassed the 10,000 dispersed throughout the rest of Canada and the United States. The Icelandic chair created at the University of Manitoba as part of the celebrations was also widely regarded as a pan-North American project. In fact, Winnipeg had acted as a cultural centre for Icelanders south of the border since the settlement era, when its Icelandic-language press served not only the city and New Iceland but also the Dakotas, Wisconsin, and Minnesota, moulding an imagined community indifferent to the international boundary. More concretely, Gimli and environs were the immediate homeland for Icelandic-American settlements like Tongue River and Sandhills in North Dakota, creating what writer David Arnason (himself a descendant of the first immigrants to New Iceland) described as the beginning of "an Icelandic diaspora in the new world."[68] Their founders had participated in both the establishment of New Iceland and subsequent exodus, so that landmark anniversaries of the founding of the Canadian colony resonated in their history, too. Further complicating the cross-border relationship, some settlers later returned to Canada, either to Manitoba or to new points in Alberta and Saskatchewan. Published in 2002, Jónas Þór's *Icelanders in North America: The First Settlers*—only the second major monograph to examine the early Icelandic-Canadian experience—underscored the continued relevance of the continental perspective. If Wilhelm Kristjanson's pioneering history in 1965 regarded the Ontario and Nova Scotian predecessors to New Iceland as a prelude to the real story on the prairies, Þór treated New Iceland as the centrepiece in a continent-wide story.[69]

\* \* \*

The idea or reality of a physical homeland, a diaspora mentality or tradition of uprooting, compatriot communities in the United States—all influenced how immigrant settler peoples on the prairies acted and defined themselves. For all but those of British origin, the country's governing elites historically considered old-world loyalties "un-Canadian" and potentially dangerous. Awareness of such attitudes never dissuaded ethno-religious groups from maintaining contacts and interests outside Canada, or sizable segments from abandoning the country altogether. At the same time, their members appreciated the perils of ingratitude and unpopular opinions and alliances, and at moments of national crisis downplayed the otherness as integral to their Canadian identity as having pioneering roots in the land. Whether the "other" cast a long or short shadow in the consciousness of immigrant settler peoples, and came from Europe or south of the forty-ninth parallel (or from a faith that knew no borders), depended on a group's peculiar immigration and settlement history and outside relationships. Thus, lived experience and the surrounding environment shaped the sense of otherness that informed ethno-religious identity on the prairies, but in other respects it touched Canada only at selected points or not at all.

**6.1.** Mounted honour guard of Hungarian "Hussars," Esterhazy-Kaposvar, Saskatchewan, early 1900s. SASKATCHEWAN ARCHIVES BOARD, R-A6204.

# Wheat, Dragon Ships, and *Baba*: Symbols of Prairie Ethnicity

WHEN HUNGARIANS AT ESTERHAZY-KAPOSVAR celebrated their golden jubilee in 1936, special guests included the Roman Catholic archbishop from Regina as well as the area's most famous son, and Saskatchewan's first minister of agriculture, the Honourable W.R. Motherwell. The dignitaries were met at the Esterhazy train station by mounted Hussars—local men in uniform, sashes across their chests, Union Jack and Hungarian flags aloft—who provided an escort along the dirt road to Kaposvar, the site of the festivities.[1] That same year Ukrainians also welcomed a visiting dignitary, Lord Tweedsmuir, governor general of Canada, to the Manitoba community of Fraserwood. An honour guard of mounted Cossacks—their dress showing individual flair, their horses festooned with blue and yellow ribbons (the Ukrainian nationalist colours), Red Ensign and Ukrainian flags flying—escorted the gubernatorial car past spectators lining the route to the school where Tweedsmuir spoke.[2] Why would two immigrant settler peoples, both of peasant origin, reincarnate in a faraway time and place the heroes of their nations' pasts to tell outsiders who they were? What do their choices say about the symbols of ethno-religious identity that emerged over more than a century on the Canadian prairies?

Certain group symbols were rooted in the prairie immigration and settlement experience and resonated most with those personally touched by it. Others, notably those drawn from the homeland, united prairie dwellers with their counterparts across Canada. Significantly, the major images of ethno-religious identity on the prairies drew less on lived experience and more on an increasingly distant homeland and homeland images removed from the historical reality of the group in western Canada. A few symbols transcended ethno-religious divisions to act as pan-regional icons, defining group members as westerners informed by a shared agricultural past. Whatever their origins and audiences, symbols thrived, often becoming fixed and sacrosanct, both because they had strong emotional appeal among insiders and because they struck a chord among the larger public. But behind their choice and popularity lay more fundamental factors: easy accessibility, instant recognition, undemanding superficiality. In fulfilling their assigned roles, symbols sometimes played loosely with fact, conveyed contradictory or ambiguous messages, and concealed complex political agenda.

In ethno-religious groups' interaction with prairie society, some symbols became "officially sanctioned" and permanent features of the public landscape and consciousness. Resistance to other symbols highlighted not only the unevenness of integration and influence but also a hierarchy of importance and appropriateness. Within ethno-religious groups, ideological or sectarian rifts, elitist versus grassroots visions, or the priorities of different immigrations and generations prevented some symbols from becoming common property, or infused common symbols with divergent meanings. Factions outside the "mainstream" of the ethno-religious community, and even circles within it, also mobilized separate symbols that addressed their particular needs but which other group members rejected as anathema or irrelevant. Occasionally, the political and emotional potency of visual images was reflected in heated debates: between old-world icons and new ones drawn from life in Canada, between grand heroic motifs and more humble domestic objects, between artifacts and themes representing the present and the future and those frozen in the past, and between rural proprietorship and urban appropriation.

## Imports: Homeland Heroes and National Stereotypes

Homelands, especially as remembered or imagined places, proved powerful sources for symbols of ethno-religious identity. The great majority involved nostalgic and sentimental images, objects and objectified figures widely recognized as a visual shorthand for particular European nations. For ideological reasons, the "mainstream" of ethno-religious groups distanced themselves from other symbols—the Nazi swastika for Germans, the Soviet hammer and sickle for eastern Europeans—with which their homelands were also widely associated. Most imported symbols of ethno-religious identity tended to be not only apolitical but also passive and static. A significant few, especially among Ukrainians and Icelanders, were self-consciously selected and manipulated to win the group legitimacy and respect in both the Canadian and western Canadian contexts.

Artificial windmills in old centres of Dutch settlement in Saskatchewan and Alberta, and the replica of Copenhagen's *Little Mermaid* at the Danish Canadian National Museum outside Dickson, Alberta, were clear examples of transplanted internationally recognized homeland icons.[3] So were Hussars, Cossacks, and Scandinavian Vikings that, unlike windmills and mermaids, appeared early in the settlement era (all in Alberta) as the names of pioneer communities.[4] Hussars as a Hungarian symbol remained limited, partly because of the group's low profile but also because they lacked the necessary authority to grasp the popular imagination on a wide scale, in Hungary and elsewhere. Yet locally a Hussar honour guard was already part of the silver anniversary celebrations of Esterhazy-Kaposvar in 1911, and in 1936 a Hussar tournament further livened that communitiy's golden jubilee.[5] However, the popularity of Cossacks and Vikings grew to embrace a variety of overlapping ceremonial, recreational, political, and commercial functions. Ukrainian farmers, for example, dressed up as Cossacks to welcome visiting bishops to their parishes.[6] Ukrainians and Icelanders also early picked their old-world heroes as the face that farmers and fishermen wished to present to their fellow citizens. The Icelandic float in Winnipeg's golden jubilee parade in 1924 was a Viking dragon ship, its sides hung with imitation shields, the banner overhead proudly proclaiming: "Icelandic Pioneers 1875 and Three Canadian-Born Descendant Generations." Three years later the Ukrainian entry in Edmonton's parade on the diamond jubilee of Confederation featured costumed Cossacks on horseback.[7]

Arguably, lithe Cossacks in tall boots, billowy trousers, and embroidered shirts executing acrobatic leaps came to symbolize "Ukrainian Canadian," and not just in the West. Promoted by outsiders as well as Ukrainians, the image advertised countless Ukrainian concerts and festivals, provided a centrepiece for public performances by Ukrainian dance troupes, and found favour in the mainstream media. Painted on the welcome sign outside the small Manitoba community of Oakburn, a female version tempered the image's essential masculinity. The young woman wore the stereotypical eastern Ukrainian folk costume of embroidered blouse, velvet tunic, knee-high red boots, and flowered headpiece with flowing ribbons.[8] Viking imagery—including the horned helmet, a nineteenth-century invented tradition—acted in similar fashion for Scandinavian Canadians, and was shared by competing claimants to the Norse heritage. Both the town of Viking in Alberta and the Manitoba town of Erickson in the old New Sweden settlement picked dragon ships as community symbols. In Erickson the wooden boat with its carved dragon head, shields, crew of two, and unfurled red-and-white sail commanded Main Street from its perch on a pile of rocks. In Viking one dragon ship originated as a mobile Canadian Centennial project to take to surrounding communities; a second, its fierce warrior's shield bearing the flags of all four Scandinavian nations, held potted flowers in Viking Troll Park. The roaming Viking draped in animal skins who captivated photographers and growling dogs at the 2002 opening of the Danish museum in Dickson was more ephemeral.[9]

Icelandic Canadians most assiduously cultivated Viking symbolism, reflecting Iceland's special relationship to Viking voyages to North America at the end of the first millennium and the role those exploits played in Icelandic collective memory and identity. By the start of the second millennium, the use of Vikings as a statement of ethnicity permeated New Iceland. They included a black metal dragon ship in full sail atop a signpost announcing "Odin's Way" in a Gimli subdivision, the Viking Motor Hotel's cuddly mascot, and an enormous horned helmet on a private lawn on Hecla Island. In 1967 the logo of the Manitoba-driven Canadian Icelandic Centennial Committee fused the official Centennial maple leaf with a Viking ship and the phrase "Vinland, the Good." That same decade the annual Icelandic festival in Gimli adopted as its logo the prow of a Viking ship, the date 1875 on its side. But for sheer physical presence nothing equalled the gigantic axe-carrying Viking in a horned helmet, Lake Winnipeg at his back, the text "Vikings, Discoverers of America 1000 A.D." at his feet, erected in Gimli by the Chamber of Commerce as the town's Centennial tribute. The president of Iceland, who also laid a wreath at the cairn to the 1875 pioneers, did the unveiling.[10]

Whatever their focus, all such community mascots either generously opened the ethnic heritage they privileged to all residents or dismissed, at least

**6.2.** Ukrainian "Cossacks" greeting clergy at Hilliard (farm) Ukrainian Catholic Church, rural Alberta, 1941. BASILIAN FATHERS MUSEUM, PH000978.

by implication, the heritages and contributions of residents of other origins. Two years after the unveiling of the Gimli statue, the man proposing the toast to Canada at the Icelandic festival regretted being unable to say a few words in Ukrainian to acknowledge Ukrainians' role in developing the area. In fact, he continued, tongue in cheek, it had been suggested that the giant Viking "hold a fish in one hand and a coobisa [*kovbasa*, ring of garlic sausage] in the other." He simultaneously defended his use of Icelandic, punning that he would speak "not in the tongue of the two founding nations but in the language of the people that found this great country of ours."[11] The Centennial gift of Canadians of Icelandic descent to the government and people of Canada underscored the Vikings' uniqueness as ethno-religious group symbols. A trilingual bronze plaque, installed in the new National Library and Public Archives building in Ottawa, reproduced "excerpts from the Graenlending saga, setting out ... the discovery of America by Leifr Eiríksson, a native of Iceland." The speeches at the unveiling confirmed the lineage of European claims to northern North America: Leifr Eiríksson, Christopher Columbus, John Cabot, Jacques Cartier.[12]

Almost a millennium separated Viking voyages to Vinland from the journeys of impoverished Icelandic immigrants to western Canada, and

**6.3.** Celebrating the Viking heritage: (from top) Scandinavian parade float, Lethbridge, Alberta, 1930s; Viking ship at the end of Main Street, Erickson, Manitoba, 2004; Giant Viking with his back to Lake Winnipeg, Gimli, Manitoba, 2004. TOP: GALT MUSEUM AND ARCHIVES, P19981000027-GP; BOTTOM: PHOTOS BY FRANCES SWYRIPA.

none of the latter arrived on dragon ships or packed horned helmets in their trunks. Most Ukrainian Canadians originated in the small western corner of Ukrainian territory, under first Polish-Lithuanian and then Austro-Hungarian rule, never exposed to the revolutionary and state-building Cossack experience that shaped the east. Why, then, did Ukrainians and Icelanders privilege these homeland icons from the distant past to express their ethnic identity? Part of the explanation lies in the accessibility, to both group members and outsiders, of simple but vivid and unambiguous national stereotypes. In this respect Cossacks and Vikings acted independently of region and the regional ethno-religious experience, even though they drew on the group's presence in the prairie West. They also lost their homeland specificity, as the Canadian prairie diaspora accessed as its own legacy aspects of a national history outside its particular experience, even at the risk of romanticizing or distorting the actual old-world past of its immigrant ancestors.

A second purpose of distant homeland symbols was to spice up an ordinary Canadian reality with the glamorous and exotic, or to give immigrants and their descendants status via figures with whom nothing in the Canadian experience, however extolled and appreciated, could compete.[13] Cossack horsemen pounding the Ukrainian steppe and seafaring Viking adventurers evoked qualities of bravery, enterprise, energy, and flamboyance that eluded humble farmers and fishermen, despite their struggles and sacrifice and success. The Cossack and Viking spirits were also understood to survive in their Canadian descendants, elevating them from commonplace to exceptional and immensely desirable. This message was largely implied in the case of the Cossacks, although *The Horsemen of Shandro Crossing*, a novel set in Alberta, conjured a parallel in a province where the cowboy allowed Ukrainians to recast the old-world Cossack in local terms.[14] The notion of a Viking spirit inherited by Icelandic Canadians was much better developed. It was envisioned as a force that drove nineteenth- and twentieth-century Icelanders overseas to create New Iceland, continuing the intrepid Viking tradition of exploration and adventure that founded Iceland and motivated Eiríksson and his companions; it spurred expansion across the continent; and it imbued subsequent generations with "vision, ... strength, and ... perseverance." Rhetoric on the seventy-fifth anniversary of the establishment of New Iceland made the connections explicit. "Modern-day Vikings" and, as "heirs of the Vikings, ... themselves Vikings of the remotest north," the 1875 immigrants triumphed over hardship to realize Eiríksson's dream in Canada and its "fabulous West."[15] In 2000 Governor General Adrienne Clarkson erased all distinctions between the heroes of long ago and Icelandic economic immigrants in Manitoba, telling her listeners that the revered sagas of old "are about real people, not knights and kings respected for their actions and titles, but farmers who are noble because of who they are."[16]

The quest for noble ancestors also marked an attempt to compete with Canada's two charter peoples: prestigious homelands, men like Wolfe and Montcalm on the Plains of Abraham, values of freedom and democracy. Common ideals and touchstones, and antecedents lodged within the traditional pantheon of Canadian heroes, enabled ethno-religious groups to claim the entire Canadian experience as co-builders of the country.[17] Personified in Leifr Eiríksson, Vikings unquestionably played a more complex and satisfying role in this respect than Cossacks, who made no voyage to Canadian shores.[18] As the founders of Iceland and the first Europeans to set foot in the future Dominion, the Vikings both tied Icelandic Canadians to the homeland and entrenched them deep in Canadian history.[19] They also gave prairie Icelanders automatic entry to the Canadian nation-building narrative as opposed to a strictly regional variant. The 197th Battalion, or "Vikings of Canada," recruited in the Scandinavian stronghold in the West during the Great War illustrated the extent to which the Anglo-Canadian world view embraced Viking valour and daring. In 1969 recognition came locally when Winnipeg, influenced by the American example and the four-year-old festival sponsored by Scandinavian organizations in the city, declared 9 October Leif Erikson Day.[20]

For Manitoba Icelanders boasting the largest Icelandic community outside Iceland,[21] the millennium celebrated worldwide in 2000 had threefold significance. It marked 1000 years since the Vikings arrived in North America, 1000 years since Iceland adopted (and exported) Christianity, and 125 years since New Iceland's first settlers landed at Willow Point.[22] The Canadian Broadcasting Corporation's New Year's Eve gala on 31 December 1999 included the waterfront in Gimli, which put on a display of ancient Icelandic traditions, as one of several globally televised Beacon Millennium communities. Most spectacularly, on the stroke of midnight a huge dragon ship constructed of ice was set ablaze, the bonfire symbolically consuming the old year, while fireworks exploded behind. A few weeks' reflection, however, produced doubts and a certain defensiveness about the event. "Gimli had the opportunity to share with the world the customs and traditions that are historically part of the Icelandic culture," reported the Winnipeg-based *Lögberg-Heimskringla*:

> Whether or not the world got this message is now a controversy amongst Gimli's people. How the viewers took the Vikings dancing around the bonfire with a bottle of Brennivín in hand, will never really be known. Sure, the Mayor of Gimli could have taken the time

to explain things better, CBC could have allowed the Consul General to speak of his family's involvement in the resurrection of these traditions, CBC could have shown us in a different light ... but that is all said in hindsight, we can't change anything now. If people saw the town of Gimli as a bunch of drunk, dressed-up hooligans, then it's their naivete that will allow them to stereotype the town as that.[23]

An earlier critique had complained that "the only [Beacon Millennium] cultural event in Canada came from the 'Icelandic capital' of Gimli, Manitoba, when the CBC gave us some glimpses of fur-clad Vikings, the horned variety, celebrating around a bonfire and a Viking ship ice sculpture on fire." Was there no Canadian culture that could have been showcased, it asked.[24]

If the Gimli celebrations caused uneasiness over the public image projected by a popularized Viking identity, and drew attention to the disjuncture between ancient symbols and Icelanders' lived Canadian experience, the millennium offered the perfect stage to reinforce the political message of the Viking legacy, or Icelanders' special place in Canadian history. Events included a re-enactment of Eiríksson's voyage in replica ships that departed Iceland on 17 June, Icelandic Independence Day, for the reconstructed Viking site at L'Anse aux Meadows in Newfoundland. The familiar claim to discovery, however, was muted. Three Native chiefs met the arriving ships and led a moment's silence in memory of the Beothuk, wiped out when Europeans came to stay centuries later. They also expressed discomfort at participating in a "Viking festival."[25] The other change was the feminization of the Viking legacy since 1967, reflecting a feminist impact in Iceland itself. It forced Eiríksson to share the spotlight with Guðríður Þorbjarnardóttir—"The First White Mother in America"—and her infant son Snorri Þorfinnsson. In the words of sculptor Ásmundur Sviensson, the replica of the statue erected in Guðríður's birthplace that Iceland presented to the Canadian Museum of Civilization "depicted Guðríður on board a Viking ship with Snorri held high on her shoulder as the newborn explorer of the New World." A well-travelled explorer in her own right and veteran of eight Atlantic crossings, Guðríður owed her fame not to her Viking prowess but to the biological functions of her sex and, even in 2000, stereotypical feminine wiles. She was "a woman of gentle beauty, yet such strength of character and such charm," wrote one admiring scribe, "that she could bend men to her will, even to the extent of taking her on voyages into the unknown."[26]

Eiríksson, Guðríður, and Snorri worked as symbols of ethnic identity in ways that Ukrainian Cossacks could not because they made the essential connection between old and new worlds. Yet Icelanders and Ukrainians also cultivated homeland figures from the immigrants' own era as vehicles for validating the group presence in the West and identifying with Canadian values. One individual was the Ukrainian serf, Taras Shevchenko, whose poetry championed freedom, human dignity, and the emancipation of his people from the imperial Russian yoke. The other was his contemporary, Jón Sigurðsson, Iceland's revered patriot and statesman who led its drive for independence from Denmark. Their symbolism played out in statues erected on the grounds of the Manitoba Legislature.

Sponsored by the nationalist umbrella organization, the Ukrainian Canadian Committee, and unveiled in 1961 by Prime Minister John Diefenbaker, the statue of Taras Shevchenko commemorated the seventieth anniversary of Ukrainian settlement in Canada and the centennial of the poet's death. The conflation of the two events stated unequivocally that Ukrainian ethnic identity looked as much to Ukraine as to Canada for substance. Shevchenko never set foot in Canada, lived under Russian not Austro-Hungarian rule, and died before mass immigration began, yet the rhetoric surrounding the statue domesticated him and his message. The poet's spirit had helped the pioneers meet the challenges of the difficult early days—clearing brush, draining swamps, breaking land, laying railway tracks, creating community institutions. Shevchenko, then, was "no stranger to Canada" but "among us," and heeding him not only brought personal success but also secured Ukrainians' claim to nation building.[27] The night before the unveiling, the Honourable Michael Starr (as Diefenbaker's minister of labour, the first Ukrainian to hold a federal cabinet post) told a youth rally how in their adopted homeland Ukrainians had realized Shevchenko's dream. "In Canada, freedom is ours; there is freedom for our institutions, freedom for our folkways and culture ... freedom for our language and freedom to participate in the democratic way of life." If the poet could be in Winnipeg that day, Starr concluded, "he would be proud ... of what has been accomplished."[28]

When the seated, brooding figure of Shevchenko took his place outside the Manitoba Legislature, he joined Queen Victoria and the Scottish bard Robert

**6.4.** Unveiling of the Jón Sigurðsson statue, Manitoba Legislature Grounds, Winnipeg, 1921. ARCHIVES OF MANITOBA, LEGISLATIVE GROUNDS/BROADWAY-STATUES-SIGURDSON 3.

Burns. The "foreign" Shevchenko's presence in this British company, and the political legitimacy the site conferred on the old-world causes of his Canadian descendants, upset segments of the still-dominant Anglo-Canadian group, evidence that acceptance still eluded Ukrainians.[29] In contrast, forty years earlier, the likeness of Icelander Jón Sigurðsson had become the first statue ever to grace the grounds of the Manitoba Legislature. Described in a later account of the unveiling as the "greatest figure in modern Icelandic history" and "Iceland's 'sword and shield' in the struggle for autonomy and representative government," Sigurðsson was remembered and admired by his compatriots in Canada as person of resolve and high ideals. As such, they had contributed financially to a statue in Iceland, erected in 1911 beside the Alþing (Parliament) in Reykjavík on the centenary of his birth. In appreciation Iceland had a second statue cast and sent to Canada, where it was installed in Winnipeg, the city at the "cultural centre" of Icelandic life in North America. It faced east, towards "the homeland of the Icelandic people, and the scene of Sigurðsson's great service in the cause of freedom and democracy."[30]

Both the Shevchenko and Sigurðsson statues tied Ukrainians and Icelanders to the homeland overseas, but the implications were less onerous for Icelandic Canadians. They respected their nation's hero for his leadership, vision, and achievements, especially as father of his country, but because his people had won their freedom, they were not called to join their brothers and sisters at home in an ongoing struggle. But the Ukrainian nation remained in captivity, Soviet communism replacing the tsars, so that in the context of the early 1960s the poet easily translated into a symbol of the Cold War, linking mainstream Canadian concerns to those of Ukrainian Canadians. At the unveiling, Diefenbaker stressed the enduring relevance, even urgency, of Shevchenko's message for eastern Europe and expressed faith in independence for Ukraine when communism inevitably collapsed. Also, as Shevchenko's children who enjoyed "the rights and privileges of Freedom and Democracy," Ukrainian Canadians had inherited the poet's torch. "It is to your great credit," the prime minister said, "that one of the tasks you have set yourselves is to keep sirens sounding to warn the nations of the dangers of appeasement, complacency or false security in the face of the monster menace of International Communism."[31] Fighting communism was thus not simply a group obligation to liberate an enslaved homeland but a mission on behalf of the Canadian state, the Western world, and their shared values.

By championing the ideals on which the Dominion was predicated and inculcating them in future generations, Shevchenko and Sigurðsson firmly attached their North American descendants to Canada. The best example of the tie was the Jón Sigurðsson Chapter of the Imperial Order Daughters of the Empire, established in 1916 to perform a wartime service and still active in the new millennium.[32] Moreover, both statues entered the ritualistic life of their respective communities, acting as pilgrimage sites not only for group members stopping privately but also visits by Icelandic and, after 1991, Ukrainian heads of state and their representatives.[33] In 1982 Manitoba Icelanders formalized the homeland tie by inaugurating an annual wreath-laying ceremony on Independence Day, which was also Sigurðsson's birthday. Delegates from Iceland plus all three levels of government in Canada participated, and speeches reiterated Sigurðsson's commitment to freedom, democracy, and equality (values, in the words of Manitoba Premier Gary Doer, "that we cherish in our own legislature").[34] Then, in 1998 Ukrainians installed a plaque beside

**6.5.** Icelandic festival at Gimli, enthroned *fjallkona* before a painted backdrop of Iceland, 1949. ARCHIVES OF MANITOBA, GIMLI-ICELANDIC CELEBRATIONS, 1949-2.

Shevchenko recalling Winnipeg as a receiving station for enemy aliens during the Great War.[35] Erected next to the Ukrainian champion of freedom and justice, in space symbolizing Canada's commitment to fairness, it registered a huge shift in the perceived boundaries of nationhood.

Over the decades, a woman in a striking dress and distinctive lace headpiece constituted a familiar figure at official ceremonies at the Sigurðsson statue. In fact, she often starred: leading the procession from the legislature on Independence Day, escorting the dignitary laying the wreath, laying the wreath herself. *Fjallkona*, or Maid (Mother) of the Mountains, she had been chosen in 1924 as the voice of Iceland at the then Winnipeg-based annual Icelandic festival. Her address in Icelandic (the first English address in the 1990s attracted criticism) customarily extolled the Icelandic spirit, heritage, and language and urged that they be preserved. Although mourning the loss of her sons and daughters, she also expressed pride in the achievements of the pioneers and their descendants.[36] After the festival's move to Gimli and the erection of the pioneer cairn in 1935, *fjallkona* also led the procession to its base and laid the wreath that ended the festival and which, "to many ... became the most powerful moment of the celebration."[37] Who was *fjallkona*, and what did a maid (or mother) of the mountains have to do with the Manitoba plain and shores of Lake Winnipeg? The personification of Iceland reciting stories from her life, she had emerged from the male imagination in an eighteenth-century poem, *Ísland*, by Eggert Ólafsson. Benedikt Gröndal's drawing for the Icelandic millennium in 1874 immortalized her visually and dictated her Canadian costume of white dress, green robe trimmed in ermine, gold belt, and white headdress and veil—evoking Iceland's meadows, fiery volcanoes, glaciers, and snowy mountaintops.

As a western Canadian figure chosen annually by the male festival board as the Icelandic mother of her overseas children, the original *fjallkona* also visually echoed her Icelandic prototype in her youth and long flowing hair. In the 1930s she started to become more mature and by the late twentieth century was invariably an older woman, until the 1970s chosen for her husband's as well as her own prominence. She also came to be accompanied by two young attendants with their own symbolism. Initially Miss Canada and Miss America, representing the two Icelandic immigrant streams in North America, they symbolized the continental identity that characterized the group. Unlike other transplanted homeland symbols, *fjallkona* herself evolved, not only adopted by Icelandic communities across Canada and in the United States but also exported back to the homeland. In both cases she played a ceremonial role similar to that in Winnipeg and Gimli. As an import to Iceland, however, *fjallkona* rejected her Canadian counterpart's increasingly matronly and nurturing image, and thus her function, through lived experience, as a model for younger generations. Addressing "her children—the Icelandic nation" in a poem or ode at the Alþing in Reykjavík, as part of Independence Day celebrations after Iceland formally separated from Denmark in 1944, Iceland's *fjallkona* was a "young, prominent actress."[38]

## Prairie Products: Group Icons and Local Mascots

Unless the prairie settlement story crucially shaped an ethno-religious group's national self-image, the construction of made-in-Canada symbols drawn from its collective experience in the West remained a regional exercise. Also, not all immigrant settler peoples found symbols in their prairie heritage to express their identity. Those that did emerge came from the settlement era and not subsequent group life in Canada, testifying to the importance of the first immigration and its roots in the land. Yet, curiously, founding fathers never translated into popular visual images to compete with old-world heroes. Despite frequent roots in the homeland, prairie group symbols crystallized and flourished because of their new-world functions and associations, and in contrast to more lofty imports from overseas were modest in nature.

Certain symbols emerging from the immigration and settlement experience were specific and unique, reflecting the impact of founding stories based on cohesive movements undertaken collectively, with clear beginnings and well-documented journeys. In such cases, the original voyage not only loomed large in the collective psyche but also provided ready images that encapsulated the passage, physically and metaphorically, from past to future and from the old life to the new. For their centennial in 1998–99, Doukhobors produced posters and greeting cards from an iconic photograph of the first contingent of immigrants sailing to Halifax aboard the SS *Lake Huron*. Russian Mennonites tied their transport symbol—the Red River sternwheeler, the *International*, that brought the first immigrants to their Manitoba landing—to arrival in the West.[39]

While still specific to individual groups, other symbols emerging from the immigration and settlement experience were more generic. The Ukrainian peasant pioneer woman, who far eclipsed her male counterpart in Ukrainian-Canadian consciousness, was the best example.[40] Maligned during the settlement era by an upwardly mobile Ukrainian intelligentsia and Anglo Canadian nation builders for perceived backwardness, she metamorphosed after the Second World War into a symbol of competing views of the Ukrainian-Canadian heritage and identity. In organized nationalist circles, she became a patriotic heroine, ranked among the great women of Ukraine, whose dedication to her language, culture, and people made her a model for her female successors in Canada regardless of when they came or where they lived. Always envisioned in her prime on a prairie homestead, the pioneer as heroine was epitomized in John Weaver's statue *Madonna of the Wheat* erected outside city hall in Edmonton. Young, slender, and beautiful, she had been commissioned by the Ukrainian Women's Association of Canada—the organization itself a product of the settlement era—and was dedicated to all pioneer women of

**6.6.** Ukrainian *Madonna of the Wheat*, dedicated to
all pioneer women of Alberta, city hall, Edmonton,
2003. PHOTO BY FRANCES SWYRIPA.

Alberta on the province's seventy-fifth anniversary.[41] *Madonna of the Wheat*
thus firmly identified Ukrainian Canadians with their beginnings in the West.
Yet her coiled braids and embroidered blouse, and the sheaf of wheat that to
Ukrainians contained the souls of long-departed ancestors, simultaneously
subsumed the generic pioneer heritage in the specific Ukrainian experience.

If the Ukrainian pioneer as heroine resembled the Icelandic *fjallkona* in her
regal bearing and identification with the homeland heritage, the same could
not be said of her popular grassroots incarnation as the old woman, or much
loved *baba* (grandmother). Neither beautiful and feminine nor conforming to

the settlement-era stereotype of the Ukrainian peasant woman as submissive and downtrodden, *baba* spoke to her direct descendants. She personified their prairie roots and sense of place as partners in nation building and a founding people of western Canada; and she personified their Ukrainian peasant heritage, even endearing traits once branded foreign and inferior. Folk art like the "Baba bell" ornament sold in a Canadiana souvenir shop in Banff depicted a plump woman in voluminous skirts and kerchief. Writers described a slightly eccentric and irreverent but confident individual. She drank beer and raised chickens in downtown Winnipeg; stored her dead husband's gallstones in a pickle jar in the kitchen; felt mildly superior to the residents of River Heights, who grew grass simply to cut it and watch it grow again; and used the onion skins in their first editions to roll her cigarettes. *Baba* also dwarfed her social-climbing daughter, ashamed of the kerchief and felt boots worn to tea in the River Heights mansion. For both folk artists and writers, in her indifference to her peasantness and its stigma in Canadian society, *baba* possessed an inviolable dignity that deserved respect and admiration.

*Baba*'s appeal lay in her gender-based functions—the heart (although not the head) of the family, and creator of the foods and handicrafts that by the late twentieth century dominated Ukrainian Canadians' ethnic identity.[42] Moreover, although she herself did not merit statues in public spaces, her prairie descendants commemorated the symbols of Ukrainian ethnicity that she expressed. Especially popular in the old Ukrainian bloc settlement in east-central Alberta, and garnering unwanted as well as wanted publicity, these monuments quickly became official or unofficial mascots of local towns and villages. They also represented, with sometimes reluctant acquiescence by non-Ukrainians whose own heritages were passed over, the regional mainstreaming of once suspect and marginalized Ukrainian immigrant culture. The first initiative, its design and construction a mathematical and engineering triumph, the gigantic metal Pysanka, or Easter egg, erected by the Vegreville and District Chamber of Commerce in 1974 honoured the 100th anniversary of the Royal Canadian Mounted Police.[43] The village of Glendon marked Ukrainians' own centennial in 1991 with the Pyrogy, a gigantic fibreglass *pyrih* or dumpling, on the tines of a fork. Dismayed at such kitsch, some residents, including Ukrainians, complained that they were a laughingstock. "It was imposed on us," said one, "like the GST," adding, in a reference to the Cree whose impassioned

**6.7.** Playful side of Ukrainian symbols—the "pyrogy" at Glendon, Alberta, 2001. PHOTO BY FRANCES SWYRIPA.

speech in the Manitoba Legislature killed the Meech Lake Accord, "Where is Elijah Harper when we need him?"[44] Lastly, in 2001 an equally controversial gigantic ring of *kovbasa*—or, quoting *Saturday Night* magazine, "The Big Banger"—sponsored by the local meat processing plant was unveiled in Mundare and immediately began pulling tourists off the highway.[45]

The Alberta statues, like the giant revolving mosquito erected in Komarno, Manitoba, as a play on the Ukrainian word for the insect,[46] revealed a grassroots sense of humour about what it meant to be Ukrainian on the prairies at the turn of the twenty-first century. In the process, the descendants of the pioneers appropriated and turned into positive symbols of ethnic identity precisely those things that had marked and condemned their immigrant ancestors as foreign and unacceptable. Against the celebrated ring of garlic sausage in downtown Mundare rang the words of the Reverend George Exton Lloyd, founding father of the English Barr Colony; in a letter to the Protestant churches of western Canada in 1928, he had demanded that the immigration of "dirty, ignorant, garlic-smelling, unpreferred continentals" be stopped.[47] The French community of St. Pierre-Jolys in Manitoba did something similar, choosing as the village mascot a grinning green frog in top hat and tails leaning on its cane. The annual summer *fête*, the St. Pierre-Jolys Frog Follies, began in 1967 when a frog-jumping competition amused the visiting Queen Elizabeth II.[48]

Historically disapproving of graven images, prairie Mennonites entered the post-Second World War era with a weak tradition of commemorative monuments and visual symbols, whether serious or lighthearted. Thus, when they decided to erect a memorial for their centennial in 1974, they debated what it should depict: their old-world heritage (the Mennonite faith) or their legacy as an immigrant settler people in western Canada. One thing was clear. The Conestoga wagon that would be so prominent in the memorial erected in Ontario in 1986 for the bicentennial of the arrival of Swiss German Mennonites after the American Revolution meant nothing to Russian Mennonites who associated coming to Manitoba with a sternwheeler and the Red River cart. Nor did the famed Mennonite quilts, gifts to Governor General Jeanne Sauvé and Ontario's lieutenant governor during the bicentennial celebrations, resound the same in their ethnic consciousness.[49] In the end prairie Mennonites entertained two concepts, both openly conscious of their regional history. Harold Funk's design featured a peaked roof suggestive of the Mennonite *darp* or village "with its elements of community and shelter" that interrupted "the strong horizontal plane of the prairies" and represented adaptation to the new environment. Using a more complex religious symbolism, Alvin Pauls envisioned a three-dimensional mural made from ordinary objects ("machinery parts, spades, forks, etc.") that was left to weather in the elements and represented the various stages in prairie Mennonite life beginning with "loss of religious freedom in Russia" and "rebirth resulting in emigration." The compromise of Funk's roof sheltering Pauls's mural never became a reality.[50]

The Mennonite debate illustrates the potential for disunity that could immobilize a community in the absence of clear, undisputed images. The old-world-style windmill built in the East Reserve in 1877 and chosen a century later to showcase the Mennonite Heritage Village in Steinbach found the necessary consensus.[51] The Mennonite debate also raised the relationship between "art," especially as abstract, and ethno-religious communities both anxious to control their public image and needful of concrete, resonating symbols (even if clichés) from the group experience. *The Commitment* by Edmonton sculptor Danek Możdżeński, commissioned by the Ukrainian Canadian Congress (Alberta) on the 100th anniversary of Ukrainian settlement in Canada for the grounds of the Alberta Legislature, recalled Pauls's Mennonite design. Packed with objects—including a *bandura*, the ubiquitous sheepskin coat, an Easter basket, a sheaf of wheat, and tools for breaking and sowing the land—it combined Ukrainians' old-world heritage and prairie pioneer experience. The guidelines for the original competition encouraged thinking along such lines. Themes like "achievement of individuals and groups in the economy, the arts and sciences, politics, education, etc." that addressed the sweep of Ukrainian life in Canada had little appeal. Far more powerful were "land, water, trees, wheat—symbols of the environment," "love of the land," "deep religious commitment," and "admiration of the risk taken on by the pioneers" that privileged the first, homesteading immigration.[52] At the same time, the statue's sponsors insisted on a site in meaningful public space in Alberta's capital rather than in the old settlement area itself.

Ukrainian discussions over the form of their centennial monument were largely private affairs. The same could not be said of the proposed monument commemorating one hundred years of Polish settlement in Alberta in 1995. By the time the project collapsed, it had received national media coverage, generated heated debate about "art" versus "cliché" and political agenda versus artistic creativity, and divided local Poles over conflicting visions of their heritage and identity.[53] The conflict underscored how the original peasant immigration had been overshadowed by later waves, especially the post-war and Solidarity immigrations. After several false starts, the Polish Centennial Society of the Canadian Polish Congress in Alberta awarded the commission (the finished product was destined for the legislature grounds) to Edmonton sculptor Ken Macklin. His undulating concrete-and-steel design depicted the three major Polish immigrant waves as well as the universality of "immigration as a human force."[54] While elements in the Polish community thought the design ugly, others criticized the sterility of an abstract form devoid of familiar symbols of Polishness. Still others argued that a cement wall twelve metres long and four metres high topped with intertwined metal bars was insensitive and inappropriate for a group whose recent memory included incarceration in Nazi concentration camps. Meanwhile, support for a rival design by Ukrainian immigrant Roman Golovatch escalated. Its two bronze wings rising in a V, inspired by the Polish cavalry in the sixteenth and seventeenth centuries, could also be seen as the wings of the eagle, Poland's supreme national symbol, which pleased those wanting the bird on any statue commemorating Polish settlement in Alberta. Also, if Golovatch's wings became a plough at the bottom of the V, as some insisted, the statue could even represent the evolution from Poland's noble past to Canadian farms, which domesticated its meaning.[55]

Nothing came of the Golovatch campaign, and the Polish community waited before trying again. The rusty metal sculpture unveiled outside Edmonton's Polish Hall in 2000—its dominant feature a lacy cone created by dozens of cut-outs viewed against the sky overhead—had symbols to satisfy everyone. The most prominent image, facing the street, was the Polish eagle. The remaining cut-outs were a potpourri of old- and new-world history. They included a map of Alberta; breaking, sowing, and harvesting the land; Our Lady of Lourdes shrine at Skaro; a grain elevator; coal miners in the Rockies; a meeting of the Canadian Polish Congress; Polish theatres of action in the Second World War; a searchlight freezing a would-be escapee from communist or Nazi terror; and a "Solidarność" banner. This all-inclusive solution reflected compromise in the face of multiple and contested symbols, but it also attested to an identity based less on the settlement era and the land than among Ukrainians or prairie Mennonites.

In the wake of the Macklin-Golovatch debacle, the *Edmonton Journal* denounced ethnic-specific memorials for dividing rather than uniting. Declaring that the last thing Alberta needed was "an army of bronze immigrants dressed in their respective period costumes," and citing Canada's cenotaphs and the American Statue of Liberty as models, it argued for a single symbol or marker to "honor all settlers" and celebrate both their contribution to the province and "the freedoms and opportunity" they found there.[56] In fact, the Polish controversy was not the first opposition to so-called ethnic statues in Edmonton public space. The chair of the jury charged with awarding the commission for the Ukrainian monument at the Alberta Legislature, and coincidentally the architect for the revamped grounds, had objected to both the precedent the statue set and its prominent position near the fountain; he preferred Parliament Hill's restriction to prime ministers and monarchs.[57] The more spirited fight focussed on the lawn outside city hall. In 1989 *Madonna of*

**6.8.** Symbols of settling the land in *The Commitment*, the Ukrainian centennial monument, Alberta Legislature grounds, Edmonton, 2001.
PHOTO BY FRANCES SWYRIPA.

*the Wheat* and a monument marking the fiftieth anniversary of Stalin's artificial famine in Soviet Ukraine in 1932–33, when several million died, had to be temporarily removed to build the new city hall. Council used the moment to propose that they be relocated to Hawrelak Park or a special ethnic heritage theme park where Edmonton's non-British, non-French communities could have their symbols without imposing on the larger public. This suggestion, in the words of one reporter, "got the Ukrainians' pyrogies in a knot,"[58] and they launched a successful campaign to have their statues restored. "What some council members may be finally sensing," the reporter mused as the row heated up, "is that Edmonton's Ukrainian community is not just another club.... Ukrainians are Edmonton's distinct society."[59] For their part, Ukrainians stressed their rights as a founding people of western Canada. They also pointed to the statue of Sir Winston Churchill in the adjoining square to counter arguments that only monuments reflecting local history belonged in a proposed protected area around city hall and that the famine memorial in particular imported "foreign" quarrels.[60]

After a century in Edmonton and Alberta, Ukrainians discovered that although they might consider themselves full-fledged members of Canadian and prairie society, there were still those who disagreed. Who was allowed into symbolically significant public space, and on what terms, identified the legitimate players in the life of the community and which of their experiences and symbols mattered. But when the dust settled, Ukrainians not only had their statues on the grounds of the legislature and in front of city hall but at that time were the *only* ethno-religious community to do so.[61] How were residents of the province and its capital, let alone members of other groups, to interpret this fact? Was the *Edmonton Sun* reporter onto something when he referred to Ukrainians in Edmonton as a "distinct society"? The two statues, whether fusing the prairie settlement story with the ethnic Ukrainian experience or commemorating homeland events, suggested that both as a separate group and as part of the regional mainstream Ukrainians *were* seen as being different from the rest.

At the other end of the spectrum, prairie Doukhobors did not seek politically potent public space for their group symbols. They also faced the problem that the images others automatically associated with "Doukhobor"— nudity, arson, hunger strikes—were negative ones linked to radical behaviour that the majority repudiated. They could neither be mobilized like the Vikings or Cossacks or turned upside down and appropriated like the Mundare sausage or St. Pierre-Jolys frog. Some of the group symbols that Doukhobors did cultivate, like the SS *Lake Huron*, emerged from the group's Canadian and prairie experience, but the most pervasive and popular images represented values whose universality could be consciously exploited.

The Doukhobor equivalent of Taras Shevchenko and Jón Sigurðsson was Count Leo Tolstoi, with the crucial difference that his personal intervention to find a haven for the persecuted sect bridged old and new worlds in real terms. In 1987 statues of Tolstoi were erected at the National Doukhobor Heritage Village in Veregin, Saskatchewan, and at the Doukhobor museum in Castlegar, British Columbia. Ironically, given the group's historical distrust of the state and fraught relationship with tsarist officials, they were gifts to the people of Canada from the Russian empire's Soviet successor, which stressed the "ideals of brotherhood among all nations" for which Tolstoi stood.[62] In 1995, the centenary of the burning of arms that set Canadian Doukhobors on a separate path, the town of Veregin acquired a statue of two doves. This peace motif in centennial iconography identified what the group considered its pivotal

**6.9.** Alberta Polish centennial monument, combining evocative homeland and settlement-era symbols, Edmonton, 2001. PHOTO BY FRANCES SWYRIPA.

contribution to not just Canada but humanity itself. Other symbols—a sheaf of wheat (the theme of the centennial statue in Lundbreck, Alberta) and the bread, salt, and water that sustained all human life—similarly both resonated in and transcended Doukhobor belief and culture.[63] Among Canadian Doukhobors the traditional offering of bread, salt, and water had special meaning as a reminder of exile overseas and the ideals for which their ancestors suffered. Before departing the Wet Mountains in Georgia in December 1898 to begin their journey to Canada, the emigrants placed "symbolic bread and water on the tables" of their abandoned homes.[64] The images on the giant painted sign erected in 1999 in Kamsack, Saskatchewan, for the Doukhobor centennial, its theme one of progress from farmers and the land to university graduates and skyscrapers, contained three overtly iconic images drawn from the Canadian experience. They were the SS *Lake Huron*; the 1917 Prayer Home with its ornate lattices and verandahs, centrepiece of the museum in Veregin; and an offering of bread, salt, and water.[65]

## The Land's Bounty: Wheat and Westerners

If one prairie symbol erased ethno-religious boundaries, it was wheat. Although less central to a group like Icelanders with their tradition of fishing on Lake Winnipeg, wheat touched everyone whose ancestors homesteaded the land. Despite repeated evidence of the wisdom of diversification, generations of farmers put their faith in the grain that the West's champions promised would make the region and its residents wealthy. For immigrant settler peoples from agricultural backgrounds, wheat also symbolized a seamless continuity between the old world and the new. And it had special poignancy for groups like Ukrainians and Doukhobors among whom it had played a ritual function for centuries. In short, ever since posters enticed settlers to the West with pictures of giant sheaves and men buried waist deep in waving fields of grain, individuals and communities embraced wheat, and in both secular and sacred contexts, as a symbol of their prairie identity.

In the late twentieth century, two phenomena illustrated wheat's everyday symbolic importance not only to westerners in their personal lives but also to the image they possessed and wished to project of their local communities. At the individual level, wheat became a favourite tombstone motif—ornamental stalks, sheaves, stooks, even swathes awaiting the combine—as rural westerners claimed their legacy and identity in the land. At official levels, wheat appeared on the signage, logos, and publicity pins of countless towns, villages, municipalities, and counties, often in tandem with the grain elevator, another all-embracing and powerful prairie symbol. A handful of local communities chose wheat as the theme of outdoor sculptures. For example, two arrangements of three towering metal stalks along the highway in Weyburn in southern Saskatchewan neatly framed the Pioneer elevator and adjacent railway track. Hundreds of kilometres to the north, a strikingly similar arrangement of three stalks next to a Red River cart advertised the dual fur trade and settlement heritage of Rosthern on the old Carlton Trail.[66] The huge cream can with three stalks of wheat protruding from its neck erected in 1988 for the 100th anniversary of the Icelandic farming community at Markerville in Alberta specifically commemorated the pioneers.

Wheat also figured in the design of official monuments, logos, and popular memorabilia produced by ethno-religious groups as they celebrated landmark

**6.10.** Roadside collage of Doukhobor symbols—including the SS *Huron*, Veregin prayer home, and traditional bread, salt, and water—Kamsack, Saskatchewan, 2002. PHOTO BY FRANCES SWYRIPA.

anniversaries. The sheaf of wheat in Ukrainians' *Madonna of the Wheat* and *The Commitment*, and both wheat and bread motifs in the Doukhobor centennial memorials, were clearly predicated upon pre-emigration folk and Christian beliefs as well as an ancient agricultural way of life. The commemorative spoon produced by the Women's Committee of the Mennonite Educational Society in Winnipeg for the prairie Mennonite centennial separated wheat symbolism from faith; the pattern featured "several heads of grain across a Bible representing the agricultural background of the people and their reliance on the biblical record as their guide in life." This imagery differed from the logo chosen for the Ontario-focussed national Mennonite bicentenary in 1986. A lone maple leaf made of intersecting lines representing ploughed furrows and a mosaic, or the group's agricultural roots and diverse cultural origins, the design brought "to mind a quilt pattern ... [the] folk art ... most readily associated with Mennonites."[67] The wheat in the official centennial logo of the Ukrainian Canadian Congress was visually implicit. The impressionistic blue and yellow background, the nationalist colours that traditionally stood for the vast Ukrainian sky and steppe, here stood for the vast Canadian sky and prairie as well.[68]

Significantly, prairie Mennonites and Ukrainians were the only ethno-religious groups to have their settlement story acknowledged by the state in the form of special commemorative stamps issued by Canada Post.[69] Its reluctance to acknowledge landmark anniversaries in the history of such peoples, while receptive to a host of other events, suggested discomfort with the recognition that this type of commemoration implied when it involved ethnicity. The four forty-cent stamps released for the Ukrainian-Canadian centennial aroused little comment—perhaps because of widespread acceptance of Ukrainians' role in opening the West; perhaps because, although regionally based, theirs was a national anniversary. Or perhaps it was because each stamp reproduced a painting by Ukrainian-Canadian artist William Kurelek from the collection of the National Gallery of Canada. In one, a family huddled together on the deck of a ship looked out over the stormy ocean. In another, a mother watched from the lit doorway as her daughter carried a plate into the winter night. Newly arrived homesteaders, the man brandishing an axe and pointing to the bush, graced the third. And in the fourth, a farmer in a hat and red shirt stood knee-deep in a field of wheat, inspecting the kernels in his hand.[70]

Almost two decades earlier, Canada Post had to be convinced that it should issue a special stamp for the prairie Mennonite centennial. "The central question," said Jake Epp, a Mennonite member of Parliament from Manitoba, of his discussions with Postmaster General André Ouellet,

> was whether this event was only of limited interest to a small ethnic group in Manitoba, or whether this event had a wider significance. I have pointed out that not only will this event be of interest to all Canadian Mennonites, but that the coming of the Mennonites to Canada in 1874 was a tangible expression of the government's decision of that day to open the vast prairies by people from all parts of Europe, not only those who were of English or French background. Evidence of this fact is seen in the multi-cultural mosaic which is evident in Canada today, and especially so in Western Canada. Since Confederation, Canada has been a haven to many who were forced to leave their homeland for religious or economic reasons.[71]

When the Post Office finally relented, the image chosen showed a group of male and female figures, the women in kerchiefs and peasant clothes, the men in black hats and jackets, that "drew attention to the Mennonite immigrants." But the Post Office pulled back from ethno-religious specificity in favour of the stamp's "honour[ing] all the ethnic groups who found their way to the prairies."[72] Seven stalks of wheat made up the centrepiece of the cancellation mark on the Day of Issue envelope.

Across the forty-ninth parallel, the United States Post Office marked the centennial of the arrival of the Russian Mennonites in that country with a stamp that paid tribute to the Turkey Red wheat they brought with them. In Canada, where the West's destiny as a breadbasket rested on the development of a quality high yield and early maturing strain suited to a short growing season, the corresponding boast belonged to Ukrainians. A subtheme in their self-image as a founding people of western Canada was that the ancestors of the famous Red Fife wheat, in the twentieth century crossed to produce the even better Marquis, came from Galicia. Red Fife had been developed in Ontario from a few kernels brought over in the 1840s from Scotland, where they had arrived by ship from Danzig. Decades later government scientists established the seeds' Galician origins. The story behind Red Fife, including the notion that the lucky survival of two stalks from the first Ontario crop saved the future for the West, received its biggest exposure in 1943 in journalist Bruce Hutchinson's award-winning *The Unknown Country*. To many Ukrainian Canadians, the knowledge that their wheat underlay western prosperity was most satisfying.[73]

Secular wheat symbolism on the prairies always flirted with the sacred, albeit more in some ethno-religious traditions than others. Yet wheat's long and multifaceted role as a Christian symbol—fruitfulness, the staff of life, or, during Holy Communion, the body of Christ—facilitated the transfer of its secular symbolism, historically rooted and place specific, into sacred space and contexts. There it could act as a pan-western phenomenon blind to ethnic and religious divisions, or it could be tied to particular groups. The sheaves of wheat and *fleurs de lys* in the stained glass windows in Ste. Philomène (later Assumption) Roman Catholic Cathedral in Gravelbourg, Saskatchewan, proclaimed the parish's prairie and French origins. At Prud'homme, another *fransaskois* community, the wrought iron Stations of the Cross and copy of Leonardo Da Vinci's *Last Supper*, their human figures rendered as stalks of wheat, worked into the cemetery fence had prairie but not ethnic French connotations.[74]

**6.11.** Nativity through prairie Doukhobor eyes, Veregin, Saskatchewan, 2004.
PHOTO BY FRANCES SWYRIPA.

The deeply religious William Kurelek expressed the universality of Christianity's message in paintings that Canadianized the biblical Nativity. Although depicting Christ's birth in settings from an Arctic igloo to Peggy's Cove, he returned repeatedly to the prairies of his boyhood: Mother and Child sheltered in his parents' barn, in a haystack in a winter field, in a boxcar or grain elevator, and, outside the settlement period, at a gas station and on a construction site. Wheat appeared via the field where it grew, the grain elevator and boxcar that turned it into a paycheque and took it to feed the world, the haystack that was left to fatten cattle. Occasionally, Kurelek's prairie Nativities had a whiff of Ukrainianness: the faint row of embroidery on Mary's blouse, the folded kerchief on her head.[75] In contrast, in the early twenty-first century, the Nativity street scene in the village of Veregin annually transformed Christ's birth into not just a prairie event but a specifically Doukhobor happening. In a deliberate evocation of place, a cutout of a grain elevator, stamped with the name "Veregin," stood beside the stable. Mary, Joseph, and the Three Wise Men (one of them a woman) wore traditional Russian peasant dress. Finally, the peace dove in the Star of Bethlehem and the gifts of bread (which the woman carried), water, and salt instead of gold, frankincense, and myrrh incorporated the symbols of Doukhoborism, including wheat, to link the message of the Nativity to the group's own beliefs.[76]

In her openness to believers regardless of ethnic background, Mary as Our Lady of the Prairies marked the pinnacle of wheat's mobilization as a western sacred symbol. European Catholicism had a long history of nationalizing the Madonna—from dedicating the nation to her service in medieval France to the modern national connotations of the Blessed Virgin of Medjugorje in Bosnia-Herzegovina, who first appeared in 1981. Thus, by once again importing saints who spoke to their specific historical experience and faith, late twentieth-century refugees from war-torn Yugoslavia further fragmented Canadian prairie Catholicism, this time in urban space. Contemporary Latin American immigrants added their dark complexioned Our Lady of Guadalupe, first seen in the visions of a local convert shortly after Spain's conquest of the Aztecs; successively patroness of New Spain, Mexico, and Latin America, she watched over and succoured the downtrodden and the colonized.[77] As a product of the new world, Our Lady of the Prairies followed in the tradition of Our Lady of Guadalupe, but on a regional and local scale and without the initial apparitions and miracles that made the Mexican Madonna famous.[78] As a product of the settlement era in the Canadian West, Our Lady of the Prairies protected and sustained the pioneers and even implied a mild martyrdom on the part of men and women of faith who toiled hard on the land and made great sacrifices.

Our Lady of the Prairies had her origins in 1916 when a boy on a Saskatchewan homestead observed his mother build a shrine to the Virgin Mary with rocks she had cleared from their land. After suffering a massive coronary as a relatively young man, he drew on the strength of her faith and promised thereafter to do good works in Mary's name. In 1957 his promise bore fruit when the Saskatchewan Legislature created Our Lady of the Prairies Foundation to assist the needy regardless of race, colour, or creed. Acknowledging its regional and agricultural roots, the foundation also sought to pay "tribute to those many prairie pilgrims who called on [Our Lady] for nurturing and guidance" and to "bring [her] and the prairie people closer to one another and to our beloved earth." In 1983 Holy Spirit Roman Catholic Church in Saskatoon erected a shrine that became the site of an annual pilgrimage. Visually, Our Lady of the Prairies resembled the secular *Madonna of the Wheat* in that she carried not the Christ Child but a sheaf or stalks of wheat. Both a Christian and Mary's personal symbol, wheat represented the merging of the sacred with the prairie experience (some said it stood for Saskatchewan specifically). Our Lady of the Prairies was also part of the land. A church calendar from the 1980s showed her crossing a swathed field, sheaf of wheat in her arms, a prairie town with its grain elevators and church spires in the background. More recently she was painted against a backdrop of rippling yellow fields awaiting harvest.[79]

* * *

Wheat, dragon ships, and *baba*. On the surface such images were uncomplicated and unambiguous, defining those to whom they mattered and serving as shorthand labels that outsiders could appreciate. They also, however, possessed deeper significance. Like dragon ships, some symbols accessed old-world pasts and figures far removed from immigrants to western Canada and their descendants, but remaining attractive for qualities or connections that reflected positively on them and that Canadians valued. Like the Ukrainian *baba*, other symbols emerged from the prairie pioneer experience and could be emotionally accessed, even among group members, solely by those whose personal roots lay in that particular time and place. Like wheat, a few symbols resonated within the group as part of an agricultural or religious tradition, but simultaneously crossed and transcended ethnic boundaries to proclaim a shared western heritage. Both adoption and display of such images depended on the group and the nature of its homeland history and prairie experience. They also involved negotiation, tension, and compromise not only within the group but also between its spokespersons and different levels of government and other Canadians. Finally, the late twentieth-century mobilization of symbols of ethno-religious identity on the prairies was part of a larger process of commemorating and preserving the pioneer past focussed on a revered immigrant generation and a return to the land, its landmarks, and its artifacts.

**7.1.** Wide street and mature trees, only remaining evidence of the Mennonite village of Hoffnungsfeld, West Reserve, 1955. ARCHIVES OF MANITOBA, MENNONITES 27.

# Returning to the Land:
# Commemoration and Preservation
# of the Past

IN THEIR GRAND NARRATIVES AND MYTH making, ethno-religious groups relied heavily on the settlement and cultivation of the land by their immigrant ancestors. They also mobilized their pioneers in more intimately symbolic ways, elevating to iconic status both the settler generation and the land that they tamed and brought into production. This process and the sentiments it reflected complemented the visual popular symbols of ethno-religious identity in which homeland images and associations dominated and the pioneer figure was noticeably absent. Although privileging one segment of the ethno-religious group, commemoration around its prairie pioneers cultivated, reinforced, and institutionalized collective memory rooted in the Canadian experience and enriched the rituals of communal life. No longer history's actors, asserting their presence and imposing order on the wilderness, the pioneers became a vehicle for furthering the agenda of ethno-religious communities acting in their name and profiting from the foundations they laid. Behind this phenomenon was a self-conscious return to the land: reasserting the pioneers' possession of it, and thus the extended group's own rights to its heritage, by preserving their stamp on their surroundings and redoing the map in their memory.

In other words, the notion of "the land" retreated from the grandiose and generic West in the abstract present in regional founding stories and claims to nation building and returned to the immediate and concrete world of the immigrant settler generation and the soil itself. As points of reference in pioneer commemoration, both place and its material culture had the potential to open their joint legacy not only to all members of the group but also, under certain circumstances, to non-members. Symbolic manipulation of the rural ethno-religious heritage also led to detachment from the land that nurtured it and gave it meaning. Transplantation into urban environments saw the countryside's artifacts removed to city museums and more intangible aspects of the past incorporated into the living cityscape.

Some initiatives and the rituals they generated were purely local in inception, design, and execution, attesting to emotional and physical continuity with the pioneers and the land at the grassroots level. Others originated with regional or national ethno-religious organizations. Their memberships might or might not be dominated by descendants of the pioneers but inevitably included those whose personal immigration stories were far removed from the rural prairies of the settlement period. In addition to bringing together disparate immigrations and generations, various initiatives also entailed, particularly at the municipal level, either tacit government cooperation and support or actual leadership and input. State involvement demonstrated that the collective experience and mythology of ethno-religious groups had entered the larger consciousness as part of both its past and its contemporary identity. It simultaneously reflected more than regional responsiveness to federal multiculturalism, as ethno-religious mainstreaming on the prairies independently acknowledged the pluralism of the West and predated Ottawa's policy. Lastly, commemorative initiatives fostered the interplay between rural and urban, whether highlighting and exaggerating their tensions or blurring their boundaries. In the process, the immigrant settler experience was vicariously brought into and legitimized in urban space, and city dwellers went into the countryside to engage with their roots.

## The Pioneer Landscape Preserved

Where once plants sat on the windowsill, smoke rose from the chimney, and chickens pecked in the dirt outside the door, by the late twentieth century only the occasional ruin in a field stood as a reminder of the homes the settler generation built. But the trained eye could also pick out more subtle signs of former human occupancy, like lone spruce trees and clumps of lilac or caragana, planted by settlers to beautify and domesticate their yards. Growing wild in the ditch, patches of tansy, used by Ukrainian peasants for medicinal purposes and spread under an open coffin to mask the smell, were more ethnically specific. As for where the pioneers came together as communities, most one-time centres of activity and identity survived only on old maps and in local memory, history books, and museums. Yet as rural schools and post offices closed, the buildings demolished or converted to granaries, halls and especially churches and cemeteries proved more resilient. One hundred years or more later, many still operated sporadically for worship services, family reunions, community anniversaries, and burials. As such, they continued to shape not only the landscape but also the imagined world through which surrounding farmers defined themselves and their neighbours. The place names of the immigrant settler generation often also remained in the collective consciousness, associated with surviving structures or the invisible patchwork of districts created by the pioneers. The names themselves, once foreign and exotic, even threatening, had become simply Canadian words, part of the region's vocabulary and fabric.

Ethno-religious pioneer commemoration took as its starting point the order imposed on the landscape by the immigrant settler generation in an attempt to preserve a record of its occupation and activity. Signposts directed the traveller off the highway to country churches and their adjacent cemeteries and halls. Cairns marked the location of long-gone community landmarks, particularly schools, or told the history of those that still existed. Metal crosses replaced the wooden ones put up by the first settlers to announce their arrival or to proclaim their faith and declare the land Christian. More privately, families erected monuments on the quarter sections their forebears had homesteaded, asserting forever their claim to this land. Such gestures overwhelmingly represented the priorities of local residents, especially descendants of the pioneers, determined that time and progress did not erase all memory of individuals and communities that once shaped the countryside. Since public memorials often engaged the larger ethno-religious group, commemorative activity was more extensive (or better orchestrated) in localities identified with the settlement of specific peoples. In those with a more generic homesteading experience, ties tended to be personal and centred on the old family farm.

Initiatives to preserve the ethno-religious pioneer presence on the land could be purely local. In 1979 a metal cross, dedicated in thanksgiving to the pioneers, replaced the second wooden cross erected to mark the arrival of

Hungarian immigrants in the Prud'homme area of Saskatchewan in 1903.[1] Exhibiting a greater consciousness of place, the Benedictines at Muenster arranged for a huge rock to be set near the site of the wooden cross erected in 1903 at the "gateway" to St. Peter's Colony. The plaque attached to its face commemorated the North-West Mounted Police station on the Carlton Trail, Hoodoo School, the original St. Benedict church, and the first Mass celebrated in the colony, in this way connecting the German Catholic settlement to the general history of the area.[2] The cairn outside Stockholm, Saskatchewan, also expressed a multilayered sense of history. The original plaque, installed in 1959 by the province, acknowledged New Stockholm church (the "first Swedish Lutheran congregation in Canada") and identified its imposing successor a mile away in the countryside as a Saskatchewan historic site. In 1994 local residents added a second plaque locating the first post office, burial grounds, schools, churches, and community halls in the surrounding Swedish settlement.[3] In Manitoba, the Ukrainian cross of freedom at Trembowla evolved from a local into a national and international group symbol. On the seventy-fifth anniversary of Ukrainian settlement in Canada in 1966, the deteriorating wooden cross was replaced by a granite one—its sole decoration an engraved *tryzub* (trident), the nationalist emblem banned in Ukraine during the harsh decades of Soviet rule. In 1977 the Ukrainian National Association in the United States erected an adjacent monument in memory of the Pennsylvania-based Reverend Nestor Dmytriw, one of its own pioneers, who had blessed the original cross in 1897 and personified the ties between Canadian and American Ukrainian diaspora communities. A Manitoba Heritage Council commemorative plaque was installed in 1984.[4]

Preserving the pioneer imprint in New Iceland also captured the imagination of a larger diaspora community. Through their practice of naming private farms, the colony's settlers had intimately ordered their surroundings, focussed on the smallest unit of land ownership. Local and personal expressions of identity, however, became internationally endorsed group symbols of the Icelandic-Canadian experience when the Icelandic League of North America undertook to erect markers identifying old properties by their original names. By the early twenty-first century over 200 of the blue-and-white aluminum signs, purchased by current or former owners, dotted New Iceland. They featured a single word beneath a falcon crest, chosen for its non-political

**7.2.** Ukrainian cross of freedom, granite replacing the original wood, Trembowla, Manitoba, 2004. PHOTO BY FRANCES SWYRIPA.

Icelandic cultural associations. Besides the articulated goal of honouring the pioneers, alerting present and future generations to their heritage, and charming tourists, the signs represented a conscious engagement by the Icelandic community with its roots in the West and the 1870s immigration. The necessity of signs also suggested that the names were being lost, involving the recovery of memory and feeding an urge to formalize and make concrete a once invisible but satisfactory system of mapping the land. As part of that process, the sign initiative generated a written record documenting the location of a property, its ownership history (many farms had stayed in one family for over a hundred years), the meaning of the name, and how it came to be chosen.[5]

Mennonite commemoration of the old Post Road in the West Reserve stressed not the pioneer "civilizing" of the Icelandic Heritage Name Sign program but a more elementary response to the land as a forbidding and sometimes deadly place. The original Post Road had been a public thoroughfare

**7.3.** Participant in the signage program to preserve old farm names in New Iceland, 2001. PHOTO BY FRANCES SWYRIPA.

that linked not only the Mennonite villages on its path but also those villages to the outside world along the Boundary Commission and North-West Mounted Police trails. The western portion of the road was ploughed under by the 1930s, except for remnants of a bridge, but the government grid absorbed the eastern portion, which continued to act as a local reference point. In 2000 the Post Road Memorial Trail became a West Reserve 125th anniversary project of the Manitoba Mennonite Historical Society. It erected replicas (with plaques) of the posts put up in the 1870s to orient travellers along the "Mennonite" section of the longer route. When completed, the Mennonite Post Road Memorial Trail formed part of the larger Boundary Trail Heritage Region.[6] For the modern traveller eager to connect with the past, a self-guided brochure mapped the road across the West Reserve, gave directions, and identified signed stopping places and points of interest.

The most ambitious commemorative scheme to preserve the pioneer imprint on the land went unrealized. A Ukrainian-Canadian centennial initiative spearheaded by the Ukrainian Canadian Congress, it envisioned a stake with the original occupant's name on every quarter section Ukrainians had homesteaded, regardless of who currently owned the property. The plan resembled the Icelandic program in its personalized identification with beginnings at their most basic level and its sense of group rights to very specific pieces of land. What made the Ukrainian project unique was the intensity of entitlement understood to have been earned by the pioneers and the political implications—public funds to support their language and culture—of the resulting group myth. Metal stakes that permanently registered as "Ukrainian" the legendary 10 million acres that represented the group's Canadian patrimony constituted the organized community's most explicit attempt to give the idea of a founding people of western Canada concrete form. Rather incongruously, given Ukrainians' pride in their role in clearing the land, the other large-scale centennial initiative was to plant thousands of trees symbolically replacing those that successful farming had demanded their ancestors cut down. The City of Calgary and local branch of the Ukrainian Canadian Congress, for example, dedicated a grove to the Ukrainian pioneers, hoping to "encourage Canadians everywhere to join ... in the spirit of 'keeping Canada green' by preserving our forests and environment for future generations."[7]

## The Pioneer Landscape Reordered and Displaced

The Ukrainian-Canadian centennial stakes and trees formed a transition between preservation of the immigrant settler generation's own imprint on the land and subsequent efforts to use the same space to pay homage to the pioneers. This second form of commemoration added a new layer of meaning to the prairie map in that its original architects were now retroactively remembered on it. Reordering and renaming the original settlement area around the pioneers revealed how later generations interpreted and accessed their history. Like the first form of commemoration, it involved local residents and direct descendants, various levels of government, and the larger ethno-religious group. Incorporation of the pioneer legacy into the modern landscape also led to displacement from the countryside into prairie urban centres. There, memorialized in city streets and parks, settlers on the land became the means for mainstreaming regional ethno-religious heritages and for connecting group members removed from the prairie pioneers to their western roots.

In some cases redoing the original settlement area map to honour the pioneers was specific and individualized. Roads in the Rural Municipality of Hanover in southern Manitoba were signposted with the surnames of pioneer settlers, largely Mennonite and Ukrainian, who lived along them. One ten-mile stretch, the "C.S. Plett Road" (named in 1996), passed the grave of the Mennonite farmer it commemorated.[8] In Saskatchewan, a sign outside the Doukhobor village of Veregin pointing north to Tolstoi Road remembered not a pioneer but the aristocratic supporter for whom the settlers named the rural school that once constituted the road's principal landmark.[9] On rare occasions redoing the map reached outside both the built environment and the European settlement experience. Kimura Lake northeast of Edmonton acknowledged the Japanese family that farmed on its shores in the midst of an otherwise strongly Ukrainian-Polish community.

In other cases the exercise was generic and generalized. Demonstrating the elasticity of the notion of pioneer, as early as 1927 Viking Hall in the Swedish settlement of New Stockholm was renamed Pioneer Hall, the site of an annual Dominion Day "Pioneer Picnic" that celebrated both Canada's birthday and the arrival of the first settlers four decades earlier.[10] More commonly, the rural cemetery, where the immigrant settler generation had claimed the land through its dead, was renamed in honour of the pioneers. For many years all that remained of the Norwegian Lutheran community at Snaasen in southern Saskatchewan was the graveyard, overrun by "lilacs, caraganas, weeds, buck brush ... a most barren and forsaken place."[11] In 1978 former members of the congregation rescued the site, erected a sign saying Pioneer Cemetery, and began gathering periodically for remembrance services. At both New Stockholm and Snaasen, ethno-religious specificity vanished from official view in that "pioneer" assimilated the two communities and their descendants into the regional story, supplanting Swedishness and Norwegianness (and

**7.4.** Nativity of the Blessed Virgin Mary Ukrainian Catholic Church, collapsing under the weight of its dome, Jaroslaw, Saskatchewan, 2009. PHOTO BY FRANCES SWYRIPA.

Lutheranism) as hallmarks of identity. In contrast, the entrance gate to New Finland cemetery, topped with the Saskatchewan tiger lily and dedicated in 1985 to the "achievements and memory of the early Finnish pioneers and their descendants," kept the old name.[12] Sometimes ethno-religious specificity did not matter. When Steinbach, in the heart of the East Reserve, renamed the original village burial ground the Pioneer Cemetery, its Mennonite identity and group associations were automatically understood.

Transplanting the rural ethno-religious heritage into prairie urban centres divorced it from its natural context. It also made place naming entirely symbolic, projecting a falsely inclusive vision of past community building onto the present. The advent of multiculturalism in the 1970s clearly galvanized city planners, backed by vote-conscious municipal politicians, who turned to ethnic "community builders" to commemorate in streets, subdivisions, public buildings, and parks.[13] Their choices reverted to the larger-than-life heroes of the settlement era, recognized by group founding stories and often familiar to outsiders as group-specific symbols. As a result, although Ukrainian settlers never thought of naming their localities after Ivan Pylypiw and Vasyl Eleniak, in 1974 Edmonton created Eleniak Road in the appropriately named complex, Pylypow Industrial. Two years later the city renamed Mayfair Park after William Hawrelak, its recently deceased and controversial mayor whose immigrant parents had homesteaded in the Ukrainian bloc to the east. Meanwhile, Edmontonians of British origin objected to the "foreignness" of the name and public erasure of their own heritage. Other names portraying Edmonton as a legitimate heir to the rural pioneer ethno-religious experience had direct historic links with the city. Kulawy Drive, for instance, honoured three Polish priests in western Canada, brothers Jan, Adalbert, and Paweł. The latter, who also served in Alberta's rural Polish parishes, founded Holy Rosary Polish Roman Catholic parish in Edmonton in 1913. Poles remembered him in a bronze plaque in the new church, both for his work among the pioneers and for his death in Auschwitz that tied the Canadian prairie diaspora to the wartime martyrdom of Poles in the homeland.[14]

## The Land and Material Culture as Symbol and Artifact

Rare evidence of a sod hut. Abandoned log cabins, the wind slowly ripping off the clapboard that had been added as money permitted. Dilapidated plastered and whitewashed cottages, their thatched roofs long replaced by less flammable shingles. One-roomed schoolhouses emptied of students. Grain elevators at risk of demolition. Well-maintained churches rising from the flat prairie or perched on a hilltop; others stripped bare and closed, their spires or domes tilting dangerously, crosses askew. Carefully tended cemeteries sheltered by rows of planted spruce; other graves enclosed by barbed wire and open to the elements or lost beneath tangled grass and brush.[15] By the 1970s, as nostalgia for the past and its artifacts gathered momentum, the material heritage of the settlement era—defining the land, recalling its human dramas—acquired unprecedented symbolic value.

Regarding pioneering as temporary, its hardships the price of future security and comfort, the settler generation attached little sentimentality to unpleasant reminders of poverty and austerity. As a result, not only local and ethno-religious communities but also federal and provincial historic sites programs had limited examples of vernacular domestic architecture with which to work. While a fortunate few private dwellings and schools survived in open-air museums, churches and cemeteries were the most secure and valued features of the pioneer landscape.[16] As secularized sites of collective memory and identity, they performed four functions. They commemorated the pioneer dead, they proclaimed the pioneers' descendants' own roots in the land, they symbolized the western (and Canadian) birthright of ethno-religious groups, and they reaffirmed these groups' ties to larger diasporas. Under the right conditions, these symbols of group heritage embraced members never touched by the prairie experience or crossed over to be appropriated by westerners and Canadians as a whole.

In the early twenty-first century, the cemeteries of ethno-religious groups on the rural prairies continued to illustrate the interlocking sense of identity and place that had always characterized them.[17] By then, however, they had long shed any connotations of exile, as the pioneers' descendants turned to them to celebrate their beginnings, remember those who preceded them, and assert their right to the land and its history. At the individual level such statements were personal and idiosyncratic, expressed best in the words and images on private tombstones. At the community level such statements stressed group membership, through commemorative cairns and monuments catering to particular ethno-religious priorities and agenda. Public space in terms of the group, cemeteries represented private space in the group's relations with the larger society. That commemoration occurred here rather than in the nearest town or village signified not only the intensity but also the exclusiveness of the group experience, as well as attachment to place.

As in the settlement period, what individuals put on their tombstones remained influenced by financial status and tombstone fashions. In that the deceased seldom chose the inscription or the ornamentation, both text and images reflected the attitudes of the living towards an earlier generation as much as they did the thinking of that generation itself. Again, as in the past, religious and cultural tradition affected how the living interacted with the dead and their burial grounds. Personalized tombstones conscious of history and place were also a manifestation of the late twentieth-century angst that gripped the rural prairies, voiced in forums from regional grassroots separatist movements to local history books with evocative titles like *Golden Memories, We Came and We Stayed*, and *This is Our Land*. More positively, landmark anniversaries of provincehood in Alberta, Saskatchewan, and Manitoba, as well as the Canadian Centennial, fostered individuals' sense of self-worth and entitlement as pioneers.[18] Lastly, not only immigrants from overseas but also migrants from within Canada developed new identities as westerners that they recorded on their tombstones. The elaborate Gagné-Hirbour monument erected in St. Pierre-Jolys traced the family from its roots in New France through the relocation to Manitoba in 1877 of its patriarch and matriarch ("parmi les fondateurs de Saint-Pierre"), ending with the couple's children and grandchildren.[19]

Most often tombstones articulated the regional roots and identity of rural westerners through romanticized, bucolic images featuring nature's abundance and nostalgic icons: a log cabin nestled in the bush beside a lake, a buck deer flashing its antlers at the forest's edge, giant fish leaping from a stream, fat cattle grazing in the pasture, a horse-drawn rack piled with hay, sheaves of wheat or combine in a field, a grain elevator. Mountains, and not just in Alberta, suggested that the regional patrimony being claimed extended well beyond the West's agricultural heritage.[20] Ultimately, and contrary to their intent, such generic images depersonalized the individual experience. Much more assertive and unique were tombstones that featured an engraving or a laser photograph of the deceased's actual farmstead. Some of these pictures clearly eulogized the past, depicting the homestead that was; others captured the moment when the person died, including details like the television antenna on the house, the van in the driveway, and the dogs barking at the gate. Aerial views most gratifyingly included not only the home and farmyard but also the sweep of land owned around them.[21] Such images certainly expressed a regional sense of place and belonging. More pointedly, they made a very personal claim to a piece of land that the deceased's family had often cultivated for a century or more. An official land description reinforced the message—the antithesis to earlier inscriptions providing a place of birth in the old country.

**7.5.** Saplings planted to identify a pioneer Mennonite grave grown into mature trees, Kronsthal, West Reserve, 1955.
ARCHIVES OF MANITOBA, MENNONITES 26.

While the above images crossed ethnic, generational, and gender lines and failed to distinguish between immigrant and migrant, they did not appeal equally to all settler peoples. Late twentieth-century Mennonite graves in the East and West reserves remained austere, virtually devoid of visual symbols identifying the dead with their regional or personal roots. Ukrainian tombstones, often highly decorated, freely used pictures to tell the story of lives lived on the land.[22] And instead of agricultural motifs, Icelanders who made their living from the depths of Lake Winnipeg preferred engravings of the lone fisherman in his boat hauling in his catch in his nets, storm clouds suspended over the vast waters.[23] Other tombstone details—Irish shamrock, Scottish thistle, Ukrainian embroidery, Viking helmet—made broad ethnic statements. But some, like the image of *fjallkona* Sigríður Hjartarson wearing the headdress in which she presided over the 1968 Icelandic festival, were highly specific.[24]

Communal commemorative cairns and monuments expressed ethnicity most forcibly, although groups differed in choosing the cemetery to pay tribute to their Canadian ancestors or confirm themselves as heirs of the community the pioneers built. Nor, despite obvious connections, did a strict parallel exist between this mobilization of the cemetery and existing rituals at graveside. Also, some groups defined community primarily as a "kingdom of God" of co-religionists, albeit with ethnic colouring; others saw it in largely secular terms, whether as something local and measurable or bigger and imagined. Finally, groups like Ukrainians, Jews, and Mennonites consciously used the symbolic potential of the dead and their resting place to remind the group in Canada that they had ties and obligations to people or nations elsewhere.

The popularity of communal commemoration in Ukrainian cemeteries and churchyards reflected in part the size and number of bloc settlements, which encouraged an exaggerated sense of belonging around land that was "theirs." Other factors included the Catholic-Orthodox rivalry, beginning in the pioneer period, that spawned rival churches and cemeteries; and the fact that Ukrainians stayed on the land through several generations, keeping their churches and cemeteries open. The traditional significance attached to the dead, the soil sheltering them, and their relationship to the living—annually reiterated in graveside services—also contributed. Crucially, it facilitated the group's self-image as a founding people of western Canada, paid for with the pioneers whose bones mingled with the prairie earth.[25] As much statements of the ethnic identity of the pioneers' descendants as testimonials to the pioneers themselves, Ukrainian memorials maintained the association with the dead and their resting places. Erected on landmark anniversaries of immigration and settlement, they also fused the group's national and diaspora narratives with the local and regional experience, and stressed settlers on the land over pioneers of faith.

Events at Patterson Lake, Manitoba, exemplify the symbolism of pioneer sacrifice and the resting place of the dead in Ukrainian group mythology.[26] In 1899 forty Ukrainian children and two adults died there of disease and exposure after residents of nearby Strathclair, fearing scarlet fever, denied the "foreigners" shelter. Marking the burial ground with wooden crosses, the survivors proceeded to their homesteads at Shoal Lake. In 1915, after cows had pastured among the graves, erasing all traces, a Ukrainian acquired and innocently ploughed up the property. Horrified to learn what he had done, he fenced off the area, where, in the 1920s, the victims' families constructed a large burial mound (*mohyla*) topped with a wooden cross. In 1941, on the fiftieth anniversary of Ukrainian immigration and settlement, the Ukrainian community appropriated the personal tragedy of the site, erecting a monument stamped with a maple leaf and the words, "Here lie 42 pioneers. Ever remembered." Over the years, the local Parkland Ukrainian Pioneer Association put up two more memorials. Then, on the group's centenary, the Ukrainian Canadian Congress (Manitoba) erected a fifth monument featuring two bowed figures burying their dead; a Ukrainian trident, a Canadian maple leaf, and a sheaf of wheat on red-and-black embroidery symbolized its sponsors' tripartite identity. "Respect and glory to the Ukrainian settlers for building and enriching Canada," read the text. "Gratitude to you for the faith, culture and traditions. God bless." Close by, St. Michael Ukrainian Catholic Church instituted annual commemorative services for the Patterson Lake dead.[27]

By the late twentieth century out-migration had long reduced Jews on the rural prairies to a handful, even in Saskatchewan. As farm families moved to western urban centres, or left the region entirely, their colonies became at best memories with only a lone synagogue, a few cemeteries, and isolated plaques to mark their one-time agricultural presence. The Jewish Historical Society of Western Canada (later the Jewish Heritage Centre of Western Canada) took the lead in preserving the community's material heritage on the land; it enlisted support, especially for cemetery recovery, from the Canadian Jewish Congress, former colonists and their descendants, and surrounding points.[28] For their cemeteries to foster a sense of place and belonging, like those of settler peoples still rooted in the communities their immigrant ancestors founded, Jews had to overcome the collective abandonment of the land that damaged their reputation and legacy as pioneers. They managed to do so because of the psychological significance of owning and cultivating the land that now sheltered their dead, fortified by a sense of pioneer labour and hardship in taming the wilderness shared with other westerners. The epitaph on a tombstone in the cemetery in Edenbridge, Saskatchewan, encapsulated this notion as a personal sentiment: "They came to toil and till the soil. Now they rest."[29]

Established in 1894, two years after the colony, Hirsch cemetery illustrated the evolution from a place for the dead defined by faith into a symbol of the

**7.6**. Former *fjallkona* (1968) remembered for her community position on her tombstone, Gimli, Manitoba, 2001.
PHOTO BY FRANCES SWYRIPA.

Jewish prairie pioneering experience for not only the pioneers' scattered descendants but also Jewish Canadians and Saskatchewan residents at large. Hirsch itself was abandoned in 1942, a victim of the Depression, but when Jews celebrated the centenary of their arrival in western Canada in 1977, they returned to pay homage to its settlers. The Canadian Jewish Congress arranged for a new sign over the cemetery gate, tidying the surviving markers, and recovering and identifying graves obliterated by drifting soil. A plaque erected by the Government of Saskatchewan in cooperation with one-time colonists and their descendants also officially recognized Hirsch colony, hailed by a former area farmer active in the rescue project as "this historic venture in Saskatchewan agriculture." Designation as a Saskatchewan historic site in 1980 strengthened the cemetery in its role of confirming Jews' birthright in the land. Events, attended by over 200 guests from as far away as Montreal and Los Angeles, included singing the Hebrew hymn for the dead and consecration of the site as the "eternal abode" of those buried there. The Honourable Norman

Vickar, minister of industry and commerce and an Edenbridge Jew, also spoke. "Standing here," he said, musing on why the day's ceremonies pulled so many back to Hirsch, "we feel the strength of history. We are in touch with our cultural and natural roots."[30] No longer a site of exclusiveness or exclusion, Hirsch cemetery had come to symbolize that Jews, through their pioneers, occupied a well-earned place in prairie history and society.

Although as immigrants they sought separation from the larger society, prairie Mennonites similarly moved towards self-inclusion. In their case, a rural way of life and longevity on the land forged deep attachment to their reserves and villages and, as focal points, pioneer burial grounds. Rosenfeld cemetery, for example, acquired both a provincial plaque commemorating Mennonite occupation of the West Reserve and a local cairn honouring village pioneers on Manitoba's centennial in 1970. Mennonites also sought to recover the names and graves of pioneer dead, both systematically and as private searches for ancestors buried anonymously, and used tombstones and communal monuments to acknowledge their predecessors.[31] One epitaph paid tribute to six members of the Hiebert family, the first of whom died in 1896, the last in 1955. "In remembrance of the pioneers," it said. "The dead in Christ shall rise first. We shall bear the image of the heavenly." In fact, Mennonite memorials acknowledged the primacy of God or hand of Providence as much as the initiative or legacy of the pioneers. The cemetery plaque erected in 1982, "in honor of our grand and great grand parents and their families who pioneered in the village of Schoenwiese, 1875–1940," illustrated the subtleties of Mennonite pioneer commemoration. The inclusion of Psalm 103:2 ("Bless the Lord, O my soul, and forget not all his benefits") stressed the spiritual. Yet in the context of the plaque—the history of Mennonite settlement on the Canadian prairies—the verse could also be read as time and place specific. "His benefits" then became the freedom of conscience and even economic prosperity that Mennonite immigrants and their descendants found in southern Manitoba. The monument in Steinbach Pioneer Cemetery, erected in memory of the men and women (named individually) who arrived "in the Providence of God" in 1874 to found the village, reinforced identification with Manitoba history. It featured a Red River cart, the traditional Métis transport used by the first Mennonites to reach their land, together with the Steinbach windmill.[32]

Historically like Mennonites in the simplicity of their burials, but openly clashing with the state, Doukhobors also came to see the commemorative value of cemeteries identified with the group's Canadian beginnings. Theirs was a delayed reaction, however, and exposed the competing claims of the prairies and British Columbia to the group experience and narrative. Centennial proposals for recognizing Doukhobor pioneers ranged from a "wall of fame" saluting contributors to Doukhobor life and the "development of Canada" to the erection of plaques in Doukhobor cemeteries.[33] Reflecting the shift in dynamics that attended the exodus from Saskatchewan to British Columbia, and the rejection of communal living by those who stayed behind, the cemetery initiative did not come from the prairies. Rather, led by the Union of Spiritual Communities of Christ, British Columbia Doukhobors both identified most closely with the project and prepared the text then sent to Alberta and Saskatchewan. They were also more apt to install the plaques, which featured the traditional symbols of Doukhoborism: two doves; bread, salt, and water; a sheaf of wheat. "Here rest the remains of Doukhobors, Christian pacifists who came to Canada from Russia in 1899 because of persecution for their life concept and refusal to bear arms," began the text:

> Guided by their belief in 'toil and peaceful life,' they and their descendants overcame hardships, maintained their spiritual and cultural integrity, and contributed to the development of the young country that gave them refuge. Now mother earth has reclaimed the remains of these Spirit Wrestlers and their souls have returned home to rest eternally in God's heavenly kingdom. May their legacy inspire future generations to continue the struggle for peace and freedom.[34]

The historically fraught relationship between Doukhobors and the Canadian state forgotten, the plaque conveyed not just gratitude and the notion of the sheltering Canadian soil but also clearly identified Doukhobor pioneers with nation building.

That Scandinavians and Germans tended to construe their pioneer cemeteries in local terms, rarely identifying with or making claims on behalf of extended ethno-religious communities, reflected group numbers plus dispersal in scattered clusters that impeded a collective consciousness. But it also illustrated that the Lutheran Church and larger faith community often

**7.7.** Successive generations of Ukrainian Canadians remember their pioneer dead at Patterson Lake, Manitoba, 2004. PHOTO BY FRANCES SWYRIPA.

constituted a major, if not the primary point of identification, making pioneer commemoration more religious than secular in emphasis. German Lutheran congregations in rural Alberta erected pioneer memorials that listed the dead in unmarked graves but were silent as to the contribution and legacy of the immigrant generation or Germanness (except by implication as part of faith).[35] The cairn in Christ Lutheran cemetery at Rhein, Saskatchewan, eschewed the notion of the secular pioneer, commemorating not the Volga Germans who settled the land but the pastors who served them and whom they produced.[36] Danish pioneer identity in Dickson, Alberta, took another direction. No memorial existed in the local cemetery, although the cairn on the site of the original Bethany Lutheran Church was dedicated to the pioneers. At the same time, the Pioneer Walk on the grounds of the Danish Canadian National Museum—honouring, by name, Danes from across Canada—stripped the idea of its prairie settlement specificity.[37] In New Iceland the pioneer cairn erected in Gimli in 1935 perhaps dulled the need for commemoration in local

**7.8.** Beth Israel Synagogue and recently erected memorial cairn, Edenbridge, Saskatchewan, 1968. ARCHIVES OF MANITOBA, JHS 1094.

cemeteries. One exception, a monument on Hecla Island "humbly" dedicated to the pioneers by their descendants marked the centennial of the establishment of Hecla village in 1876. It paid tribute to "the Icelandic settlers who through perseverance, strength of character and an enduring faith in God and their adopted island, turned a remote dream into a thriving community of which we were an integral part and which we will always cherish in our memory."[38] The roll of honour inside the adjacent Lutheran church, identifying those who served "King and Country" between 1939 and 1945, claimed broader Canadian ties.

Missing in the rural pioneer cemeteries of immigrant settler peoples were communal monuments to local sons killed in Canada's two world wars. Proliferating across the country after 1918 and altered after 1945 to accommodate new names, cenotaphs tended to go up in towns and villages in high profile and symbolically significant public space.[39] Communities of British or mixed Allied origin saw the logic of this decision. The unity of purpose, sacrifice, and patriotism that war generated cut across both narrow geographic and ethnic boundaries to bind countryside and the local railway centre emotionally as well as economically. In contrast, the absence of war memorials in the cemeteries of eastern Europeans underscored that, despite the overarching pioneering experience, they existed outside and at odds with the dominant culture. As pacifists, Mennonites and Doukhobors had made their conscientious objector status a condition for coming to the prairies, while in 1914 unnaturalized Ukrainians, as subjects of Austria-Hungary, became enemy aliens forbidden to enlist. By 1945 the natural place to remember second-generation Ukrainians who died for their country was with their comrades on the inclusive memorial in the town or village then replacing the rural clusters that had been the core of local Ukrainian identity. Yet immigrant settler peoples from eastern Europe cultivated independent traditions of honouring their war dead. Remembrance went beyond the traditional soldier, blurred the distinction between rural past and urban present, and metaphorically brought groups' European dead to Canadian soil.

Despite the lack of Canadian war memorials in their pioneer cemeteries, Ukrainians and Poles both remembered their Canadian war dead in private ethnic space. After the Second World War, Poles in Alberta and Saskatchewan erected twin monuments at the entrance to the Our Lady of Lourdes shrines at Skaro and Rama. One acknowledged area pioneers and founders of the parish, the other local men, buried in Europe, "who gave their lives for their country." In St. Peter's Colony, Our Lady of Lourdes at Lake Lenore was also dedicated to Second World War servicemen, including those who died in battle.[40] Ukrainian commemoration—at the heritage village Selo Ukraina outside Dauphin, Manitoba, created in conjunction with Canada's National Ukrainian Festival— involved less obviously sacred space. Dedicated to "Ukrainian Canadians who fought and died for Canada," the Tomb of the Unknown Ukrainian Soldier formed the centrepiece of a symbolic place of the dead, the Ukrainian Centennial Memorial Park. Over the years the cenotaph was joined by monuments to the pioneers, those interned as enemy aliens during the Great War, and, from the same conflict, Filip Konowal, winner of the Victoria Cross.[41] Also highlighting the importance of separate remembrance, the cenotaph to Ukrainian-Canadian veterans erected at the Edmonton Norwood (Ukrainian) branch of the Royal Canadian Legion in 2000 represented the centralization of commemoration in the city. Tellingly, the Norwood memorial simultaneously claimed membership in two additional communities, paying tribute to "the Ukrainian pioneers who with courage and perseverance helped build Alberta" and to "all Canadians who gave up their lives for freedom as we know it."[42]

Prairie Jews likewise honoured their Canadian war dead, choosing sites— the cemetery over other group space, the city over the rural colonies—that reflected not only marginalization but also Jewish settlement and lifestyle preferences. In the monument to the "memory of Jewish citizens of Edmonton who gave their lives for freedom and democracy in the war, 1939–1945," in Edmonton's Hebrew cemetery, honouring blood sacrifice around shared Canadian values had a purely local focus. The memorial erected in Shaarey Zedek cemetery in Winnipeg by the General Monash (Jewish) branch of the Royal Canadian Legion was less restricted to place, remembering by name simply those Jews who "offered the supreme sacrifice" in the two world wars.[43] A second monument in the Edmonton cemetery—to victims of the Holocaust, naming the camps where they perished—attested to local Jews' identification with their people and their dead as part of world Jewry. They reaffirmed the ties annually, gathering in the place of their Canadian dead to remember the fate of millions who had stayed in Europe. The Manitoba Holocaust memorial, in contrast, erected in 1990 by the Winnipeg Jewish Community for Holocaust Survivor Families in Manitoba, sat on the legislature grounds, its vertical walls, rising from the arms of a Star of David set into the lawn, recording the names of the perished.

Mennonites and Ukrainians also identified strongly with their overseas dead, but as originally rural settler peoples the eventual choice of urban space for collective commemoration illustrated shifting dynamics not at issue among Jews. The Mennonite Heritage Village in Steinbach accessed old-world dead on two levels. First, both Johann Bartsch and Jakob Höppner, leaders of the exodus from Prussia to the Russian empire, figuratively relocated to Manitoba. Negotiations with Soviet authorities saw the obelisk from Bartsch's grave in southern Ukraine moved to the museum grounds in 1968. Höppner's marker, complete with wrought-iron fence, followed in 1973 as his grave on the island of Chortitza was levelled for a park.[44] Second, a monument at the entrance to the museum grounds remembered Mennonite victims of violence, including women specifically, in the Russian empire and then the Soviet Union. The Ukrainian diaspora consciousness, constructed around old-world dead, and

**7.9.** Bricks outlining where St. Onuphrius Ukrainian Catholic Church once stood, rural Alberta, 2003. PHOTO BY FRANCES SWYRIPA.

fed by the post-1945 displaced persons, produced memorials like that to Ukraine's freedom fighters in Edmonton's St. Michael Ukrainian cemetery, or those to the artificial famine in Soviet Ukraine in 1932–33 outside Edmonton and Winnipeg city halls. The Ukrainian Centennial Memorial Park at Selo Ukraina also remembered both the famine and victims of Soviet tyranny more generally, bringing to the Canadian countryside an event in the homeland that never personally touched the families of pioneers with origins in western Ukraine. In the late twentieth century, the churchyards and cemeteries of the old rural settlement area modestly echoed this politicized and old-world Ukrainianness. Both Catholic and Orthodox commemorated the millennium of Christianity in Ukraine in 1988, sometimes in conjunction with the pioneers. In other instances, the Ukrainianness articulated was purely secular—a trident added to the entrance gate, Ukraine's flag alongside Canadian and provincial flags, or, less aesthetically, the stones of the cairn erected for the golden jubilee of Ukrainian settlement in 1941 painted patriotic blue and yellow.[45]

Through its special relationship with the dead, the cemetery evolved into a major site of pioneer commemoration, connecting the immigrant generation with its successors and them both with a number of interlocking communities. But as a physical presence on the land, the rural church eclipsed the cemetery as *the* symbol of ethno-religious settlement and identity on the prairies. Moreover, the surviving buildings not only acquired iconic status but also became themselves "the pioneer" (the artifact, as opposed to the person) being commemorated. Their preservation, then, both as local landmarks and as symbols of a more intangible legacy for future generations, was important. Yet out-migration left aging and dwindling congregations and churches no longer, or infrequently, used for services. What was to be done with empty or emptying houses of worship transformed into settlement-era ethnic icons, to which faith was often secondary? This question beset local communities, parish committees, and church hierarchies across the prairies. In the early twenty-first century, for example, the oldest Ukrainian Catholic church in Saskatchewan, at Jaroslaw south of Yorkton, stood open to the elements, sagging under the weight of the central cupola, the wood inside buckling and rotting away.[46] Should such structures be converted to other uses? Should they be burned, demolished, or, less drastically, allowed to decay and, slowly reclaimed by the land, serve a heritage industry enamoured of ruins?[47]

The 2004 compendium of over 300 closed Lutheran churches in Saskatchewan preserved a paper record of buildings that once helped define the prairie landscape and residents' lives. For their part, Ukrainians' prairie churches had been systematically documented since 1941, decades before nostalgia for a disappearing past gripped westerners, and in subsequent years projects not just to collect data but to paint and photograph increasingly cherished group symbols escalated.[48] An attractive solution, and one that validated ethno-religious groups and their heritages within the larger prairie context, was to secure municipal, provincial, or even federal historic site or heritage resource status for surviving buildings.[49] Some, like the majestic Ukrainian Catholic Church of the Immaculate Conception at Cooks Creek, Manitoba, were chosen for architectural significance and played no independent historical role in the collective group consciousness. In fact, provincial (1986) and national (2004) recognition raised the Cooks Creek church's profile in the Ukrainian community. The Doukhobor Prayer Home at Veregin had been a major group symbol since constructed in 1917, both as a place of worship and as the leader's residence, so that becoming a Saskatchewan heritage property in 1982 reinforced but did not create its importance. Other buildings, like the

1915 Hegre Norwegian Lutheran church outside Camrose, an Alberta historic site since 1997, had only local significance.[50] But while government recognition meant acceptance and heightened odds of survival, mainstreaming within the context of prairie heritage secularized and commodified houses of worship as historical artifacts, much like the grain elevator or, from an earlier era, the fur trade post. Pioneer prairie churches thus acquired yet another function, as tourist attractions luring visitors to the countryside to buy gas, food, local crafts, and ethnic antiques to boost the area economy.

Whether the impact was local or regional or national, and confined to the pioneers' descendants or encompassing later immigrations, place mattered in the preservation and elevation of prairie pioneer churches to group symbols. If moved from its commanding position above the valley to the north, Hungarians' imposing stone Our Lady of Assumption Roman Catholic Church at Kaposvar would lose much of its aura and authority. Other structures also belonged where they stood, part of the land and its history: the Doukhobor Prayer Home at Veregin; the Benedictines' twin-towered cathedral at Muenster; the white clapboard Icelandic Lutheran church a few metres from Lake Winnipeg on Hecla Island; and the oldest Mennonite church in the West on the wide street dissecting Reinland, Manitoba.[51] But as Edenbridge's Beth Israel Synagogue showed, place turned contentious when segments of the ethno-religious group spurned the land yet valued its artifacts. Established in 1906, and celebrating its silver jubilee during the Great Depression with a parade and speeches, the small Jewish farming community no longer had a *minyan* (quorum for prayer) by the late 1960s when it erected a memorial cairn beside the synagogue. The following decade the Winnipeg-based Jewish Historical Society of Western Canada proposed relocating the building from its isolated site to the Manitoba capital, especially since many of the colony's descendants lived there. Outraged, Edenbridge residents insisted that their synagogue remain in Saskatchewan, perhaps moved to Saskatoon. In the end, it stayed put, and in 1976, on the seventieth anniversary of Edenbridge's founding, a 500-strong pilgrimage marked the synagogue's designation, together with the cemetery, as a provincial historic site.[52]

Separation of the pioneer artifact from its surroundings did occur in the case of tiny St. Onuphrius Ukrainian Catholic Church, built in 1906 north of Smoky Lake, Alberta. Dismantled, its parts catalogued and shipped thousands of kilometres, St. Onuphrius was reassembled and reconsecrated in 1996 as the focal point of the prairie section of Canada Hall in the Canadian Museum of Civilization in Hull, Quebec, across the river from Ottawa. Being showcased on such a national stage transformed the Ukrainian prairie pioneer heritage. It signalled ultimate mainstream appropriation and internalization of the Ukrainian pioneer church as a prairie icon, emblematic of the region's settlement past.[53] It simultaneously legitimized Ukrainians, through their own symbols, as a regional founding people and partners in nation building. No longer part of the land or the West but still evocative of time and place, St. Onuphrius served, in the museum's words, as a "visible symbol ... of the multicultural mosaic that came to typify the [prairie] region" and paid "tribute to the major role that Ukrainians played in developing this country."[54] The inescapable message—that "prairie" was "Ukrainian" and vice versa—privileged the pioneers at the expense of interwar, displaced person, and post-Soviet immigrations; and Catholic at the expense of Orthodox. To outsiders, fixated on the visual stereotype and the historical context it represented, such considerations did not matter.

Yet because St. Onuphrius stayed a living church, displacement led to a new role in the religious calendar of Ottawa-area Ukrainians. On the Feast of Theophany (19 January) a procession to the Ottawa River for the ritual blessing of the waters under an ice cross followed a special service in the museum church. Some worshippers were transplanted westerners reconnecting with their roots; others had never been exposed to the Ukrainian prairie experience but now accessed its heritage as part of their spiritual lives. However, if St. Onuphrius escaped secularization and commodification as a historical artifact, a "museum event" open to the casual public and media cameras threatened to commercialize faith. (When descendants of the pioneer parish had their baby baptised in the church in 2008, staff kept museum visitors out).[55] Meanwhile, at the end of the tree-lined trail leading to St. Onuphrius cemetery and bell tower in the Alberta countryside, only a plaque and a brick outline on the ground marked where the church once welcomed its rural congregation.

\*   \*   \*

From a simple cairn on the old family homestead to an entire church rebuilt on the Ontario-Quebec border, commemorating and preserving the pioneer past of immigrant settler peoples on the prairies had a single goal—to ensure that memory of the pioneers, their achievements, and their presence on the land survived. When a generic pioneer figure and heritage dominated as part of a common western legacy, local and regional identities tended to merge and ethno-religious consciousness was muted. Emphasis on the pioneer and pioneer heritage as ethno-religious phenomena reflected and reinforced a group narrative and identity whose ties extended beyond the immediate locality and region. It also embraced and mobilized group members other than the pioneers' descendants, confirming the larger importance of the Canadian prairie settlement experience, while facilitating its separation from the land to which it belonged. Finally, ethnicity and religion came to inform the West's own self-image and identity, as well as the stereotypes of outsiders, with diversity understood to be integral to the regional fabric.

**8.1.** Detail of *Landing at Willow Point*, Arni Sigurðsson's iconic painting of arrival in New Iceland in 1875. ARCHIVES OF MANITOBA, N21194.

# Pilgrimage: The Land as "Sacred Ground" and Gathering Point

ONE AUTUMN DAY THREE WOMEN, all related but from different generations, packed a lunch and walked two and one-half kilometres along the shore of Lake Winnipeg south of Gimli to the spot they had selected for a picnic. The beach, when they reached it, was sandy, marshy, and strewn with reeds, but comfort mattered little as they headed for the rock that loomed over the lapping water to unwrap and share the food they had prepared. The date was 21 October 1975. Exactly 100 years earlier the first Icelandic immigrants, and the women's own ancestors, had stepped onto dry land here at Willow Point and been sheltered by White Rock until they struck out, on foot, to find a suitable settlement site. On this historic occasion, the trio completed their personal pilgrimage by retracing their steps, and those of their forebears, back into Gimli.

The notion of pilgrimage in conjunction with millennial anniversaries of immigration and settlement captured the imagination, well beyond this private journey, as return to and gathering on the land became part of community commemoration and ritual. But unlike the preservation of material cultural heritages, pilgrimage in western Canada focussed not on the entire territory associated with an ethno-religious group, but on specific landmarks within that space central to its collective memory and identity. Some peoples elevated the point of first arrival or a particular settlement site to "sacred ground," marked with cairns and formally revisited on special occasions. The most elaborate traditions crystallized around Willow Point, where a private grassroots gesture evolved into a public event; and, representing organized community initiatives, the junction of the Rat and the Red rivers in Manitoba (Mennonites), the Edna-Star colony in Alberta (Ukrainians), and the village of Veregin in Saskatchewan (Doukhobors). Moreover, a handful of traditional sacred pilgrimage sites acquired auxiliary secular functions tied to a group's settlement history. Each of the big immigrant shrines—Our Lady of Lourdes at Skaro, Our Lady of Mount Carmel in St. Peter's Colony, and the Grotto Golgotha in Mundare — illustrated this interplay among faith, the land, and ethnicity. A third gathering point involved the grave sites of a group's founding fathers. For many peoples, the placement and wording of the tombstone paid homage enough. Others, intent on greater communal recognition, erected monuments in the cemetery or churchyard. A select few transformed the grave into a place of pilgrimage and exploited its symbolism as a physical link to both their Canadian prairie roots and the homeland. As with other forms of commemoration and preservation of the past, pilgrimage embraced a return to the land that united different immigrations and generations, the city and the countryside, and westerners with group members in other parts of the country.

## Landing Sites and Settlement Sites as "Sacred Ground"

Elevating landing sites and settlement sites to "sacred ground" asserted a group's claim to a particular piece of the prairies for all time and against all comers. Always part of the collective consciousness or entering it years later, large or small, accessible or remote—the site was significant because of its association with beginnings. This privileging of place around a group's prairie origins created a situation reminiscent of the impact of the St. Lawrence Valley on the French-Canadian psyche.[1] Although such prairie homelands increasingly meant little in practical terms, especially with out-migration from the old rural settlements, they continued to pull people back to them. Individual pilgrims no doubt came for primarily sentimental and nostalgic reasons, curious about their personal roots or wishing to connect more generally with their people and their history. For the organized ethno-religious community, the journey constituted a ritual whose broader elements served often complex group agenda and identities.

When the flatboats carrying Icelandic settlers were cut adrift from the steamboat towing them and the occupants poled their way to the western shore of Lake Winnipeg, the landing at Willow Point heralded the beginnings of New Iceland. Both landing and site always figured in the Icelandic-Canadian story, burned into the collective memory of generations and immortalized in poetry, song, pictures, and monuments. Equally integral to the story, White Rock marked not only where the tired newcomers quit their transport, sought protection from the elements, and erected their tents, but also where, according to legend, that night they welcomed the first child born to the colony. Over the decades no other prairie settler people interacted with their landing or settlement site with the ritualized regularity and intensity of Icelandic Canadians. Their attachment testified to the emotional impact of place and beginnings, certainly, but also to the unambiguous claims of Willow Point and White Rock and the continued concentration of the settlers' descendants in New Iceland and vicinity.

The catalyst for large-scale official mobilization of Willow Point in community life and mythology was the seventy-fifth anniversary of the founding of New Iceland in 1950, although nothing then predicted the enduring popularity of two by-products of the celebration. The first, Frank Olson's poem "Willow Point" hailing arrival "in the promised land," would be reprinted and recited on important occasions to become itself one of the rituals of commemoration. The poem paid homage to the "Vikings in the West" who tamed the frontier, introduced democracy, created prosperous farms, preserved their cultural heritage, and dispatched their descendants across Canada.[2] The second by-product, Arni Sigurðsson's oil painting *Landing at Willow Point*, soon metamorphosed into an iconic image comparable to the onion-domed pioneer church among Ukrainians. But unlike the generic Ukrainian image, the Icelandic painting evoked and visually froze a specific moment in time, tied directly to the group's founding story. So important did this picture become that in 1973 the original was acquired on behalf of the community by the Icelandic Cultural Corporation, later the New Iceland Heritage Museum in Gimli, where it would hang. A copy in the reading room of the Icelandic Collection at the University of Manitoba's Dafoe Library also dignified symbolic group space. In 2000 the potential viewership of *Landing at Willow Point* was consciously broadened to coincide with New Iceland's 125th anniversary. The actual painting went temporarily to the Manitoba Museum of Man and Nature in Winnipeg for its millennium exhibit, while large canvas reproductions allowed people to own and display the picture in their homes. As well, the image appeared on an official commemorative stamp issued in Iceland by the Postal Administration on 9 October, with first day cancellations featuring a Canadian maple leaf and the date.[3]

Both the landing and Willow Point were also incorporated directly into Icelandic community ritual. The pioneer cairn in Gimli, originally proposed for New Iceland's golden jubilee (and made of stones picked from the beach), was unveiled on 21 October 1935, the anniversary of the landing. And, when the president of Iceland visited Manitoba during Canada's Centennial, wreath-laying ceremonies occurred not only at the statues of Jón Sigurðsson at the legislature and the Viking statue in Gimli but also at White Rock, rededicated after receiving a new base. The most meaningful ritualization of the landing site, however, emerged from the now historic walk of Connie Magnusson, her mother Sigga Benedicktson, and her aunt Herdis Einarsson, upset that Willow Point had no role in the Icelandic centennial celebrations. The women subsequently made their pilgrimage a yearly one, others joined, and by the 125th anniversary of the founding of New Iceland, the "Walk to the Rock" had become a formalized event sponsored by the Gimli chapter of the Icelandic National League. For several years local schoolchildren had been bused to the site to participate in the ceremonies, while in the classroom they learned about its history and significance. In 2000 walkers braved a bitter wind to watch the prime minister of Iceland lay a wreath and praise the courage and faith of his countrymen who came "ashore at this location and persevered through great hardships ... to make their dream of better life come true." A descendant of the pioneers articulated the point of the excursion and emotional pull of White Rock more explicitly. "It was very good," she reflected, "to remember, in this very visceral way, our forebears, who, with this journey, began our journey in North America."[4]

Finally, Gimli itself became a pilgrimage destination for Icelandic Canadians. That it would acquire such a mantle was never guaranteed given its remote location, especially prior to rail (announced only in 1905) and road connections with the south. Then, too, it faced a competitor in Winnipeg, which by the early twentieth century had almost twice as many Icelandic residents as New Iceland.[5] Gimli's victory over Winnipeg as the Icelandic mecca ended the first rural-urban rivalry for control of a settler people's imagination and

**8.2.** Dappled light playing on the gateway to the monument at the junction of the Rat and Red rivers where in 1874 the first Mennonites disembarked, 2001.
PHOTO BY FRANCES SWYRIPA.

identity. It also cemented the pre-eminence of New Iceland in group memory and ritual; even Icelandic Americans with new-world roots in the settlement, but no emotional attachment to Winnipeg, came "home" to participate in events. Crucial to the shift of focus from metropolis to hinterland, in 1932 the annual Icelandic festival, held in Winnipeg since 1889, moved to Gimli "in the heart of New Iceland [and] within reach of smaller Icelandic communities" in hopes of reversing a decline in interest. Over 3000 people attended the first Gimli festival, three times more than in its final years in Winnipeg. Besides a large contingent from the city, participants included hundreds of area residents "who had seldom bothered to make the trip to Winnipeg" and felt excluded from the mainstream of community life there. The festival's new home, Gimli Park, was an identifiably Icelandic space, which consolidated the ethnic character and role of the event. It also facilitated the transformation of Gimli into an annual gathering point—for local residents, returning descendants, and interested Icelanders from across Canada and the United States—to celebrate

**8.3.** Ukrainian-Canadian centennial monument, blending into the land, erected in 1991 in Edna-Star, 2003. PHOTO BY FRANCES SWYRIPA.

their origins and heritage and to honour the pioneers.[6] A new feature for the millennium festival in 2000, "Thingvellir Nýja Ísland," reinforced Gimli's attractiveness and function as a pilgrimage destination. It appropriated the notion of the ancient Icelandic place of assembly to create a series of tents, each representing a single Icelandic settlement, that acted as Homecoming Headquarters for visitors to "connect with family and friends."[7]

Prairie Mennonites, like Icelanders, celebrated an unambiguous starting point for their unfolding prairie story. From the moment the initial party of sixty-five families reached the junction of the Rat and the Red and abandoned the sternwheeler *International* for dry land, this modest spot assumed symbolic proportions. However unimpressive and unwelcoming the river bank in reality, it represented a final break with the suffering and broken promises of the past and a definitive step towards the hopes and dreams of the future. Among both Mennonite pioneers and their descendants, the junction of the Rat and the Red thus functioned similarly to Willow Point and White Rock, albeit without quite the same connotations of "sacred ground." But physical differences between Mennonite and Icelandic landing sites affected their evolution as group symbols. Just outside Gimli, Willow Point lay at the symbolic heart of New

Iceland; the junction of the Rat and the Red, in contrast, lay not on Mennonite land in the East Reserve but several kilometres west near the French community of Ste. Agathe.

The question of the role that the Rat and the Red might play in prairie Mennonite community life emerged in conjunction with the group's centennial celebrations in 1974. As one flashpoint, the controversy over the proposed anniversary monument concerned not only its form and imagery but also the best venue to convey its message. At issue was the relative symbolism of the inconspicuous meeting of the waterways where the celebrants' ancestors first stepped onto prairie soil versus a high-profile public location on the Manitoba Legislature grounds. Although those approached to execute the project favoured the historically significant group space, the urban site and mainstream legitimacy it conferred prevailed. "What more meaningful a place to commemorate our centennial," remonstrated one unhappy commentator, "than the very spot our forefathers first landed one hundred years ago?"

> But no, it seemed our leaders felt a certain economic threat from developing this location, a threat to the museum at Steinbach where such a large investment had already been made. It had already been decided that the site of the monument was to be on the grounds of the Manitoba Legislative Building, "at the crossroads of Manitoba life." Here we would take our rightful place, as part of the Manitoba mosaic, along with the other ethnic groups (Queen Victoria, Robby Burns, Taras Shevchenko, and Louis Riel?).[8]

The Rat and the Red were, in fact, incorporated into the centennial celebrations with a "dramatized meditation" on 1874 staged near the spot where the rivers joined. As the spirits of the first arrivals welcomed their descendants to the "historic ground" that began "the adventure in faith for which you are honoring us today," they confirmed the Janus-like symbolism of the site in looking backward and forward at once. A journey half way around the world "undertaken in answer to God's command, in hopes of a brighter future, in the faith that with God's help all present and future obstacles would be overcome," the spirits said, following the script their descendants penned, "both ended and began on this river bank."[9]

When prairie Mennonites celebrated their 120th anniversary two decades later, the junction received the official recognition denied in 1974, with the creation of a small park cut among the vegetation along the east bank of the Red after it swallowed the Rat. At this out-of-the-way spot, unmarked from the secondary highway that provided access, Governor General Edward Schreyer (a former premier of Manitoba) unveiled a granite monument at the end of a tree-lined path. Beneath an engraving of the iconic *International*, a lengthy text explained the meaning of the site and outlined the immigration and settlement history of Mennonites "from German-speaking colonies in south Russia (Ukraine)." It also paid tribute to the pioneers who had been "among the first Europeans to establish farm communities on open prairie," the successful transplantation of "their nonresistant church-centered ways of life," and a legacy of "courage and faith in God."[10] Whatever Mennonites thought of their memorial's sentiments, it attracted unwanted attention from visitors holding a different view of history. By fall 2001 the monument had been vandalized; someone, presumably with Ukrainian territorial or nationalist sympathies, had chiselled out "Russia" to leave only "Ukraine" as the Mennonite homeland.

Nothing in the story of Ukrainian origins in Canada compared to the role that the Rat and the Red or Willow Point played in Mennonite or Icelandic consciousness. Winnipeg, the obvious landing site in the West, aroused few emotions, serving for most immigrants as a temporary stop and transfer point that marked the start not the end of the prairie leg of their journey. That Ukrainians felt the absence of a clear, symbolically charged landing site to officially date their beginnings became apparent during the centennial celebrations of 1991, when the Ukrainian Canadian Congress erected a commemorative statue not in Quebec, where Ivan Pylypiw and Vasyl Eleniak landed, but the city of Halifax. There, a short distance from Pier 21, where thousands of immigrants of all sorts entered Canada, a stylized human figure extended the traditional Ukrainian welcome of bread and salt.[11] Within the prairies, Ukrainians received no tract of land, legally defined and set aside, to gravitate to and identify as theirs. Vigorous and competing nuclei across the West also blunted the status of "first" and "oldest" claimed by the settlement of Edna-Star in Alberta. Yet that status, bolstered by Dr. Osyp Oleskiv's endorsement of the area for emigrating Ukrainian peasants, and the fact that both founding fathers settled there, guaranteed the colony's pre-eminence in the Ukrainian-Canadian imagination.

**8.4.** Doukhobors mark *Petrov Den* and fifty years in Canada in front of the Prayer Home in Veregin, Saskatchewan, 1949. SASKATCHEWAN ARCHIVES BOARD, S-B9644.

The impact of the Ukrainian bloc east of Edmonton could be seen in the unparalleled attention the area received over the decades from professional and popular historians, folklorists, novelists, and others. The Ukrainian Canadian Congress acknowledged the significance of Edna-Star in 1991 by launching its national centennial celebrations in Alberta, choosing Edmonton for the big showcase events but the countryside for quieter, more symbolic gatherings.[12] A 100-kilometre torch relay, retracing the trek of the first settlers to their homesteads, went from Old Strathcona, where Ukrainian immigrants detrained before construction of a railway in central Edmonton north of the river, to Lamont in the heart of the old bloc. Several hundred people then joined a fifteen-kilometre "fun run" to the first settlement site at Star; others did the more sedate "Pioneer Walk" from the nearby Russo-Greek Orthodox Church of the Holy Transfiguration. At the site, Canada's deputy prime minister and local member of Parliament, Don Mazankowski, ignited a centennial flame, using the torch lit that morning in Edmonton by descendants of Pylypiw and Eleniak. The unveiling of a permanent marker followed. Lying flat against the ground on a flat piece of land surrounded by grain fields, the slab blended into the landscape, almost invisible from the road a few metres away. Its design—a world map with an arrow from the immigrants' native village of Nebyliv to their new home at Star, and a second map plotting Ukrainian settlement in Canada—captured the importance of place to Ukrainian-Canadian identity. The text then narrowed this identity to the individual homestead. "In commemoration," it read,

> of Ivan Pylypow and Wasyl Eleniak whose arrival in 1891 led to the first permanent settlement of Ukrainians in Canada, as follows: Mykhailo Pullishy, May 7, 1894 on N.W. 22-56-19 W4 and followed within one month by Wasyl Feniak on S.E. 22 and Fedor Melnyk on N.E. 22. Together, these families spent the first winter within a few meters of this marker. Ivan Pylypow settled on S.W. 22 in September 1894.[13]

On a day full of symbolism, the most palpably patriotic gesture was the collective reaffirmation by those present of their Canadian citizenship, two judges of Ukrainian origin presiding over the oath.

Two final settlement sites to acquire broad group connotations and functions as "sacred ground" evolved quite differently. Being divinely chosen as the site of a temple immediately declared the Mormon town of Cardston in southern Alberta special. According to a descendant of founding father Charles Ora Card writing at the end of the twentieth century, both this temple and Card's nearby log house performed important group roles, "symboliz[ing] home, durability and permanence."[14] Yet, by then, Canadian Mormonism and its birthplace had long transcended not only their original associations with prairie immigration and settlement but also their American cultural roots. Pilgrims to Cardston accessed a common religious identity and heritage but represented great ethnic diversity. The Doukhobor village of Veregin shared similarities with Cardston. It, too, immortalized the group's founding father, Peter "the Lordly" Verigin; and it, too, housed the group's pre-eminent religious structure, the 1917 Prayer Home where Doukhobors worshipped and two generations of Verigins lived on the upper floor. It was here, as well, that Doukhobors gathered on Petrov Den for special communal prayers and thanksgiving on both the fiftieth and 100th anniversaries of life in Canada. Unlike Cardston, Veregin the village was not part of group beginnings, having

**8.5.** Lighted candles at the Skaro shrine honour local Poles killed overseas during the Second World War, Feast of the Assumption, 2005.
PHOTO BY FRANCES SWYRIPA.

emerged only with the railway, but it became their physical symbol, consciously reinforced in 1980 when the National Doukhobor Heritage Village opened. Its centrepiece, the Prayer Home was designated a provincial historic property two years later, at which time the government of Saskatchewan stressed its "traditional position as the cultural and religious centre for Doukhobors in the nation."[15]

As symbols of beginnings, some prairie landing or settlement sites—like Boian for Alberta Romanians, or Hirsch and Edenbridge for descendants of their Jewish founders—never entertained national aspirations. The claims on the larger group consciousness of other sites varied. At one extreme, although celebrated as the cradle of Hungarian life in Canada, displacing the earlier Huns Valley, Esterhazy-Kaposvar never captured the Hungarian-Canadian imagination in the manner of Willow Point or Edna-Star. As a focal point for group commemoration and pilgrimage, Kaposvar with its stone church and rectory, cemetery, and shrine acted on local and regional levels. The addition of cairns and plaques, Stations of the Cross in memory of the pioneers, and heritage buildings (moved from the surrounding countryside in the 1980s) reaffirmed this limited identity.[16] That Kaposvar failed to become associated with beginnings among the group as a whole in the manner of Ukrainian and Icelandic sites reflected in part the disjuncture in the group history that saw urban Ontario so decisively undercut rural Saskatchewan. At the other extreme, the tiny Alberta hamlet of Dickson at the centre of the first Danish settlement on the prairies shed its local and regional profile for new nationwide prominence. Supported by the Federation of Danish Associations in Canada, a local heritage initiative grew into the Danish Canadian National Museum, which depicted the Danish experience, past and present, from across the country. The museum's grand opening in 2002 illustrated this pan-Canadianism. "Honoured pioneer" encompassed all "senior Danish-Canadian immigrants," regardless of when they came or where they settled, and, with the exception of the dedication of the small church, official speeches conveyed little sense of time and place.[17] Yet assurances that Dickson was the right location for a national Danish museum privileged a particular time and place in the group story and consciousness, based on its roots and enduring presence in the land in the West.

## Pioneer Shrines as Secularized and Politicized Sites

If landing and settlement sites acquired quasi-spiritual characteristics, the major immigrant shrines of the pioneer era pushed the relationship among faith, the land, and ethnicity in a secular direction. Over the decades, in addition to their roles as deeply spiritual places and foci for worship, the shrines at Skaro, Mount Carmel, and Mundare helped mark milestone anniversaries of immigration and settlement. The line between sacred and secular was most blurred, and the group in question most circumscribed, in the case of Mount Carmel's identification with St. Peter's Colony of German Catholics. Skaro, in contrast, represented Alberta Poles' provincial ethnic identity and history, while Mundare reflected the merger of regional prairie and national founding narratives in Ukrainian consciousness. Skaro also fused ethnic community and Catholic faith, but religion excluded Orthodox Ukrainians from Mundare. Nonetheless, all three shrines highlighted the need to observe landmark anniversaries by communally returning to sacred space identified with beginnings. As gathering places for the faithful, both Skaro and Mount Carmel expanded beyond their Polish and German bases to tear down the walls that ethnicity had erected within settlement-era Roman Catholicism. Ukrainians' Byzantine rite hampered the same development at Mundare.

In some ways, Our Lady of Lourdes shrine at Skaro substituted for a Polish settlement or landing site in community commemoration and ritual because it lacked competition from a secular provincial founding narrative. When Alberta Poles celebrated their centennial in 1995, Skaro figured not only among the multiple images in the monument eventually erected in Edmonton but also in events themselves. A special jubilee Mass during the annual pilgrimage attested to the shrine's iconic stature, past and present, uniting rural descendants of the original settlers with recent immigrants in the city. The fact that Poles had gathered in this holy place on the Feast of the Assumption for seventy-six of their 100 years in Alberta assisted its transformation into *the* symbol of the group's pioneering credentials and birthright in the land. It also gave the surrounding Polish settlement priority of place against potential rivals in the provincial story. By eliminating the problem of contested or exclusionary sites, denominational unity—where Catholicism historically defined Polishness—reinforced the shrine's status in Polish beginnings and life.

Skaro's secular outreach had other dimensions. By the early twenty-first century, the candlelight procession during the pilgrimage saw glowing candles placed not only on ancestral graves in the adjacent cemetery but also, attesting to a broader Canadian identity, at the foot of the cairn to local men lost in the Second World War. In 1967 beautification of the shrine and grounds had been a Canadian Centennial project. Identification with Poland and Polish Catholicism also had specific expressions. In 1966 Skaro drew 6000 worshippers on the millennium of Christianity in Poland and shortly thereafter welcomed the unknown Polish cardinal, Karol Wojtyła, soon to become Pope John Paul II. At times the pilgrimage included a Ukrainian Divine Liturgy. This openness towards Poles' immediate neighbours, regardless of ethnicity or rite, graduated to the incorporation of Our Lady of Lourdes into the rituals of mainstream prairie Catholicism. Skaro, for example, was chosen for a special pilgrimage marking the seventy-fifth anniversary of the establishment of the Catholic Women's League in the Archdiocese of Edmonton.[18]

The evolution of Our Lady of Mount Carmel both echoed and diverged from the path adopted by Our Lady of Lourdes. Most significantly, the strong sense of identity characterizing St. Peter's Colony from its inception meant that as a participant in landmark anniversaries of immigration and settlement the Saskatchewan shrine predated its Polish counterpart in Alberta. The marble statue of Mary was blessed already on the colony's silver jubilee in 1928. Fifty years later, the annual July pilgrimage constituted one of two highlights of its seventy-fifth anniversary, to which, in keeping with the settlement's American and ecclesiastical roots, the head of the Benedictines' mother abbey in Pennsylvania was invited. Like Skaro, Mount Carmel acquired secular Canadian patriotic associations when, in 1967, the recently closed Conception parish donated the huge bell it had acquired in 1927 as a Centennial gift. And, like Skaro, Mount Carmel reached out to its Byzantine-rite Ukrainian neighbours, a sign of greater openness to come. Yet Germanness receded to the background, so that of the three shrines under discussion, Mount Carmel least identified with its ethnic roots. It also early integrated into mainstream prairie Catholicism, attracting 12,000 pilgrims to inaugurate the Saskatchewan Family Rosary Crusade in 1948.[19]

With construction of the Grotto Golgotha in Mundare in the 1930s, the much older pilgrimage on the Feast of Sts. Peter and Paul immediately refocussed around the shrine. Under the Basilian Fathers, both pilgrimage and shrine helped sensitize the village to secular Ukrainian landmarks in the surrounding countryside, including the historical significance of Edna-Star. They also lifted Mundare above dozens of similar centres in the Ukrainian blocs as a natural headquarters for collective commemoration and celebration. On the fiftieth anniversary of Ukrainian immigration and settlement in 1941, a mammoth two-day celebration in honour of the pioneers attracted over 7000 participants. Dressed in a suit and clutching several stalks of wheat in his hand, octogenarian Vasyl Eleniak rode down Main Street on a float laden with symbols of Ukrainian homesteading: miniature plastered, whitewashed, and thatch-roofed cottage; outdoor clay oven; wattle fence woven from willow branches; sheaves of grain. The Ukrainian Catholic bishop travelled from Winnipeg to officiate at a Divine Liturgy at the grotto, when Eleniak again received special recognition. Ten years later 10,000 people came for the sixtieth anniversary of Ukrainian immigration and settlement, requiring a special train from Edmonton to transport outside guests. In 1991 so many people crowded into Mundare for the annual pilgrimage, its theme the Ukrainian-Canadian centennial, that the town ran out of food. The broadened base of post-war participants at anniversary services at the grotto underscored Mundare's role in communal rituals of remembrance derived from its association with both immigrant beginnings and a tradition of religious pilgrimage. Most obvious were the ranks of Edmonton youth in the uniform of the Ukrainian scouting organization Plast, introduced to Canadian cities by the displaced persons immigration but foreign to the rural blocs of the settlement era.[20]

The custom among some settler peoples to announce their arrival on the prairies, and proclaim their faith and interest in the land, by erecting private crosses or family shrines disappeared with their descendants. Nonetheless, the latter often assumed responsibility for maintaining or replacing what they inherited. It was also extremely rare for surviving settlers or their children, even when still on the land, to equate their personal immigration and settlement stories with landmark anniversaries of the larger ethno-religious group by erecting new crosses or shrines. An exception in its timing (built the year before Ukrainians' golden jubilee), the stone "jubilee pioneer chapel" next to the road on the family farm northeast of Mundare immortalized Petro and Paraska Siracky. Left open for passersby, by the late twentieth century the chapel had acquired a guest book and the ambiance of "public property" as a stop on the itinerary of chartered buses touring area churches.[21]

## Grave Sites as "Sacred Sites" and Places of Pilgrimage

Community commemoration and ritual around the grave sites of ethno-religious groups' founding fathers signalled the deliberate transformation of private into public space. The two developments involved permanent statements on the landscape (special markers, tombstone inscriptions, and monuments) as well as pilgrimages where group members gathered to pay their respects or celebrate landmark events. The form adopted depended on several factors. Most immigrant settler peoples were too few, too scattered, or too localized in their history and identity to produce a single dominant figure of homage focussed on place of burial. Yet a handful not only celebrated founding fathers whose influence ranged from local to national but also appreciated the

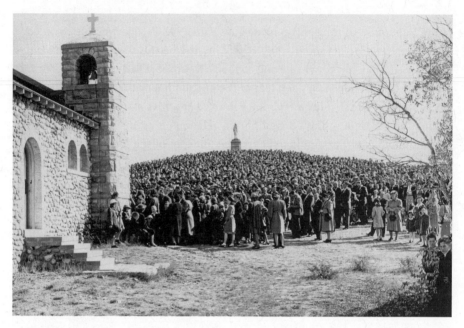

**8.6.** Saskatchewan Family Rosary Crusade, Our Lady of Mount Carmel shrine, St. Peter's Colony, 1948. ARCHIVES OF THE ORDER OF ST. BENEDICT, ST. PETER'S ABBEY.

symbolic potential of their bodies and resting places. Three pioneer peoples—Icelanders, Doukhobors, and Ukrainians—possessed not one but two figures and grave sites to attract monuments, pilgrims, and community rituals.

Some grave sites—like that of David J. Kautonen in New Finland cemetery, his tombstone inscribed simply "Our First Settler, 1888"—had purely local significance and made minimal fuss.[22] There were also individuals who, although widely regarded as founding fathers, left no grave sites to attract either pilgrims or monuments. The Reverend (later Bishop) George Exton Lloyd stayed in the Barr Colony a mere two years and died in Victoria; "Count" Paul O. d'Esterhazy visited the prairies, and his colony, only briefly; Mormon Charles Ora Card returned to Utah after falling ill; and Baron Maurice de Hirsch of the Jewish Colonization Association never set foot in Canada. The absence of a grave site did not necessarily exclude formal remembrance. Jews at Edenbridge, for example, marked the centennial of the birth of their benefactor in 1931 with a program in the local hall. On a stage decorated with his "huge portrait ... [surrounded by] sheaves of grain, adorned with stalks of corn," speeches and songs celebrated the tangible results of Hirsch's dream of putting Jews on the land.[23] Recognition of regional Mennonite founding fathers, who often doubled as religious leaders, involved both cemetery commemoration and monuments in lieu of grave sites. Years after his death in 1897, the tombstone of the Reverend Heinrich Wiebe, one of the scouting party of 1873 who eventually settled in the West Reserve, where he died, was moved to a cairn near Gretna. Another cairn, unveiled in 2000 in Rosengart cemetery, remembered the leadership of Johann Wiebe, whose grave had no marker, alongside "the pioneer congregation he served." Finally, a cairn at nearby Shanzenfeld honoured Ontario Mennonite Jacob Shantz, who had recommended Manitoba to Mennonites from the Russian empire.[24]

The German Catholic descendants of St. Peter's Colony, the largest and most cohesive ethno-religious settlement with a purely regional identity, also had religious leaders as founding fathers. That two priests vied for the title reflected the colony's dual origins as a joint German Catholic and agricultural initiative. One candidate was Father Bruno Doerfler, whose 1902 scouting mission secured official approval for the venture, from both the Canadian government and his Order of St. Benedict in the United States, and determined the colony's location. The other candidate, Prior Alfred Mayer, presided over the transfer of the Benedictine community at Cluny, Illinois, to Saskatchewan. Although he returned to the United States after three years, Mayer was closely identified with the history of the spiritual community of Benedictine monks, and thus with St. Peter's Colony as a specifically religious enterprise. Doerfler was associated with the genesis and early life of the colony more broadly, but after replacing Mayer as prior and then becoming abbot of the elevated St. Peter's Abbey in 1911, he acquired special status in the Benedictine narrative as well.

Falling unexpectedly ill in spring 1919, Abbot Bruno was one of the first pioneer monks to die. His funeral at the new church at Muenster attracted some 3500 mourners as well as a Saskatchewan government representative and Catholic prelates (including the Ukrainian bishop, Nykyta Budka) from across the prairies. Commemoration came swiftly if anonymously, when Berthold Imhoff, who had just begun painting the church's interior, chose the face of the monk he much admired for St. Paul high in the nave.[25] Abbot Bruno was buried in the parish cemetery, but in 1923, on the twentieth anniversary of the founding of St. Peter's Colony, was reinterred in the monastic cemetery at the abbey under a black granite monument. After a Requiem Mass at the cathedral for the repose of the souls of Abbot Bruno and departed settlers, a parade depicting the history of the colony wound through Muenster to the abbey, followed by a short service at the new grave site. *St. Peter's Messenger* praised the life and work of the man "sprung from sturdy German stock" who, like other pioneer priests, had helped open the West, and whose legacy lay in the prosperity of the colony he founded, led, and promoted. Although the abbey complex figured prominently in subsequent landmark anniversaries, official events at Abbot Bruno's grave did not. Yet the monastic cemetery possessed far-reaching symbolic significance for the Benedictines. In 1929, almost two decades after his death, the remains of Prior Oswald Moosmueller, founder of their original community at Cluny, were exhumed and reburied at St. Peter's Abbey. Thus, the man whose death set in motion the relocation of his monks north of the forty-ninth parallel came to his final rest on the Canadian prairies.[26]

Without dominating founding father figures, Scandinavians had no grave sites to exploit as group symbols or to incorporate into community ritual. Icelanders were the exception. As the first head of New Iceland's council, and an active participant in the controversies that rent the young colony, Sigtryggur Jónasson had a complicated relationship with his fellow immigrants and the settlement's formative years. It affected his reputation both then and among future generations. Looking back on the 125th anniversary of the landing at Willow Point, local historian Nelson Gerrard lamented Jónasson's marginalization during his lifetime. "There is irony," he wrote,

> in the fact that this great man spent his last years humbly, his achievements increasingly forgotten or unknown. Though he was honoured by his contemporaries on more than one occasion over the years, Sigtryggur outlived most of those who had been the direct beneficiaries of his personal acts of kindness and charity, and at the time of his death at age 90 in 1942, his modest funeral provided scant evidence that he was being borne to the grave one of the most noble and accomplished Icelandic Canadians of all time.[27]

**8.7.** Landscaped and well-tended Ukrainian Catholic shrine at Mundare, Alberta, c. 1955. BASILIAN FATHERS MUSEUM, PH000220.

The tombstone marking Jónasson's grave in Riverton cemetery along the Icelandic River identified the occupant as "Capt." Sigtryggur Jónasson, "Father of the First Icelandic Settlement of Canada." Blind to the claims of earlier settlements in Nova Scotia and Ontario, or the distant Vikings, those few words reaffirmed the primacy of New Iceland in the group origins story and subsequent narrative. More public recognition of Jónasson—through a community monument in the cemetery or collective homage at his grave as part of the festival or landmark anniversary celebrations focussed on nearby Gimli—never materialized. He was, however, acknowledged with a plaque in Gimli and, in 1976, on the centennial of the founding of the village, a memorial in Riverton itself.[28]

What Jónasson failed to achieve the Alberta homesteader and poet Stephan G. Stephansson reaped. Moreover, the Icelandic-born Stephansson—who lived in Wisconsin and Dakota Territory before homesteading at Markerville in

**8.8.** Grave of Abbot Bruno Doerfler, founder of St. Peter's Colony, Benedictine cemetery, Muenster, Saskatchewan, 2009. PHOTO BY FRANCES SWYRIPA.

**8.9.** Grave of poet Stephan Stephansson, popular with Icelandic visitors to his nearby homestead, Markerville, Alberta, 2002. PHOTO BY FRANCES SWYRIPA.

1889—was revered as much, if not more, in his homeland as among Icelanders in Canada. In the 1990s, for example, President Ólafur Ragnar Grímsson chose one of his poems for the traditional ceremony accompanying the oath of office, while a Reykjavík hotel featured Stephansson in one of its literary-themed rooms.[29] The man known in Iceland as the Poet of the Rocky Mountains also received a monument, erected by the government in 1953 on the centenary of his birth and unveiled by his Canadian daughter. Constructed of rocks, it was located near his birthplace of Vatnsskarð atop a stony outcrop thinly covered with vegetation and ringed by mountains.[30] The Historic Sites and Monuments Board of Canada had acknowledged Stephansson three years earlier, with a cairn on the edge of Markerville in a picnic and sports ground that provided no visibility. The restoration and opening to the public of Stephansson House (an Alberta Provincial Historic Resource since 1976) on the family homestead a few miles to the north in 1982 remedied the situation.[31] Stephansson himself died in 1927 at age seventy-three and was buried close by in a small private cemetery. The large stone cairn erected by family, friends, and admirers bore a stanza from one of his most loved poems, stressing the emigrant's bond with the homeland:

> Though you have trodden in travel
> All the wide tracts of the earth,
> Bear yet the dreams of your bosom
> Back to the land of your birth.

Stephansson's grave never became a site of ritualized pilgrimage among Icelanders in Canada, but it attracted casual visitors. It also attracted visitors from Iceland: ordinary tourists, the ambassador who called his homage a "religious experience," his successor who insisted that the grave be added to his itinerary. Perhaps President Grímsson, who came to Canada in 1999 and laid a wreath at the cairn over the grave of the poet who spoke at his inauguration, said it best. Stephansson, he told those present, was "a farmer who after a long day of tilling the earth wrote poems in the Icelandic language. His life is an enduring testimony to the triumph of the soaring spirit."[32]

Even though he stripped the prairies of supremacy in group life, few founding fathers had the impact in life or death as the Doukhobors' Peter

Verigin. In 1924, amid escalating factional tensions, and sixteen years after he led the Christian Community of Universal Brotherhood to British Columbia, Verigin died in a mysterious explosion aboard a train. Many blamed the Sons of Freedom, although the Russian Bolsheviks, and, in some Doukhobor circles, the Canadian government were also suspects. Verigin's funeral attracted 7000 mourners—Community, Independent, Sons of Freedom— including a contingent from the prairies; Prime Minister Mackenzie King sent condolences. A monument (its motif a sheaf of wheat) eventually marked the spot in the mountains at Farron where Verigin died, but his tomb near Brilliant entered Doukhobor ritual as a magnet for both ceremony and conflict. Its symbolic potential was apparent six months after the funeral when 4000 Doukhobors gathered at his grave and with bowed heads selected his son as his successor, just as Verigin had himself been selected leader at the grave of Lukeria Kalmykova.[33] While Community Doukhobors thereafter held annual memorial services at his tomb on the anniversary of their leader's death, in 1931 the Sons of Freedom committed the first of many acts of vandalism and blew up its marble cover, leading to construction of a protective fence topped with barbed wire around the site. Other Sons of Freedom incorporated Verigin's grave into protests against the Canadian state, marching to the tomb, for example, to demonstrate opposition to national registration during the Second World War.[34] More recently, and specifically during their centennial, mainstream Doukhobors gathered for prayers at Verigin's grave on Petrov Den to commemorate the burning of arms in 1895.

Engraved on the rock face hanging above his tomb, in poetic Russian but awkward English, Verigin's epitaph read:

> Dedicated to Peter w Lordly. This blessed rocky bluff casts its mournful sad look on a grave sufferingly mournful, holy, to convey people truth of a story. Here flowed once in Doukhobor tears a coffin with body of a leader strong, mighty with mournful prayer of spiritual wrestlers. Into the bowels of earth grievously lowered. His spirit—arise for memory everlasting in many loving hearts. He bequeathed to us in holy covenant "toil and peaceful life" with Christ.[35]

Reflecting Doukhobors' emphasis on the religious life and spirit within, the epitaph unsurprisingly ignored the secular and material world. Given the

**8.10.** Massed mourners at the funeral of Peter "the Lordly" Verigin, Brilliant, British Columbia, 1924. SASKATCHEWAN ARCHIVES BOARD, S-B9557.

disillusionment and restlessness of Verigin's prairie co-religionists who followed him into new, self-imposed exile in the Kootenays, the absence of any reference to the man who led the sect during its years in Saskatchewan was also not surprising. But if distance or ideology alienated prairie Doukhobors from aspects of the great leader's grave, Saskatchewan, as the cradle of Canadian Doukhoborism, provided an alternative. The grave in question drew not on the Canadian story but on the crucial events of Petrov Den 1895, when army conscript Matvei Lebedev, one of the first Doukhobors to lay down his weapons, ripped off his corporal's epaulets and exhorted other soldiers to do the same. Arrested, court-martialled, and treated brutally in a penal battalion, Lebedev then came to Canada, settling in the South Colony.[36] He did not join the exodus to British Columbia, and when he died in 1937 was buried in Nadezhda cemetery north of Veregin. "Fighter for the cause of the people," his tombstone said, and "eternal memory for all those who suffered to keep the ideal alive." Lebedev personified, and brought to Canadian soil, both Canadian Doukhobors' old-world martyrs who refused to disobey God's edict against

**8.11.** Ivan Pylypiw and Vasyl Eleniak commemorated during the Ukrainian-Canadian centennial in their native village of Nebyliv, Ukraine, 2003. PHOTO BY FRANCES SWYRIPA.

killing and the defining moment in their separate history abroad. Ceremonies organized for Veregin on Petrov Den in 1995, the centennial of the burning of arms, acknowledged his symbolism with the decision to fix up and hold a commemorative gathering at his grave. In the end rain forced cancellation of the service in the cemetery down a rutted trail in a field.[37]

Ukrainians also elevated their founding fathers to national group symbols, albeit without Verigin's contemporary prominence and influence. The graves of Vasyl Eleniak and Ivan Pylypiw each received very different treatment, although neither site evolved into more than an erratic pilgrimage destination.

The differences reflected the divergent paths the two men took, paths that penalized Pylypiw and favoured Eleniak (who also outlived his travelling companion by twenty years). In 1954 the lieutenant governor of Alberta unveiled a granite monument—its sentiments those of industry, progress, providence, and thanksgiving—beside St. Mary Ukrainian Catholic Church in Chipman, celebrating Eleniak as the first Ukrainian in Canada.[38] It depicted occupation and cultivation of the land as an uncompromisingly male enterprise. On one side, below the date 1891, a cross's rays blessed a muscular man in a cowboy hat, sleeves rolled to the elbow, shirt open at the neck, wielding a scythe. The text, in Ukrainian, read: "To the Ukrainian pioneers from their grateful sons." On the reverse, beneath the year 1954, a farmer drove his self-propelled combine. This text, in English, was more conscious of place: "In commemoration of the Ukrainian pioneers in Canada by their grateful sons." When Eleniak died two years later, he was buried in the adjacent cemetery. His tombstone reiterated, in both languages, his status as the first Ukrainian settler in Canada.

Pylypiw, who died in 1936, was buried in the cemetery of the Russo-Greek Orthodox Church of the Holy Transfiguration at Star, Alberta. Bearing eloquent testimony to the delayed and uncertain evolution of the Ukrainian-Canadian founding myth in which he figured, his tombstone featured the now-famous photograph of the grizzled peasant in his sheepskin coat, and told his personal story, but made no first or founding claims. "Came to Canada to look over country 1890," the bilingual epitaph began. "Went back to Austria brought back his family to Canada to stay in 1893." Someone later corrected 1890 to 1891, the actual year of Pylypiw's first voyage, but left the original zero still visible to the sharp eye. Pylypiw also had to wait more than half a century after his death for a monument comparable to the one Eleniak received in his lifetime. Even then, in the centennial cairn erected in the Star churchyard, Pylypiw (and his wife Maria) shared the limelight with the three other couples, identified like them by name and photographs, who settled together on nearby homesteads. The detailed inscription personalized the Ukrainian immigration story while preserving the grand narrative, and allowed women a modest role while continuing to privilege men. "They were the first of thousands from all parts of Ukraine," it concluded, "who came and played a large part in the development of western Canada. They were also part of the founding members of this parish and, along with many others who settled in this area, are resting in this cemetery."[39]

Following Ukraine's independence in 1991, newly restored relations with the homeland produced some of the most symbolically charged events of the Ukrainian-Canadian centennial. The first postage stamp issued by the new Ukrainian state honoured the Canadian anniversary, while Canadian Governor General Ramon Hnatyshyn, the first Ukrainian to hold the vice-regal position, visited his ancestral homeland in his official capacity. But the village of Nebyliv from which Pylypiw and Eleniak set out so long ago attracted the greatest attention. Erected in the school grounds, a monument commemorating the start of emigration featured reliefs of the "first Ukrainians in Canada," plus the kneeling figure of a peasant in traditional dress, hat in hand, hand over his heart. By 2003 the statue was seriously cracked, but that did not deter a busload of University of Saskatchewan students, who delayed a scheduled tour of the school to take each other's pictures beside this symbol of their roots, Ukrainian and Canadian. In the school's history room, they saw another reminder of those roots—packets of earth from the graves of Pylypiw and Eleniak presented to the people of Nebyliv by Ukrainians in Canada. The prairie pioneers had thus come home, their symbolic remains treasured in special boxes surrounded by pictures of the traditional heroes of Ukrainian history.[40]

\* \* \*

Regardless of the impetus—religious or secular, private or communal, casual or ritualized—return to the land for the purpose of pilgrimage represented a spiritual journey in the quest for roots. For descendants of the immigrant settler generation, the journey was personal and at least somewhat familiar. Enlarging their frame of reference beyond family homesteads and graves, they sought a place in the land that tied them to the group to which they and their ancestors belonged. For group members who had never set foot in the rural West, whether from choice or circumstance, and who possessed different immigration and settlement histories, the journey was a step into the unknown. They sought to access a symbolic place and a Canadian prairie birthright that were theirs vicariously, but no less theirs. In equating both personal and group identity with ethno-religious space in the land, pilgrimage made two additional statements. It reaffirmed the enduring relevance and far-reaching repercussions of ethnicity, and ethnicity shaped by faith, to prairie society and identity. And it reaffirmed, through the elevation of selected sites to iconic status, both the inseparability of ethno-religious identity from the prairie settlement era and the persisting relevance of the ethno-religious imprint the pioneer generation imposed on the prairie map.

# Conclusion

IN IMPORTANT RESPECTS, THIS BOOK is an unfinished project. As I completed the revisions in spring 2009, the Historic Sites and Monuments Board of Canada prepared to add its plaque to the cluster of pioneer memorials on the grounds of Our Lady of Assumption Roman Catholic Church at Kaposvar. It planned similar plaques for St. Peter's Colony and the Ukrainian stronghold of Mundare. They would commemorate, respectively, the founding of Esterhazy's Hungarian colony in 1886, the establishment of the German Catholic settlement under the Benedictines in 1903, and the arrival of the first permanent Ukrainian Catholic clergy in east-central Alberta in 1902. All had been designated "events of national historical significance," officially entrenching their regional, even localized group stories and place in the land in an evolving national narrative. Such recognition could conceivably alter how group members accessed these sites and their history, and how they situated them within a hierarchy of group landmarks and stories. It could also affect how outsiders assessed the ethno-religious imprint on the West and through it the nation.

I hoped to attend all three unveiling ceremonies. I would not, however, go as an innocent observer. I had not only worked closely with the communities in question to submit the original nominations but had also been involved in the wording of the plaques and was slated to speak at Kaposvar.[1] Insights gleaned from researching and writing this book thus influenced the resulting perceptions of "national significance"—Saskatchewan as the cradle and long-time centre of Hungarian-Canadian life, the uniqueness of St. Peter's Colony as a dual religious/settlement venture and an Abbacy Nullius, and the Mundare mission as the foundation of the Ukrainian Catholic Church in Canada. Those insights would also shape public perceptions of the three sites and what they stood for. In other words, the prairie child curious about her backyard who became a historian was now a player in shaping regional identity. While the historian probed the relevance of the land, place, and region through the eyes of the peoples involved, the player actively promoted the connection between land and narrative, region and nation, ethno-religious group and place.

That said, land, place, and region did figure prominently in the ethno-religious identity of immigrant settler peoples on the prairies, and engaged in a complex series of interlocking relationships. To the immigrant generation, the land meant the soil, rocks, trees, water, and wildlife (including the hated mosquito) on their homesteads. It also meant the larger, still local landscape, at first disorienting and alien, which they collectively claimed and ordered, creating communities that served the living, the faithful, and the dead. Occupation of the land transformed a space into places, whose physical landmarks—stores, schools, churches, cemeteries, grain elevators—were the product of human imagination and cultural experience interacting with the prairie environment. Places irretrievably changed the landscape, just as being rooted and living in place shaped individual and group identities around existing ethnic and religious touchstones augmented by new western Canadian sensibilities. Place to the pioneers also meant something more abstract. As a legal land description, it symbolized the tiny piece of the immense prairies that belonged to them personally. As the name of their community, it immortalized a shared homeland, immigration and settlement experience, or hopes for the future. Most importantly, place names defined the space where "we" lived and established boundaries between "us" and "them" (even close neighbours and members of the same ethno-religious group).

Over time the understanding of place in the land changed. For the immigrants' descendants still living where their ancestors settled, practicality and progress vied with sentimentality. While the latter stimulated efforts to remember and acknowledge the pioneers' presence and contribution, even renaming points on the map in their honour, the former represented reality. An empty school was safer demolished than sitting derelict, a potential fire hazard; an abandoned farmstead ploughed under increased the acreage for cash-generating crops; a church used twice a year weighed on its few parishioners. Moreover, rural residents wanted modern comforts and conveniences—storing their grain in galvanized metal bins, not converted log houses; cladding old buildings in easy-maintenance vinyl siding; installing electricity and carpeting in their churches; and straightening and widening roads made scenic but dangerous by vision-blocking turns and trees. Those of the immigrants' descendants who had moved away often found the changes disconcerting and misguided. For them, the personally displaced, place in the land was nostalgic, compromised by progress. It was somewhere to visit to re-energize and reconnect with roots but not somewhere to live. Displacement, plus a remembered or romanticized past unimpaired by responsibility for the everyday care of its material heritage, exaggerated the importance of preserving pioneer landmarks. Finally, attachment to place in the land came to characterize ethno-religious groups as part of their collective identity and memory. Group attitudes towards the legacy of the prairie pioneers were dictated less by regret for what had been, or anxiety over what had been lost, than interest in what remained and how surviving buildings and sites could be mobilized for the present.

Displacement, especially from the land, has often been described as a form of death, or memory and culture loss that impoverished both the individual and collective self.[2] Its repercussions could be observed in migrants from the old rural settlement areas and their offspring, particularly in their need to go back to places left behind and the anxiety about what they would find (or not find). Emigration itself entailed displacement, and, in the case of immigrant settler peoples in western Canada, often without any realistic option to return to their old world, even to visit. But if leaving home for the unknown prairies represented a death of sorts, even among those already feeling displaced because of prejudice or persecution or recurrent migration, the prairie experience also negated that death. Had emigrants-turned-immigrants not resolutely recreated place, and invested heavily in it emotionally, neither their descendants nor the larger ethno-religious group would have identified with the land as they did. All immigrants recreate place to some extent, but the intensity of belonging witnessed on the Canadian prairies reflected a unique combination of circumstances. Millions of acres of "empty" land, thousands of people needed and lured in a short span to make it productive, easy terms of ownership, and a fluid frontier setting in which everyone counted, and was conscious at some level of building a society together, made these newcomers participants in *the* western formative experience. Traditional agricultural peoples, former factory workers, perpetual wanderers, those whose rural settlements ultimately collapsed—all developed a strong sense of place based on land ownership and pioneering in common. A rented tenement in Winnipeg and waged labour enriching someone else, or a hard-fought niche among established farming communities in Ontario or Quebec sparked nothing comparable.

During the settlement period, which of the local communities that the immigrant generation created would grow into villages, towns, and occasionally cities with sometimes significant hinterlands, and which ones would fade away, could not have been predicted. Clearly, location mattered—a rail line as opposed to a crossroads in the countryside, for example. But not all railway service centres would thrive equally, and size and economic importance could not eradicate the sentimental appeal of rural clusters that progress passed by. Nor were all the physical landmarks constructed by immigrant settler peoples valued equally, then or later. Chinked log houses or plastered and whitewashed cottages provided crucial shelter, but homestead after homestead had one; far more rare churches both fed the spirit and, from the start, aimed to impress visually. Yet lack of value virtually erased dwellings from the landscape, so that the remaining structures joined surviving churches as the embodiment of the pioneer experience and legacy. Precisely which buildings, or landmarks, acquired a second life among later generations rested in part on accident. Lightning might destroy a beloved or grand landmark, or neglect or poverty leave an unprepossessing structure untouched to attract exaggerated attention. Other buildings had been widely regarded as special since their construction, facilitating the transition from settlement-era functionality to heritage symbol.

All such landmarks derived much of their power from their location on the land, just as all of them both helped to define and were defined by the landscape. However, only those enjoying elevated status among the immigrant generation itself tended to be inseparable from the sites, equally treasured, on which they stood. In fact, the pioneer physical settings—as ultimate localized places—that became focal points of individual and ethno-religious group identity and community ritual often existed independently of human construction. These places, most often landing or settlement sites, represented a more fundamental interaction with the environment. In such instances, the choice of location had perhaps initially been inadvertent or random, but once made, it was irrevocable, unchangeable, and irreplaceable.

Inevitably, members of ethno-religious groups who journeyed together to the prairies and congregated in reserved tracts or blocs where their kind predominated understood both place in the land and the immigration and settlement experience that nurtured it as involving more than themselves or their immediate surroundings. Undercutting pioneering's universal and unifying character, and the individualism of the frontier thesis, their version of the prairie narrative organized the opening of the West around ethnicity and religion and the initiative and contribution of groups. This emphasis considered ethno-religious diversity—which generations of nation builders had lamented—based on occupation and ownership of the land as the core of the regional identity and distinctiveness. It also distinguished the Canadian West from its American counterpart. The continuing importance, into the twenty-first century, of the traditional prairie West to the self-image of members of ethno-religious groups whose prairie origins lay in the land underscored the region's continued existence and relevance, even if only in the imagination. At the same time, the disjuncture between the past that the traditional West celebrated and the reality of the modern urban West produced tensions that coloured how place in the land was commemorated, preserved, and accessed.

All immigrant settler peoples inserted themselves into the regional story. Yet not all ethno-religious groups incorporated their prairie pioneers and their sense of place in the land into the larger group identity, narrative, or community ritual. Those groups whose Canadian origins lay in the prairie West during the formative decades of large-scale immigration and settlement developed a special attachment to the region that transcended the actual pioneers and their descendants. Continuing concentration in the prairie provinces, despite out-migration or later immigrant waves favouring other parts of the country, reinforced that attachment. Among groups for whom the prairies were marginal to the overall group experience, or who had an alternate group experience in a different part of the country, attachment to the prairies was solely regional in nature. It also remained limited to group members for whom it resonated personally, and competed with group narratives rooted elsewhere in Canada. Regardless of the specific scenario, the ensuing relationship between the group as a whole and its prairie fragment once again remarked on the significance of ethnicity and religion, this time to understanding the interplay between region and nation in Canada. The active intervention of the Historic Sites and Monuments Board of Canada (and co-opted historians) in defining and publicizing the "national historical significance" of ethno-religious heritages on the prairies—sites, events, individuals—injected another player into the process with unknown results.

# NOTES

## INTRODUCTION

1   Frederick Jackson Turner's much published "The Significance of the Frontier in American History" was originally presented to the American Historical Society in 1893. The literature on frontierism and metropolitanism in the Canadian West is extensive, ranging from case studies on ranching and the North-West Mounted Police to more general works represented, among others, by G.F.C. Stanley, J.M.S. Careless, and Ramsay Cook. Recent contributions include Robert Irwin, "Breaking the Shackles of the Metropolitan Thesis: Prairie History, the Environment and Layered Identities," *Journal of Canadian Studies* 32, 3 (1997): 98–118; R. Douglas Francis, "Turner versus Innis: Bridging the Gap," *American Review of Canadian Studies* 33, 4 (2003): 473–85; William Katerberg, "A Northern Vision: Frontiers and the West in the Canadian and American Imagination," *American Review of Canadian Studies* 33, 4 (2003): 543–63; and Lorry Felske and Beverly Rasporich, eds., *Challenging Frontiers: The Canadian West* (Calgary: University of Calgary Press, 2004), esp. the introduction.

2   J.M.S. Careless, "'Limited Identities' in Canada," *Canadian Historical Review* 50, 1 (1969): 1–10; and "Limited Identities—Ten Years Later," *Manitoba History* (1979–80): 3–9.

3   Royden Loewen, "On the Margin or in the Lead: Canadian Prairie Historiography," *Agricultural History* 73, 1 (1999): 27–45, argues that while the new rural history in the United States stressed the socioeconomic function of farm families, women, and the environment, its prairie counterpart in Canada, reflecting greater urban and capitalistic influences, focussed on things like ethnicity, culture, and comparative settlement patterns.

4   Gerald Friesen wrote the now classic *The Canadian Prairies: A History* (Toronto: University of Toronto Press, 1984). His evolving views on the West can be traced in "The Prairies as Region: The Contemporary Meaning of an Old Idea," in his *River Road: Essays on Manitoba and Prairie History* (Winnipeg: University of Manitoba Press, 1996), 165–82, which reprinted the article from 1992; and his presidential address, "Space and Region in Canadian History," *Journal of the Canadian Historical Association* (2005): 1–22. Also useful here is R. Douglas Francis, "Regionalism, Landscape, and Identity in the Prairie West," in Felske and Rasporich, *Challenging Frontiers*, 29–49.

5   Benedict Anderson, *Imagined Communities: Reflections on the Origin and Spread of Nationalism*, rev. ed. (1983; London: Verso, 2006).

6   Invented traditions are defined, and examined both for their assumed invariance and ancient derivation and the conditions under which they are constructed, in Eric Hobsbawm and Terence Ranger, eds., *The Invention of Tradition* (1983; Cambridge: Cambridge University Press, 1992), 1–14.

7   David Lowenthal, *The Heritage Crusade and the Spoils of History* (London: Viking, 1996), xi; see also his influential *The Past is a Foreign Country* (Cambridge: Cambridge University Press, 1985).

8   The phrase "storied landscapes" was inspired by the "storied places" of Brian Osborne's "Landscapes, Memory, Monuments, and Commemoration: Putting Identity in Its Place," *Canadian Ethnic Studies* 33, 3 (2001): 39–77. A growing and excellent literature on heritage, collective memory, commemoration, landscape, and identity is both theoretical in scope and draws on case studies from across the globe. For example, Jonathan Vance's *Death So Noble: Memory, Meaning, and the First World War* (Vancouver: University of British Columbia Press, 1997) is the best Canadian study of war, while the Second World War in Europe has alone generated numerous monographs—from Michael Steinlauf's *Bondage to the Dead: Poland and the Memory of the Holocaust* (Syracuse, NY: Syracuse University Press, 1997) to Henry Rousso's *The Vichy Syndrome: History and Memory in France since 1944*, trans. Arthur Goldhammer (Cambridge, MA: Harvard University Press, 1991), originally published in French in 1987.

## Chapter One

1   Visited 26 July 1998. Also see Howard Palmer and Tamara Palmer, eds., *Peoples of Alberta: Portraits of Cultural Diversity* (Saskatoon: Western Producer Prairie Books, 1985); Dorene Zawadiuk et al., eds., *Romanians in Alberta* (Edmonton: Canadian Romanian Society of Alberta, 1998); *Vegreville in Review: History of Vegreville and Surrounding Area, 1880–1980* (Vegreville: Vegreville and District Historical Society, 1980); and Uriel Rosenzweig, comp. and ed., *The First Century of Jewish Life in Edmonton and Northern Alberta, 1893–1993* (Edmonton: Jahsena, 2000).

2   On the evolving image of the West and its role in Confederation, see Doug Owram, *Promise of Eden: The Canadian Expansionist Movement and the Idea of the West, 1856–1900* (1980; rpt. Toronto: University of Toronto Press, 1992). William L. Morton, "The Bias of Prairie Politics," *Transactions of the Royal Society of Canada* 3, 49 (1955): 57–66, was the first articulation of western alienation by a professional historian.

3   On Quebec attitudes to the settlement-era West, see Arthur Silver, *The French-Canadian Idea of Confederation, 1864–1900*, 2nd ed. (Toronto: University of Toronto Press, 1997), esp. chs. 4 and 7–9.

4   Friesen, *Canadian Prairies*, 244, claims that the "unique status" of the British and French on the prairies "derives more from linguistic and historical precedence, ... than from officially sanctioned cultural privileges. In other words, English and French, like all other peoples, were immigrants to western Canada and behaved as members of ethnic groups." Yet he also says that despite "decades of European immigration, the cultural standards of prairie society remained British; social and economic leadership rested firmly in the hands of the British Canadian; and even in politics, where notions such as socialism and social credit were bandied about, British institutions and principles were as yet unshaken" (273).

5   Unless otherwise specified, all statistics come or are derived from the decennial Canadian census or the special censuses of the prairie provinces taken in 1916, 1926, and 1936.

6   Cecilia Wetton, *The Promised Land: The Story of the Barr Colonists*, 2nd ed. (1953; Lloydminster: Lloydminster Times, 1979); Helen Reid, *All Silent, All Damned: The Search for Isaac Barr* (Toronto: Ryerson, 1969); Kathryn Ivany, "The History of the Barr Colonists as an Ethnic Experience, 1903–1928" (M.A. thesis, University of Alberta, 1985); Lynne Bowen, *Muddling Through: The Remarkable Story of the Barr Colonists* (Vancouver: Douglas and McIntyre, 1992); and Franklin Foster, *The Trail of 1903: An Account by the Rt. Rev. George Exton Lloyd* (Lloydminster: Foster Learning, 2002).

7   See, for example, C.A. Dawson, *Group Settlement: Ethnic Communities in Western Canada* (Toronto: Macmillan, 1936), 335–74, which looks at "two representative areas" (335), St. Albert in Alberta and Ste. Rose in Manitoba. Gravelbourg became a major French centre in Saskatchewan; see Georges Hébert, *Les débuts de Gravelbourg: Son fondateur, ses pionniers, les institutions, 1905–1965* (Gravelbourg: n.p., 1965).

8   See David Hall, "Clifford Sifton: Immigration and Settlement Policy, 1896–1905," in *The Settlement of the West*, ed. Howard Palmer (Calgary: University of Calgary Press, 1977), 60–85 and 243–51.

9   James S. Woodsworth, *Strangers within Our Gates, or Coming Canadians* (Toronto: Stephenson for the Missionary Society of the Methodist Church, 1909), is a succinct handbook to the crystallizing ethnic hierarchy. Robert England, *The Central European Immigrant in Canada* (Toronto: Macmillan, 1929) draws on the impressions of Anglo-Canadians teaching in the "more backward non-English speaking districts" (vii) of Saskatchewan to promote its assimilationist agenda.

10  See Dawson, *Group Settlement*, 95–161; Frank Epp, *Mennonites in Canada, 1786–1920: The History of a Separate People* (Toronto: Macmillan, 1974); Harry Loewen, "A House Divided: Russian Mennonite Nonresistance and Emigration in the 1870s," in *Mennonites in Russia: Essays in Honour of Gerhard Lohrenz*, ed. John Friesen (Winnipeg: CMBC Publications, 1989), 127–43; William Janzen, *Limits on Liberty: The Experience of Mennonite, Hutterite, and Doukhobor Communities in*

*Canada* (Toronto: University of Toronto Press, 1990), 1–15, 19–35, and 88–115; and Harry Loewen, "Mennonites," in *Encyclopedia of Canada's Peoples*, ed. Paul R. Magocsi (Toronto: University of Toronto Press for the Multicultural History Society of Ontario, 1999), 957–62.

11 See S.J. Sommerville, "Early Icelandic Settlement in Canada," *Papers of the Historical and Scientific Society of Manitoba* (1944–5): 25–9; Wilhelm Kristjanson, *The Icelandic People in Manitoba: A Manitoba Saga* (1965; rpt. Winnipeg: R.W. Kristjanson, n.d.), quoted 31; Jónas Þór, *Icelanders in North America: The First Settlers* (Winnipeg: University of Manitoba Press, 2002); and Anne Brydon, "Icelanders," in Magocsi, *Encyclopedia of Canada's Peoples*, 685–8.

12 See Dawson, *Group Settlement*, 175–272; Brigham Card et al., eds., *The Mormon Presence in Canada* (Edmonton: University of Alberta Press, 1990); and Brigham Card, "Mormons," in Magocsi, *Encyclopedia of Canada's Peoples*, 979–83.

13 See Erna Paris, *Jews: An Account of Their Experience in Canada* (Toronto: Macmillan, 1980), 211–72; Cyril Leonoff, *The Jewish Farmers of Western Canada* (N.p.: Jewish Historical Society of British Columbia and Western States Jewish Historical Association, 1984); Gerald Tulchinsky, *Taking Root: The Origins of the Canadian Jewish Community* (Toronto: Lester, 1992); Yossi Katz and John Lehr, "Jewish Pioneer Agricultural Settlements in Western Canada," *Journal of Cultural Geography* 14, 1 (1993): 49–68; and some three decades of articles by Abraham Arnold in *Western Jewish News* and *Canadian Jewish News*.

14 See Andrew Marchbin, "Early Immigration from Hungary to Canada," *Slavonic Review* 13 (1934): 127–38; N.F. Dreisziger et al., *Struggle and Hope: The Hungarian-Canadian Experience* (Toronto: McClelland and Stewart, 1982); Martin Kovacs, *Esterhazy and Early Hungarian Immigration to Canada: A Study Based upon the Esterhazy Immigration Pamphlet* (Regina: Canadian Plains Research Center, 1974); and Nandor Dreisziger, "Hungarians," in Magocsi, *Encyclopedia of Canada's Peoples*, 660–4.

15 See Gulbrand Loken, *From Fjord to Frontier: A History of Norwegians in Canada* (Toronto: McClelland and Stewart, 1980); Henning Bender and Birgit Larsen, eds., *Danish Emigration to Canada* (Aalborg, Denmark: Danes Worldwide Archives with the Danish Society for Emigration History, 1991); and in Magocsi, *Encyclopedia of Canada's Peoples*, Loken's "Norwegians," 1014–5, and Christopher Hale's "Danes," 407–9, and "Swedes," 1218–25.

16 See Jaroslav Petryshyn, *Peasants in the Promised Land: Canada and the Ukrainians, 1891–1914* (Toronto: Lorimer, 1985); Orest Martynowych, *Ukrainians in Canada: The Formative Period, 1891–1924* (Edmonton: Canadian Institute of Ukrainian Studies Press, 1991); Julian Stechishin, *A History of Ukrainian Settlement in Canada*, trans. Isidore Goresky (Saskatoon: Ukrainian Self-Reliance League of Canada, 1992); and Frances Swyripa, "Ukrainians," in Magocsi, *Encyclopedia of Canada's Peoples*, 1281–311.

17 See n. 1; Victor Turek, *Poles in Manitoba* (Toronto: Polish Alliance Press, 1967); Andrzej Kobos and Jolanta Pękacz, eds., *Polonia in Alberta, 1895–1995: The Polish Centennial in Alberta* (Edmonton: Polish Centennial Society and Canadian Polish Congress, Alberta Branch, 1995); and in Magocsi, *Encyclopedia of Canada's Peoples*, Henry Radecki's "Poles," 1056–60, and James Patterson's "Romanians," 1092–4.

18 See Dawson, *Group Settlement*, 1–91; George Woodcock, *The Doukhobors* (London: Faber and Faber, 1968); Janzen, *Limits on Liberty*, 1–15, 36–59, and 116–41; Carl Tracie, *"Toil and Peaceful Life": Doukhobor Village Settlement in Saskatchewan* (Regina: Canadian Plains Research Center, 1996); and Koozma Tarasoff, "Doukhobors," in Magocsi, *Encyclopedia of Canada's Peoples*, 422–5.

19 See Dawson, *Group Settlement*, 275–332 (St. Peter's and St. Joseph's colonies); George Aberle, *From the Steppes to the Prairies: The Story of the Germans Settling in Russia on the Volga and Ukraine; also, the Germans Settling in the Banat, and the Bohemians in Crimea, Their Resettlement in the Americas—North and South America and in Canada* (Dickinson, ND: Bismarck Tribune,

1964); Joseph Height, *Paradise on the Steppe: The Odyssey of a Pioneering People* (Bismarck, ND: North Dakota Historical Society of Germans from Russia, 1973), esp. 237–46, and *Homesteaders on the Steppe: The Odyssey of a Pioneering People* (Bismarck, ND: North Dakota Historical Society of Germans from Russia, 1975), esp. 321–9; and Heinz Lehmann, *The German Canadians, 1750–1937: Immigration, Settlement and Culture*, trans. and ed. Gerhard Bassler (St. John's: Jesperson Press, 1986).

20 Anderson, *Imagined Communities*.

21 Ukrainian population data come from the census calculations in William Darcovich and Paul Yuzyk, eds., *A Statistical Compendium on the Ukrainians in Canada, 1891–1976* (Ottawa: University of Ottawa Press, 1980).

22 Myron Gulka-Tiechko, "Ukrainian Immigration to Canada under the Railways Agreement, 1925–30," *Journal of Ukrainian Studies* 16, 1–2 (1991): 29–60.

23 On post-war immigration and nation building, see Franca Iacovetta, *Gatekeepers: Reshaping Immigrant Lives in Cold War Canada* (Toronto: Between the Lines, 2006).

24 Bruno Doerfler, OSB, *Quest for a New Homeland: The Founding of St. Peter's Colony in Saskatchewan* (Muenster, SK: St. Peter's Press, 1988), 70 ("Mr. Barr started out in the autumn [of 1902] to select the colony. Having travelled west of Battleford for a day or two, and not finding the weather agreeable for the trip, he turned back and selected the site for the colony on paper"); and Reid, *All Silent, All Damned*, 84.

25 For Card's own version of his activities, see *The Diaries of Charles Ora Card: The Canadian Years, 1886–1903*, ed. Donald Godfrey and Brigham Card (Salt Lake City: University of Utah Press, 1993).

26 A facsimile of Doerfler's account of his journey first published in 1903 (in English) in Minnesota as *Across the Boundary* is reprinted, with his handwritten notes, in *Quest for a New Homeland*, 1–107.

27 See, for example, the history of the German-Russian Hope Congregation of the Evangelical and Reformed Church at Stony Plain, AB, in Reuben Bauer, *One of Many* (Edmonton: Author, 1965), which has sections on both immigrant families and the congregation's pastors.

28 The characterization is Epp's (*Mennonites in Canada, 1786–1920*, 191).

29 Figures from Kristjanson, *Icelandic People in Manitoba*, 69–70 and 142–3.

30 See Marshall Nay, *Trailblazers of Ukrainian Emigration to Canada: Wasyl Eleniak and Ivan Pylypow* (Edmonton: Brightest Pebble, 1997) for a popular rendering of the two men's story; Vladimir J. Kaye, *Early Ukrainian Settlements in Canada, 1895–1900: Dr. Joseph Oleskow's Role in the Settlement of the Canadian Northwest* (Toronto: University of Toronto Press, 1964); and Oleskiv's influential 1895 pamphlet, *Pro vilni zemli* (About free lands), reprinted by the Ukrainian Free Academy of Sciences (Winnipeg: 1975).

31 A facsimile of the English-language version of Esterhazy's 1902 pamphlet is reproduced in Kovacs, *Esterhazy and Early Hungarian Immigration to Canada*, 61–130; Kovacs's detailed annotations follow.

32 For a contemporary account of the Doukhobor journey to Canada, see L.A. Sulerzhitskii, *To America with the Doukhobors*, trans. Michael Kalmakoff with an introduction by Mark Mealing (Regina: Canadian Plains Research Center, 1982); Aylmer Maude provides a second participant's perspective in *A Peculiar People: The Doukhobors* (London: Archibald Constable, 1905).

33 On the decline of Doukhobor communal villages in Saskatchewan, reflecting the departure of both the radicals and the independently minded, already by 1913, see Tracie, *"Toil and Peaceful Life,"* 152–206. Of fifty-nine villages established in the Mennonite East Reserve and seventy in the West Reserve, most had disappeared by 1900; Epp, *Mennonites in Canada, 1786–1920*, 212.

34 See, for example, Radomir Bilash, "Ukrainian Rural Communities in East Central Alberta before

1930," in *Continuity and Change: The Cultural Life of Alberta's First Ukrainians*, ed. Manoly Lupul (Edmonton: Canadian Institute of Ukrainian Studies and Alberta Historic Sites Service, 1988), 60–70; and, for the same area, Lubomyr Luciuk and Bohdan Kordan, *Creating a Landscape: A Geography of Ukrainians in Canada* (Toronto: University of Toronto Press, 1989), 20–1.

35  Michael Usiskin, *Uncle Mike's Edenbridge: Memoirs of a Jewish Pioneer Farmer*, trans. Marcia Usiskin Basman (Winnipeg: Peguis, 1983), 27.

36  See, for example, Ellenor Ranghild Merriken, *Looking for Country: A Norwegian Immigrant's Alberta Memoir*, with an introduction by Janice Dickin (Calgary: University of Calgary Press, 1999), 88 and 100.

37  For example, both Norwegian and Swedish entries in Magocsi, *Encyclopedia of Canada's Peoples*, are vague as to first comers.

38  See, for example, Charles Anderson et al., eds., *Circle of Voices: A History of the Religious Communities of British Columbia* (Lantzville, BC: Oolichan Books, 1983), 136–48. Since the Second World War, various Christian fundamentalist groups, including ones tied to post-war Dutch immigrants, have been attracted to British Columbia, creating enclaves in the interior (105–7).

39  See Jane McCracken, *Stephan G. Stephansson: The Poet of the Rocky Mountains* (Edmonton: Alberta Culture, 1982); Carolyn Dearden and Laurel Andersen, *From Fire and Ice: A Markerville History* (N.p.: Stephan G. Stephansson Icelandic Society, 1995); and W.J. Lindal, *The Saskatchewan Icelanders: A Strand of the Canadian Fabric* (Winnipeg: Columbia Press, 1955).

40  On Mexico and Paraguay specifically, see Frank Epp, *Mennonites in Canada, 1920–1940: A People's Struggle for Survival* (Toronto: Macmillan, 1982), 94–138; and T.D. Regehr, *Mennonites in Canada, 1939–1970: A People Transformed* (Toronto: University of Toronto Press, 1996), 134–8.

41  Vadim Kukushkin, "Back in the USSR," *Beaver* 86, 4 (2006): 33–6. Preliminary research suggests some 500 returnees in total.

42  See http://www.rootsweb.com/~cansk/Saskatchewan/ethnic/finnish-saskatchewan.html (accessed 12 August 2005). More generally, see Reino Kero, "The Canadian Finns in Soviet Karelia in the 1930s," in *Finnish Diaspora*, ed. Michael Karni (Toronto: Multicultural History Society of Ontario, 1981), 203–13; and Ronald Harpele et al., eds., *Karelian Exodus: Finnish Communities in North America and Soviet Karelia during the Depression Era*, a special issue of *Journal of Finnish Studies* 8, 1 (2004).

43  Henry Srebrnik, "Red Star over Birobidzhan: Canadian Jewish Communists and the 'Jewish Autonomous Region' in the Soviet Union," *Labour* 44 (1999): 129–47; and his "Such Stuff as Diaspora Dreams are Made On: Birobidzhan and the Canadian-Jewish Communist Imagination," *Canadian Jewish Studies* 10 (2002): 75–107.

44  Joseph Glass, "The Settlement of Prairie Jews in Palestine, 1917–39," *International Journal of Canadian Studies* 16 (1997): 215–44; and his "Isolation and Alienation: Factors in the Growth of Zionism in the Canadian Prairies, 1917–39," *Canadian Jewish Studies* 9 (2001): 85–123.

45  See *Icelandic Canadian* 25, 4 (1967): 19.

46  Epp, *Mennonites in Canada, 1920–1940*, 2. There were 202,500 Mennonites in the United States, 120,000 in the Soviet Union, 70,000 in the Netherlands, and 58,800 in Canada; India (20,000) and China and Java/Sumatra (10,000 each) came next.

47  The 30,000 and BC/prairie figures come from Tarasoff, "Doukhobors," 424. Some 11,000 Doukhobors were said to live in the late Soviet Union. Keith Crim, ed., *The Perennial Dictionary of World Religions* (San Francisco: Harper and Row, 1989), 231, gives the Canadian Doukhobor population as 20,000 and the world figure as an unexplained 50,000.

48  Ann Pawliczko, ed., *Ukraine and Ukrainians throughout the World: A Demographic and Sociological Guide to the Homeland and Its Diaspora* (Toronto: University of Toronto Press, 1994), 9, figures from shortly after Ukraine's independence. Canada had an estimated 963,310 to 1,000,000 Ukrainians, the United States 730,056 to 1,300,000.

## CHAPTER TWO

1   While admitting that Ottawa and its agents dictated the location of some colonies, John Lehr argues that Ukrainians themselves often selected poor land: see "Government Coercion in the Settlement of Ukrainian Immigrants in Western Canada," *Prairie Forum* 8, 2 (1983): 179–94; "Rural Settlement Behaviour of Ukrainian Pioneers in Western Canada, 1891–1914," in *Western Canadian Research in Geography: The Lethbridge Papers*, ed. Brenton Barr (Vancouver: Tantalus, n.d.), 51–66; and "Peopling the Prairies with Ukrainians," in *Canada's Ukrainians: Negotiating an Identity*, ed. Lubomyr Luciuk and Stella Hryniuk (Toronto: University of Toronto Press, 1991), 30–52.

2   Early works were *Place-Names of Alberta* (1928) and *Place-Names of Manitoba* (1933) published by the Department of the Interior for the Geographic Board of Canada; and Z.M. Hamilton, *Place Names of Saskatchewan* (Regina: Department of Natural Resources and Industrial Development, 1949). Westerners eager to recover and record their history sparked later interest: see J.B. Rudnyc'kyj, *Manitoba Mosaic of Place Names* (Winnipeg: Canadian Institute of Onomastic Sciences, 1970); E.T. Russell, *What's In a Name: The Story Behind Saskatchewan Place Names*, 3rd ed. rev. (1968; Saskatoon: Western Producer Prairie Books, 1980); and Eric Holmgren and Patricia Holmgren, *2000 Place Names of Alberta* (Saskatoon: Modern Press, 1972). In the 1990s Alberta Community Development and the Friends of the Geographic Names of Alberta Society produced four volumes under the title *Place Names of Alberta*. See also *Geographical Names of Manitoba* (Winnipeg: Manitoba Conservation, 2000), a government project; and Bill Barry's *People Places: Saskatchewan and Its Names* (Regina: Canadian Plains Research Center, 1997) and *People Places: The Dictionary of Saskatchewan Place Names* (Regina: Author, 1998).

3   See Haraldur Bessason in *Lögberg-Heimskringla*, 1 June 1967. Another landform with local ethno-religious roots was Kaposvar Valley in Saskatchewan, named for the Hungarian settlement.

4   John Rempel and William Harms, *Atlas of Original Mennonite Villages, Homesteaders, and Some Burial Plots of the Mennonite West Reserve, Manitoba* (Altona, MB: Authors, 1990), 5. They suggest that the founders of the villages of Schoenwiese and Reinland along the Post Road selected the sites precisely because of the trail's links to the outside world (48).

5   For the twenty-five Manitoba place names of Icelandic origin approved by the Canadian Board of Place Names, see Bessason, in *Lögberg-Heimskringla*, 1 June 1967.

6   Ibid. Bessason identifies the fifty most common topographical elements in New Icelandic farm names. More comprehensively, see *Örnefni í Nýja Íslandi* (N.p., n.d.), Nelson Gerrard's compilation of New Icelandic farm names and their origins/meanings; the examples published in *Lögberg-Heimskringla* in 2001–2; and Kristiana Magnusson, "Place-Names of Breiðuvík District—Hnausa," *Icelandic Canadian* 33, 4 (1975): 33–7, and 34, 1 (1975): 38–43.

7   Woodcock, *Doukhobors*, 186.

8   Chinatowns represented the ultimate division between "them" and "us." Using Vancouver as her case study, Kay Anderson argues that they were constructs of white society and governments interested in their own hegemony; see "The Idea of Chinatown: The Power of Place and Institutional Practice in the Making of a Racial Category," *Annals of the Association of American Geographers* 77, 4 (1987): 580–98. David Chuenyan Lai, *Chinatowns: Towns within Cities in Canada* (Vancouver: University of British Columbia Press, 1988), 87–95, 135–46, and 154–7, describes the cycles of prairie Chinatowns.

9   Iaroslav B. Rudnytskyi, "Kanadiiski heohrafichni nazvy ukrainskoho pokhodzhennia," in *Propamiatna knyha Ukrainskoho narodnoho domu u Vynypegu*, comp. Semen Kovbel and ed. Dmytro Doroshenko (Winnipeg: Ukrainskyi narodnyi dim, 1949), 765–819.

10  Thomas Flanagan, *Louis "David" Riel: "Prophet of the New World,"* rev. ed. (Toronto: University of Toronto Press, 1996), 81–104.

11  See, for example, Benjamin Smillie, ed., *Visions of the New Jerusalem: Religious Settlement on the Prairies* (Edmonton: NeWest Press, 1983); and A.W. Rasporich, "Utopian Ideals and Community Settlements in Western Canada, 1880–1914," in *The Canadian West: Social Change and Economic Development*, ed. Henry Klassen (Calgary: University of Calgary Press, 1977), 37–62.

12  Peter Windschiegl, OSB, *Fifty Golden Years, 1903–1953: A Brief History of the Order of St. Benedict in the Abbacy Nullius of St. Peter, Muenster, Saskatchewan* (Muenster, SK: St. Peter's Abbey, 1953), 15 and 29.

13  The striking Ste. Philomène became a cathedral in 1930, was renamed Our Lady of the Assumption in 1965, and acquired national historic site status in 1995; see *La Cathédrale: Notre-Dame-de-l'Assomption, Gravelbourg, Saskatchewan, Canada* (1998).

14  See, for Kaposvar, the Saskatchewan History and Folklore Society plaque installed in 1991 (visited 11 August 2002); for Cooks Creek, Basil Rostoff et al., *Monuments to Faith: Ukrainian Churches in Manitoba* (Winnipeg: University of Manitoba Press, 1990), 90, and the Manitoba Provincial Historic Sites website at http://www.gov.mb.ca/chc/hrb/prov/p023.html (accessed 6 January 2002); and for Muenster, Marcella Hinz, *St. Peter's Cathedral: The Inside Story* (Muenster, SK: St. Peter's Press, 1995).

15  See http://www.city.lloydminster.ab.ca (accessed 31 October 2005) for St. John Anglican, now at the Barr Colony Heritage and Cultural Centre; and for the Morinville church, an Alberta Provincial Historic Resource since 1974, the undated brochure, *Welcome to St. Jean Baptiste Parish, Morinville, Alberta: A Brief History* (author's private collection). St. John's popularity can be glimpsed in the Ukrainian *Propamiatna knyha z nahody zolotoho iuvileiu poselennia ukrainskoho narodu v Kanadi* (Yorkton, SK: "Holos Spasytelia" for the Episcopal Ordinariat, 1941) and *Zbirnyk materiialiv z nahody iuvileinykh sviatkuvan u 50-littia Ukrainskoi hreko-pravoslavnoi tserkvy v Kanadi* (Winnipeg: Consistory of the Ukrainian Greek Orthodox Church of Canada, 1968); and the multiethnic Lois Munholland, *Pulpits of the Past: A Record of Closed Lutheran Churches in Saskatchewan up to 2003* (Strasbourg, SK: Three West Two South Books, 2004).

16  *Prayerbook in Honor of St. Theresa (The Little Flower) on the Occasion of the Golden Anniversary of the Erection of Her Shrine at Wakaw, Saskatchewan, Canada, and of the Annual Pilgrimage in Her Honor at This Shrine* (N.p., 1973), 5–6.

17  See the folk song collected in Rama, SK, tapping an old Ukrainian proverb to beseech the help of St. Nicholas in crossing to the new land; Robert Klymasz, *An Introduction to the Ukrainian-Canadian Immigrant Folksong Cycle* (Ottawa: National Museums of Canada, 1970), 25–8.

18  For St. Elizabeth of Hungary, see Polonia in Manitoba (1902) and Stockholm in Saskatchewan (1905), dates from commemorative plaque (Polonia), visited 28 May 2004, and historical panels (Stockholm), Our Lady of Assumption Roman Catholic Church, Kaposvar, visited 11 August 2002. The Kaposvar church contains both a statue of St. Elizabeth of Hungary and, on the rear wall, the Hungarian coat of arms with its Crown of St. Stephen. For St. Laszlo, see the rural church north of Prud'homme, SK, visited 9 June 2004.

19  For Sts. Volodymr and Olha, see Wroxton in Saskatchewan (1909) and Valley River in Manitoba (1924), both Catholic, in *Propamiatna knyha z nahody zolotoho iuvileiu poselennia ukrainskoho narodu v Kanadi*, 166 and 223; and Vegreville in Alberta (1929), Orthodox, in *Zbirnyk materiialiv*, 66–7. For St. Olaf, see Govan (1910), Admiral (1913), and Oungre (1927), all in Saskatchewan, in Munholland, *Pulpits of the Past*, 4, 91, and 180.

20  For St. Stanislaus, see Round Hill in Alberta (1907), in William Makowski, *The Polish People in Canada: A Visual History* (Montreal: Tundra Books, 1987), 176; and for St. Casimir, Krakow in Alberta (1902), in Anthony Sylla, "Kraków: Father Olszewski's Settlement (1899–1910)," in *Polish Settlers in Alberta: Reminiscences and Biographies*, ed. Joanna Matejko (Toronto: Polish Alliance Press, 1979), 270–1.

21  Windschiegl, *Fifty Golden Years*, 175, 183, and 215; and *Journey of Faith: St. Peter's Abbacy, 1921– 1996* (Muenster, SK: Muenster Diocese, 1996), 95–6.

22  Wintonyk shrine, visited 26 May 2004 (buildings gone, leaving the shrine in a clump of bush in a field). My thanks to Elizabeth Holinaty (descendant), Edmonton, and Slavko Omelan (owner), Wakaw, SK.

23  Borys shrine, visited 16 November 2003; the hoped-for church was never built, although annual services were held at least into the 1930s. For the facts of the Borys shrine I am indebted to Jerritt Pawlyk, "An Evolving Symbol: An Examination of the Borys Roadside Shrine" (unpublished paper, 5 November 2001, author's private collection); see also Harry Pshyk, ed., *Pioneers and Progress: Calmar and District* (Calmar, AB: Calmar and District Historical Society, 1980). An old man erecting a cross (inscribed with his and his wife's names) prior to leaving for Canada is the focus of Vasyl Stefanyk's short story available in translation in *The Stone Cross* (Toronto: McClelland and Stewart, 1971), 21–32.

24  Hungarian (Miskolczi) cross, visited 9 June 2004; see also the handwritten note attached to the wooden replacement cross in nearby St. Laszlo Roman Catholic Church.

25  Windschiegl, *Fifty Golden Years*, 132; and *Journey of Faith*, 53–4.

26  Rogation crosses, St. Anthony Roman Catholic Church, Grosswerder, SK, visited 7 May 2005. Quote from *Prairie Legacy* (Grosswerder, SK: Grosswerder and Districts New Horizons Heritage Group, 1980), 34.

27  Cross of freedom, Trembowla, MB, visited 27 May 2004; and Nestor Dmytriv, *Kanadiiska Rus': Podorozhni vspomyny* (Mt. Carmel, PA: Svoboda, 1897), 19–20. See also Stechishin, *History of Ukrainian Settlement in Canada*, 141–8; and Michael Marunchak, *The Ukrainian Canadians: A History* (Winnipeg and Ottawa: Ukrainian Free Academy of Sciences, 1970), 100–1, and *Kanadiiska Terebovlia* (Winnipeg: Zahalna biblioteka "UKT," 1964).

28  Lac Ste. Anne shrine, visited 24 July 2005; and E.O. Drouin, OMI, *Lac Ste-Anne Sakahigan* (Edmonton: Éditions de l'Ermitage, 1973), 52–63. See also Steve Simon, *Healing Waters: The Pilgrimage to Lac Ste. Anne* (Edmonton: University of Alberta Press, 1995), a photographic essay of the annual July event that draws thousands of Natives from local Cree to Dene in the north and US pilgrims in the south.

29  Skaro shrine, visited 14 August 2005. See also Anthony Sylla, *Memoirs: Sketches on Early Polish Settlements and the Polish Roman Catholic Church in Western Canada*, ed. Andrzej Kobos (Toronto: Oblates of Mary Immaculate, Assumption Province, 1997), 241–87, reprinted in part in Matejko, *Polish Settlers in Alberta*, 414–16; Kobos and Pękacz, *Polonia in Alberta*, xi and xxii, and esp. Pękacz, "Skaro Shrine: The Polish Contribution to the Marian Worship in Alberta (after Fr. Antoni Sylla)," 57–63 (quote, 60); and *50th Anniversary—Skaro Shrine, Star Alberta. Replica of the Grotto of Lourdes* (1969). Sylla's architect was Fr. Philip Ruh, an Oblate who trained in Galicia to work among Ukrainian Catholics in Canada. Ruh designed some of their most impressive churches, including Immaculate Conception at Cooks Creek and, in the 1950s, its Grotto of Our Lady of Lourdes.

30  Mount Carmel shrine, visited 8 August 2002; Hoffmann quoted from *Naicam Progress*, February 1948, http://www.collections.ic.gc.ca/humboldt/stpeters (accessed 12 December 2001). See also Windschiegl, *Fifty Golden Years*, 89–95; and *Journey of Faith*, 310–3.

31  See Windschiegl, *Fifty Golden Years*, 89–90; the girl is identified as Hatty/Henrietta MacKay and her

story comes from the man who made her coffin and helped bury her. In J.A. Prud'homme, "Carmel, A Legend of the Cree Tribe," *St. Peter's Messenger*, 24 July 1924 (see also *Colony Post*, May 1978), a devout Cree girl whom visiting fur traders called Carmel poisoned herself as she fled with her loving parents from an unwanted Cree suitor, religion unknown; her parents buried her beside the cross she fashioned from two branches just before she died. In his 1948 memoir in *Naicam Progress*, Fr. Hoffmann noted reports from the 1870s that Roman Catholic missionaries, or even a bishop, had erected the cross.

32 Mundare shrine, visited 17 February 2002. See also *Propamiatna knyha z nahody zolotoho iuvileiu poselennia ukrainskoho narodu v Kanadi*, 72–3 and 325; and Basilian Fathers, *Monder uchora i sohodni/Mundare Yesterday and Today* (Toronto: Basilian Press, 1969), 64, 74–5, 134, 137, 144, and 154.

33 Rama shrine, visited 9 August 2002. See also Makowski, *Polish People in Canada*, 151–2; and http://www3.sk.sympatico.ca/ourlady/shrines.html (accessed 10 December 2001).

34 Cudworth shrine, visited 8 August 2002. The story of the shrine's origins, reproduced on publicity materials for the annual pilgrimage (see the 2002 poster, author's private collection), is quoted from http://www.carltontrail.sk/ca/webpage/mempages/rmhoodoo/cudworth/cutatt.htm (accessed 12 December 2001).

35 On the Webster shrine, see Makowski, *Polish People in Canada*, 176–7 and 286; Leonard Ostaszewski, "Poles in Sexsmith and Webster (1827–1975)," in Matejko, *Polish Settlers in Alberta*, 316–8; and Izabella Wilk and Roman Wozniak, "Conquering the Peace River Country," in Kobos and Pękacz, *Polonia in Alberta*, 90. Maria Kozakiewicz, "Indestructible Elements: The Church, Religious Tradition, and the Polish Community of Alberta," in Kobos and Pękacz, *Polonia in Alberta*, 67, notes how not only Polish pioneers but she herself in 1988 packed pictures of Our Lady of Częstochowa in their immigrant luggage.

36 In 2001 the International Marian Research Institute identified some thirty Marian shrines on the prairies; see http://www.udayton.edu/mary/resources/shrines/canada.html (accessed 25 October 2005). The Canadian Catholic Enchiridion (http://ca-catholics.net/shrines/canada.htm, accessed 10 December 2001) gave a more conservative nineteen shrines in total. The most recent edition (2002) of *The Novalis Guide to Canadian Shrines* has entries on over forty prairie shrines.

37 Gabrielle Roy, "Where Will You Go, Sam Lee Wong?" in *Garden in the Wind*, trans. Alan Brown (Toronto: McClelland and Stewart, 1977), 48–104.

38 This section relies heavily on cemetery visits throughout the prairie provinces over two decades, with more systematic fieldwork conducted between 1999 and 2005 to obtain a good mix of ethnic and ethno-religious groups.

39 Merriken, *Looking for Country*, 116.

40 See the grave of Israel Berner, who died aged twenty in November 1918, probably a victim of the Spanish flu (Hebrew cemetery, Hirsch, SK, visited September 2003); and, for glass mosaics, St. Michael Ukrainian Catholic cemetery, Roblin, MB, visited 27 May 2004.

41 St. Anthony Roman Catholic cemetery, Grosswerder, SK, and Holy Rosary Roman Catholic cemetery, Reward, SK, visited 7 May 2005. On the transplanted iron cross tradition on the American plains and Canadian prairies, see Nicholas Vrooman and Patrice Marvin, eds., *Iron Spirits* (Fargo, ND: North Dakota Council on the Arts, 1982); and the documentary, Timothy Kloberdanz, writer/narrator, and Bob Dambach, producer, *Prairie Crosses, Prairie Voices: Iron Crosses of the Great Plains* (Fargo, ND: Prairie Public Television and North Dakota State University Libraries, 2002).

42 See, for example, "Caroline Kaiser, born Tbwardboski on 18 September 1828 in Rauschen, Ostrode district, Riga, East Prussia, Germany; died on 23 September 1927 at Wetaskiwin" (in German), St. John Lutheran cemetery, west of Wetaskiwin, AB, visited August 2000.

43 Visited 11 August 2002. On the local Welsh community, see *Bangor and District: History Book* (Bangor, SK: Bangor History Book Committee, 2002).

44 See, for example, Anton Alfred Rollander (died in Canada 20 July 1912), Evangelical Mission (Swedish) cemetery, Stockholm, SK, visited 12 August 2002; and Vasilii Andreivich Bavulin (misspelt "razhden v Konadi 1907"), Tombovka cemetery, Kamsack, SK, visited 27 May 2004.

45 *St. Peter's Bote*, 24 December 1908.

46 G746a, Provincial Archives of Alberta (PAA), Edmonton.

47 On Ukrainian cemeteries and tombstones, see Luciuk and Kordan, *Creating a Landscape*, 14–15; A.M. Kostecki, "Crosses of East Slavic Christianity among Ukrainians in Western Canada," and Bohdan Medwidsky, "Ukrainian Grave Markers in East-Central Alberta," *Material History Bulletin* 29 (1989): 55–8 and 72–5; and James Darlington, "The Ukrainian Impress on the Canadian West," in Luciuk and Hryniuk, *Canada's Ukrainians*, 69–70.

48 Conversation, Henry Ens, Reinland, MB, 24 September 2001. On pioneer Mennonite cemeteries, burial plots, and funeral customs, see the comments about rural Hoffungsort, SK, in Russell, *What's in a Name*, 141; Rempel and Harms, *Atlas*, esp. the cemetery index (145–7 and C1–C39), which identifies known interred by name; Linda Buhler, "Mennonite Burial Customs," *Preservings* 7 (December 1995): 51–2, and 8 (June 1996): 48–50 (the latter issue also discusses two private family cemeteries); and Jacob G. Guenter, "Early Traditional Mennonite Funeral," in *Hague-Osler Mennonite Reserve, 1895–1995* (Hepburn, SK: Hague-Osler Reserve Book Committee, 1995), 634.

49 Conversation, Alex Ewashen, president, Canadian Doukhobor Society, Calgary, 15 September 2001.

50 Nicoli Wasilovitch Shcuratoff, Tolstoi cemetery, Veregin, SK, visited 10 August 2002. See also the epitaph of Ivday Moojalsky: "Free Christian, born in Kawkaz in the province of Tiflis, Russia. Suffered for liberty, repudiated the Russian government, was banished from his native city for 3 years. Refused to serve Russian militarism himself and did not allow his sons to serve. Came to Canada May 6, 1899, died May 9, 1920, at the age of 71 years. Exiled by the Russian autocratic government."

51 The date 1907 comes from the International Association of Jewish Genealogical Societies Cemeteries Project website, http://iajgs.org/cemetery/ (accessed 26 October 2005). A sign offering a reward for information about vandals in a c. 1915 photograph (A2605, PAA) showed how some Edmontonians saw the cemetery as alien space in which to remind Jews of their marginality.

52 Shaarey Zedek cemetery, Winnipeg, visited 21 September 2001.

53 Specifically on rural Jewish cemeteries on the prairies, see, for example, Clara Lander, "Saskatchewan Memories or How to Start a Jewish Cemetery," *American Jewish Archives* 27, 1 (1975): 5–7, and "Starting a Jewish Cemetery in Saskatchewan, Canada," *Western States Jewish History* 31, 2–3 (1999): 168–71; and Scott de Groot, "Jewish Cemeteries in Manitoba," *Jewish Life and Times* 9 (2009)

54 Catherine Cole and Ann Milovic, in *Standing on New Ground: Women in Alberta*, ed. Catherine Cavanaugh and Randi Warne (Edmonton: University of Alberta Press, 1993), 28, mention this initiative in passing.

55 Bill Jessiman, quoted in Rempel and Harms, *Atlas*, 101.

## CHAPTER THREE

1 Andrzej Strzelecki, "The Plunder of Victims and Their Corpses," in *Anatomy of the Auschwitz Death Camp*, ed. Yisrael Gutman and Michael Berenbaum (Bloomington and Indianapolis: Indiana University Press with the United States Holocaust Memorial Museum, 1998), 251; see also Danuta Czech, "The Auschwitz Prisoner Administration," 369–70.

2 Maria Adamowska, "Beginnings in Canada," in *Land of Pain, Land of Promise: First Person Accounts by Ukrainian Pioneers, 1891–1941*, trans. Harry Piniuta (Saskatoon: Western Producer Prairie Books, 1978), 57.

3 See the multifaceted discussion, although the perspective of non-English-speaking immigrants is underrepresented, in R. Douglas Francis and Chris Kitzan, eds., *The Prairie West as Promised Land* (Calgary: University of Calgary Press, 2007).

4 For the Polish position, see Mieczslaw Haiman, *Ślady Polskie w Ameryce* (Chicago: Dziennik Zjednoczeniz, 1938); and Victor Turek, "Poles among the de Meuron Soldiers," *Transactions of the Historical and Scientific Society of Manitoba* 3, 9 (1954): 53–68. The Ukrainian case is found in Paul Yuzyk's review of Turek in *Slavica Canadiana 1954*, ed. J.B. Rudnyc'kyj (Winnipeg: Ukrainian Free Academy of Sciences, 1955), 26; Marunchak, *Ukrainian Canadians*, 25; and Stechishin, *History of Ukrainian Settlement in Canada*, 61–5. Even Belarusians, never a force on the prairies, entered the debate; see *Belaruski holas*, July 1962; and John Sadouski, *A History of the Byelorussians in Canada* (Belleville, ON: Mika, 1981), 39–41. Lithuanians also claimed some of the soldiers without identification with Red River; P.R. Gaida et al., *Lithuanians in Canada* (Ottawa and Toronto: Lights Printing and Publishing, 1967), 21–4.

5 Turek, quoted in Henry Radecki and Benedykt Heydenkorn, *A Member of a Distinguished Family: The Polish Group in Canada* (Toronto: McClelland and Stewart, 1976), 37.

6 Yuzyk, in *Slavica Canadiana 1954*, 26.

7 Peter D. Zacharias, *Reinland: An Experience in Community*, 2nd ed. (Reinland, MB: Reinland Centennial Committee, 2001), 43.

8 Woodcock, *Doukhobors*, 189.

9 The event is identified on the photograph hanging in the National Doukhobor Heritage Village, Veregin, SK (visited 20 August 2008). During celebrations in nearby Kamsack in 1969 on the seventieth anniversary of Doukhobor immigration and settlement, the burning of arms was purely symbolic and staged indoors (S-B9514, Saskatchewan Archives Board, Saskatoon).

10 Letter (Mae Popoff, Saskatoon), Canadian Doukhobor Society *Sheaf*, July 1999; editorial, Canadian Doukhobor Society *Newsletter*, June 1996; annual coverage in both periodicals; and the panel "How the Doukhobors Came to Canada" (quote) in the National Doukhobor Heritage Village. For an earlier period, see, for example, the fiftieth-anniversary poem "Jubilee" by Ivan Gr. Bondarev (Blaine Lake, SK), *Iskra*, 15 April 1949. Josh Sanborn, "Pacifist Politics and Peasant Politics: Tolstoi and the Doukhobors, 1895–1995," *Canadian Ethnic Studies* 27, 3 (1995): 52–71, argues that "the Doukhobor rebellion of 1895 was a carefully orchestrated political act" to attract Tolstoi to their cause. On the enduring importance of the burning of arms, see also Julie Rak, *Negotiated Memory: Doukhobor Autobiographical Discourse* (Vancouver: University of British Columbia Press, 2004).

11 Nelson Gerrard of Arborg, MB, in *Lögberg-Heimskringla*, 28 July 2000 (quotes); and the provincial government pamphlet, *Sigtryggur Jonasson* (Winnipeg: Manitoba Culture, Heritage, and Recreation, 1984).

12 For the landing at Willow Point and psychological importance of Gimli, see July–October issues of the newspapers *Lögberg* and *Heimskringla* on landmark anniversaries of New Iceland's founding in 1925, 1935, and 1950; *Lögberg-Heimskringla* for 1975 and 2000 celebrations; and the journal *Icelandic Canadian*, beginning with the colony's seventy-fifth anniversary in 1950.

13 On Gimli as capital or cradle, see the speech by Neil Bardal, honorary consul general for Iceland in Gimli, in *Lögberg-Heimskringla*, 4 February 2000; and on the seventy-fifth anniversary of immigration and settlement, "Editorial," *Icelandic Canadian* 8, 4 (1950): 9–10, and Jon Laxdal, "New Iceland, 1875–1950," *Icelandic Canadian* 9, 1 (1950): 17–20 and 45–50. W. Kristjanson, "The Influence of Environment on the Icelandic People in Winnipeg," *Icelandic Canadian* 9, 2 (1950): 13–17, makes a case for the advantages of the southern city.

14 *Almanac of the Hungarian Golden Jubilee of Kaposvar-Esterhazy, Saskatchewan, Canada, 1886–1936* (N.p., n.d.), 22; *Kanadai Magyar Újság*, 7 April 1936, profiling the Kaposvar pioneers; and Jean Pask, ed., *Kaposvar: A Count's Colony, 1886–1986* (Esterhazy, SK: Kaposvar Historic Site Society, 1986), 25, 35 (quoting G.V. Dojcsak from *Saskatchewan History*, 1973), and 108.

15 Doerfler, *Quest for a New Homeland*, 71–2.

16 On the Barr Colony founding story and the roles of Barr and Lloyd, see Grant MacEwan in the *Western Weekly Supplement*, 15 May 1963, on its diamond jubilee; the article by Linda Goad in *Homecoming '75*, 27 July 1978, on its seventy-fifth anniversary; and the centennial booklet, *Lloydminster, 1903–2003* (Lloydminster, AB: Meridian Booster, 2003), 14 (quote).

17 Donald Godfrey, "'Canada's Brigham Young': Charles Ora Card, Southern Alberta Pioneer," *American Review of Canadian Studies* 18, 2 (1988): 223–38; and "A History of the Church of Jesus Christ of Latter-Day Saints in Cardston and Area in 1950," http://www.telusplanet.net/public/mtoll/lds.htm, quoting *Chief Mountain Country*, 173–82 (accessed 27 October 2005).

18 See Archives of Manitoba (AM), Winnipeg, Abraham Arnold Papers, P5105, file 64.4; and, on the Hirsch settlement specifically, Arnold's articles in *Canadian Jewish News*, 24 October, 28 November 1975, 27 February 1976, and *Western Jewish News*, 23 October, 6 November 1975.

19 Nancy Schelstraete, *Life in the New Finland Woods: A History of New Finland, Saskatchewan* (Rocanville, SK: New Finland Historical and Heritage Society, 1982), 7–9 and 155–6.

20 Loken, *From Fjord to Frontier*, esp. chs. 6 and 7.

21 Zawadiuk, *Romanians in Alberta*, preface, 92, and 123; and Kobos and Pękacz, *Polonia in Alberta*, 6 and 11.

22 For mainstream coverage of the celebrations, see *Edmonton Bulletin*, 26, 29, 30 June, 3 July 1928; and *Edmonton Journal*, 26, 27, 29, 30 June, 3 July 1928.

23 *Kanadiiskyi farmer*, 1 August 1928; *Zakhidni visty*, June–July 1928, gives the local Ukrainian perspective on the jubilee and Ukrainian Pioneers (Old-Timers) Association.

24 The articles appeared in the calendar almanacs *Providnyk* (1933), published by the St. Raphael's Ukrainian Immigrants' Welfare Association, and *Kaliendar Kanadiiskoho farmera* (1937). See also Bobersky's papers in the Ukrainian Cultural and Educational Centre, Winnipeg; and Pylypiw's obituary, *Ukrainskyi holos*, 28 October 1936.

25 Minutes, Golden Jubilee Working Committee, 18 April 1955, 69.220/1-4, PAA. On initial exclusion of Native "pioneers" from recognition, see Frances Swyripa, "1955—Celebrating Together, Celebrating Apart: Albertans and Their Golden Jubilee," in *Alberta Formed—Alberta Transformed*, vol. 2, ed. Michael Payne et al. (Edmonton: University of Alberta Press and Calgary: University of Calgary Press, 2006), 601–2.

26 James Opp, "Prairie Commemorations and the Nation: The Golden Jubilees of Alberta and Saskatchewan, 1955," in *Canadas of the Mind: The Making and Unmaking of Canadian Nationalisms in the Twentieth Century*, ed. A. Chapnick and N. Hillmer (Montreal and Kingston: McGill-Queen's University Press, 2007), 214–33.

27 Pask, *Kaposvar: A Count's Colony*, 126 (photograph).

28 *Ukrainski visti*, 18 April, 5 September 1955; scrapbook, Michael Luchkovich Papers, Ukrainian Canadian Archives and Museum of Alberta, Edmonton; and *Ukrainskyi pionir*, January, March, September 1955. These sentiments carried into the Ukrainian-Canadian centennial in 1991, in the text to the monument erected by Alberta Ukrainians on the legislature grounds. "Jews Lived in Sask., Alberta, 20 Years before Provincehood" (*Canadian Jewish News*, 7 August 1980) illustrates the importance of timing among other groups; reminiscent of Slavic de Meurons in Red River, it identifies potential pre-settlement-era arrivals, including a Silverman at Fort Edmonton in 1869 prospecting for gold.

29 Philip Petursson, quoted in *Lögberg-Heimskringla*, 27 August 1970; see also ibid., 23 July 1970.

30 On Saskatchewan, see the article by Brother Methodius (Koziak), *Saskatoon Star-Phoenix*, 13 April 1955. On Alberta, see the Ukrainian Catholic bishop of Edmonton, *Ukrainski visti*, 12 September 1955; the member of the Legislative Assembly for Vegreville, Michael Ponich, in the Alberta Legislature, *Vegreville Observer*, 6 April 1955, and *Edmonton Journal*, 12 March 1955; and various pieces in *Ukrainskyi pionir*, January, March, September 1955.

31 Bobersky, in *Kaliendar Kanadiiskoho farmera*, 130; also the passenger list, including W. Ilillik and I. Pylpiwsky, of the SS *Oregon* landing in Quebec on 7 September 1891, http://www.collectionscanada.ca/archivianet/passenger (accessed 13 August 2007). The most authoritative source giving Halifax is Martynowych, *Ukrainians in Canada*, 60.

32 In contrast, *The Diaries of Charles Ora Card* and Lloyd's 1940 memoirs (see Foster, *Trail of 1903*) appeared too late to affect early formulations of Mormon and Barr Colonist founding stories.

33 Sulerzhitskii, *To America with the Doukhobors*, originally published in 1905 as *V Ameriku s dukhoborami*.

34 Abraham Arnold, untitled typescript dated 11 April 1990 (paper presented to Manitoba Historical Society, 11 May 1990), 10–11, in Arnold Papers, P5106, file 65.2, AM.

35 Much Doukhobor music has since been recorded. See, for example, Kenneth Peacock, ed., *Songs of the Doukhobors: An Introductory Outline* (Ottawa: National Museums of Canada, 1970), a National Museums of Canada project; A.P. Markova and P.P. Legebokov, *Sbornik dukhoborcheskikh pslamov, stikhov i pesen* (Grand Forks, BC: Union of Spiritual Communities of Christ, 1978); N.N. Kalmakov, comp., *Dukhovnye stikhi i narodnye pesni dukhobortsev v Kanade* (Richmond, BC: N.N. Kalmakoff, 1991); and the commercial CDs *Saskatoon Doukhobor Choir 2002* and *Saskatchewan Doukhobor Centennial Choir 2005*.

36 Kristjanson, *Icelandic People in Manitoba*, 494. The strength of the saga tradition, and the extensive documentation it left from the pioneering period, perhaps discouraged a secondary literature. Kristjanson's book was the first to utilize some of this data. Þór, *Icelanders in North America*, appeared over three decades later; it neither dealt solely with Canada nor tackled the sweep of Icelandic-Canadian history.

37 See *Manitoba Morning Free Press*, 23 December 1902; and the "aboard ship" photograph reproduced in Woodcock's *Doukhobors*.

38 Offprint, Sigtryggur Jónasson, "The Early Icelandic Settlements in Canada," *Transactions of the Historical and Scientific Society of Manitoba* 59 (22 March 1901).

39 On the Swedish-American impact, see, for example, Viveka Janssen, "Bibliography of Swedish Settlement in Alberta, 1890–1930," *Swedish-American Historical Quarterly* 33, 2 (1982): 124–9, and "Swedish Settlement in Alberta, 1890–1930," ibid., 33, 2 (1982): 111–23. When the Lakehead Social History Institute in Thunder Bay, ON, undertook to produce the first history of Swedes in Canada in the early 2000s, a bundle of its brochures inviting public input were placed in the guest-book receptacle beside the highway cairn to the New Stockholm settlement in Saskatchewan; visited 12 August 2002. The only book-length history of Norwegians in Canada, Loken's *From Fjord to Frontier*, tells a prairie-driven, settlement-era story.

40 Epp, *Mennonites in Canada, 1786–1920*; and Martynowych, *Ukrainians in Canada*.

41 *Souvenir of the Silver Jubilee of St. Peter's Colony, 1903–1928, Zum Andenken an das Silberne Jubiläum der St Peters-Kolonie* (N.p., n.d.); and *Almanac of the Hungarian Golden Jubilee of Kaposvar-Esterhazy*.

42 Pask, *Kaposvar: A Count's Colony*; and, for St. Peter's Colony, n. 44. Unlike the 1936 Hungarian history, the golden jubilee cairn erected at Kaposvar individually named (male) "pioneer settlers" alongside the colony's "archbishops, missionaries and parish priests."

43 Kobos and Pękacz, *Polonia in Alberta*; and Zawadiuk, *Romanians in Alberta*. See also the earlier Matejko, *Polish Settlers in Alberta*. Turek, *Poles in Manitoba*, and the National Museums of Canada research report, G. James Patterson, *Romanians in Saskatchewan: Four Generations of Adaption* (Ottawa: National Museums of Canada, 1977) had quite different stimuli.

44 Doerfler, *Quest for a New Homeland*, ii; *The Best of Humboldt, Centennial Edition: Including Burr, Carmel, Fulda and Marysburg* (Humboldt, SK: Humboldt and District Book Committee, 2006), which celebrated the centennial of both city and province; and *LeRoy and District: Saskatchewan Centennial, 1905–2005* (LeRoy, SK: LeRoy and District Heritage Museum, 2005), which included local celebrations on Saskatchewan's golden jubilee in 1955. On the 1955 provincial anniversary specifically, see also Lindal, *Saskatchewan Icelanders*.

45 Paul Yuzyk, *Ukrainians in Manitoba: A Social History* (Toronto: University of Toronto Press, 1953) competed with overviews of the Ukrainian experience in Alberta as diverse as the three community history volumes published by the Ukrainian Pioneers Association of Alberta between 1970 and 1981, Myrna Kostash's influential and controversial *All of Baba's Children* (Edmonton: Hurtig, 1977), and Helen Potrebenko's *No Streets of Gold: A Social History of Ukrainians in Alberta* (Vancouver: New Star Books, 1977). No overview exists of Saskatchewan. In the 1970s scholarly research on Alberta was stimulated by the creation of the Canadian Institute of Ukrainian Studies at the University of Alberta and the provincial Ukrainian Cultural Heritage Village.

46 N. Flak, "A Brief History of the Ukrainian Pioneers Association of Alberta," in *Ukrainian Pioneers in Alberta, Canada*, ed. Joseph Lazarenko (Edmonton: Ukrainian Pioneers Association of Alberta, 1970), 81–5; and Abraham Arnold Papers, P5111, file 152.1, AM.

47 See Arnold, untitled typescript, Arnold Papers, P5106, file 65.2, AM, on the possibility of non-Jewish neighbours naming New Jerusalem; Smillie, *Visions of the New Jerusalem*, on the theme more generally; Doerfler, *Quest for a New Homeland*, 95; Deuteronomy 8:7–10, quoted by the local member of the Legislative Assembly, Galician-born Nicholas Bachynsky, in *Kalendar Ukrainskoho holosu* (1937), 127; and correspondence (V.A. Sukharev, Grand Forks, BC), *Iskra*, 24 December 1948.

48 Debbie Anne Seipert, "Follow Me, Stanisław Sarnecki, 'The Moses of Rabbit Hill,'" in Kobos and Pęckacz, *Polonia in Alberta*, 38–45; in that volume, see also Andrzej Kobos and Aleksander Matejko, "Jadwiga and Rajmund (Ray) Pierzchajło: From *A World Apart* to the Promised Land of Canada," 248–53, about post-Second World War immigrants. Allusions to Moses could also be oblique and group focussed, as in the chapter "Canadian Exodus," in Woodcock, *Doukhobors*, 130–51; and, by an insider for a later period, Frank Epp, *Mennonite Exodus: The Rescue and Resettlement of the Russian Mennonites since the Communist Revolution* (Altona, MB: Canadian Mennonite Relief and Immigration Council, 1962).

49 W. Kristjanson, "1875—Westward to Manitoba," *Icelandic Canadian* 33, 4 (1975): 18; see also, for example, Laxdal, "New Iceland," 17–20 and 45–50. The best discussion of the biblical exodus/promised land motif in the Icelandic founding story, including the now often ignored role of John Taylor as Moses, is Kirsten Wolf, "Emigration and Myth Making: The Case of the Icelanders in Canada," *Canadian Ethnic Studies* 33, 2 (2001): 1–15.

50 Petryshyn, *Peasants in the Promised Land*. The ultimate biblical parallel—Pylypiw and Eleniak as latter-day Moses leading their people across the ocean—appeared in conjunction with the

centennial monument proposed for the Alberta Legislature grounds (author's private collection). For the communist minority, see, officially, Association of United Ukrainian Canadians and Workers Benevolent Association, *A Tribute to Our Ukrainian Pioneers in Canada's First Century* (Winnipeg: Association of United Ukrainian Canadians and Workers Benevolent Association, 1966), 87–90; and, by a sympathizer, Nay, *Trailblazers of Ukrainian Emigration to Canada.*

51 Epp, *Mennonites in Canada, 1786–1920*, 188–9.

52 Friðjón Friðriksson, address of welcome to Lord Dufferin, in *Framfari*, 17 November 1877.

53 *Almanac of the Hungarian Golden Jubilee of Kaposvar-Esterhazy*, 14 and 20.

54 See Frank Epp, "In Search of Utopia: Mennonites in Manitoba" (paper presented to the Twenty Club, 1956), P5985, AM; E.K. Francis, *In Search of Utopia: The Mennonites in Manitoba* (Altona, MB: D.W. Friesen, 1955); and Koozma Tarasoff and Larry Ewashen, *In Search of Utopia: The Doukhobors*, 3ʳᵈ ed. rev. (Castlegar, BC: Spirit Wrestlers Associates, 1994), plus their film of the same name. The quest motif also appears in *Pioneers and Pilgrims* (Steinbach, MB: DFP Publications, 1990), a history of Steinbach in the East Reserve, and in the chapter with the same title in Woodcock, *Doukhobors*, 152–81.

55 Esterhazy, quoted in Kovacs, *Esterhazy and Early Hungarian Immigration to Canada*,13; Fr. E. Krasitsky, quoted in *Kanadiiskyi ukrainets*, 3 July 1929; and Shirley Adrener, "Arson, Nudity, and Bombs among the Canadian Doukhobors," in *Threatened Identities*, ed. Glynis Breakwell (Chichester and New York: Wiley, 1983), 248.

56 "Emigrants to North America," *Icelandic Canadian* 56, 1 (2000): 16. See also, for example, Guttormur Guttormsson's poems, "Homesteading" (trans. Paul Sigurdson) and "Indian Festival" (trans. Watson Kirkconnell), in *Áróra/Aurora*, ed. Heather Ireland (N.p., n.d.), 5 and 118–22.

57 Ryan Eyford, "Quarantined within a New Colonial Order: The 1876–7 Lake Winnipeg Smallpox Epidemic," *Journal of the Canadian Historical Association* (2006): 55–78. The point about the Vikings is discussed in ch. 6, especially in the context of the Viking statue in Gimli.

58 Elder Wilhelm Ewert, quoted in *Mennonite*, 8 January 1974; see also Epp, *Mennonites in Canada, 1786–1920*, 191–2 and 305.

59 See, for example, *Mennonite*, 26 February, 9 April, 3 September 1974, and Leo Driedger in *Mennonite Quarterly Review*, July 1972; also, for similar soul searching on the Canadian Centennial, *Mennonite Brethren Herald*, 27 January 1967, and *Canadian Mennonite*, 17 January, 13 June 1967. Comparing Manitoba, Oklahoma, Paraguay, and Mexico, Calvin Redekop, "Mennonite Displacement of Indigenous Peoples: An Historical and Sociological Analysis," *Canadian Ethnic Studies* 14, 2 (1982): 71–90, argues that Mennonites "did not overtly displace  indigenous peoples" but were "indirectly responsible" for the violation of human rights in that they accepted, appealed to, and profited from state policy.

60 Canadian Doukhobor Society *Sheaf*, November 1996. See also the photograph, "Doukhobor Village Museum was the site of a large native gathering in October where borshch was introduced as part of the sacred ritual feast," in Canadian Doukhobor Society *Newsletter*, September 1997, regarding British Columbia.

61 Sigtryggur Jónasson dismissed the possibility of an all-Icelandic colony in the United States and warned New Icelanders that if they did not persist where they were, they would likely never receive similar exclusivity elsewhere in Canada; *Framfari*, 8 February 1879.

62 *Framfari*, 6 March, 5, 12, 17 April 1878, 23 June, 17 July 1879. The newspaper (September 1877–September 1879) covered the charges, countercharges, and acrimony from all angles, pledging not only to keep settlers informed but also to help them make up their own minds. Not everyone approved, maintaining that *Framfari* exacerbated dissension in the colony.

63 On the pros and cons of New Iceland as a wise settlement site, see *Framfari*, 30 September, 22 December 1877, 27 February, 6, 13 March, 21 June, 5, 16 July, 23 December 1878, 8, 15 February, 6 March, 23 June, 17 July 1879.

64 Nelson Gerrard of Arborg, MB, in *Lögberg-Heimskringla*, 28 July 2000 (quote). On the government loan and Jónasson's involvement, see *Framfari*, 10 December 1877, 7 January, 8 February, 28 March, 9, 23 April, 14, 31 May, 2, 23 June, 9, 17, 29 July, 22 August, 2, 23 September, 29 October 1879.

65 Contemporary picture drawn from *Framfari*, 30 September 1877, 5, 17 April, 14 June, 8 August, 11, 23 December 1878, 8 (quote), 15 February, 6 March, 14 May 1879. For later expression of the heroic Icelandic pioneering spirit, see "Editorial," 9–10; and Laxdal, "New Iceland," 17–20 and 45–50.

66 *St. Peter's Bote*, 11 October 1904. On settler rejection of the notion of the Promised Land, see also ibid., 11 February 1904 ("St. Peter's Colony is no paradise. Besides, the original paradise is lost and is no where to be found").

67 See, for example, *St. Peter's Bote*, 11, 18 February, 8, 15 March 1904.

68 *St. Peter's Bote*, 11 February 1904.

69 See, for example, *St. Peter's Bote*, 11, 18 February, 26 April, 24, 31 May 1904.

70 "Retrospective Glances," *Souvenir*, n.p.

71 See Jean Pask, "History of Kaposvar," in Pask, *Kaposvar: A Count's Colony*, 7.

72 Rufus Stephenson, quoted in Pask, "History of Kaposvar," 7–8.

73 Kovacs, *Esterhazy and Early Hungarian Immigration to Canada*, 54; the volume's introduction offers the best account of his involvement with the colony (on Esterhazy the man, see esp. 2–3, 31–8, and 48). In Pask, *Kaposvar: A Count's Colony*, see also the reprint of G.V. Dojcsak, "The Mysterious Count Esterhazy," 30–6; and, on the Julius Vass affair, Pask, "History of Kaposvar," 7–8 and 10–14.

74 See the letter, 19 July 1911, cited in *Almanac of the Hungarian Golden Jubilee of Kaposvar-Esterhazy*, 13; L.R. Flook, "Kaposvar: Canada's First Hungarian Colony," in ibid., 22–4; Pask, "History of Kaposvar," 2–26; and Dojcsak, "The Mysterious Count Esterhazy," 30–6.

75 The betrayal of Canada or Gold Mountain also fed a Chinese counter myth, predicated in part upon elusive riches (coalescing around disregard for Chinese lives during construction of the Canadian Pacific Railway), in part upon elusive equality and citizenship. See, for example, Anthony Chan, *Gold Mountain: The Chinese in the New World* (Vancouver: New Star Books, 1983); and Paul Yee, *Tales from Gold Mountain: Stories of the Chinese in the New World* (Vancouver: New Star Books, 1989).

76 See, for example, the contribution to the debate of Martin Johansson, a logger in British Columbia and labourer on Alberta farms, in Eva St. Jean, "'Letters from the Promised Land': The Ambiguous Radicalization of a Swedish Immigrant, 1928–34," *Labour* 53 (2004): 203–21.

77 Larry Warwaruk, *Red Finns on the Coteau*, 2nd ed. (1984; rpt. Muenster, SK: St. Peter's Press, 2004); and Finnish Saskatchewan Genealogical Roots at http://www.rootsweb.com/~cansk/Saskatchewan/ethnic/finnish-saskatchewan.html (accessed 11 August 2007). On the Karelian episode generally, see, by child participant Mayme Sevander, *Red Exodus: Finnish-American Emigration to Russia* (Duluth, MN: Oscat, 1993) and *Soviet Bondage* (Duluth, MN: Oscat, 1996); and the research project by the University of Minnesota at http://www.d.umn.edu/hist/karelia/index2.html (accessed 31 March 2003).

78 See Association of United Ukrainian Canadians and Workers Benevolent Association, *Tribute to Our Ukrainian Pioneers*, the proceedings of the convention at which Pylypiw's son William was guest of honour. Nay, *Trailblazers of Ukrainian Emigration to Canada*, 122–53, discusses both the collapse of Pylypiw and Eleniak's friendship and their posthumous fortunes.

## CHAPTER FOUR

1 Editorial, *Canadian Mennonite*, 13 June 1967.

2 This chapter benefits from discussions with Aya Fujiwara, whose "From Anglo-Conformity to Multiculturalism: The Role of Scottish, Ukrainian, and Japanese Ethnicity in the Transformation of Canadian Identity, 1919–1971" (Ph.D. dissertation, University of Alberta, 2007) explores some of its themes in a different context.

3 Agnes Laut, *The Canadian Commonwealth* (Indianapolis: Bobbs-Merrill, 1915), ch. 7 (quote 113).

4 Dawson, *Group Settlement*, 102; and Epp, *Mennonites in Canada, 1786–1920*, 195.

5 Cited by Earle Waugh, in *Edmonton Journal*, 1 September 1990.

6 Gerhard Wiebe, *Ursachen und Geschichte der Auswanderung der Mennoniten aus Russland nach Amerika* (Winnipeg, 1900), 27, cited in Epp, *Mennonites in Canada, 1786-1920*, 183 (see also 191).

7 Speech (S.F. Rybin, Blaine Lake, SK), *Iskra*, 2 July 1949, quote; and correspondence (Ivan Gr. Bondarev, Blaine Lake), ibid., 26 August 1949. See also Victoria's portrait and its caption, National Doukhobor Heritage Village, Veregin, SK, visited 9 August 2002.

8 Woodcock, *Doukhobors*, 134.

9 LAE, "The Centennial Page," Canadian Doukhobor Society *Newsletter* 2, 2 (1997).

10 Dufferin on Mennonites drawn from Epp, *Mennonites in Canada, 1786-1920*, 217–9; *Manitoba Free Press*, 23 August 1877; and C. Henry Smith, *The Coming of the Russian Mennonites* (Berne, IN: Mennonite Book Concern, 1927), 182–6.

11 *Framfari*, 17 November 1877; Kristjanson, *Icelandic People in Manitoba*, 71–5, based heavily on the *Framfari* account; and *Manitoba Free Press*, 17 September 1877.

12 Adrienne Clarkson during the visit of Iceland's president to Winnipeg, quoted in *Lögberg-Heimskringla*, 25 August 2000. For earlier examples of Dufferin's mobilization, see Laxdal, "New Iceland," 20; and the chronology of North American Icelandic history in *Lögberg-Heimskringla*, 1 June 1967.

13 Ólafur Ragnar Grímsson, president of Iceland, in *Lögberg-Heimskringla*, 4 February 2000.

14 On New Iceland as a "virtual sovereign state" and "democracy or republic," see Laxdal, "New Iceland," 46. Nelson Gerrard, who cites research by Wilhelm Kristjanson and W.J. Lindal, offers an effective critique in *Lögberg-Heimskringla*, 1 December 2000; his evidence includes New Iceland's leaders assuring Dufferin in 1877 that they were loyal British subjects.

15 *Framfari*, 17 November 1877.

16 Paul Yuzyk, *Ukrainian Canadians: Their Place and Role in Canadian Life* (Toronto: Ukrainian Canadian Business and Professional Federation, 1967), 85. *Kalendar Ukrainskoho holosu* (1937), 125–9, printed Tweedsmuir's speech and the official welcome by a member of the Legislative Assembly, Nicholas Bachynsky, who stressed the freedoms and opportunities of Canada compared to the homeland. See also the Ukrainian press on Tweedsmuir's death, February 1940.

17 *Kalendar Ukrainskoho holosu*, 125–9; and Laut, *Canadian Commonwealth*, 113.

18 Arbitrarily, see Kristjanson, *Icelandic People in Manitoba*, 380–5 and 518; Marunchak, *Ukrainian Canadians*, 349–50 and 723; Loken, *From Fjord to Frontier*, 124; Louis Rosenberg, comp., *Chronology of Canadian Jewish History* (N.p., [1959]), 19 and 24; and Turek, *Poles in Manitoba*, 137–41.

19 The Jon Sigurdsson Chapter, Imperial Order Daughters of the Empire, in Winnipeg published three volumes: *Minningarrít Islenzkra Hermanna* (1923), *Veterans of Icelandic Descent, World War II, 1939–1945* (1990), and *A Supplement to Veterans of Icelandic Descent, World War II, 1939–1945* (1993). For Ukrainians, see *Almanakh kanadiiskykh ukrainskykh voiakiv* (Winnipeg: Buduchnist natsii, 1946); and V.J. Kaye, *Ukrainian Canadians in Canada's Wars* (Winnipeg: Ukrainian Canadian Research Foundation, 1983).

20 J.J. Bíldfell, cited in Jónas Þór, *Islendingadagurinn: An Illustrated History* (Winnipeg: Icelandic Festival of Manitoba, 1989), 35. For Ukrainians, see the "Address to the Canadian People" adopted at a mass rally in Winnipeg, *Winnipeg Free Press*, 17 July 1916; *Kanadiiskyi farmer*, 2 February, 9 March 1917; and *Kanadyiskyi rusyn*, 14 November 1917.

21 Friðjón Friðriksson, quoted in *Framfari*, 17 November 1877.

22 See Kristjanson, *Icelandic People in Manitoba*, 204–12 (quotes 210, 212); his "Northwest Rebellion," *Icelandic Canadian* 54, 5 (1998): 169–73, first published in 1953; his "The Influence of Environment on the Icelandic People in Winnipeg," *Icelandic Canadian* 9, 2 (1950): 13–17; and Watson Kirkconnell's translation of Kristinn Stefansson, "The Ninetieth Battalion" (first printed in *Leifur*, 24 July 1885), in *Icelandic Canadian* 54, 5 (1998): 174.

23 See, for example, from the nationalist camp, Yuzyk, *Ukrainian Canadians*; and from the communists, Association of United Ukrainian Canadians and Workers Benevolent Association, *Tribute to Our Ukrainian Pioneers in Canada's First Century*.

24 See, for example, A.J. Arnold in *Jewish Post*, 21 September 1967 (also *Western Jewish News*, 31 August 1967) on the Canadian Jewish Congress's Centennial exhibition in Winnipeg; and in *Western Jewish News*, 21 April 1977.

25 Holy Rosary Roman Catholic Church, Edmonton, visited 10 September 1997; John Huculak, *History of the Holy Rosary Parish in Edmonton, 1913–1988* (Edmonton: Holy Rosary Parish, 1988), 15–35; and scroll, PAA.

26 On the Blaine Lake discussions, see *Iskra*, 28 January, 20 May, 26 August 1949; Creston, BC, celebrated on Dominion Day because it was a Friday, hoping a long weekend would boost attendance (*Iskra*, 27 May 1949).

27 *Globe and Mail*, 4 January 1947. The self-congratulatory messages often boasted that the national citizenship ceremony included every nationality in the Dominion. The *Calgary Herald* (reprinted *Saskatoon Star-Phoenix*, 3 January 1947), however, noted that Canadian citizenship also meant discrimination against Chinese, Japanese, East Asians, and Natives. These groups were not represented at Ottawa (although local Winnipeg ceremonies included a Chinese businessman; *Winnipeg Free Press*, 4, 11 January 1947).

28 On Mynarski, see *Globe and Mail*, 4 January 1947; and *Winnipeg Free Press*, 2, 4, 6 January 1947. Relying on official sources for their information, regional coverage of all three prairie representatives varied little in the big western dailies.

29 On Ens and Eleniak, see *Globe and Mail*, 4 January 1947; *Saskatoon Star-Phoenix*, 2 January 1947; and (Eleniak quotes) *Edmonton Journal*, 14 December 1946, 4 January 1947.

30 Locally, Ens is commemorated at the entrance to Rosthern Centennial Park; Rosthern, SK, visited 6 August 2002. Epp, *Mennonites in Canada, 1786–1920*, 311–12 and 403, draws on the *Saskatoon Star-Phoenix* (2 January 1947) for Ens's career; it also notes his sympathies for the Lutheran dissenter Swedenborg, who attracted a following among Canadian prairie Mennonites.

31 *Edmonton Journal*, 17 December 1947.

32 Of the two big pioneer newspapers, both Winnipeg based, *Ukrainskyi holos* (22 January 1947) carried the standard account of the Ottawa ceremony and Eleniak; *Kanadiiskyi farmer* (8 January

1947) ran a front-page photograph and summary of his life, ending with the successes of his grandchildren. Both newspapers serialized Judge W.J. Lindal's *Canadian Citizenship and Our Wider Loyalties* (June and July 1946). The communist *Ukrainske slovo* (8 January 1947) covered the Ottawa events and named Eleniak but stressed how Ukrainians had earned their citizenship by "back-breaking labour" and despite prejudice and discrimination.

33  Quoted in *Novyi shliakh*, 1 June 1946. For other mainstream venues, see the local music teacher in *Saskatoon Star-Phoenix*, 6 January 1947; the editor of *Novyi shliakh* in *Winnipeg Free Press*, 7 January 1947; and the Ukrainian Catholic bishop at special Catholic citizenship services for Manitoba, St. Boniface cathedral, *Winnipeg Free Press*, 6 January 1947.

34  *Mennonite Mirror*, December 1974; see also the centennial issue, January–February 1974.

35  Editorial, *Carillon*, 31 July 1974. On Mennonites' national bicentennial, see *Mennonite Reporter*, 31 March, 18 August 1986.

36  *Israelite Press*, 6 January 1967; and *Western Jewish News*, 23 March 1967. See also *Canadian Jewish News*, 30 June 1967. The Proclamation of Faith and Thanksgiving, read before the House of Commons and various provincial legislatures, had expressed similar sentiments; see *Commemorative Report on National Bicentenary of Canadian Jewry, 1759–1959* (Montreal: Canadian Jewish Congress, 1959), inside cover, also 4, 6, and 27–33 for tributes by Prime Minister John Diefenbaker, Governor General Georges Vanier, and members of the Commons, Senate, and provincial assemblies.

37  Carl Berger, *The Sense of Power: Studies in the Ideas of Canadian Imperialism, 1867–1914* (Toronto: University of Toronto Press, 1970), 78–108. Murray Barkley, "The Loyalist Tradition in New Brunswick: The Growth and Evolution of an Historical Myth, 1825–1914," *Acadiensis* 4, 1 (1975): 3–45, sees the Loyalist tradition there as a form of regional patriotism, especially in times of crisis; yet by preserving ideals and institutions forming the "cornerstones of Canadian nationality," New Brunswick Loyalists also became founding fathers of Canada.

38  See Owram, *Promise of Eden*, esp. 214–6 (quotes); also Frits Pannekoek, "The Historiography of the Red River Settlement, 1830–1868," *Prairie Forum* 6, 1 (1981): 75–85.

39  *Kanadiyskyi ranok*, 21 May 1921; Ludwik Kos-Rabcewicz-Zubkowski, *The Poles in Canada* (Ottawa and Montreal: Polish Alliance Press, 1968), 192; and Loken, *From Fjord to Frontier*, 211.

40  Plaudits by Canadian establishment figures range from Lieutenant Governor S.W. Bowles's remarks about Icelanders on Manitoba's centennial, *Lögberg-Heimskringla*, 27 August 1970, to the scroll and letter from Prime Minister Jean Chrétien on the Doukhobor centennial, Canadian Doukhobor Society *Newsletter* 1, 5 (1996). For groups' own enumeration of their virtues, see, at random, Dreisziger, *Struggle and Hope*, 228–30; Loken, *From Fjord to Frontier*, 44–101; Yuzyk, *Ukrainians in Manitoba*, 40–5 and 52; and, on mainstream and group landmark occasions, the ethno-religious press.

41  Turek, *Poles in Manitoba*, 93; Slavic settlers, Turek said, would have achieved even more had they received only "a part of funds ... spent on sponsoring the colonization by the immigrants from the British Isles, and other settlers of Anglo-Saxon origin." See also Radecki and Heydenkorn, *Member of a Distinguished Family*, 221; and William Makowski, *History and Integration of Poles in Canada* (Niagara Peninsula, ON: Tundra Books, 1967), 48.

42  See Abraham Arnold, "The Contribution of the Jews to the Opening and Development of the West," *Transactions of the Historical and Scientific Society of Manitoba* 3, 25 (1968–9): 23–37; his untitled typescript revisiting New Jerusalem (Manitoba Historical Society Conference, 1990), Abraham Arnold Papers, P5106, file 65.2, AM; and in *Canadian Jewish News*, 16 May, 11 July 1975, 27 February 1976, 19 August 1982.

43  Yuzyk, *Ukrainian Canadians*, 11–12; see also his "75th Anniversary of Ukrainian Settlement in Canada," *Ukrainian Review* 14, 1 (1967): 81.

44 In Pierre Berton's *The Promised Land: Settling the West, 1896–1914* (Toronto: McClelland and Stewart, 1984) Ukrainians moved to the centre of the national narrative, opening the prairie saga. See also James MacGregor's sympathetic *Vilni Zemli/Free Lands: The Ukrainian Settlement of Alberta* (Toronto: McClelland and Stewart, 1969), the first Anglo-Canadian work since Charles Young's more scholarly (and more critical) *Ukrainian Canadians: A Study in Assimilation* (Toronto: T. Nelson, 1931).

45 In *All of Baba's Children*, 30–1, Myrna Kostash criticizes the sons and daughters of the pioneers for their complacent view of the past as a parade of "firsts" and success stories. To relieve their marginality, she argues, they had to make "good" Canadians of the peasants in sheepskin coats and ignore the discrimination and pressures to assimilate. See also Yar Slavutych, *The Conquerors of the Prairies* (Edmonton: Slavuta Publishers, 1984), 5–6 and 22–5.

46 Woodcock, *Doukhobors*, 152–260 (quote 174), remains the best account of the prairie exodus and subsequent relations with the state.

47 Ibid., 198, 203, and 204.

48 From Doukhobors' golden jubilee, see correspondence, *Iskra*, 25 March 1949 (Roman B. Chursinov, Kamsack, SK), 3 June 1949 (Malania I. Popova, Midway, BC), 10 June 1949 (P.D. Arishchenkov, West Grand Forks, BC), 22 July 1949 (Petr Negreev, Canora, SK), 16 September 1949 (Fedor D. Fillipov, Prekrasnoe, BC). From the Doukhobor centennial, see, for example, Koozma Tarasoff on the land issue in Saskatchewan, Canadian Doukhobor Society *Newsletter* 2, 4 (1997); and the flyer for the book *Spirit-Wrestlers' Voices* (author's private collection).

49 Canadian Doukhobor Society *Sheaf* 4, 2 (1999).

50 No monograph exists on Ukrainians in Ontario or Quebec, only a special issue of *Polyphony* by the Multicultural History Society of Ontario, and a collection of essays, Alexander Biega and Myroslaw Diakowsky, eds., *The Ukrainian Experience in Quebec* (Toronto: Basilian Press, 1994).

51 Iwan Perederyj, comp. and ed., *Centennial of the First Ukrainian Settlement in Canada, 1891–1991: Commemorative Philately, Memorabilia, and Architecture* (Cornwall, ON: Author, 1995–6), 11, 34, 36, 39, and 50.

52 This point is discussed more thoroughly in ch. 5.

53 See, for example, the toast to Canada by Robert Winters, minister of trade and commerce, at Canadian Centennial celebrations in Gimli, *Icelandic Canadian* 26, 1 (1967): 19–20; *Lögberg-Heimskringla*, 1 June 1967; and Kristjanson's *Icelandic People in Manitoba*.

54 Winters, *Icelandic Canadian*, 20, for 1967; and *Lögberg-Heimskringla*, 1 (quote), 22, 29 September, 6 October 2000, for commemoration of Kinmount and Markland. The political implications of the nationalization of the prairie narrative in the Icelandic and Ukrainian communities differed considerably. Although Manitoba, and especially New Iceland, established Icelanders' pioneering claims in the West, Denmark's recognition of Iceland as a sovereign state in 1918 precluded the need for a prairie-based founding myth that demanded state support for group survival (see, for example, Kristjanson, *Icelandic People in Manitoba*, 517).

55 *Mennonite Mirror*, February 1975 (quote); and *Mennonite*, 8 July 1986.

56 Gerard Jennisen, Manitoba Legislative Assembly, quoted in *Preservings* 8 (June 1996): 50.

57 Editorial, *Mennonite Mirror*, January–February 1974.

58 See *Mennonite Brethren Herald*, 31 October 1986, on both the original trek and one family's re-enactment; *Mennonite Reporter*, 31 March (Vineland memorial), 28 July (historical dramas) 1986; and *Mennonite*, 12 August 1986.

59 *Mennonite Reporter*, 31 March 1986; see also the request to bring stones to the Conference of Mennonites in Canada meeting in Steinbach in 1974, *Mennonite*, 3 September 1974.

60  *Mennonite Brethren Herald*, 25 July 1986; *Mennonite*, 11 February 1986; and Kathy Shantz Good, in *Mennonite Reporter*, 31 March, 15 September 1986.

61  See, for example, Gerald Tulchinsky, *Taking Root: The Origins of the Canadian Jewish Community* (Toronto: Lester Publishing, 1992) and *Branching Out: The Transformation of the Canadian Jewish Community* (Toronto: Stoddart, 1998).

62  See, on Quebec's appropriation of Ezekiel Hart, Canadian Jewish Congress, *Commemorative Report*, 9; on Jews at the conquest, Rosenberg, *Chronology*, 2 and 3; and on parallels between Aaron Hart and Italians' Giovanni Caboto, Roberto Perin, "Making Good Fascists and Good Canadians: Consular Propaganda and the Italian Community in Montreal in the 1930s," in *Minorities and Mother Country Imagery*, ed. Gerald Gold (St. John's: Institute of Social and Economic Research, Memorial University, 1984), 136–58.

63  On Toronto and the bicentenary, see *Canadian Jewish News*, 12 February 1960.

64  Rosenberg, *Chronology*, 12–14. On the prairies in jubilee schema and rhetoric, see also *Jewish Post*, 24 December 1959; *Israelite Press*, 11 December 1959; and Canadian Jewish Congress, *Commemorative Report*.

65  *Western Jewish News*, 1 October 1959.

66  Ibid.; and *Israelite Press*, 2 October 1959 (quote). See also *Canadian Jewish News*, 8 April 1960.

67  *Israelite Press*, 6, 13 January 1967 (republished 22, 29 September 1967).

68  Report by A.J. Arnold and Harry Gutkin, Abraham Arnold Papers, P5111, file 152.5, AM. Harry Gutkin, *Journey into Our Heritage: The Story of the Jewish People in the Canadian West* (Toronto: Lester and Orpen Dennys, 1980) is based on the exhibit.

69  Based on Abraham Arnold Papers, P5110, file 151.2; and P5111, file 152.1, AM.

70  *Jewish Post and News*, 18 July 1990.

71  Abraham Arnold, in *Canadian Jewish News*, 24 January 1980; see also *Western Jewish News*, 11 February 1982.

72  A.J. Arnold, in *Western Jewish News*, 3, 10 (quote) June 1982; see also editorial, *Jewish Post*, 4 November 1982.

73  Dreisziger, *Struggle and Hope*, 66.

74  *Almanac of the Hungarian Golden Jubilee of Kaposvar-Esterhazy*, esp. 22–6; and Pask, *Kaposvar: A Count's Colony*. Neither book carried greetings from other Hungarian communities in Canada; the 1936 volume included messages from Saskatchewan's lieutenant governor and premier, and the Saskatchewan Archives Board provided the foreword in 1986.

75  On psychological and other differences among Independent, Community, and Sons of Freedom Doukhobors, see Harry Hawthorn, ed., *The Doukhobors of British Columbia: Report of the Doukhobor Research Committee* (Vancouver: University of British Columbia, 1952), 100, 121, 162–4, and 325.

76  *Western Producer*, 25 June 1959.

77  Woodcock, *Doukhobors*, 241.

78  *Kavalkada*, summarized in *Iskra*, 2 September–4 November 1949. See also the editorial, *Iskra*, 22 July 1949; and, for a later period, Woodcock's *Doukhobors*.

79  J.J. Verigin, telephone conversation, 31 August 2001. As Doukhobors began their second century in Canada, world events helped them focus around global peace. See, in particular, the discussions about a mission statement, Doukhobor Unity Conference, Calgary, 15 September 2001 (author's notes, with thanks to J.J. Verigin for the invitation to attend).

## Chapter Five

1 Open letter, I.F. Stuchnov (Penticton, BC) to Ivan Gr. Bondarev (Blaine Lake, SK), *Iskra*, 19 August 1949.

2 *Cardston News*, 7 July (Hillspring Ward), 4 August (Aetna) 1955.

3 On commemorating Shevchenko in Canada, see the Ukrainian-language press for March (the month in which he was born and died), beginning with 1914, the centenary of his birth.

4 Baron Segismund Perenyi, quoted in *Almanac of the Hungarian Golden Jubilee of Kaposvar-Esterhazy*, 15.

5 Guðni Ágústsson, minister of agriculture for Iceland, quoted in *Lögberg-Heimskringla*, 5 July 2002.

6 Henry Provisor, "London, Broadcasts about the Chair of Icelandic," *Icelandic Canadian* 8, 3 (1950): 9–10; W.J. Lindal, "Distinguished Visitors from Iceland," *Icelandic Canadian* 9, 2 (1950): 18–20; and Kristjanson, *Icelandic People in Manitoba*, 466 and 477–82 (quote 482).

7 See, for example, Kristjanson, *Icelandic People in Manitoba*, 2–6 and 11–12; "Editorial," *Icelandic Canadian* 8, 4 (1950): 9–10; and Wolf, "Emigration and Mythmaking," 1–8.

8 Sigtryggur Jónasson, in *Framfari*, 8 February 1879.

9 Conversation, Sigrid Johnson, University of Manitoba, January 2003.

10 Ingibjörg Jónsson (address as *fjallkona*, 1951), quoted in *Lögberg-Heimskringla*, 27 July 2001; and ibid., 5 July 2002. See the Icelandic-Canadian press, late summer/early fall, for both the toast to Iceland and the *fjallkona*'s speech, traditionally delivered in Icelandic; *fjallkona* herself is discussed in ch. 6.

11 Thanks to Ryan Eyford for this observation.

12 Loken, *From Fjord to Frontier*, 120–4.

13 For the delicate retelling of the group's wartime story, see Dreisziger, *Struggle and Hope*, 160–2 and 169–73. On downplaying the attraction of Hitler and National Socialism for some Mennonites, see Epp, *Mennonites in Canada, 1920–1940*, 548.

14 Turek, *Poles in Manitoba*, 136–45 (quotes 137 and 145).

15 On Ukrainian input into multiculturalism, see Bohdan Bociurkiw, "The Federal Policy of Multiculturalism and the Ukrainian-Canadian Community," in *Ukrainian Canadians, Multiculturalism, and Separatism: An Assessment*, ed. Manoly Lupul (Edmonton: Canadian Institute of Ukrainian Studies, 1978), 98–128; community briefs (author's private collection); Ukrainian Community Development Committee (Prairie Region), *Building the Future: Ukrainian Canadians in the 21ˢᵗ Century: A Blueprint for Action* (Edmonton: n.p., 1986); and Manoly Lupul, *The Politics of Multiculturalism: A Ukrainian-Canadian Memoir* (Toronto: Canadian Institute of Ukrainian Studies Press, 2005).

16 Donald Dawson, "Community Power Structure and the Rise of Ethnic Language Programs in Public Schooling" (Ph.D. dissertation, University of Alberta, 1982), esp. 98–144 and 172–215; Manoly Lupul, "The Canadian Institute of Ukrainian Studies," in *Ethnic Canadians: Culture and Education*, ed. Martin Kovacs (Regina: Canadian Plains Research Center, 1978), 445–9 (quote); and Lupul, *Politics of Multiculturalism*, 233–60.

17 Manoly Lupul, "The Tragedy of Canada's White Ethnics: A Constitutional Post-Mortem," *Journal of Ukrainian Studies* 7, 1 (1982): 3–15; see also his "The Political Implementation of Multiculturalism," *Journal of Ukrainian Studies* 17, 1 (1982): 93–10, and *Politics of Multiculturalism*, 301–21 and 438–82.

18  Association of United Ukrainian Canadians and Workers Benevolent Association, *Tribute to Our Ukrainian Pioneers.*

19  See A.M. Shlepakov et al., *Ukrainian Canadians in Historical Ties with the Land of Their Fathers (Dedicated to the 100ᵗʰ Anniversary of Ukrainian Settlement in Canada)*, trans. Viktor Kotolupov and Viktor Ruzhitsky (Kyiv: Dnipro Publishers, 1991), the unplanned swan song of Soviet-era scholarship; Petro Kravchuk, ed. and comp., *Z ridnoho hnizda: Diaspora—100 rokiv emihratsii ukraintsiv do Kanady* (Kyiv: Firma "Dovira," 1992), which plays with the concept of diaspora; Iu.Iu. Slyvka, ed., *Ukrainska emihratsiia: Istoriia i suchasnist—Materialy mizhnarodnykh naukovykh konferentsii prysviachenykh 100-richchiu emihratsii ukraintsiv do Kanady* (Lviv: Kameniar, 1992); and my extended review in *Journal of Ukrainian Studies* 22, 1–2 (1997): 219–24.

20  The Doukhobor figures were Canada and the former Soviet Union 30,000 each, United States 500; invitation, centennial exhibit, "Spirit Wrestlers: The Doukhobors," Canadian Museum of Civilization, Hull, QC, 18 January 1996–12 October 1997 (author's private collection). For Mennonites, see Gerard Jennisen, addressing the Manitoba Legislative Assembly, quoted in *Preservings* 8 (June 1996): 50.

21  See, for example, Owram, *Promise of Eden*; Smillie, *Visions of the New Jerusalem*; and the most recent reprint of Rasporich's "Utopian Ideals and Community Settlements in Western Canada, 1880–1914," in Francis and Kitzan, *Prairie West as Promised Land*, 127–54.

22  *Martyrs Mirror* is available in English at http://www.homecomers.org/mirror. See also, for example, Cornelius Krahn, *The Witness of the Martyr's Mirror for Our Day* (Newton, KS: Bethel College, 1974); Aaron Toews, *Mennonite Martyrs: People Who Suffered for Their Faith, 1920–1940*, trans. John Toews (Winnipeg and Hillsboro, KS: Kindred Press, 1990) on the Soviet era; Rod Sider's sermon, in *Mennonite Brethren Herald*, 31 October 1986, on the national bicentennial; and, for the 200-year-old leather-bound copy in a Springfeldt, SK, home, Russell, *What's In a Name*, 290.

23  During the prairie Mennonite centennial, see, for example, Paul Erb, in *Mennonite*, 26 February 1974; H.L. Sawatzky (Department of Geography, University of Manitoba), in *Mennonite Life*, midyear 1974; and Al Reimer, in *Mennonite Mirror*, December 1974.

24  Jim Coggins, in *Mennonite Brethren Herald*, 16 May 1986; see also the comments by Robert Kreider, of Russian Mennonite descent, in *Mennonite Mirror*, January–February 1974.

25  *Mennonite Mirror*, January–February 1974. See also Frank Epp, in *Mennonite Brethren Herald*, 12 July 1974; and Rev J.H. Neufeld, in *Mennonite Mirror*, April 1974.

26  Sales of Vladimir Chertkov's *Christian Martyrdom in Russia*, published in 1897, were influential in raising money to finance the Doukhobor emigration to Canada.

27  Hawthorn, *Doukhobors of British Columbia*, 51.

28  On martyrs during the golden jubilee, see *Iskra*, 6, 27 May, 19 August 1949, all involving British Columbia. On the Canadian repertoire of hymns recalling old-world martyrdom, see, for example, Peacock, *Songs of the Doukhobors*, 61, 79–86, and 89–95, and *Twenty Ethnic Songs from Western Canada* (Ottawa: National Museum of Canada, 1966), 32–7; and for contemporary prairie performances of historical hymns, the CD *Saskatoon Doukhobor Choir* (2002), esp. recordings 5–9. More generally for topics discussed in this chapter, see Rak, *Negotiated Memory*.

29  Frank Epp, in *Mennonite Mirror*, January 1975; and Woodcock, *Doukhobors*, 10–11.

30  Kukushkin, "Back in the USSR."

31  Glass, "The Settlement of Prairie Jews in Palestine, 1917–1939," 215–43.

32  Rose Albano, "The Manteca Russian Colony," *Manteca Bulletin*, 11 May 1997, http://www.doukhobor.org (accessed 4 June 2007); and Woodcock, *Doukhobors*, 168–9.

33 Hawthorn, *Doukhobors of British Columbia*, tried both to explain Doukhobor attitudes and behaviour and to find a solution to problems posed by the sect, especially Sons of Freedom; see 12, 18–57, 122, 143, 150–3, 158–61, 172–3, 183, 256, and 330. See also Woodcock, *Doukhobors*, 308–61.

34 On return to and relations with the homeland, both before and after 1917, see, for example, Hawthorn, *Doukhobors of British Columbia*, 330; Woodcock, *Doukhobors*, 261–83 and 293; J.L. Black, *Canada in the Soviet Mirror: Ideology and Perception in Soviet Foreign Affairs, 1917–1991* (Ottawa: Carleton University Press, 1998), 3–4, 42–3, 239, 326–7, and 338; and, in Andrew Donskov et al., eds., *The Doukhobor Centenary in Canada* (Ottawa: Slavic Research Group/Institute of Canadian Studies, University of Ottawa, 2000), the articles by Eli Popoff, Jack McIntosh, Koozma Tarasoff, and Julie Rak.

35 *Iskra*, 14 January, 29 April, 13 May, 15, 22 July, 12, 19 August, 16 September 1949.

36 *Toronto Star*, 28 May 1989.

37 Epp, *Mennonites in Canada, 1786–1920*, 195.

38 Frank Epp, in *Mennonite Brethren Herald*, 12 July 1974; and address, David Schroeder (Canadian Mennonite Bible College), to the centennial celebration in the Winnipeg Arena, 28 July, in *Carillon* (Steinbach), 25 November 1974.

39 Adolf Ens, in *Mennonite Reporter*, 25 November 1974; emphasis in original.

40 Editorial, *Mennonite Mirror*, January–February 1974.

41 Leo Driedger, *Mennonite Identity in Conflict* (Lewiston, NY, and Queenston, ON: Edwin Mellen Press, 1988), 99–102.

42 For this paragraph, see editorial, *Canadian Mennonite*, 13 June 1967 (Canada's "goodness"); Vic Penner, in *Mennonite Mirror*, December 1974, on contemporary Manitoba martyrs; the works of Leo Driedger, including *Mennonite Identity in Conflict* (50–9, 77, and 204); Peter Wiebe and Leo Driedger, in *Canadian Mennonite*, 13 June 1967 ("good, positive middle-class acceptance by the world may yet kill us"); and, for a more appreciative view of Canada's middle-class blessings, John Redekop, in *Mennonite Brethren Herald*, 9 June 1967.

43 *Ottawa Citizen*, January–June 1996. Similar distancing from the radicals by mainstream Doukhobors occurred during the fiftieth anniversary of the group's immigration and settlement; see, for example, *Iskra*, 13 May, 15 July, 29 August 1949.

44 Doukhobor Unity Conference, Calgary, 15 September 2001 (author's notes).

45 Rudy Friesen with Sergey Shmakin, *Into the Past: Buildings of the Mennonite Commonwealth* (Winnipeg: Raduga Publications, 1996), 8. See also, for example, the Doukhobor pilgrimage to Russia described by participant Allan Markin, in *Trail Times*, 22 October 2004.

46 Alex Ewashen, in Canadian Doukhobor Society *Sheaf* 3, 4 (1998); see also his report, as Canadian Doukhobor Society president, in *Sheaf* 7, 3 (2001): 1, in support of the still unrealized project, which, he regretted, the society had supported less than the Union of Spiritual Communities of Christ.

47 *Write It in Your Heart and Proclaim It in Song* (Aprelevka Sound Inc.) was the English translation of the album, available from Spirit Wrestlers Associates in Castlegar, BC (brochure, n.d., author's private collection).

48 Koozma Tarasoff, "More Doukhobors Move from Georgia to Russia," http://www.doukhobor. org/stories.html (accessed 25 May 2008). Relocation was still in progress in 2007–8; on the same site, see Jonathan Kalmakoff's "Georgian Doukhobors Relocate to Tambov, Russia" (2007) and "More Georgian Doukhobors Move to Tambov" (2008). More generally, see Svetlana I. Inkova, "Doukhobors of the USSR at the End of the 1980s," *Canadian Ethnic Studies* 27, 3 (1995): 181–95.

49  Thanks to Jars Balan for use of his paper, "California Dreaming: Agapius Honcharenko's Role in the Formation of a Pioneer Ukrainian Canadian Intelligentsia" (June 2007, author's private collection).

50  *Edmonton Bulletin*, 4 February 1901.

51  "Introduction," in Card, *Mormon Presence in Canada*, xix.

52  Woodsworth, *Strangers within Our Gates*, 78–86. Woodsworth concluded that Mormons, "though American, are in no true sense American, and their presence is a serious menace to our Western civilization" (83).

53  See the birthday greetings and pioneer obituaries (including reprints in the column "30 Years Ago") carried in the *Cardston News* during Alberta's golden jubilee in 1955.

54  For a local perspective, see the editorial ("We're Different Than the Americans"), *Cardston News*, 20 January 1955. Scholarly views on the continental context of Mormonism, Canadian-American comparisons, and ethno-religious peoplehood can be found in Card, *Mormon Presence in Canada*; and Peter Morris, "Charles Ora Card and Mormon Settlement on the Northwestern Plains Border," in *The Borderlands of the American and Canadian Wests: Essays on Regional History of the Forty-Ninth Parallel*, ed. Sterling Evans (Lincoln, NB: University of Nebraska Press, 2006), 172–82.

55  Per Rudling, "Scandinavians in Canada: A Community in the Shadow of the United States," *Swedish-American Historical Quarterly* 57, 3 (2006): 152–60, compares American and Canadian numbers and notes immigrants' desirability, assimilability, and delayed movement to Canada.

56  Windschiegl, *Fifty Golden Years*, 47–61.

57  Myron Kuropas, *The Ukrainian Americans: Roots and Aspirations, 1884–1954*, published in Canada (Toronto: University of Toronto Press, 1991), was the first real American study since 1914. Orest Subtelny, *Ukrainians in North America: An Illustrated History* (Toronto: University of Toronto Press, 1991) treated Canada and the United States separately; the conference, Cross-Stitching Cultural Borders: Comparing Ukrainian Experience in Canada and the United States, University of Toronto, 1998, examined interaction as well as similarities and differences.

58  See the booklet *Ukrainians in North Dakota*, originally published in *North Dakota History* 53, 3 (1986), which relies on Canadian scholarship for contextualizing the North Dakota experience; participation by local youth in Ukrainian dance competitions in Manitoba and Saskatchewan, *Journal of the Ukrainian Cultural Institute* 23, 1 (2003): 1, and program, Ukrainian Festival, Dickinson, ND, 18–20 July 2003; in the same program, Canada as the source of a *pyrohy*-making machine; and Andriy Nahachewsky, "Eat, Dance, and Be Ukrainian: The Dauphin (Manitoba) and Dickinson (North Dakota) Summer Festivals," presented at Cross Stitching Cultural Borders

59  Oleh Gerus, "The Reverend Semen Sawchuk and the Ukrainian Greek Orthodox Church of Canada," *Journal of Ukrainian Studies* 16, 1–2 (1991): 67–77.

60  Virgil Lundquist, *A Century of Faith: New Stockholm Lutheran Church, 1889–1989, Stockholm, Saskatchewan* (Stockholm, SK: Centennial Committee, New Stockholm Lutheran Church, [1989]), 3, 8–9, 11, 14, and 16. At the church's golden jubilee in 1939, the prairies and northwestern Ontario dominated the Canadian conference.

61  Loken, *From Fjord to Frontier*, 127–46 (quote 130), 165, and 200–6; Loken himself had a lengthy institutional relationship with Camrose Lutheran College. Rudling, "Scandinavians in Canada," 161–3, notes, but does not pursue, the pan-North American character of Scandinavian religious life; he also notes the pervasive influence of the Scandinavian-American press.

62  Loken, *From Fjord to Frontier*, 178–80.

63  Epp, *Mennonites in Canada, 1786–1920*, 195.

64  Calgary historian J.B. Toews, in *Mennonite Life*, midyear 1974. Drawing on the memoirs of Elder

Gerhard Wiebe, Toews described conservative attitudes, which created a predisposition for emigration, as "an inability to understand the changes Russia had undergone by 1870; a strong suspicion of the outside world, especially government officials; a cultural isolation which involved an ignorance of the Russian language; a negativistic pacifism which rejected war but refused to assume any positive obligations and duties" (9). See also, for example, Loewen, "A House Divided," 127–43.

65　Royden Loewen, *Family, Church, and Market: A Mennonite Community in the Old and New Worlds* (Urbana: University of Illinois Press, 1993); and his "'The Children, the Cows, My Dear Man and My Sister': The Transplanted Lives of Mennonite Farm Women, 1874–1900," *Canadian Historical Review* 73, 3 (1992): 344–73.

66　H.L. Sawatzky and Peter Penner, in *Mennonite Mirror*, February, March 1975.

67　Beverly Suderman, in *Mennonite*, 11 February 1986.

68　David Arnason, in David Arnason and Vincent Arnason, eds., *The New Icelanders: A North American Community* (Winnipeg: Turnstone Press, 1994), 6.

69　See Provisor, "London, Broadcasts about the Chair of Icelandic," 9–10; Kristjanson, *Icelandic People in Manitoba*, esp. 274; Þór, *Icelanders in North America*, 163–79; and important dates in North American Icelandic history, in *Lögberg-Heimskringla*, 1 June 1967.

# Chapter Six

1　*Esterhazy Observer*, 9 July 1936; see also Pask, *Kaposvar: A Count's Colony*, 49, 53, 56, and 199 (from the silver jubilee).

2　"General-gubernator Kanady mizh ukraintsiamy," *Kalendar Ukrainskoho holosu* (1937), 125.

3　Edam, SK, visited 6 November 2004 (its windmill honoured the province's seventy-fifth anniversary); Neerlandia, AB, visited 8 May 2004; Dickson, AB, visited 26 May 2002. Dickson plans included a miniature castle and drawbridge, Viking ship, and figures from Hans Christian Anderson's fairy tales (undated flyer, author's private collection). See also the useful *Scandinavian Connections: A Guide to Sites in Alberta* (Edmonton: Scandinavian Trade and Cultural Society, 2007).

4　Hussar had German roots and Viking was in a Norwegian area. Cossack could have been chosen as a surname; Rudnytskyi, "Kanadiiski heohrafichni nazvy ukrainskoho pokhodzhennia," 787.

5　Pask, *Kaposvar: A Count's Colony*, 48 and 54.

6　*Propamiatna knyha z nahody zolotoho iuvileiu poselennia ukrainskoho narodu v Kanadi*, 280 and 293; see also the documentary, *Real Communities: Local Culture and Diversity on the Prairies* (Friends of the Ukrainian Folklore Centre, University of Alberta, 2005).

7　*Icelandic Canadian* 33, 4 (1975); and *Propamiatna knyha z nahody zolotoho iuvileiu poselennia ukrainskoho narodu v Kanadi*, 253.

8　On Cossack symbolism, see the posters, souvenir programs, and media coverage from Canada's National Ukrainian Festival (est. 1966) in Dauphin, MB, and the Pysanka Festival (est. 1974) in Vegreville, AB. Oakburn, MB, visited 28 May 2004.

9　Viking, AB, visited 5 October 2003 (see also *Centennial Bulletin*, Edmonton, February 1967); Erickson, MB, visited 28 May 2004.

10　Gimli and Hecla Island, MB, visited 22 September 2001. See, for the Centennial logo, *Icelandic Canadian* 25, 4 (1967): cover; for the Viking statue, designed by Gussur Eliasson, *Icelandic*

*Canadian* 25, 4 (1967): 19–22, and "Icelandic Day Celebration 1967," *Icelandic Canadian* 26, 1 (1967), 22–4; and for Viking festival imagery, Þór, *Íslendingadagurinn*, 96–102.

11 Frank Arnason, quoted in *Lögberg-Heimskringla*, 27 August 1969.

12 "Centennial Report," *Icelandic Canadian* 25, 1 (1966): 44 (quote); Haraldur Bessason, "Leifr Eiriksson," *Icelandic Canadian* 25, 2 (1966): 11–16; "The Leifr Eiriksson Plaque," *Icelandic Canadian* 25, 3 (1967): 23; and on the unveiling, *Icelandic Canadian* 25, 4 (1967): 28–37. Erickson, MB, was named for its postmaster; Rudnyc'kyj, *Manitoba Mosaic of Place Names*, 64.

13 The ultimate Ukrainian-Canadian appeal to the past was to medieval Rus', when Kyiv's princes forged dynastic ties across Europe and participated in European affairs as equals. The notion that the marriage of King Harold's daughter to Grand Prince Volodymyr Monomakh "gave the present Queen Elizabeth II of England and Canada an infusion of Ukrainian blood" (Michael Czuboka, *Ukrainian Canadian, Eh? The Ukrainians of Canada and Elsewhere as Perceived by Themselves and Others* [Winnipeg: Communigraphics/Printers Aid Books, 1983], 1) especially comforted those still sensitive to the stigma of second-class status.

14 Yuri Kupchenko, *The Horsemen of Shandro Crossing* (Edmonton: Tree Frog Press, 1989).

15 *Lögberg-Heimskringla*, 5 July 2002; Albert Halldorsson, "A Toast to Canada" (poem), *Lögberg*, 17 August 1950; and Prof. Skuli Johnson, in *Icelandic Canadian* 9, 1 (1950): 16. See also Johnson's poem, "Canada of the Vikings," *Lögberg*, 27 August 1925, written for New Iceland's golden jubilee; Kristjanson, *Icelandic People in Manitoba*, 2–12; and Wolf, "Emigration and Myth Making," 1–15.

16 Adrienne Clarkson, in *Lögberg-Heimskringla*, 25 August 2000.

17 See Italian mobilization of Giovanni Caboto: for example, early twentieth-century coal miners in the Rockies naming their organization; interwar immigrants in Montreal challenging Jacques Cartier as "discoverer of Canada"; and, in the late twentieth century, naming an Edmonton park.

18 Popular Ukrainian-Canadian mythology boasts that one of the first Ukrainians in North America, tsarist diplomat Petro Poletyka in the United States from 1818 to 1822, came from a prominent Cossack family; Andrew Gregorovich, *A Chronology of Ukrainian Canadian History* (Toronto: Ukrainian Canadian Committee, 1974), 6. In 1924 the Geographic Board of Canada named a mountain in honour of this man who helped resolve the Alaskan boundary dispute; Rudnytskyi, "Kanadiiski heohrafichni nazvy ukrainskoho pokhodzhennia," 804–5.

19 For other groups locating their ancestors among the Vikings, on sometimes shaky evidence, see Dreisziger, *Struggle and Hope*, 26, on behalf of poet Stephen Parmenius; and more generalized claims, despite entrenchment in the nation's history and elites making symbolic validation via the Vikings unnecessary, in W. Stanford Reid, ed., *The Scottish Tradition in Canada* (Toronto: McClelland and Stewart, 1976), ix.

20 Kristjanson, *Icelandic People in Manitoba*, 380; and *Lögberg-Heimskringla*, 15 October 1969.

21 Comments, Icelandic Minister of Foreign Affairs, in *Lögberg-Heimskringla*, 4 February 2000.

22 See official recognition of this conjuncture in ibid., by both Governor General Adrienne Clarkson and Iceland's president (Ólafur Ragnar Grímsson) and prime minister (Davið Oddsson).

23 Leslie Bardal, in *Lögberg-Heimskringla*, 28 January 2000 (Miguel Joyal sculpted the ship).

24 G. Isfeld, in *Lögberg-Heimskringla*, 21 January 2000.

25 *Lögberg-Heimskringla*, 16 June, 11, 18 August 2000.

26 On the historical Guðríður and Snorri and their millennium mobilization, see *Lögberg-Heimskringla*, 4, 18 February, 10 (quote), 24 March, 14, 28 April, 21 July 2000, 6 (quote), 13, 20 December 2002; and Kristiana Magnusson Clark, "Guðríður Þorbjarnardóttir—A Woman of Destiny," *Icelandic*

*Canadian* 56, 1 (2000): 18–23. On Canada's Centennial, the story of European discovery by Dr. Valdimar J. Eylands mentioned Snorri but not Guðríður; *Lögberg-Heimskringla*, 1 June 1967.

27  *Ukrainskyi holos*, 9 August 1961; *Postup*, 16 July 1961; and *Zhinochyi svit*, July/August 1961. See also Premier Duff Roblin, quoted in *Winnipeg Free Press*, 10 July 1961.

28  *Winnipeg Free Press*, 10 July 1961.

29  On the symbolism of the Shevchenko statue in Winnipeg, see Frances Swyripa, "History, Ethnic Legitimacy, and Public Space: The Shevchenko Statues in Winnipeg and Washington" (presented at Cross-Stitching Cultural Borders). While the Winnipeg Shevchenko functioned primarily within the context of Canadian nation building, Americans saw his Washington counterpart (1964) as an anti-Soviet ally during the Cold War.

30  Kristjanson, *Icelandic People in Manitoba*, 376–9.

31  *Ukrainskyi holos*, 26 July 1961. Diefenbaker also evoked the now familiar touchstones of the group mythology, but in the 1960s heady recognition of Ukrainians' role in nation building: Ivan Pylypiw and Vasyl Eleniak; the struggles, hardships, and triumph of anonymous pioneers; their descendants' success.

32  Kristjanson, *Icelandic People in Manitoba*, 386–90. The Shevchenko Medals, awarded annually by the Ukrainian Canadian Congress (formerly Committee) since 1962, operate differently, although open to non-Ukrainians; Diefenbaker was the first recipient.

33  In 2000, for example, the consul general of Iceland laid a wreath at Sigurðsson's feet, while Ukraine's minister of foreign affairs placed wreaths at both the Shevchenko statue and the monument at city hall to the 1932–3 artificial famine in Ukraine under Stalin. *Novyi shliakh*, 24 June 2000; and http://www.iceland2000org/site/schedule (accessed 27 January 2002).

34  See, for example, *Lögberg-Heimskringla*, 18 June 1982, 5 July (quotes) 2002.

35  The plaque was "Placed by the Province of Manitoba in cooperation with the Ukrainian Canadian Civil Liberties Association, the Ukrainian Canadian Foundation of Taras Shevchenko, and the Ukrainian community of Manitoba."

36  For change and continuity in *fjallkona*'s speech, see the addresses half a century apart (1951, 2000) in *Lögberg-Heimskringla*, 15 September 2000, 27 July 2001.

37  Þór, *Íslendingadagurinn*, 61; published for the festival's centennial, the book discusses the history, selection, and role of *fjallkona*, 38–42. See also *Fjallkonas of Íslendingadagurinn, 1924–1989: Sixty-Six Years of Tradition* (Winnipeg: Icelandic National League, 1989); and *Fjallkonan í Winnipeg og að Gimli, 1924–1964* (Winnipeg: n.p., 1964), whose official portraits illustrate the shift to more mature women.

38  *Lögberg-Heimskringla*, 20 July 1967; also 12 May 2000. On *fjallkona* as a female/feminist symbol, see Inga Björnsdóttir, "Nationalism, Gender and the Contemporary Icelandic Women's Movement" (Ph.D. dissertation, University of California, 1993), 81–188; and Anne Brydon, "Mother to Her Distant Children: The Icelandic Fjallkona in Canada," in *Undisciplined Women: Tradition and Culture in Canada*, ed. Pauline Greenhill and Diane Tye (Montreal and Kingston: McGill-Queen's University Press, 1997), 87–100.

39  Doukhobor posters and greeting cards (author's private collection); see also the Mennonite monument, junction Rat and Red rivers, MB, visited 23 September 2001.

40  The pioneer woman's symbolism is developed in Frances Swyripa, "Baba and the Community Heroine: Two Images of the Ukrainian Pioneer Woman," *Alberta* 2, 1 (1991): 59–46, and *Wedded to the Cause: Ukrainian-Canadian Women and Ethnic Identity, 1891–1991* (Toronto: University of Toronto Press, 1993). On Ukrainian-Canadian symbols generally, including from the prairies, see Manoly Lupul, ed., *Visible Symbols: Cultural Expression among Canada's Ukrainians* (Edmonton: Canadian Institute of Ukrainian Studies, 1984), esp. 129–41 and 162–6.

41 *Madonna of the Wheat*, Edmonton, various visits.

42 See Wsevolod Isajiw, "Symbols and Ukrainian Canadian Identity: Their Meaning and Significance," in Lupul, *Visible Symbols*, 119–28.

43 Pysanka statue and plaque, Vegreville, AB, various visits. See also the undated pamphlets by the Town of Vegreville and local Chamber of Commerce, *Welcome to Vegreville, Home of the World's Largest Pysanka* and *The World's Largest Pysanka* (author's private collection).

44 Pyrogy statue, Glendon, AB, visited 2 May 2004. On the unveiling, see *Edmonton Journal*, 24, 30, 31 (quote) August 1991.

45 Kovbasa statue, Mundare, AB, various visits. See also Shannon McKinnon, "The Big Banger," *Saturday Night*, 9 June 2001, 38–9; *Edmonton Journal*, 9 June 2001; Natalia Shostak, "Local Ukrainianness in Transnational Context: An Ethnographic Study of a Canadian Prairie Community" (Ph.D. dissertation, University of Alberta, 2001), esp. ch. 2; and Lisa Grekul's reflections in *Leaving Shadows: Literature in English by Canada's Ukrainians* (Edmonton: University of Alberta Press, 2005), 193–204.

46 Mosquito statue, Komarno, MB, visited 22 September 2001.

47 Published in the *Advocate*, 15 February 1929; see also Michael Luchkovich, *A Ukrainian Canadian in Parliament* (Toronto: Ukrainian Canadian Research Foundation, 1965), 61–2.

48 St. Pierre-Jolys, MB, visited 23 September 2001; and http://www.redrivervalley.com/_events/august.htm (accessed 5 November 2001).

49 Barbara Fauth's Vineland memorial on the site of the first meeting house in Canada combined religious and pioneer elements; see *Mennonite Reporter*, 31 March 1986, supplement. For a critique of the ethnic content of many 1986 events, including the quilt presentation and a festival "to explain Mennonitism to the people of Toronto" through "readings, ethnic cooking and handcrafts [sic]," see *Mennonite Brethren Herald*, 16 May 1986.

50 R.P. Friesen, writing in *Mennonite Mirror*, March 1975. Pauls's modified design subsequently won first place at the Mennonite Festival of Art and Music in Winnipeg, and the Women's Committee of the Mennonite Educational Society tried to install it in a public building in the city.

51 See http://www.mennoniteheritagevillage.com (accessed 30 May 2007).

52 *The Commitment*, Edmonton, various visits; see also Commemorative Monument Committee, Alberta Ukrainian Canadian Centennial Committee of the Ukrainian Canadian Congress (Alberta), 1991–2 (author's private collection).

53 See Polish Alberta Centennial Collection, Archives of the Canadian Polish Congress (Alberta), Edmonton; *Globe and Mail*, 6 August, 4, 17 December 1996; *Edmonton Journal*, 3, 6, 8, 11 December 1996, 24 January 1998; *Panorama Polska*, May 1995, August, September, October 1996, September 1997; *Widzanie z Whyte Avenue*, 22 July, 14 August 1996; and *Biuletyn Kongresu Polonii Kanadyjskiej (Okreg Alberta)*, 1992–6.

54 This universality was what attracted the jury; see architect Janusz Najfeldt, jury chair, in *Edmonton Journal*, 6 August 1996.

55 The observations about Golovatch's design come from Danek Możdżeński, 24 August 2001; the conclusions are my own.

56 *Edmonton Journal*, 8 December 1996.

57 John McIntosh, jury chair, in *Edmonton Journal*, 17 September 1993.

58 Neil Waugh, in *Edmonton Sun*, 20 December 1989. In the City of Edmonton Archives, see Council

Minutes, 13, 26 April 1983; letter, Ukrainian Canadian Committee, 12 December 1989; City Hall Steering Committee Report #1 and enclosures, 10 January 1990; and records of the Public Affairs Committee, 10, 17, 24 April 1990. Press coverage can be found in *Edmonton Journal*, 14–28 April, 8 May, 20–24 October 1983, 7, 8 December 1989, 10, 11 January, 15, 18, 25 April 1990; and *Edmonton Sun*, 6 October, 20 December 1989.

59 Neil Waugh, in *Edmonton Sun*.

60 John Geiger, in *Edmonton Journal*, 7 December 1989.

61 In 1986 the Hindu Society of Alberta sponsored a bust of Mahatma Gandhi behind the library off Churchill Square. The lack of outcry no doubt reflected the stress on Gandhi's message of serenity and peace, the modest space, and the British tie that legitimized Indian history among "non-ethnic" Edmontonians; see *Edmonton Journal*, 27 August 1986.

62 See http://www.doukhobor-homepage.com (accessed 27 January 2002). Veregin, SK, visited 8 August 2002.

63 Telephone conversations, Larry Ewashen, Castlegar, BC, 23 August 2001, and J.J. Verigin, Grand Forks, BC, 31 August 2001. See also the doves, loaf of bread, salt shaker, and water pitcher on the centennial sign at the prayer home, Blaine Lake, SK; visited 8 August 2002.

64 Woodcock, *Doukhobors*, 139.

65 Kamsack, SK, visited 9 August 2002.

66 Weyburn, SK, visited 11 October 2001; Rosthern, SK, visited 6 August 2002.

67 *Mennonite*, 12 March 1974 (Margaret Quiring, Winnipeg, was the artist); and *Mennonite Reporter*, 31 March 1986, supplement (Glenn Fretz, Toronto, designed the logo).

68 The logo was designed by Nicola Dubensky, Winnipeg, for the Ukrainian Canadian Centennial Commission appointed by the Ukrainian Canadian Congress.

69 See the Scott stamp catalogue, Canada Stamp Nos. 501 onward (1969–).

70 See Canada Scott Nos. 1326-91; also, on initiatives by Ukrainians in Canada and independent Ukraine (the Ukrainian-Canadian centennial stamp was the first stamp issued by the Ukrainian Post Office), Perederyj, *Centennial of the First Ukrainian Settlement in Canada*, 4–25. The Canada Post stamps were issued 29 August 1991 in Edmonton; the Day of Issue envelope featured men in western clothes and women in kerchiefs building a log house.

71 *Mennonite Mirror*, January/February 1974, special centennial issue.

72 *Mennonite Brethren Herald*, 4 October 1974, quoting Member of Parliament Joseph Guay (a picture of the Day of Issue envelope and stamp, 28 August 1974, is included); see also Canada Scott No. 643.

73 See Isydore Hlynka, *The Other Canadians* (Winnipeg: Trident Press, 1981), 118–20, quoting *The Unknown Country*; M.L. Borowsky, *Plants from Ukraine in Canada* (Winnipeg: Ukrainian Free Academy of Sciences, 1975); and "Wheat," *Canadian Encyclopedia* (Edmonton: Hurtig, 1985), 1936. Dr. Thorvaldur Johnson's survey of the history of wheat in Canada, *Lögberg-Heimskringla*, 1 June 1967, makes the Ukrainian link explicit.

74 Gravelbourg, SK, visited 11 August 2002; see also *La Cathédrale*, 8 and 21. Prud'homme, SK, visited 9 June 2004; ironmonger Hervé Poilievre, designer Cora Poilievre.

75 William Kurelek, *A Northern Nativity* (Toronto: Tundra Books, 1976); and *The World of William Kurelek/Svit Vasylia Kurylyka* (New York: Ukrainian Museum, 1987), 58.

76 Veregin, SK, visited 27 May 2004.

77  See, for example, Ena Campbell, "The Virgin of Guadalupe and the Female Self-Image: A Mexican Case History," in *Mother Worship: Theme and Variations*, ed. James Preston (Chapel Hill: University of North Carolina Press, 1982), 5–24; William Taylor, "The Virgin of Guadalupe in New Spain: An Inquiry into the Social History of Marian Devotion," *American Ethnologist* 14 (1987): 9–25; Stafford Poole, *Our Lady of Guadalupe: The Origins and Sources of a Mexican National Symbol, 1531–1797* (Tucson, AZ: University of Arizona Press, 1995); and, in Catholic literature, *A Handbook on Guadalupe* (New Bedford, MA: Our Lady's Chapel, 1996).

78  For a wide-ranging personal perspective, see Joan Skogan, *Mary of Canada: The Virgin Mary in Canadian Culture, Spirituality, History, and Geography* (Banff, AB: Banff Centre for the Arts, 2003); Our Lady of the Prairies is briefly discussed on 194.

79  See http://www3.sk.sympatico.ca/ourlady.history.html (accessed 10 December 2001); http://www. ourladyfoundation.org/contactus.php (accessed 21 November 2005, quote from "Our Vision"); and Leonard St. John, *The Novalis Guide to Canadian Shrines* (Ottawa: Novalis, St. Paul University, 2002), 178–9. Calendar, St. Michael Roman Catholic Church, St. Michael, AB, mid 1980s; painting by Carol Tremblay. See also the mosaic, Our Lady of the Prairies Catholic Elementary School, Edmonton, visited 18 October 2005 (quote from plaque).

## CHAPTER SEVEN

1  The cross "is maintained in perpetuity by the Miskolczi family" (handwritten note, St. Laszlo Roman Catholic Church); visited 9 June 2004. A nearby rock in memory of Janos and Anna Miskolczi, who emigrated from Hungary in 1903 and homesteaded on the quarter section, was dedicated during a family reunion in 1993.

2  "Gateway" rock, visited 8 August 2002. A local family and the Saskatchewan History and Folklore Society sponsored a cairn on the actual site of the cross; *Journey of Faith*, 53–4. The Benedictines erected a cairn on the site of the first Mass celebrated later in 1903 on their own homestead.

3  Swedish cairn, visited 12 August 2002; the second plaque was "donated and placed by Ohlen '86, the Swedish Historical Society, Stockholm, Saskatchewan."

4  Cross of freedom, Trembowla, MB, visited 27 May 2004; see also the Manitoba government pamphlet, *The Cross of Freedom* (Winnipeg: Manitoba Culture, Heritage, and Recreation, 1984).

5  See, on the Heritage Name Sign program, *Lögberg-Heimskringla*, 27 April, 25 May 2001 (subsequent issues carried brief entries on individual signs); and, on the documentation of farm names, old or new, Gerrard, *Örnefni í Nýja Íslandi*.

6  Manitoba Mennonite Historical Society, *The Post Road—The Mennonite West Reserve Post Road Memorial Trail Tour* (brochure, 2000) author's private collection. The points of interest were Fort Dufferin; the Post Road memorial sign; the Mennonite villages of Edenburg, Neubergthal, Neuanlage, Neuhorst, Schoenwiese, Reinland, Hochfeld, Osterwick, and Waldheim; and Mountain City. See also Conrad Stoesz, "The Post Road," *Mennonite Historian* (June and September 2000), at http://old.mbconf.ca/old/historian (accessed 27 December 2003); *Saturday Winnipeg Free Press*, 17 June 2000; *West Reserve 125*[th] *Anniversary*, 26 June 2000, a supplement inserted in southern Manitoba newspapers; and Zacharias, *Reinland*, supplement (10).

7  See "Program Overview: Centennial of Ukrainians in Canada," conference of the Ukrainian Canadian Congress, Edmonton, 1 September 1990 (author's private collection); and Perederyj, *Centennial of the First Ukrainian Settlement in Canada*, 48.

8  See http://www.mts.net/~delplett/book/chapter_nine.html (accessed 31 December 2003).

9   Tolstoi school (1929–60) stood on SE 29-30-1-W2; see http://www.doukhobor.org/pn-details. html?rec=155 (accessed 31 December 2003).

10  Swedish cairn, "New Stockholm Settlement," visited 12 August 2002.

11  Information on the Snaasen cemetery and memorial services, including quote, comes from http:// cap.estevan.sk.ca/cemetery.records/snaasen/history.html (accessed 13 July 2001); see also http://cap. estevan.sk.ca/cemetery.records/snaasen/memorial.html (accessed 13 July 2001).

12  New Finland (New) cemetery, visited 11 August 2002. Psalm 117:2 ("For his merciful kindness is great toward us: and the truth of the Lord endureth for ever. Praise ye the Lord") appears in Finnish on the adjacent plaque.

13  Of some 3000 entries in J.B. Rudnyc'kyj, *Mosaic of Winnipeg Street Names* (Winnipeg: Canadian Institute of Onomastic Sciences, 1974), only a handful—like Hekla Avenue, Valhalla Drive, and Sawchuk Bay (after National Hockey League goalie Terry Sawchuk) reflected Manitoba's non-British, non-French heritage. On Edmonton place names, see Historic Sites Committee, Edmonton Historical Board, *Naming Edmonton: From Ada to Zoie* (Edmonton: University of Alberta Press, 2004).

14  Holy Rosary Roman Catholic Church, Edmonton, visited 20 September 1997. On the Kulawys, see Gaston Carrière, *Dictionnaire biographique des Oblats de Marie-Immaculée au Canada*, tome II (Ottawa: Éditions de l'Université d'Ottawa, 1977), 209–10; John Huculak, *History of the Holy Rosary Parish in Edmonton, 1913–1988* (Edmonton: Holy Rosary Parish, 1988); Matejko, *Polish Settlers in Alberta*, 15, 109–11, 204, 270–300, 312–5, and 424–5; and Kobos and Pęckacz, *Polonia in Alberta*, 3–71.

15  The quest for roots has fed massive cemetery recovery and tombstone inscription projects, many sponsored by ethno-religious communities, others by provincial bodies. The Saskatchewan Genealogical Society's (SGS) database of over 3200 cemeteries and burial sites can be accessed at http://www.saskgenealogy.com/cemetery/cemetery.htm; actual files are kept in the SGS library. See http://www.abgensoc.ca/nameindex.html on accessing over 700,000 surnames in the Alberta Genealogical Society index. The Manitoba Genealogical Society (MGS) has transcribed data (available at the MGS Resource Centre) from over 1400 cemeteries; see http://www.mbgenealogy. com.

16  The oldest and best outdoor museums are the government-operated Ukrainian Cultural Heritage Village east of Edmonton, where Ukrainians gather every August under the auspices of the Ukrainian Canadian Congress (Alberta), and the Mennonite Heritage Village in Steinbach, MB; see http://tapor. ualberta.ca/heritagevillage/ and http://www.mennoniteheritagevillage.com (accessed 15 June 2005).

17  See ch. 2, n. 38.

18  Titles from *Alberta's Local Histories in the Historical Resources Library*, 6th ed. (Edmonton: Alberta Culture, 1986). On pioneer mythology in local histories generally, see Joanne Stiles, "Descended from Heroes: The Frontier Myth in Rural Alberta," *Alberta* 2, 2 (1990): 27–46. On the centrality of the pioneer in Alberta's fiftieth anniversary celebrations plus its intersection with ethnicity, see Swyripa, "1955—Celebrating Together, Celebrating Apart," 589–612.

19  Roman Catholic cemetery, St. Pierre-Jolys, MB, visited 23 September 2001.

20  See, for example, the David and Rena Robertson marker in Yellow Grass village cemetery on the bald prairie south of Regina; visited 12 October 2001.

21  See, for example (all Ukrainian), Kozmak and Soldan farms, cemetery, Two Hills, AB, visited 12 August 2001; and Bogdanski and Pawluk farms, Sts. Peter and Paul Ukrainian Catholic cemetery, Mundare, AB, visited 12 August 2001.

22  East and West reserves, MB, visited 23–4 September 2001.

23 See, for example, Sigurður and Guðlaug Peterson, Johanes and Ingibjorg Isfeld, and George and Helga Bristow, town cemetery, Gimli, MB, visited 22 September 2001.

24 See, for example, Orest Krasey (Ukrainian embroidery framing Leonardo da Vinci's *Last Supper*), Assumption of the Blessed Virgin Mary Ukrainian Catholic cemetery, Meleb, MB, visited 22 September 2001; and Mundi Goodman (helmet) and Sigriður Hjartarson (*fjallkona*), Gimli cemetery.

25 For Ukrainians' birthright in the land holding the bones of their pioneers, see Volodymyr Plaviuk, *Prypovidky abo ukrainsko-narodnia filosofiia* (Edmonton: n.p., 1946), introduction.

26 Patterson Lake, MB, visited 28 May 2004. See also Stechishin, *History of Ukrainian Settlement in Canada*, 174–9; Marunchak, *Ukrainian Canadians*, 44 and 61; Kaye, *Early Ukrainian Settlements in Canada*, 255–63; and Perederyj, *Centennial of the First Ukrainian Settlement in Canada*, 42 (most recent monument). In 1990 the Rural Municipality of Rossburn declared the burial ground a heritage site, http://www.gov.mb.ca/chc/hrb/mun/m045.html (accessed 4 December 2001).

27 For the Ukrainian-Canadian centennial, Ukrainians in east-central Alberta built a symbolic *mohyla* evoking the burial mounds of the ancient Scythians that dot the Ukrainian steppe and which, under the Cossacks, functioned as strategic points. With Ukraine's independence in 1991, *mohyly* became popular as memorials to the nationalist insurgents of the 1940s and 1950s. Erected on property owned by the town of Lamont, the Canadian Mohyla was "dedicated to the Ukrainian people who cast themselves like seeds unto the wind to settle, and take root upon this land, so generations might flourish" (official sign, visited 5 September 2001). See also Hania Martyniuk, "The Mohyla, A Living Monument" (publicity sheet, 1999), author's private collection.

28 Minutes, Jewish Historical Society of Western Canada, 12 May 1974, Abraham Arnold Papers, P511, file 152.3, AM.

29 Isaac and Dora Cohen, Hebrew cemetery, Edenbridge, SK, visited 7 August 2002.

30 Hirsch Community Jewish cemetery, Hirsch, SK, visited 1 October 2003; http://cap.estevan.sk.ca/ cemetery.records/ hirsch/index.html (accessed 18 September 2004), quotes by A.S. Muscovitch and N. Vickar; *Western Jewish News*, 17 July 1980; and *Canadian Jewish News*, 24 July 1980. See also *Canadian Jewish News*, 16 December 1999; on discovering Hirsch cemetery, Toronto-based Myriam Shechter wrote: "As a designated historic site, the cemetery is now a reminder of an important period in the history of the Jewish people and Saskatchewan. For the descendants of the original colonists, it serves as a focal point, a concrete way to stay in touch with their cultural and historical roots."

31 On recovery, see Rempel and Harms, *Atlas*, esp. the cemetery index (145–7 and 61–4 "39) which identifies known interred by name; both Hiebert and Schoenwiese examples come from this volume. Rosenfeld, MB, visited 24 September 2001.

32 More incongruously, the cairn in the Mennonite Heritage Village in Steinbach dedicated to the Russian Mennonite immigration of the 1920s featured a Red River cart alongside a hand plough and spinning wheel; Steinbach, MB, visited 23 September 2001.

33 Telephone conversation, J.J. Verigin, Grand Forks, BC, 31 August 2001.

34 From British Columbia, see *Iskra*, December 2000, 24–6, 66–7, and 85–7, on Champion Creek cemetery; and *Iskra*, November 2000, 25–7, on Sion, Outlook, and Sleepy Hollow cemeteries.

35 See, for example, St. Paul Lutheran cemetery, Ellerslie, AB, and St. John Lutheran cemetery, west of Wetaskiwin, AB, visited August 2000; and Grace Lutheran cemetery, Gnadenthal, AB, visited 1 July 2001.

36 Christ Lutheran cemetery, Rhein, SK, visited 10 August 2002.

37 Dickson, AB, visited 26 May 2002; reports (1990s plus) on the Dickson museum in the proceedings of the annual Danish Canadian Conference, Federation of Danish Associations in Canada; and, for a detailed analysis of the museum's exhibits and mindset, Crystal Willie, "Ethnicity and the Pioneer in Alberta's Community Museums" (M.A. thesis, University of Alberta, 2003).

38 Lutheran church and cemetery, Hecla, MB, visited 22 September 2001.

39 "We Will Remember: War Monuments in Canada," http://www.stemnet.nf.ca/monuments (accessed 24 August 2001) provides details on local war memorials in Alberta, Saskatchewan, and Manitoba, representing three construction phases: 1920s to 1930s, post-World War II, and 1980s to 1990s (increasingly including all veterans, not just war dead). Both communities and surnames highlight the West's British heritage; many plaques expressly include "and district"; few memorials were originally erected in the cemetery.

40 Skaro shrine, visited 14 August 2005; Rama shrine, visited 9 August 2002; Lake Lenore, SK, visited 4 August 2004.

41 Selo Ukraina, Dauphin, MB, visited 28 May 2004; erecting the tomb reflected the decision of the 1985 World Congress of Free Ukrainians in Edmonton to declare 1986 "Year of the Ukrainian Soldier." See also Perederyj, *Centennial of the First Ukrainian Settlement in Canada*, 41; and http://www.city.dauphin.mb.ca/UK/tomb.htm (accessed 4 December 2001).

42 Dedication program, 7 May 2000 (author's private collection); the words on the cenotaph differ slightly. In contrast to Ukrainian speeches at the unveiling, mainstream dignitaries (Department of Veterans' Affairs, Province of Alberta, City of Edmonton, Royal Canadian Legion) ignored the specific Ukrainian-Canadian military service and record.

43 Shaarey Zedek cemetery, Winnipeg, visited 21 September 2001.

44 Zacharias, *Reinland*, 18; also http://www.mennoniteheritagevillage.mb.ca (accessed 27 January 2002).

45 See St. Nicholas Ukrainian Catholic Church, Sarto, MB, visited 23 September 2001; St. Elias Ukrainian Orthodox Church, Luzan-Toporiwtzi, AB, visited 12 August 2001; Ukrainian Catholic Church of Spasa/Muskalik, AB, visited 1 August 1998; and Transfiguration of Our Lord Ukrainian Catholic Church, Round Hill, AB, visited 26 November 2005.

46 Nativity of the Blessed Virgin Mary Ukrainian Catholic Church, Jaroslaw, SK, visited 11 August 2002; the commemorative cairn, dedicated to the church, was erected for the millennium of Christianity in Ukraine.

47 On decay and the past, including the merits of ruins versus restoration, see Lowenthal, *The Past is a Foreign Country*, esp. ch. 4.

48 Munholland, *Pulpits of the Past*. For a Ukrainian sampling, see *Propamiatna knyha z nahody zolotoho iuvileiu poselennia ukrainskoho narodu v Kanadi; Zbirnyk materiialiv*; Diana Thomas Kordan, *Historical Driving Tour: Ukrainian Churches in East Central Alberta* (Edmonton: Canadian Institute of Ukrainian Studies and Alberta Culture and Multiculturalism, 1988); Rotoff, *Monuments to Faith*; Parasia Iwanec's paintings, Ukrainian Canadian Archives and Museum of Alberta, and her *Ukrainski tserkvy Alberty u mystetskykh tvorakh i v opysi Parasi Ivanets: Slidamy ukrainskykh pioneriv po Alberti* (Priashiv: Pryvatpress, 1991); William Sinclair's paintings, University of Alberta Collections, Edmonton; and Anna Kovch-Baran, *Ukrainian Catholic Churches of Saskatchewan* (Saskatoon: Ukrainian Catholic Council of Saskatchewan, 1977) and *Ukrainian Catholic Churches of Winnipeg Archeparchy* (Saskatoon: Archeparchy of Winnipeg, 1991).

49 For provincial and municipal sites, see www.cyr.gov.sk.ca/, esp. "Heritage Properties Search" (Saskatchewan); http://www.gov.mb.ca/chc/hrb/prov, esp. "Historic Resources" (Manitoba); and http://hermis.cd.gov.ab.ca/ARHP (Alberta). In 2003 the Historic Sites and Monuments Board of Canada began to address the underrepresentation of ethno-cultural groups on the prairies with

workshops in Edmonton, Saskatoon, and Winnipeg (author's private collection). At all three government levels, churches are overrepresented in ethnic commemoration.

50 Ukrainian Catholic Church of the Immaculate Conception, Cooks Creek, MB, http://www.gov. mb.ca/chc/hrb/prov and http://www.pc.gc.ca/docs/pc/rpts/heritage/prot51_e.asp (accessed 18 December 2005); plaque, Doukhobor Prayer Home, Veregin, SK, visited 9 August 2002; and plaque, Hegre Norwegian Lutheran Church, visited 11 May 2002.

51 Kaposvar, SK, visited 11 August 2002 (church, municipal historic site, Rural Municipality of Fertile Belt, 1999); Veregin, SK, visited 9 August 2002; Muenster, SK, visited 8 August 2002 (church, municipal historic site, Rural Municipality of St. Peter, 1984); and Reinland, MB, visited 24 September 2001 (plaque, unveiled on village centennial, 19 July 1975).

52 Minutes, Board of Directors, Jewish Historical Society of Western Canada, 20 April 1975, in Abraham Arnold Papers, P511, file 152.4, AM; *Canadian Jewish News*, 11, 18, 25 June 1976; and *Western Jewish News*, 21 August 1975, 3, 10, 17 June 1976.

53 The foundation already existed. See Iwanec of the Ukrainian displaced persons immigration and Sinclair of the Alberta Supreme Court (n. 48); also invitation, Louis Dupuis exhibit, "Prairie Icons," Agnes Bugera Gallery, Edmonton, 2004 (author's private collection).

54 See http://www.civilization.ca/hist/phase2/mod6e/html (accessed 14 January 2003); similar sentiments on Ukrainian churches in Manitoba are found in Rotoff, *Monuments to Faith*, vii.

55 Canadian Museum of Civilization media release for the Feast of the Theophany in 2002; http://www. civilization.ca/media/show (accessed 14 January 2003); and baptism, *Ottawa Citizen*, 21 August 2008. Original site, St. Onuphrius Ukrainian Catholic Church, visited 23 October 2003; Canadian Museum of Civilization, Gatineau, QC, visited 20 February 2003.

## CHAPTER EIGHT

1 The most potent settlement-as-pilgrimage-site among "non-charter" peoples is Africville in Halifax, NS, a 150-year-old Black community razed to the ground in the 1960s. Evacuees and descendants gather annually at the site—a symbol of not only white racism and indifference but also Black spirit and fortitude—both to remember and to celebrate. See Africville Genealogy Society, *The Spirit of Africville* (Halifax: Formac Publishing, 1992); and the 1989 National Film Board documentary, *Remember Africville* (Shelagh Mackenzie, director), produced in association with the Canadian Broadcasting Corporation.

2 Frank Olson, "Willow Point," *Icelandic Canadian* 9, 1 (1950): 12; and, reprinted for the Icelandic centennial, in *Icelandic Canadian* 33, 4 (1975): 22.

3 On the painting *Landing at Willow Point* by Arni Sigurdsson, see *Lögberg*, 3 August 1950; *Icelandic Canadian* 9, 1 (1950): 12; and *Lögberg-Heimskringla*, 21 July, 15 December 2000.

4 Quotes, *Lögberg-Heimskringla*, 1, 8 December 2000. On mobilization of Willow Point and the landing anniversary, see also *Lögberg-Heimskringla*, 24 August 1967, 11 August, 6 October, 3 November 2000; W. Kristjanson, "The Icelandic Day Celebration and the Visit of the President of Iceland," *Icelandic Canadian* 26, 1 (1967): 22–4; and John S. Matthiasson, "The White Rock of Willow Island: A Symbol of New Iceland," *Icelandic Canadian* 55, 4 (2000): 338–9.

5 Sigtryggur Jónasson estimated that in 1901 some 4000 Icelanders lived in Winnipeg, 2000 in New Iceland; Kristjanson, *Icelandic People in Manitoba*, 300.

6 The preceding discussion is based on Þór, *Islendingadagurinn*, 34–61 (quotes 42 and 52). See also the Gimli reference in Brydon, "Mother to Her Distant Children," 95–6, drawing in part on the documentary made on the centennial of the Icelandic festival.

7   *Lögberg-Heimskringla*, 28 July 2000.

8   *Mennonite Mirror*, March 1975.

9   *Mennonite Mirror*, December 1974.

10  Junction, Rat and Red rivers, visited 23 September 2001; on the unveiling, see *Mennonite Historian*, 1994.

11  On the statue in Cornwallis Park, see http://www.multiculturaltrails.ca/level_3/number134. html (accessed 21 January 2006). A re-enactment on Canada Day 1991 of the landing of the first Ukrainians was planned to coincide with the annual convention of the Ukrainian Business and Professional Federation of Canada, held that year in Halifax.

12  On the entire package of events, see *Edmonton Journal*, 1 September 1991; *Ukrainski visti*, September 1991; and *Celebrate!: Official Souvenir Program, National Opening Ceremonies, Ukrainian Canadian Centenary, Edmonton, Alberta, and Area, August 29–September 1, 1991* (author's private collection).

13  Centennial marker, Star, AB, visited 21 September 2003; see also Perederyj, *Centennial of the First Ukrainian Settlement in Canada*, 43.

14  See http://www.telusplanet.net/public/mtoll/lds.htm, quoting *Chief Mountain Country*, 173–82 (accessed 27 October 2005); and Brigham Card, "Charles Ora Card and the Founding of the Mormon Settlements in Southwestern Alberta, North-West Territories," in Card, *Mormon Presence in Canada*, 77.

15  On golden jubilee celebrations in Veregin and Kamsack, see the 1949 documentary by the Doukhobor Society of North Eastern Saskatchewan, *Ternistyi put/Thorny Road*; the full rationale for designating the Prayer Home a provincial heritage property appears in the "Statement of Historical Significance" at http://www.cyr.gov.sk.ca/index.cfm?page=78 (accessed 5 February 2006).

16  Kaposvar, SK, visited 11 August 2002, 26 November 2004.

17  Speeches by presidents, Federation of Danish Associations in Canada and Danish Canadian National Museum, at the museum's grand opening, 26 May 2002 (author's notes); and Rolf Christensen, "A Short History of the Danish Canadian National Museum," *21st Danish Canadian Conference, Red Deer, 23–6 May 2002* (Gloucester, ON: Federation of Danish Associations in Canada, 2002), 34–42.

18  Pilgrimage, Skaro shrine, 14 August 2005. See also Kobos and Pękacz, *Polonia in Alberta*, xi and xxii; Huculak, *History of the Holy Rosary Parish in Edmonton*, 34–7 and 77; *50th Anniversary—Skaro Shrine*; and Magdalene Medynski, "Recollections of the Skaro Mission," in *We Praise God with Blessed Mary* (1993), 8–15. See also Jason Kovacs, "Sanctifying Ethnic Memory and Reinforcing Place Attachment: Cultural Identity, Sacred Place, and Pilgrimage in Esterhazy, Saskatchewan," *International Journal of Canadian Studies* 36 (2007): 245–65.

19  See *Prairie Messenger*, 25 July 1928; the five seventy-fifth anniversary issues of *Colony Post*, 1976–8; and *Journey of Faith*, 197–8 and 310–25.

20  *Propamiatna knyha z nahody zolotoho iuvileiu poselennia ukrainskoho narodu v Kanadi*, 267–76 and 324–7; Basilian Fathers, *Monder uchora i sohodni*, 74–6 and 144; photograph collection, Basilian Fathers Museum, Mundare, AB; the National Film Board of Canada's *New Home in the West*, produced for the 1941 jubilee and including the Mundare celebrations; jubilee coverage in *Ukrainski visti*, organ of the Ukrainian Catholic Exarchate/Eparchy of Edmonton; and conversations, Bishop Lawrence Huculak, OSBM, Ukrainian Catholic Eparchy of Edmonton, Edmonton, 2002–3.

21  Siracky chapel, visited 28 June 2003; the phrase "jubilee pioneer chapel" comes from Bishop Neil Savaryn, in *Propamiatna knyha nahody zolotoho iuvileiu poselennia ukrainskoho narodu v Kanadi*, 327.

22 New Finland (Old) cemetery, New Finland, SK, visited 11 August 2002.

23 Usiskin, *Uncle Mike's Edenbridge*, 136–9.

24 Rempel and Harms, *Atlas*, 18 (H. Wiebe); Rosengart, MB, visited 24 September 2001, and Zacharias, *Reinland*, supplement (10) (J. Wiebe); and Shanzenfeld, MB, visited 24 September 2001 (Shantz, monument in school grounds not cemetery).

25 St. Peter Roman Catholic Cathedral, Muenster, SK, visited 2 June 2004; and Hinz, *St. Peter's Cathedral*, 4 and 17.

26 Quote, *St. Peter's Messenger*, 26 July 1923. See also Windschiegl, *Fifty Golden Years*, 43–6; *St. Peter's Messenger*, 14, 28 June, 5 July 1923; and *St. Peter's Abbey Newsletter* 23, 3 (2001): 7. On Prior Oswald Moosmueller's remains, see Windschiegl, *Fifty Golden Years*, 96; and *St. Peter's Abbey Newsletter* 23, 2 (2001): 2.

27 *Lögberg-Heimskringla*, 28 July 2000.

28 Riverton, MB, visited 29 May 2004; by telephone, Nelson Gerrard queried the "Captain" on Jónasson's tombstone. See also the Manitoba government pamphlet, *Sigtryggur Jonasson*.

29 Documentary, Jay Stewart, director, *The Journey Home: Iceland—Stephansson* (Edmonton: Going Home Productions, 2001). See also Murray Lundberg, "Stephan G. Stephansson: An Icelandic Poet in Canada," at http://www.explorenorth.com/library/weekly/aa071400a.htm (accessed 8 October 2004).

30 Rosa Benediktson, Stephansson's youngest daughter, was invited to Iceland to unveil the monument (*Stephan G. Stephansson Icelandic Society Newsletter*, February 1996); for a good photograph, see http://www.studiozero.com/iceland/iceland_19.html (accessed 8 October 2004).

31 On the Historical Sites and Monuments Board of Canada unveiling, see "The Stephan G. Stephansson Monument," *Icelandic Canadian* 9, 1 (1950): 21–3; and Prof. Skuli Johnson, "Stephan G. Stephansson (1853–1927)," *Icelandic Canadian* 9, 2 (1950): 9–12 and 44–56 (main speech). See also Jane McCracken, *Stephan G. Stephansson: The Poet of the Rocky Mountains* (Edmonton: Alberta Culture, Historical Resources Division, 1982), prepared in connection with the acquisition of Stephansson House by the Province of Alberta; her "Stephan G. Stephansson: Icelandic-Canadian Poet and Freethinker Canadian," *Canadian Ethnic Studies* 15, 1 (1983): 33–53, and "Stephan G. Stephansson: A 'West Icelander,'" *Prairie Forum* 8, 2 (1983): 195–210; and translations of Stephansson's poetry in *Stephan G. Stephansson: Selected Prose and Poetry* (Red Deer, AB: Red Deer College Press, 1988).

32 Markerville, AB, visited 20 May 2002, Grímsson quote, *Stephan G. Stephansson Icelandic Society Newsletter*, Winter 1999; and, on Stephansson's grave as a site of pilgrimage by visiting Icelandic dignitaries, comments by Stephansson House guide Annamarie Bruseker (23 November 2001) and facility supervisor Olga Fowler (24 September 2004).

33 *Nelson Daily News*, 3, 4 November 1924; Woodcock, *Doukhobors*, 186, 257–60, and 316, also illustrations; and photograph of the funeral crowd, 2 November 1924, in the Doukhobor Prayer Home, National Doukhobor Heritage Village, Veregin, SK, visited 9 August 2002.

34 Hawthorn, *Doukhobors of British Columbia*, 316; also *Vancouver Sun*, 27 March 1944.

35 For a description of Verigin's grave and picture of the inscription above, see Nancy Millar, *Once Upon a Time: Stories from Canadian Graveyards* (Calgary: Fifth House, 1997), 33–4.

36 On Lebedev's resistance and treatment and his posthumous appeal to the Sons of Freedom in the 1940s, see Woodcock, *Doukhobors*, 97–8 and 323.

37 Nadojda (Nadezhda) cemetery, north of Veregin, SK, visited 9 August 2002. On the burning of arms celebrations, see the brochure, *100 Years as Doukhobors*, and the program insert for both the

morning memorial at Lebedev's grave and afternoon events at the National Doukhobor Heritage Village (author's private collection).

38 On the unveiling, see *Edmonton Journal*, 24 July 1954.

39 Russo-Greek Orthodox Church of the Holy Transfiguration, Star, AB, visited 21 September 2003, at which time the images of the four couples had gone for repairs. See also Perederyj, *Centennial of the First Ukrainian Settlement in Canada*, 46.

40 Nebyliv, Ukraine, visited 23 July 2003 (with the University of Saskatchewan summer school at the Ukrainian Catholic University, Lviv); thanks to Natalia Khanenko Friesen for first drawing the packets of Canadian earth to my attention. On the stamp issued by the Post Office of Ukraine, see Perederyj, *Centennial of the First Ukrainian Settlement in Canada*, cover, 6.

## CONCLUSION

1 My involvement with the Historic Sites and Monuments Board of Canada began in 2003 in conjunction with three prairie workshops organized by Parks Canada to address the underrepresentation of ethno-cultural communities in HSMBC commemorations. I subsequently participated in another workshop soliciting nominations for a second underrepresented group, women in the West.

2 For this and other related points on place and displacement, see Edward S. Casey, *Getting Back into Place: Toward a Renewed Understanding of the Place-World* (Bloomington and Indianapolis: Indiana University Press,1993), esp. ch. 2.

# INDEX

A
Arnason, David, 156–57
Arnold, Abraham, 95, 130

B
Banach, Maria, 91
Banach, Stanisław, 91
Barr, Isaac, 15, 23, 87, 101
Barr Colony, 15, 23, 87, 96, 101, 124
Bartsch, Johann, 212
Belgians, 50
Benedicktson, Sigga, 222
Benedictines: impact of US on, 153; local
    commemoration initiatives, 194, 283n2;
    and Mount Carmel, 63; published history
    of, 97; and St. Peter's Colony, 56–57, 87,
    235–36
Bobersky, Ivan, 91–92, 94
Bodnar, Petro, 64
Borys, Ivan, 60–61
Bowles, S.W., 271n40
British: churches of, 58; collective identity
    of, 27, 31, 124; founding story, 87;
    immigration to Canada, 15, 23, 30; place
    names, 46–47
British Columbia, 35, 145
Budka, Nykyta, 235
Bunko, John, 63
burial customs, 66–74. See also cemeteries;
    graves

C
Canada: as beacon of democracy, 110–14;
    citizenship celebrations, 117–18,
    270n27, 270n32; immigrant dreams of,
    77; immigration patterns in, 32, 34–35;
    importance of war service in, 115–16, 118;
    nation-building myths, 119–23; national
    celebrations, 115, 116–17
Canada, Government of: and Doukhobors,
    35, 122; and Hungarian immigration, 26,
    104–5; and Icelandic immigration, 102;
    and immigrants' homeland ties, 139–41;
    and National Policy, 14–19; and preferred
    immigration, 21–22; and Ukrainian
    immigration, 25
Canadian Jewish Congress (CJC), 130, 205,
    206

Canadian Jewish Historical Society (CJHS),
    130
Canadian Pacific Railway, 26, 105
Card, Charles Ora: home of, 93, 228;
    honouring of, 54; land scouting of, 23;
    later life, 234; as leader of Canadian
    Mormons, 88; on Mormons as part of
    national narrative, 111
Catholicism: building and naming churches,
    56–60; and pre-1916 immigration, 20;
    and shrines, 60–66. See also specific ethnic
    groups
cemeteries, 201–10, 220. See also graves
Chinese, 268n75, 270n27
Chrétien, Jean, 271n40
Clarkson, Adrienne, 113, 165
commemoration initiatives: and cemeteries,
    201–10; and focus on pioneers, 191–93;
    local, 194–97; maintaining landmarks,
    200–201; renaming settlement areas,
    197–99; transplanting heritage, 199–200;
    and war dead, 210–12. See also specific
    ethnic groups
The Commitment (Możdżeński), 178, 180
community life, 27–29, 66–67
Cossacks as symbol, 159, 161, 163, 164–65,
    278n18, 285n27
Cyprus, 36

D
Danes: commemorating dead, 209; early
    immigration of, 18, 27; immigration
    distribution, 30, 33, 34, 37; and national
    museum, 230; regional homeland of, 40;
    symbols of, 161, 162
Davies, Johanna Jenkins, 69
Dawson, C.A., 111
Derksen, Henry, 109
Dickson, AB, 37, 209, 230
Diefenbaker, John, 168, 170, 280n31, 280n32
Dmytriw, Nestor, 61, 194
Doer, Gary, 170–71
Doerfler, Bruno: as founder of St. Peter's
    Colony, 23, 235–36; gravesite, 238;
    honouring, 59, 87, 88; published history
    of, 94, 98
Dominion Day celebrations, 115, 116–17
Doukhobors: burial customs, 71–72; burning